Japan's Pan-Asian

This book is a study of how the theories and actual practices of a Pan-Asian empire were produced during Japan's war, 1931–1945.

As Japan invaded China and conducted a full-scale war against the United States in the late 1930s and early 1940s, several versions of a Pan-Asian empire were presented by Japanese intellectuals, in order to maximize wartime collaboration and mobilization in China and the colonies. A broad group of social scientists – including Rōyama Masamichi, Kada Tetsuji, Ezawa Jōji, Takata Yasuma, and Shinmei Masamichi – presented highly politicized visions of a new Asia characterized by a newly shared Asian identity. Critically examining how Japanese social scientists contrived the logic of a Japan-led East Asian community, Part I of this book demonstrates the violent nature of imperial knowledge production which buttresses colonial developmentalism. In Part II, the book also explores questions around the (re)making of colonial Korea as part of Japan's regional empire, generating theoretical and realistic tensions between resistance and collaboration.

Japan's Pan-Asian Empire provides original theoretical perspectives on the construction of a multi-ethnic and multi-cultural empire. It will appeal to students and scholars of modern Japanese history, colonial and postcolonial studies, as well as Korean studies.

Seok-Won Lee is Associate Professor of History at Rhodes College, USA. His areas of research include twentieth-century Japanese intellectual history, colonialism, and imperialism in East Asia.

Routledge Studies in the Modern History of Asia

For a full list of available titles please visit: www.routledge.com/Routledge-Studies-in-the-Modern-History-of-Asia/book-series/MODHISTASIA

Japan's Pan-Asian Empire

Wartime Intellectuals and the Korea Question, 1931–1945

Seok-Won Lee

Routledge
Taylor & Francis Group

LONDON AND NEW YORK

First published 2021
by Routledge
2 Park Square, Milton Park, Abingdon, Oxon OX14 4RN

and by Routledge
52 Vanderbilt Avenue, New York, NY 10017

*Routledge is an imprint of the Taylor & Francis Group, an informa
business*

British Library Cataloguing-in-Publication Data
A catalogue record for this book is available from the British Library

Library of Congress Cataloging-in-Publication Data
A catalog record for this book has been requested

ISBN: 978-0-367-42783-2 (hbk)
ISBN: 978-1-003-00030-3 (ebk)

Typeset in Times New Roman
by Apex CoVantage, LLC

This book is dedicated to my wife Eunil Bae and my children Yejun Lee, Joshua Lee and Daniel Lee.

Contents

Acknowledgments

My first meeting with J. Victor Koschmann at Cornell University in 2003 was followed by a series of encounters with insightful scholars and a caring community of graduate students. This book is the outcome of my doctoral studies in East Asian intellectual history, among these exceptional people. When I was struggling with my doctoral dissertation topic, Professor Koschmann encouraged me to expand my interests to the intellectual history of the Japanese Empire. Professor Naoki Sakai has always been a thought-provoking teacher as well as a colleague who has stimulated my ideas. Without the wonderful teaching of Professor Sherman Cochran, I would not be able to discuss Chinese history seriously in my book project. Professor Hirano Katsuya helped me increase the sophistication of my inquiries into colonialism and minorities in my research project.

Together with these mentors, I must say that being surrounded by a group of wonderful colleagues is one of the best strokes of luck in the academic world. I believe that I have been one of these lucky scholars. From the beginning of my graduate studies in Seoul, Korea and Ithaca, New York to this day, I have received a great deal of support and intellectual inspiration from many wonderful colleagues. I just want to express my deepest gratitude to all of them collectively, instead of listing each of their names on this page.

The Rhodes College Department of History has been the most nurturing intellectual community in my life since I entered the real academic world. Joining Rhodes in Fall 2011, I have not ony received much financial and administrative support from the College, but I have also been intellectually stimulated by the wonderful historians around me and the College's focus on a liberal arts education. Together with this book, my research on Asian intellectual history has been extended to the topics of Afro-Asian encounters and Asian-American history. As a result of being in Memphis, one of the most dynamic cities in the United States, and surrounded by an atmosphere of critical thinking at Rhodes College, I must say that this book project has been greatly improved, and I owe a large debt to my colleagues in the Department of History and the entire Rhodes community.

My research and writing grew with my family and their love. First and foremost, Eunil Bae, the love of my life, has been the one who has supported me at every stage of my academic career. I hope that I can at least show my gratitude to her through this book. While I have been turning this dissertation into a book manuscript, three wonderful boys – Yejun, Joshua and Daniel – came into our family and they have been an invaluable source of joy in my life. Finally, this book is dedicated to my mother and my parents-in-law for their ongoing and unconditional support.

Earlier versions of several chapters were previously published. Parts of Chapters 1 and 2 appeared in the summer issue of the Korean journal *Yoksamunjeyongu* and the January 2014 issue of *Social Science Japan Journal*. Chapter 3 was contributed to the 2008 winter issue of the Korean journal *Yoksamunjeyongu*, and Chapter 4 was published in the summer 2016 issue of *The Review of Korean Studies*. These chapters have been revised substantially and are included in this book with permission from the journal publishers. Finally, as is always the case in my writing, all the errors in this book are mine.

Introduction

Empire Beyond Empire: Pan-Asianism and Regionalism in Modern Japan

In September 1937, W.E.B. Du Bois, one of the most influential African American intellectuals of the twentieth century, contributed an article to *The Pittsburgh Courier* on the recent outbreak of the Sino-Japanese War. Criticizing England, France and America, Du Bois predicted that the Sino-Japanese War would be "one of the great deciding wars of the world" and boldly concluded that "the future of [all] colored people is bound up with it."[1]

Du Bois's endorsement of Japan's invasion of China as a war of racial liberation was not an uninformed reaction. He had produced numerous articles in which he showed a keen interest in a Japan-led Asian order since the 1910s. His visit to Japan and Manchukuo in 1936, Imperial Japan's 1930s laboratory for Pan-Asian colonialism, convinced him that Japan's Pan-Asian empire provided a parallel example in support of his speculative idea for a Pan-African international community. But Du Bois had little access to independent sources regarding the iniquitous reality of Japanese imperialism and colonialism. As such, he overestimated the munificent quality of the Japanese plan for Asia, particularly in considering it as analogous to his own idealistic vision for the political enjoinment of Africa and its diaspora. At the heart of Du Bois's optimistic appraisal of the seemingly emancipatory value of Japanese imperial expansion was the clear deployment of a politics of racial liberation in statements by the Japanese government.

This development began with the establishment of Manchukuo, and the official use of the slogan the "harmony of five races (*gozoku kyowa*)" in government propaganda. Such official proclamations were only the surface manifestation of the various profound sets of theories regarding the top-down construction of a Pan-Asian community. This was the deeper intellectual context that provided the epistemological limits to the official position regarding racial harmony in the new imperial Japanese version of Asia. Unfortunately, this was a context of scholarly thought and argument that Du Bois was unable to consider in his assessment of the Japanese empire, or critically advance within his own pan-African perspective.

By 1931, Japan was an established imperial power whose sphere of control spanned from northeast China through the Korean peninsula and down to Taiwan. In September 1931, the Japanese Kwantung Army realized the nation's long-term imperial ambition of occupying northern China. The 1931 Manchurian Incident (or the Manchurian Crisis) began with a staged explosion on the South Manchurian Railway and then rapidly proceeded to vastly alter the topography of the Japanese empire. The Japanese government claimed that this explosion was an attack by anti-Japanese Chinese forces, and in response the Kwangtung Army carried out a large-scale military operation and eventually occupied most of northeast China. Most Western imperial powers, including the United States, were openly hostile to this military invasion, but in March 1932, Japan established the imperial state of Manchukuo, a new geopolitical entity between mainland China and the Korean peninsula.

Manchukuo provided an experimental site for the practice of new forms of Japanese imperial ideology. The rhetoric of the "harmony of five races," which Du Bois found attractive, epitomized the "utopian" conceptual dimension of Japan's ambitious empire-building project. The apparently "reformist" approach to the Japanese colonial project was in part due to the observation by Japanese bureaucrats and intellectuals that the possibility to build an empire in the historically conventional sense was over. They were attentive to the political, economic and demographic changes occurring inside and outside the region of their control, and one of the most conspicuous symptoms of the collapse of the old Japanese imperial structure was the unprecedented influx and outflow of population between the imperial metropole and her colonies. According to *zainichi* historian Park Kyung Sik, the number of Korean subjects in Japan proper skyrocketed from 419,009 to 881,347 between 1931 and 1937,[2] and the same was true of Japanese residents who moved to Manchukuo, Taiwan and Korea.[3] These migrations created new social divisions and lines of conflict within the Japanese empire. Since most colonial immigrants to Japan proper occupied the low-wage jobs that low-class Japanese workers previously held, they often competed and eventually conflicted with these similarly economically disenfranchised Japanese workers. Socio-political changes driven by this unprecedented population mobility suggest that the rhetoric of "racial harmony" was initially deployed to cover up various politico-economic tensions in reality. For instance, the growing number of Korean workers and unions in Japan competed directly with low-class Japanese workers. This resulted in aggravating the existing negative images of Koreans held by ordinary Japanese people, and intensified racism against migrants in Japan.[4] Recent historical studies of migrant subjects within the Japanese empire illustrate how various differing agencies and interests combined to form the contours of the imperial society. This appreciation for the full diversity of factors involved in influencing migration patterns across the empire renders the traditional narrative of the hierarchal empire-colony power structure unable to usefully account for the complex social dynamics shaping the wartime Japanese empire.[5]

These rapidly changing and threatening circumstances called for a more effective method of governance to maintain the stability of the empire. First and foremost, the political and theoretical grounds for a sense of unity that might encompass and address all Asian people and minimalize inter-ethnic socio-economic conflicts were urgently called for. Japan had become internationally isolated in the aftermath of the 1931 Manchurian Crisis. After fierce debates over how to handle diplomatic pressure from Western imperial powers regarding imperial expansion in China, Japan made the aggressive decision to withdraw from the League of Nations in 1933. As Hotta's recent work shows well, Japan's isolation from the international order partly explains why Pan-Asian regionalism first gained a currency among intellectuals and politicians as an alternative *diplomatic* approach to maintain Japan's hegemony in East Asia.[6] In that respect, it would be correct to consider wartime Japanese Pan-Asianism as a response to her exclusion from the Euro-centric world order. Perhaps the official slogan of the "Greater East Asia Co-Prosperity Sphere (*daitōa kyōeiken*)," first coined in the early 1940s, represents the apex of imperial Japan's desire to create a new international order against the West.[7] At issue here is the problematic historical tendency to conceive of the "Greater East Asia Co-Prosperity Sphere" as deceptive fantasy bearing no relationship to real imperial aims and desires. This has arguably precluded students of Japanese and East Asian history from comprehensively and seriously addressing the broad scope of regional Pan-Asian thought and practice during the twentieth century.

This book will trace the intellectual trajectories of Pan-Asianist theories and practices during the wartime period, 1931–1945, focusing on Japanese and colonial social scientists, Korean social scientists in particular. Recent studies of Pan-Asianism have more usefully provided a different perspective on how and why the idea and practice of an Asian unity has actually offered a powerful resource for Asian people to define their lives during the twentieth century. These new studies, in spite of their different methodological orientations, share the common thesis that Pan-Asian regionalism was not merely reducible to being a floating idea or superficial piece of rhetoric. Instead, they would consider it as an influential stream of *thought* that has had a profound impact on the self-conception and everyday life of Asian people.[8]

The fact that Pan-Asianism has received little attention among students of East Asian history was partly due to the common perception that it was premised upon blood-oriented, intrinsic and thus irrational concepts of Asia. The result of this reductive rendering is that the complex discourse behind Japanese imperial Asian regionalism is characterized as a simplistic configuration in which the concept of Pan-Asia unconditionally designates an anti-modern, anti-Western ideology and signifies a fundamentalist zeal for returning to a traditional Asia. The irony of the coexistence between dormant anti-Western sentiments and the Japanese search for modernization culminated in the late 1920s and 1930s, when imperial Japan's transformation into a multi-ethnic and multi-cultural empire resulted in the eruption of various Asian regional discourses that were oftentimes contradictory. For instance, until the 1920s, the Japanese advocates of anti-Westernism had mainly targeted European powers as the primary object of their ideological attacks. However, the question of the United States as part of the ultimate Western foe to be overcome had always existed since, Yoshimi Shunya has argued, Americanism had quickly penetrated the cultural sectors of everyday life in 1920s Japan.[9] Under these circumstances, a number of Japanese imperial intellectuals adhered to this form of "spiritual Pan-Asianism" during the wartime period. Spiritual

Pan-Asianists' agitation for an upcoming war between Japan and the West had received public attention in Japan proper in the 1920s,[10] when tensions between the United States and Japan were aggravated. However, a fundamental limit within spiritual Pan-Asianist thought was the absence of concrete means of creating a realistic politico-economic structure of a new East Asian empire, other than calling for spiritual and cultural bonds that were at best applicable to *Japanese* citizens within Japan proper. It was at this point that more concretized, rational and even scientific visions of a Pan-Asian empire were produced and gained currency among both Japanese and Korean intellectuals. This book explores these newly emerging Pan-Asianists, who were clearly aware of the urgency to overcome the traditional empire-colony power structure to forge a new empire.

Pan-Asian empire beyond old empire: the rise of "rationalist" Pan-Asianism

Challenging simplistic misconceptions of Pan-Asian thought, this book offers a substantially different narrative of how various Pan-Asianist theories and theorists were often at rival variance in wartime Japan, and how among these, a scientific, rational and futuristic notion of an Asian unity actually prevailed in academic circles as well as in the field of real politics. To this end, the following investigation pays particular attention to a broad group of Japanese and Korean social scientists who proposed a new vision of Pan-Asian community. Rōyama Masamichi, Kada Tetsuji, Takata Yasuma, Shinmei Masamichi, Ezawa Jōji and Moritani Katsumi, these intellectuals belonged to separate established disciplines in the field of social sciences – political science, economics, sociology and geography. Crucially, many of them shared the common influence of Marxism and other radical thoughts during the Taisho period despite being trained in non-Marxist mainstream social sciences. Beginning in the early 1930s, this collection of scholars independently undertook investigations into the shared trans-disciplinary social scientific question of how to overcome the limits of a liberal capitalist economy and democracy: The dominant social structure which was presumed to have provided the backbone of the modern nation-state system and the existing imperial order. At the heart of this inquiry was the need to *rationalize* Japan's transition to becoming a new multi-ethnic empire. In this endeavor, these scholars became influential within the imperial intellectual sphere and their notion of a multi-ethnic empire, often called the East Asia Community (*tōa kyōdōtai*) rapidly gained currency among both Japanese and colonial thinkers, and Korean intellectuals in particular, during the late 1930s and early 1940s.[11]

This book pays special attention to the question of why "rationalist" and once liberal and progressive intellectuals, mostly social scientists, occupied the forefront of Pan-Asian imperial discourses in the early 1930s. These scholars came to dominate the Japanese academy during the wartime period, specifically through their notion of a Pan-Asian community. This investigation follows the imperative set by Katō Shūichi and other scholars in their considering wartime Japan as the continuation of prewar Japan.[12] It is important to note that the practical approach to constructing a new Pan-Asian community originated in the academic observation that a new paradigm was necessary to enable the reconstruction of Japanese society during the time of total war. To understand the mentality of these social scientists as self-defined "social pioneers," one needs to understand the "problem-solving" pragmatic concern of Japanese social science in the early twentieth century. Social scientists in Japan, prior to turn of the century, were prized and privileged citizens as they provided the ideological direction as well as the practical knowledge to support the nation's modernization during the Meiji period. However, the critique of social scientists as uncritical servants of state-led, top-down and authoritative modernization programs grew at the turn of the twentieth century. In response, liberal and progressive intellectuals called for the national discipline of social science to reform its focus and address the concerns of the socially disenfranchised. This tendency was related to the fact that the shadow of Japan's rapid and top-down modernization – economic inequality between the rich and poor, imbalance between metropole and rural areas, *zaibatsu*-oriented economy and so on – was increasingly conspicuous in the 1910s and the 1920s. The escalation of internal inconsistencies in early-twentieth-century Japanese society gave rise to a new influential group of social scientists. This circumstance historian Andrew Barshay categorized as the moment of "pluralization" in the Japanese social sciences.[13] These newly empowered intellectuals and academics called variously for social reforms to the democratic system, a free-market economy independent of state intervention, and sometimes even a full-scale Marxist social revolution. Through this thinking process, young Japanese social scientists now considered it their ontological task to provide solutions for social problems. For them, the term and idea of society was a newly "discovered" space in which different class, religious, economic and political interests collided, and solutions to these conflicts might be created.[14]

However, the geographical scope of interest for these social scientists in the 1920s was largely confined to Japan proper. Only a few intellectuals were acutely aware that Japan's social issues were inseparable from its imperial structure. Therefore, the rise of progressive and liberal intellectuals in early-twentieth-century Japan does not necessarily tell us that Japanese social scientists had armed themselves with a critique of imperialism, except for a small group of radical Marxist scholars. As Andrew Gordon demonstrates, the development of democracy and capitalism at home became paradoxically associated with endorsing national interests abroad. Consequently, imperialism and democracy co-habited the national political terrain for a considerable time.[15] External and internal changes to Japanese society in the early 1930s suddenly deconstructed the mutually inclusive coexistence of imperialism abroad and the optimistic liberal and progressive atmospheres at home. The "crisis mentality" that had originated in Europe in the aftermath of the First World War and the Great Depression quickly arrived in Japan. On the other hand, Japan's position in the international order was jeopardized as it invaded northern China in 1931. All in all, Japanese intellectuals had become increasingly aware that the challenges that imperial Japan faced could no longer be solved by solely "domestic" prescriptions. It was at this point that Japanese intellectuals who had been overwhelmed by Taisho liberal atmospheres looked beyond the national border and became involved in imperial projects abroad.

First of all, they were convinced that without creating a new theoretical basis for empire, imperial Japan could not cope with the numerous challenges threatening social stability, from ethnic conflict to economic crisis. These social scientists were convinced that imperial Japan could not simply stick to the conventional logic of empire and ape the ways in which European powers governed their colonies. As European governments took colonies as sites for economic exploitation, serious measures to minimize the physical and cultural interaction between the colonizer and the colonized were also created. Population mobility was restrained, and if colonial subjects migrated within the empire, they always faced severe ethnic discrimination in the metropolitan center. Interracial interaction was also largely shunned by white settlers in the colony. Ann Stoller has explored the question of how white European residents in Southeast Asia created and maintained rigid tensional spaces of interaction in racial and economic hierarchies.[16] Within such a power structure, it was almost impossible to envision an empire of intimacy:[17] a conceptual community where both the colonizer and the colonized subject could become jointly incorporated under a new, shared form of imperial identity, and a common sense of destiny. Imperial Japan also adopted similar ethnic hierarchy-oriented governing structures in its early stages, but as I have discussed, the massive influx and outflow of population from the early 1930s on made it impossible for Japan to maintain separatist policies of racial exclusion. Most importantly, Japan's overt expansionist moves invited criticism and resistance from European powers. The rise of Pan-Asianism in defense of a new, Japan-led Asian order demanded actual changes that would politically distinguish Japan's empire from the European form of imperialism.

Under these circumstances, these intellectuals witnessed and partially incepted the end of the old imperial order and heralded the coming of the new: a process this book terms as "empire beyond empire." As political scientist Sakai Tetsuya has noted, liberal Japanese scholars during the Taisho period were convinced that a pluralist internationalist thinking should replace the nation-state framework that had sustained the balance of power up until the early twentieth century.[18] Several strong nation-states in the European continent, with the recent addition of the United States, were the major global imperial powers and divided the world into their spheres of interest. However, various predictions of the end of the Euro-centric order appeared in the wake of the destruction of the Great War and the Great Depression, and they were in different contexts, pointing to the advent of non-Western regional power. In this regard, many Japanese intellectuals were influenced by geopolitical theorists such as Alfred Mahan, who anticipated that an Asia-based regional power would threaten the Euro-centric hegemony.[19] Accordingly, they strove to disseminate the newness and validity of a Pan-regionalist thinking within the conceptual reconstruction of the Japanese empire. To be sure, it was an opinion held not just by these rationalist social scientists but also by conservative and so-called *Japanist* intellectuals that a new Asian empire must incorporate Chinese and other Asian colonial subjects. However, the significant difference between rational social scientists and spiritual Japanist Pan-Asianists was that the former were clearly aware that a new, Japan-led regional empire would only be possible by drawing on *voluntary* participation from Chinese and colonial subjects, not by spiritual and biological ties such as the Imperial Way or racial similarities among Asian subjects. To this end, it was stressed that realistic and favorable social and political policies should be put into practice to maximize mobilization from within the colonial territories. For this reason, racist colonial governance was criticized for jeopardizing the stability of the empire. As sociologist Kada Tetsuji argued in his 1938 best-selling book *Race, Nation and War*, racism is not rigidly part of social science.[20] Vehemently criticizing the blood-centered ethnic nation-building project of Alfred Rosenberg, the icon of racist theory in Nazi Germany, Kada reconfirmed that Japan's new empire building should be based on the creation of *minzoku*, a socially, politically and culturally constructed Asian community.[21] At stake was the question of what socio-political and economic engineering processes should be embarked on in binding these Asian subjects to a Japan-led East Asian empire. Here, these Japanese and colonial social scientists became closely involved in creating a new body of imperial knowledge that ranged from theories such as racism, national socialism and communitarianism to most practical issues of colonial economic development and the geographical reconstructing of imperial territories.

The social scientists this book explores insisted that a developmental perspective should be applied to the colonial economy. In other words, reducing the economic gap between metropole and colony was prioritized in their empire-building project. Instead of relentlessly repeating the logic of anti-Westernism and anti-modernism, they suggested that people in the colony could be incorporated into a Pan-Asian community by embracing the notion of the "community of destiny," that is, their future was bound with the developing picture of a Pan-Asian community. In this conception, it was stressed that what was important was not the abstract repetition of Asian commonness, but that subjects in both Japan and the colony could share in the futuristic vision that their life would be improved over the course of together building a new Pan-Asian empire. Based on these observations, they put forward the notion of the East Asian Community (*tōa kyōdōtai*) and this group of *kyōdōtai* social scientists formed one of the most influential streams of Pan-Asian discourse in the interwar period.

Contesting Pan-Asianism

To capture the historical significance of this rational, scientific and developmentalist notion of Pan-Asianism advocated by wartime Japanese social scientists, it is important to understand why they cast a skeptical eye on the existing logic of an Asian unity. As I have discussed, Pan-Asian regionalism was not a new theory invented by Japanese social scientists during the wartime period. Different types of Pan-Asianism, either as political ideology or cultural discourse, existed in the late nineteenth and early twentieth centuries.[22] Okakura Tenshin, for example, advocated Asia as a single regional unit as early as 1903.[23] His early Pan-Asianist thinking was, however, premised on the essentialist idea that Asians shared the same cultural heritage. In that respect, although it was not his main goal to analytically interrogate the origins and sources of the idea of an essential Asian commonality, he was preoccupied with rediscovering the original aspects of a mythical Asian unity.[24] This type of early Pan-Asianism was characterized by an emphasis on locating the cultural and intrinsic similarities that would constitute the 'Asian spirit' and thus discern Asians as a group distinct from the rest of world, notwithstanding that each Pan-Asian discourse was contingently shaped in close association with particular local political atmospheres.

As is well known, Okakura's resort to Asian unity operated with the overt intention to reveal the superiority of the Japanese cultural tradition to the West. This politically contextualized appropriation of Pan-Asian thought existed elsewhere. For instance, Sun Yat-sen's "Greater Pan-Asianism" illuminates how Pan-Asianism was closely associated with traditional sinocentric ideology. In a famous speech given to a Japanese audience in Kyoto in 1924, Sun Yat-sen introduced his idea of Pan-Asianism with a global context of modernization, tradition and racism. Criticizing Western hegemony as the "Rule of Might," he asserted that a harmonious, ethical and thus inclusive source of political thought and governance was absent in the European tradition.[25] On the contrary, Sun believed that the Eastern tradition of governance could be symbolized as the "Rule of Right" and suggested that Japan's successful modernization and China's vast spiritual tradition should be combined to form a twentieth-century version of a Pan-Asian community.[26] Among other issues, Sun problematically used the historical Chinese tributary system as the basis for his long history of Pan-Asianism in East Asia. He argued that all Asian people had voluntarily subordinated themselves to the Han-Chinese tributary system, and that it represented the diplomatically institutionalized order of sinocentric ideology. Sun's ambitious zeal for conceptually enjoining all East Asian people together, to offer a strong regional defense in the era of Western imperialism, was ironically premised on the singular ethnic superiority of the Han-Chinese people. Unsurprisingly, therefore, this concept of Pan-Asianism also permitted Sun to call for the elimination of "the remnants of the Manchus," the rival "barbarian" ethnic group to the Han who had established the Qing dynasty.[27]

In contrast, the rise and consumption of Pan-Asianism in early-twentieth-century Japan took on a much more subtle political form. Ironic as it may sound, Pan-Asianism was often appropriated by conservative and even ultranational fascists in early-twentieth-century Japan. To understand this paradoxical relationship between Pan-Asianism and Japanese fascism, one needs to consider how Japan's position in the international order had a profound impact on domestic conservatism. Immediately after Japan invaded northeast China in 1931 and established Manchukuo in 1932, most European powers who had endorsed Japan's position in East Asia turned hostile for fear of Japan becoming a regional superpower. This diplomatic conflict resulted in Japan's withdrawal from the League of Nations in 1933. The sense of crisis in national security stimulated conservatives and ultranationalists who held deep-rooted anti-modern and anti-Western sentiment. Japan's now hostile relationship with the Western powers gave them the ideological excuse to fundamentally problematize the national path toward Western modernization. Their alternative proposal was the "Imperial Way," in which Japan was refigured as a totalitarian society. For these fundamentalist ultranationalists, the direction of Japan's new order was designed to substitute Western social organizations and structures with Asian ones. Toward this purpose, they intentionally appropriated the concept of Asian commonality, in biological and cultural terms, as an ideological means to incorporate the colonies and the Chinese people into the Japanese empire-building project. Therefore, it was not surprising that many of these ultranational fascists also became advocates of Pan-Asianism in the early 1930s. For instance, Mistukawa Kametarō and Kanokogi Kuzunobu associated their Imperial-Way ideology with a Pan-Asian order.[28] According to them, the ultimate dignity of the Japanese Emperor will be at last realized as his reign reaches the "eight corners of the world under one roof (*hakkō ichiu*)." As such, the main task for these ultranationalists was to associate spiritual pan-Asianism with imperial-way Japanism and denounce Western values, such as individualism and rationality, as detrimental to Asian unity.

Lacking in both sinocentric and ultranationalist essentialist approaches to Pan-Asianism was any notion of how to cope with the contingent economic and political issues that would preclude Asians from forming a politically coherent regional community. In this respect, these early-twentieth-century versions of Pan-Asianism should perhaps be more properly considered as a "political manifestation" of underlying desires for an ethnically oriented idea of regional hegemony. Unsurprisingly, they often turned to a notion of the common ethnic sentiment among Asian people as the basis for their Pan-Asianist logic, and ironically so given that their Pan-Asian thinking was born out of particular ethnic hierarchies within the region. Roughly speaking, wartime Japanese ultranationalist Pan-Asianism was in no way different from these early twentieth-century versions of Pan-Asianism in that it was based on Japanese racial superiority.

A "rational" Pan-Asian Empire: the "community of destiny" and modernization

If the assertion of Asian commonalities or a zeal for restoring Asian value systems, both of which regurgitated an idea of Asia as the past or traditional, was not enough to construct a new regional community, what other perceptions of Asia could be used or discovered and put forward instead? This was the primary inquiry that many social scientists shared in the interwar period, and this book explores their ideas. Their first priority was to call for fundamental epistemological transformations to enable them to contrive a new theory of Pan-Asianism. They rejected the notion of Pan-Asianism in regard to any biological or intrinsic ahistorical affinity among Asian people. Rather than return to the past as a source for a new Asian unity, these intellectuals intended to contrive a Pan-Asian theory that looked to the future. They hoped such a theory might appeal to the Chinese and colonial subjects, and provide a "forward-looking" picture of a new Asia. Considering that if each ethnic community steadfastly adhered to the concept of biological race such as Chinese, Korean and Japanese, a new, shared subjectivity could not be formed, ethnic nationalism should therefore be transcended, to realize the future of a Pan-Asian empire where a multi-ethnic population could be endorsed and the possibility of being an "East Asian" citizen would become openly inclusive and fluid. Additionally, these scholars were not interested in reasserting the value of the traditional Asian modes of life that had historically constituted the agriculture-oriented economic conditions in East Asia. Instead, they argued that economic development was urgent in the colonies to reduce the economic gap between the colony and metropole, as they believed that this disparity had generated a destructive unevenness.[29] The recognition that the widening economic gap between Japan and the colony would eventually become detrimental to the stability of the empire indicates that these social scientists maintained a certain level of sensitivity to colonial problems based on their pluralist perspective.

A vivid example of the social sensitivity that differentiated these imperial social scientists from the conservative, ultranational Imperial-Way fascists was their resolute stance against racist governance. Vehemently criticizing Nazi Germany's racism, they railed against Japanese ultranationalists who intended to strengthen racial hierarchies during the wartime period. Precisely for this reason, these social scientists' regionalist thinking created lines of conflict with both advocates of the Imperial-Way and right-wing bureaucrats, even though none of them ever directly challenged the Japanese emperor-system. The most evident example of this tension appeared in their critiques of *naisenittai* (Japan and Korea as one body). This was a brutal policy that aimed to incorporate Koreans as subjects of the Japanese emperor based on the supposed racial and cultural origins shared between the two nations. As Capiro's recent study well shows, imperial Japan's basic approach to Korean subjects was to assimilate them into the Japanese empire while maintaining an ethnic hierarchy between the metropole and the colony.[30] To accomplish this seemingly impossible goal, various deceptive theories disguised as science were presented. The notion of *naisenittai* was one part of imperial Japan's ethnic engineering projects and traceable to the theory of *nissendōsoron* (Japanese and Koreans as having the same ancestor) which proliferated immediately after Japan's annexation of Korea. The idea that Koreans and Japanese shared similar physical and cultural characteristics was frequently revisited by Japanese intellectuals to justify Japan's annexation of Korea, and used as the basis of a plan to transform Koreans into Japanese subjects in linguistic and cultural terms during the wartime period.[31] The seemingly impossible task to incorporate colonial subjects equally within the imperial project and also maintain ethnic hierarchies offers a clear reason why the formation of ethnic subjectivity emerged as a most urgent issue in Japan's new empire building.

The imperial scholars this book examines vehemently criticized the unscientific and irrational aspects of any biological concepts of Asian commonness. Instead, they grappled with the question of creating a socio-political subjectivity that was both constructive and fluid. For instance, Shinmei Masamichi imagined a "United

States of East Asia." This was a new concept of an "East Asian nation" in which Asians might believe that they belonged to one grand East Asian nation (*minzoku*), while each ethnic group – Chinese, Japanese and Koreans – would not have to denounce their indigenous identity. Shinmei and like-minded intellectuals such as Takata Yasuma and Kada Tetsuji were well aware that the key to realizing their optimistic vision of a multi-ethnic Pan-Asian community was to convince both Japanese and colonial subjects that they potentially shared a sense of the "community of destiny (*unmei kyōdōtai*)," a concept that frequently appeared in Pan-Asian discourses in wartime Japan. While spiritual Pan-Asianists interpreted the "community of destiny" as a revisiting of traditional Asian values or devoting oneself to the "Holy War" led by the Japanese emperor, these scientifically trained academics presented a different definition. Rōyama Masamiachi was a political scientist and one of the main advocates of the rationalist notion of a Pan-Asian regional bloc. He contended that a regional community in East Asia must share "something other than natural and perpetual elements or cultural unification" and that the destiny of all Asian people was contingent on the creation of a new form of East Asian identity, not a conception of intrinsic commonness.[32]

How, then, could a sense of unity be created not by resorting to "natural and perpetual elements"? This question was inseparable from the problem of how modernization and Westernization were delineated in wartime Pan-Asian discourses. As I have discussed, the more intellectuals articulated spiritual Pan-Asianism in their diatribes of blood-oriented, intrinsic Asian sameness, the deeper they became complicit with the rhetoric of "overcoming the West" or "overcoming modernity" as an anti-thesis, and the rhetoric of anti-modernity, anti-individualism and anti-capitalism was continuous in academic writing, novels, government propaganda, and other cultural and visual materials.[33] The "war of thought (*shisōsen*)" formulated a clear-cut battleground between Japan and the "decadent" West, and involved itself in the psychological and epistemological processes of affirming an independent historicity in the East.[34] As the term "overcoming" suggests, this logic in many cases employed the retrospective observation that Japan and the Japanese had historically striven relentlessly to catch up with Western modernity. For this reason, what needed to be overcome was not just the West as an actual enemy but, more importantly, the influence of Western thought within Japan.

This book does not aim to denigrate the historical significance of anti-modern and anti-Western Pan-Asianism during the wartime period. In fact, recent studies of Asianism in colonial Korea show how strongly anti-Western Pan-Asianism penetrated the mindset of not only Japanese intellectuals but also colonial Korean intellectuals. By displacing the West and repositioning Korea in a Japan-led Asian empire, these Korean Pan-Asianists attempted to overcome the reality of their prolonged colonization and obtain subjectivity as the citizen of imperial Japan.[35] Importantly, they did not find that indigenous Korean culture was contradictory to the idea of a spiritual Pan-Asianism. Instead, they dexterously rediscovered similarities between Japanese and Korean culture. For instance, they insisted that the famous *mu* (nothingness) spirit later sophisticated by Japanese philosophers such as Nishida Kitarō[36] or *bushido* existed both in Korea and Japan. This was to demonstrate that a collective form of the Pan-Asian culture or spirit could be constituted by exploring the common aspects that existed in each ethnic group.[37] The discursive influence of anti-modern and anti-Western Pan-Asianism also explains why a prefix of "Pan-Asia" was attached to most regionalist theories in the wartime period. However, Korean intellectuals did not accept Japan-originated Pan-Asian philosophical theories as such. As Jung's recent study shows, wartime Korean intellectuals such as Seo In Sik were aware of the limits of a culturalist Pan-Asian ideology that eventually attempted to mobilize Korean subjects for Imperial Japan's "holy" war. Instead of responding to the utopian vision of a Pan-Asian empire put forth by Japanese intellectuals, they grappled with the question of how the cultural ground shared by colonial Korea and Japan would be converted into energies that would replace problematic Western modernity with a new type of Asian modernity.[38]

Based on these observations, this book argues that subsuming all wartime pan-Asian discourses under the monolithic notion of "overcoming modernity" would fail to reveal the complexity of Japanese and colonial intellectuals' various encounters with the notion of a Pan-Asian empire. The most extreme example of this tendency might be the affirmation of the war as an action of significant historical progress which might liberate Asians from the oppression of white supremacy.[39] More importantly, anti-modern and anti-Western Pan-Asianism in many cases operated at the level of idealized and speculative writing limited to an intellectual readership. Lacking in this tenacious return to a notion of Asia was a sense of the practical need to cope with the realistic problem of the political and economic imbalance between Japan and the colony. In this regard, those such as the "overcoming the modern" group led by the Kyoto School of Philosophy, remained trapped by modernity, since they insisted that Japanese cultural primacy in Asia was due to its regionally unique economic and technological development in the twentieth century. This perspective rendered their notion of the Japanese "overcoming" of modernity only a reaffirmation of it.[40]

Pan-Asianism as developmentalism: the "Korea problem"

In contrast to these philosophers, the social scientists this study explores were not preoccupied with the concept of overcoming modernity, although they largely shared the recognition that a new Pan-Asian empire should replace the old Eurocentric imperial structure. But nor were they convinced that the building of a Pan-Asian empire would be possible through the total rejection of Western and modern values. In addition, they were aware that the economic gap between Japan and the colony, and between metropolitan and rural areas of the empire, could not be addressed simply by advocating anti-capitalism and renouncing modernization in theory. In this respect, instead of tracing the trajectories of the philosophical development of "overcoming modernity," they shared a common inquiry as to how a developmentalist perspective might serve to incorporate both Japanese and colonial subjects into a new empire.

For example, Ezawa Jōji, the rationalist geopolitician, who is one of the central intellectuals in Chapter 3, addressed the principle of constructing East Asian space to realize the "community of destiny." According to him, Asian space is neither a given nor a natural object, but one where countless different memories and experiences occurred simultaneously and ubiquitously. But he believed that through the project of constructing a new space – for example, through national land planning – these different experiences could converge with the common goal to build an East Asian community where economic unevenness and colonial hierarchies would no longer exist. Therefore, Ezawa argued that by creating a new space, people in the colony might obtain a promoted status within the empire-building process. This led him to emphasize the necessity of a developmentalist approach in reconstructing the new imperial territory to narrow the gap between metropole and colony. At the center of this new social scientific thinking, which Ezawa conceptualized as East Asian geopolitics, was his new interpretation of space not as a physical substance, but as an active force to be deployed toward shaping the destiny of any given community.[41]

In this way, these social scientists aimed to rationalize the construction of an East Asian Community, calling for domestic reforms and the deconstruction of the traditional forms of empire-colony hierarchies. The primary purpose of their particular theory of empire building was to appeal to the Chinese people. While they attempted to convince the Chinese of the historical significance of creating a Pan-Asian community, these social scientists also criticized the obstinate fixed concept of Asia propagated by the ethnic Chinese, often called the "central kingdom mentality" or the sinocentric world order. To theoretically challenge this notion, both rational social scientists and conservative intellectuals conducted extensive research on China. In so doing they created the field of China studies as an independent discipline within the Japanese academy.

While considering China as both a geographical and an epistemological unit in investigating the historical significance of wartime Pan-Asian discourses, this study pays special attention to colonial Korea. Many of these rational social scientists took it for granted that Taiwan and Korea were already part of the Japanese empire. In that respect, the rationalist Pan-Asian discourses by the Japanese social scientists that this book explores did not contain sophisticated plans or agendas for colonial Korea or Taiwan, although they revealed a clear understanding of the need to reduce the economic gap between metropole and colony as their primary concern. This discursive and political vacuum in the colony was filled by conservative and imperial-way ultranationalists who attempted to completely eliminate indigenous colonial language and culture in their fantasized goal of incorporating colonial subjects as faithful citizens of imperial Japan. The systematic implementation of *naisenittairon* (Theories of Japan and Korea as one body) during the wartime period in colonial Korea tells us the extent to which culturalist and spiritual Pan-Asianism prevailed in the colony as well.

However, this study argues that illuminating such total assimilation-oriented colonial policies by imperial Japan shows only a partial reality of colonial Korean subjects' responses to Japan's empire building. Projecting sympathy with the call to create an Asian regionalist bloc on the one hand, these Korean intellectuals were much more concerned with promoting the advent of a new Asian empire as a way of enhancing the political and economic status of colonial Korea. Precisely for this reason, recent studies of Japan's total war in colonial Korea have shown the complex nature of its Pan-Asian project.[42] These Korean intellectuals in the wartime period were also clearly aware of the paradoxical absence of other colonial voices in Japanese Pan-Asian discourses. However, this blindness toward Japan's colonial hegemony on the part of Japanese intellectuals ironically produced an important space for identity politics in Korea. The rhetoric of a universal empire was appropriated by a group of colonial Korean intellectuals as a way to overcome both the empire-colony power structure and the limits of local capitalist modes of production at the same time.

Under these circumstances, it was natural that rationalist Pan-Asianism, such as the notion of the East Asia Community, gradually gained currency among Korean intellectuals, since on the surface it called for expanding political spaces for colonial subjects as well as bringing economic development to the colony. In Jeong Sik, the primary subject of Chapter 5, was convinced that Korea's status would be improved by the creative re-interpretation of the idea of constructing a rational empire and collaborating with Imperial Japan. He believed that Korea's capability to produce more rice than it needed and its vast labor power would fuel the total mobilization needed to sustain Japan's war efforts. But he also argued that Japan must reconstruct Korea's agriculture and develop its industry to transform the latent potential of colonial Korea into a real force. In's writing vividly illustrates how a developmental perspective penetrated not only the notions of Japanese intellectuals, but also those of colonial intellectuals.

The specter of modernization: the Asia-Pacific War and its aftermath

In this way, Japanese social scientists' rationalist support for a Pan-Asian community was closely associated with wartime mobilization through its developmentalist logic. This, they believed, would provide the optimal way to exploit material resources and mobilize Chinese and colonial subjects for Japan's war effort. An acute sense of historicity therefore indicates that these Japanese intellectuals produced knowledge and presented actual policies in clear support of the empire. In similar fashion to Immanuel Wallerstein's identification of the birth of cold war area studies in the United States in the 1950s and 1960s, the social scientists this book will explore were in a true sense "area specialists." They accumulated vast amounts of knowledge with the aim to universalize the Japanese empire.[43] For this reason, they appropriated the social scientific notion of rationality to disguise their positioning as pro-imperial and colonial social scientists. Sociologist Max Weber defined rationalization as the driving force behind modern society. According to him, the intellectual turn to rationality diminished the explanatory power of religious, supernatural and metaphysical human activities, all of which are considered as "irrational." Rationality is instead comprised of social and institutional forces controlled by reason, calculation and goal-oriented activities.[44] Importantly, rational choice or rational action is not necessarily accompanied by social justice or politico-economic development. Rationality as a purely social scientific concept is often intertwined with a highly teleological sense of human life. In the social sciences, the term "rationalization" has denoted the optimization of effectiveness and productivity, and precisely for this reason it has been considered as one of the core values of modern society.

In this respect, imperial social scientists in interwar Japan experimented with this new notion of rationality. They were particularly interested in the application of the concepts of increased effectiveness and enhanced productivity to the colony. They hoped to extend the realm of social rationality outside Japan proper in the name of a Pan-Asian community. However, their ambitious challenge to the Euro-centric order and their production of seemingly progressive policies and theory was also part of a reflexive answer to the problem of the old imperial structure in crisis. In that respect, they were sincere imperialists who were deeply concerned about the uncertain future of the Japanese empire. Therefore, the reason this book pays special attention to these social scientists is that the partially deceptive logic of a multi-ethnic empire and colonial development was not simply a form of political rhetoric that only existed during the wartime period and became extinct afterwards. As illustrated above, these scholars put forward this logic to renovate the imperfect present and construct a new Pan-Asian society premised on the sense of the "community of destiny." The developmentalist perspective that defined their Pan-Asianism was a revised version of the government-led modernization program that was based on individual spontaneous participation. Importantly, the logic of mobilization did not fade away with the end of the war and the empire in 1945. State-driven top-down modernization was adopted by all national parties, and on both sides of the new cold war divide in Taiwan, South Korea and Japan on one side, and China and North Korea on the other. Pseudo-democratic governments in South Korea and Japan carried out rapid economic development plans, spurred on and supported by America's ambition to become the new regional power in East Asia. This explains why many of these imperial intellectuals in wartime Japan not only survived, but continued to exert a strong academic influence in 1950s and 1960s Japan. In a different context, the same legacies of wartime mobilization and an intellectual commitment to the Japanese empire also had a strong impact on the making of postcolonial South Korea. All these developments reconfirm why it is so important to retrace the intellectual trajectories of Pan-Asianism in interwar Japan, as this history offers a means to understand the issues of (post)colonialism and modernization in contemporary East Asia.

Notes

1 W.E.B. Du Bois, "China and Japan," *The Pittsburgh Courier*, Sep. 25, 1937.
2 Park Kyung Sik, *Zainichi Chōsenjin ni kansuru sogo chosa kenkyu* [A Comprehensive Research on Korean Residents in Japan] (Tokyo: Shin Gigensha, 1979), 15, 18, 28, 29.

3 About Japanese peasants' migration to Manchukuo in the 1930s, see Part IV in Lou-ise Young, *Japan's Total Empire: Manchuria and the Culture of Wartime Imperialism* (Berkeley: University of California Press, 1998).

4 Michael Weiner, *Race and Migration in Imperial Japan* (London: Routledge, 1994), 139–140.

5 For recent studies of migrant subjects who moved to empire or the colony, see Ken C. Kawashima, *The Proletarian Gamble: The Korean Workers in Interwar Japan* (Dur-ham: Duke University Press, 2009); Uchida Jun, *Brokers of Empire: Japanese Settler Colonialism in Korea* (Cambridge, MA: Harvard University Asia Center, 2011).

6 Eri Hotta, *Pan-Asianism and Japan's War 1931–1945* (New York: Palgrave Macmil-lan, 2007).

7 The term "Greater East Asia Co-Prosperity Sphere" was presented as early as the late 1930s and different versions of "co-prosperity sphere" existed until it was officially promulgated by Imperial Japan in the early 1940s.

8 Yonetani Masafumi, *Ajia/nihon* [Asia/Japan] (Tokyo: Iwanami Shoten, 2006); J. Victor Koschmann and Sven Saaler, eds., *Pan-Asianism in Modern Japanese History: Colo-nialism, Regionalism and Borders* (London: Routledge, 2006); Cemil Aydin, *The Poli-tics of Anti-Westernism in Asia: Visions of World Order in Pan-Islamic and Pan-Asian Thought* (New York: Columbia University Press, 2007). Svan Saaler and Christopher W. Szpilman recently published a collection of primary sources on Pan-Asianism in twentieth- century Asia. Svan Saaler and Christopher W Szpilman, *Pan-Asianism, A Documentary History* (Lanham, MD: Rowman and Littlefield, 2011), 2 vols. Jeremy A. Yellen, *The Greater East Asia Co-Prosperity Sphere: When Total Empire Met Total War* (Ithaca: Cornell University Press, 2019).

9 See Chapter I in Yoshimi Shunya, *Shinbei to Hanbei* [Pro-America or Anti-America?] (Tokyo: Iwanami Shoten, 2007).

10 Sekai shizo kenkyūkai, ed., *Senso ka heiwa ka* [War or Peace?] (Tokyo: Nihonhyōronsha, 1921).

11 For recent studies of the East Asia Community, see Chapter 5 in Jung Sun Han, *An Imperial Path to Modernity: Yoshino Sakuzō* (Cambridge, MA: Harvard University Asia Center, 2012); Chapter 2, in Tessa Morris Suzuki, *Re-inventing Japan, Time, Space and Nation* (New York: M.E. Sharpe, 1998). Also see William Miils Fletcher, *The Search for a New Order: Intellectuals and Fascism in Interwar Japan* (Durham: University of North Carolina Press, 1982).

12 Katō Shūichi, "Taisho Democracy as the Pre-Stage for Japanese Militarism," in *Japan in Crisis: Essays on Taisho Democracy*, eds. Bernard S. Silberman and Harry Haroo-tunian (Princeton: Princeton University Press, 1974), 217–236.

13 Andrew Barshay, *The Social Sciences in Modern Japan* (Berkeley: University of Cali-fornia Press, 2004), 36–71.

14 In a 1926 book titled *Reading Society*, economist Nagai Toru argued that the term *shakai* [society] was "discovered" since class groups appeared in human relations and class-oriented human relations were developed independent of state-individual rela-tions. As long as class struggles exist, social movements including radical movements, he stressed, would continue in modern nations. Nagai Toru, *Shakaitokuhon* [Reading Society] (Tokyo: Nihonhyoronsha, 1926), 15.

15 Andrew Gordon, *Labor and Imperial Democracy* (Berkeley: University of California Press, 1991). Also see Part I in Sheldon Garon, *Molding Japanese Minds: The State in Everyday Life* (Princeton: Princeton University Press, 1997).

16 Ann Laura Stoller, *Carnal Knowledge and Imperial Power Race and the Intimate in Colonial Rule* (Berkeley: University of California Press, 2010).

17 The concept of "intimacy" has recently received attention in the field of colonial Korean literature and cultural studies. See Aimee Nayoung Kwon, *Intimate Empire: Collaboration & Colonial Modernity in Korea and Japan* (Durham: Duke University

Press, 2015); Su Yun Kim, *Imperial Romance: Fictions of Colonial Intimacy in Korea, 1905–1945* (Ithaca: Cornell University Press, 2020).

18 Sakai Tetsuya, *Kindai nihon no kokusai jitsujoron* [Theories of International Order in Modern Japan] (Tokyo: Iwanami Shoten, 2007).

19 Alfred Mahan, *The Problem of Asia and its Effect on International Polices* (Boston: Little, Brown and Company, 1900).

20 Kada Tetsuji, *Jinshu, minzoku, sensō* [Race, Nation and War] (Tokyo: Keio Shobo, 1938).

21 Ibid., 95–106.

22 Hotta explains the rise and development of Pan-Asianism in Japan in three different ways: (1) Asian commonalities based on philosophical dimension of Asian civilization, (2) a theory of Asian alliance and (3) wartime Pan-Asianism associated with Japan's expansionist ultranationalist thinking. Eri Hotta, *Pan-Asianism and Japan's War 1931–1945*, 7.

23 Okakura Tenshin's work was published in England in 1903 as *The Ideals of the East with Special Reference to the Art of Japan.*

24 For a detailed analysis of Okakura's Pan-Asian thought, see Brij Tankha, ed., *Okakura Tenshin and Pan-Asianism* (Leiden: Brill, 2008).

25 Sun Yat-sen, "Greater Asianism," in *China and Japan: Natural Friends, Unnatural Enemies: A Guide for China's Foreign Policy* (Shanghai: China United Press, 1941), 141–151, also available in *Pan Asianism: A Documentary History*, eds. Sven Saaler and Christopher Szpilman (Lanham, MD: Rowman & Littlefield Publishers, 2011), 75–85.

26 Sun Yat-sen, "Greater Asianism," 144–146.

27 Ibid. For a recent study of Chinese ethnic nationalism and "Chineseness," see Thomas Mullany, *Coming to Terms with the Nation: Ethnic Classification in Modern China* (Berkeley: University of California Press, 2011); also see Xiaowei Zang, *Ethnicity in China: A Critical Introduction* (Cambridge: Polity, 2015).

28 For a recent study of Mitsukawa Kametarō, Christopher W. Szpilman, "Between Pan-Asianism and Nationalism: Mitsukawa Kametarō and his Campaign to Reform Japan and Liberate Asia," in *Pan-Asianism in Modern Japanese History: Colonialism, Regionalism and Borders*, eds. J. Victor Koschmann and Svan Saaler (London: Routledge, 2006), 85–100; Christopher W. Szpilman, "Kanokogi Kazunobu: Pioneer of Platonic Fascism and Imperial Pan-Asianism," *Monumenta Nipponnica* 68, no. 2 (2014): 233–280; also see Christopher W. Szpilman, *Kindai Nihon no kakushinron to Ajia shugi: Kita Ikki, Ōkawa Shūmei, Mitsukawa Kametarō ra no shisō to kōdō* [Radical Thought and Asianism in Modern Japan: Thoughts and Behaviors in Kita Ikki, Ōkawa Shūmei and Mitsukawa Kametarō] (Tokyo: Ashi Shobō, 2015).

29 Mimura's recent work examines how the so-called Japanese reform bureaucrats (*kakushin kanryo*) mapped out a government-led new empire. However, Mimura's concept of "planning" is geographically confined to Japan proper and does not discuss how the issue of colonial development became increasingly important in building an empire. Janis Minura, *Planning for Empire* (Ithaca: Cornell University Press, 2012).

30 Mark Capiro, *Japanese Assimilation Policies in Colonial Korea* (Seattle: University of Washington Press, 2009); George Akita and Brandon Palmer, *The Japanese Colonial Legacy in Korea, 1910–1945: A New Perspective* (Portland: MerwinAsia, 2015).

31 For a study of *nissendōsoron* in early-twentieth-century Japan, see Mitsui Takashi, "Kindai academizushigaku no nakano<*nissendōsoron*> [The Theory of Japan and Korea having the Same Ancestor in the Field of Modern History Scholarship]," *Chosenshikenkyu kaironbunso* 42 (Oct. 2004): 42–76. Oguma Eiji has also extensively written on the issue of racial integration in imperial Japan. Oguma Eiji, *A Genealogy of Japanese Self-Images* (Melbourne: Trans Pacific Press, 2002).

32 Rōyama Masamichi, "Tōa kyōdōtai no rironteki kiso [A Theoritical Basis for the East Asian Cooperative Community]," in *Azia mondai kōza* 1 (Tokyo: Sōgensha, 1939), also in Rōyama Masamichi, *Tōa to sekai: shin chistujō e no ronsaku* [East Asia and the World: Exploring a New Order] (Tokyo: Kaizōsha, 1941), 156–157.

33 Koyama Iwao, *Sekashi no tetsugaku* [The Philosophy of World History] (Tokyo: Iwanami Shoten, 1941); Hiromatsu Wataru, *Kindai no chōkokuron: shōwashisoshi no ichidansō* [Overcoming Modernity: A Thought on the Intellectual History of Showa Japan] (Tokyo: Asahi Shuppansa, 1980). The "Overcoming Modernity" symposiums in 1942 have recently been translated into English. Richard F. Calichman, ed., *Overcoming Modernity* (New York: Columbia University Press, 2008). About the "overcoming the modern" discourses by the Kyoto School of Philosophy, see Chapter 2 in Harry Harootunian, *Overcome by Modernity: History, Culture, and Community in Interwar Japan* (Princeton: Princeton University Press, 2000), 34–94; Karatani Kojin, "Overcoming Modernity," in *Contemporary Japanese Thought*, ed. Richard F. Calichman (New York: Columbia University Press, 2005), 101–118.

34 About a recent study of "war of thought" and censorship in interwar Japan, see Barrack Kushner, *The Thought War: Japanese Imperial Propaganda* (Honolulu: University of Hawaii Press, 2007); Max Ward, *Thought Crime: Ideology and State Power in Interwar Japan* (Durham: Duke University Press, 2019).

35 Jung Jong Hyun, *Tongyangnon kwa singminji Chosŏn munhak: chegukchŏk chuch'e rŭl hyanghan yongmang kwa punyŏl* [Discourses on the Orient and Literature in Colonial Korea] (P'aju-si: Ch'angbi, 2011); Cha Seung Ki, *Pan'gŭndaejŏk sangsangnyŏk ŭi imgyedŭl: singminji Chosŏn tamnonjang esŏ ŭi chŏnt'ong, segye, chuch'e* [The Critical Point of Anti-Modern Imagination: Tradition, the World and Subject in the Discursive Space of Colonial Korea] (Seoul: P'urŭn Yŏksa, 2009).

36 Nishida Kitarō, *Last Writings: Nothingness and the Religious Worldview*, trans. David Dillworth (Honolulu: University of Hawaii Press, 1993).

37 In this respect the Kyoto School of Philosophy, which articulated a profound discussion of "overcoming the modern" in the interwar period, has recently drawn attention from scholars in Japan and the English-speaking world. See Naoki Sakai, *Translation and Subjectivity: On "Japan" and Cultural Nationalism* (Minneapolis: University of Minnesota Press, 1997); Christopher Goto Johns, *Political Philosophy in Japan: Nishida, the Kyoto School and Co-prosperity* (London: Routledge, 2010); James Heisig, *Philosophers of Nothingness: An Essay on the Kyoto School* (Honolulu: University of Hawaii Press, 2002); Richard Calichman, *Overcoming Modernity: Cultural Identity in Wartime Japan* (New York: Columbia University Press, 2008); Viren Murthy, Fabian Schafer and Max Ward, eds., *Confronting Capital and Empire: Rethinking Kyoto School Philosophy* (Leiden: Brill, 2017); Harumi Osaki, *Nothingness in the Heart of Empire: The Moral and Political Philosophy of the Kyoto School in Imperial Japan* (Albany: SUNY Press, 2019).

38 Jung Jong Hyun, *Tongyangnon kwa singminji Chosŏn munhak*, 115–117.

39 David Williams, *Defending Japan's Pacific War: The Kyoto School Philosophers and Post-White Power* (London: Routledge Curzon, 2004).

40 Harry Harootunian, *Overcome by Modernity*, 35–94.

41 Ezawa Jōji, *Kokudokeikaku no kisoriron* [Basic Theories of National Land Planning] (Tokyo: Nihonhyōronsha, 1942).

42 A number of important works written in English, Japanese and Korean deserve mention including Pang Kie-Jung, "Ilbonpasizum insik ui hondonkwa jaeinsikui banghyang [The Confusion of Analyzing Japanese Fascism and a Direction for New Understanding]," in *Sikminji pasizum ui yusankwa kukbokui kwaje* [The Legacy of Colonial Fascism and the Question of Overcoming It], ed. Pang Ki-Jung (Seoul: Hyean, 2006), 21–66; Takashi Fujitani, *Race for Empire: Koreans as Japanese and Japanese as Americans during World War II* (California: University of California

Press, 2011); Carter Eckert, *Offspring of Empire: The Kochang Kims and the Colonial Origins of Korean Capitalism, 1876–1945* (Seattle: University of Washington Press, 1991); Gi-Wook Shin and Michael Robinson, eds., *Colonial Modernity in Korea* (Cambridge: Harvard University Press, 1999); Brandon Palmer, *Fighting for the Enemy: Koreans in Japan's War 1937–1945* (Seattle: University of Washington Press, 2013).
43 Immanuel Wallerstein, "The Unintended Consequences of Cold War Area Studies," in *The Cold War and the University*, ed. Noam Chomsky (New York: The New Press, 1997), 195–232.
44 Max Weber, *From Max Weber: Essays in Sociology*, trans and ed. H. H. Gerth and C. Wright (New York: Oxford University Press, 1946), 267–359; Max Weber, *The Theory of Social and Economic Organization*, ed. Taclcott Parsons (New York: Oxford University Press, 1947), 8–29.

Bibliography

Akita, George and Brandon Palmer. *The Japanese Colonial Legacy in Korea, 1910–1945: A New Perspective*. Portland: MerwinAsia, 2015.
Aydin, Cemil. *The Politics of Anti-Westernism in Asia: Visions of World Order in Pan-Islamic and Pan-Asian Thought*. New York: Columbia University Press, 2007.
Barshay, Andrew. *The Social Sciences in Modern Japan*. Berkeley: University of California Press, 2004.
Calichman, Richard F., ed. *Overcoming Modernity: Cultural Idenity in Wartime Japan*. New York: Columbia University Press, 2008.
Capiro, Mark. *Japanese Assimilation Policies in Colonial Korea*. Seattle: University of Washington Press, 2009.
Cha, Seung Ki. *Pan'gŭndaejŏk sangsangnyŏk ŭi imgyedŭl: singminji Chosŏn tamnonjang esŏ ŭi chŏnt'ong, segye, chuch'e* [The Critical Point of Anti-Modern Imagination: Tradition, the World and Subject in the Discursive Space of Colonial Korea]. Seoul: P'urŭn Yŏksa, 2009.
Du Bois, W.E.B. "China and Japan." *The Pittsburgh Courier*, Sep. 25, 1937.
Eckert, Carter. *Offspring of Empire: The Kochang Kims and the Colonial Origins of Korean Capitalism, 1876–1945*. Seattle: University of Washington Press, 1991.
Ezawa, Jōji. *Kokudokeikaku no kisoriron* [Basic Theories of National Land Planning]. Tokyo: Nihonhyōronsha, 1942.
Fletcher, William Mills. *The Search for a New Order: Intellectuals and Fascism in Interwar Japan*. Durham: University of North Carolina Press, 1982.
Fujitani, Takashi. *Race for Empire: Koreans as Japanese and Japanese as Americans during World War II*. Berkeley: University of California Press, 2011.
Garon, Sheldon. *Molding Japanese Minds: The State in Everyday Life*. Princeton: Princeton University Press, 1997.
Gordon, Andrew. *Labor and Imperial Democracy*. Berkeley: University of California Press, 1991.
Goto Johns, Christopher. *Political Philosophy in Japan: Nishida, the Kyoto School and Co-Prosperity*. London: Routledge, 2010.
Han, Jung Sun. *An Imperial Path to Modernity: Yoshino Sakuzō*. Cambridge, MA: Harvard University Asia Center, 2012.
Harootunian, Harry. *Overcome by Modernity: History, Culture, and Community in Interwar Japan*. Princeton: Princeton University Press, 2000.

Heisig, James. *Philosophers of Nothingness: An Essay on the Kyoto School.* Honolulu: University of Hawaii Press, 2002.

Hiromatsu, Wataru. *Kindai no chōkokuron: shōwashisoshi no ichidansō* [Overcoming Modernity: A Thought on the Intellectual History of Showa Japan]. Tokyo: Asahi Shuppansa, 1980.

Hotta, Eri. *Pan-Asianism and Japan's War 1931–1945.* New York: Palgrave Macmillan, 2007.

Jun, Uchida. *Brokers of Empire: Japanese Settler Colonialism in Korea.* Cambridge, MA: Harvard University Asia Center, 2011.

Jung, Jong Hyun. *Tongyangnon kwa singminji Chosŏn munhak: chegukchŏk chuch'e rŭl hyanghan yongmang kwa punyŏl* [Discourses on the Orient and Literature in Colonial Korea]. P'aju-si: Ch'angbi, 2011.

Kada, Tetsuji. *Jinshu, minzoku, sensō* [Race, Nation and War]. Tokyo: Keio Shobo, 1938.

Karatani, Kojin. "Overcoming Modernity." In *Contemporary Japanese Thought,* edited by Richard F. Calichman, 101–118. New York: Columbia University Press, 2005.

Katō, Shūichi. "Taisho Democracy as the Pre-Stage for Japanese Militarism." In *Japan in Crisis: Essays on Taishō Democracy.* Princeton: Princeton University Press, 1974.

Kawashima, Ken C. *The Proletarian Gamble: The Korean Workers in Interwar Japan.* Durham: Duke University Press, 2009.

Kim, Su Yun. *Imperial Romance: Fictions of Colonial Intimacy in Korea, 1905–1945.* Ithaca: Cornell University Press, 2020.

Koschmann, J. Victor and Sven Saaler, eds. *Pan-Asianism in Modern Japanese History: Colonialism, Regionalism and Borders.* London: Routledge, 2006.

Koyama, Iwao. *Sekashi no tetsugaku* [The Philosophy of World History]. Tokyo: Iwanami Shoten, 1941.

Kushner, Barrack. *The Thought War: Japanese Imperial Propaganda.* Honolulu: University of Hawaii Press, 2007.

Kwon, Aimee Nayoung. *Intimate Empire: Collaboration and Colonial Modernity in Korea and Japan.* Durham: Duke University Press, 2015.

Mahan, Alfred. *The Problem of Asia and Its Effect on International Polices.* Boston: Little, Brown and Company, 1900.

Minura, Janis. *Planning for Empire.* Ithaca: Cornell University Press, 2012.

Mitsui, Takashi. "Kindai academizushigaku no nakano<*nissendōsoron*> [The Theory of Japan and Korea Having the Same Ancestor in the Field of Modern History Scholarship]." *Chōsenshikenkyū kaironbunso* 42 (Oct. 2004): 42–76.

Morris-Suzuki, Tessa. *Re-inventing Japan: Time, Space and Nation.* New York: M. E. Sharpe, 1998.

Mullany, Thomas. *Coming to Terms with the Nation: Ethnic Classification in Modern China.* Berkeley: University of California Press, 2011.

Murthy, Viren, Fabian Schafer and Max Ward, eds. *Confronting Capital and Empire: Rethinking Kyoto School Philosophy.* Leiden: Brill, 2017.

Nagai, Toru. *Shakaitokuhon* [Reading Society]. Tokyo: Nihonhyoronsha, 1926.

Nishida, Kitarō. *Last Writings: Nothingness and the Religious Worldview.* Translated by David Dillworth. Honolulu: University of Hawaii Press, 1993.

Oguma, Eiji. *A Genealogy of Japanese Self-Images.* Melbourne: Trans Pacific Press, 2002.

Okakura, Tenshin. *The Ideals of the East: With Special Reference to the Art of Japan.* Rutland: Tuttle Company, 1903.

Osaki, Harumi. *Nothingness in the Heart of Empire: The Moral and Political Philosophy of the Kyoto School in Imperial Japan*. Albany: State University of New York Press, 2019.

Palmer, Brandon. *Fighting for the Enemy: Koreans in Japan's War 1937–1945*. Seattle: University of Washington Press, 2013.

Pang, Kie-Jung, ed. *Sikminji pasizum ui yusankwa kukbokui kwaje* [The Legacy of Colonial Fascism and the Question of Overcoming It]. Seoul: Hyean, 2006.

Park, Kyung Sik. *Zainichi Chōsenjin ni kansuru sogo chosa kenkyu* [A Comprehensive Research on Korean Residents in Japan]. Tokyo: Shin Gigensha, 1979.

Rōyama, Masamichi. "Tōa kyōdōtai no rironteki kiso [A Theoritical Basis for the East Asian Cooperative Community]." *Azia mondai kōza* 1. Tokyo: Sōgensha, 1939. Also in Rōyama Masamichi, *Tōa to sekai: shin chistujō e no ronsaku* [East Asia and the World: Exploring a New Order], 152–168. Tokyo: Kaizōsha, 1941.

Saaler, Svan and Christopher W. Szpilman, eds. *Pan-Asianism: A Documentary History*. Lanham, MD: Rowman and Littlefield, 2011, 2 vols.

Sakai, Naoki. *Translation and Subjectivity: On "Japan" and Cultural Nationalism*. Minneapolis: University of Minnesota Press, 1997.

Sakai, Tetsuya. *Kindai nihon no kokusai jitsujoron* [Theories of International Order in Modern Japan]. Tokyo: Iwanami Shoten, 2007.

Sekai shizo kenkyūkai, ed. *Senso ka heiwa ka* [War or Peace?]. Tokyo: Nihonhyōronsha, 1921.

Shin, Gi-Wook and Michael Robinson, eds. *Colonial Modernity in Korea*. Cambridge: Harvard University Press, 1999.

Shunya, Yoshimi. *Shinbei to Hanbei* [Pro-America or Anti-America?]. Tokyo: Iwanami Shoten, 2007.

Stoller, Ann Laura. *Carnal Knowledge and Imperial Power: Race and the Intimate in Colonial Rule*. Berkeley: University of California Press, 2010.

Sun, Yat-sen. *China and Japan: Natural Friends, Unnatural Enemies: A Guide for China's Foreign Policy*. Shanghai: China United Press, 1941.

Szpilman, Christopher W. "Kanokógi Kazunobu: Pioneer of Platonic Fascism and Imperial Pan-Asianism." *Monumenta Nipponnica* 68, no. 2 (2014): 233–280.

———. *Kindai Nihon no kakushinron to Ajia shugi: Kita Ikki, Ōkawa Shūmei, Mitsukawa Kametarō ra no shisō to kōdō* [Radical Thought and Asianism in Modern Japan: Thoughts and Behaviors in Kita Ikki, Ōkawa Shūmei and Mitsukawa Kametarō]. Tokyo: Ashi Shobō, 2015.

Tankha, Brij, ed. *Okakura Tenshin and Pan-Asianism*. Leiden: Brill, 2008.

Wallerstein, Immanuel. "The Unintended Consequences of Cold War Area Studies." In *The Cold War and the University,* edited by Noam Chomsky, 195–232. New York: The New Press, 1997.

Ward, Max. *Thought Crime: Ideology and State Power in Interwar Japan*. Durham: Duke University Press, 2019.

Weber, Max. *From Max Weber: Essays in Sociology*. Translated and edited by H. H. Gerth and C. Wright. New York: Oxford University Press, 1946.

Weber, Max. *The Theory of Social and Economic Organization*. Edited by Taclcott Parsons. New York: Oxford University Press, 1947.

Weiner, Michael. *Race and Migration in Imperial Japan*. London: Routledge, 1994.

Williams, David. *Defending Japan's Pacific War: The Kyoto School Philosophers and Post-White Power*. London: Routledge Curzon, 2004.

Yellen, Jeremy A. *The Greater East Asia Co-Prosperity Sphere: When Total Empire Met Total War*. Ithaca: Cornell University Press, 2019.

Yonetani, Masafumi. *Ajia/nihon* [Asia/Japan]. Tokyo: Iwanami Shoten, 2006.

Young, Louise. *Japan's Total Empire: Manchuria and the Culture of Wartime Imperialism*. Berkeley: University of California Press, 1998.

Zang, Xiaowei. *Ethnicity in China: A Critical Introduction*. Cambridge: Polity, 2015.

Part I

Theories of a Pan-Asian empire

1 Toward a new imperial order

Pan-Asian regionalism in interwar
Japan

The period of anxiety

In June 1933, the renowned Japanese philosopher Miki Kiyoshi published an essay titled, "The Thought of Anxiety and its Overcoming." In this writing, Miki first introduced the concept of period in history in which he insisted that a new period had begun since the end of the First World War.[1] This period, he stressed, is characterized by anxiety and he diagnosed that the thought of anxiety gave rise to fundamental skepticism toward self-evident modern values that had been sustained by individuals until the outbreak of the First World War.[2] Not surprisingly, Miki's speculation was a philosophical approach to what Edward Hallett Carr later termed "Twenty Years' Crisis."[3] Miki asserted that overcoming anxieties would not be possible by searching for objective truth and instead suggested that constructive and creative subjectivities must be established by individuals.[4]

While Miki centered his analysis on the field of literature and philosophy, the sense of crisis had already been a widespread phenomenon among Japanese and Western intellectuals in the early 1930s. Various theoretical attempts were made by European intellectuals in order to replace the limits of *laissez-faire* capitalism and democracy. In the field of diplomacy and international politics, a much bolder blueprint was provided to preclude the single-nation-state-oriented world from experiencing another world war. In May 1930, Aristide Briand, a renowned French diplomat, called for the necessity of creating a "United States of Europe" to rescue Europe from being dismantled and to avoid a tacit endorsing of the United States of America as a sole superpower in the international order. To be sure, Briand's blueprint for a new international order clearly reflects the growing sense of anxiety, as well as France's strategic decision to appropriate Germany's situation as a way of promoting her influence in Europe vis-à-vis Great Britain. German politicians and intellectuals also showed sympathy for Briand's new international order theory, hoping for a restoration of its wounded national pride in the wake of the Great War and the reinstatement of German national leadership in Europe.

For Japanese intellectuals in the 1930s, the sense of crisis took on much more profound colors than any imperial powers in the world. As Koyasu Nobukuni and others have argued, liberal and progressive intellectuals had focused their "constructive" and "creative" powers on the critiques of the preponderance of the Japanese nation-state, since they observed that the total process of modernization since 1868 had resulted in the reduction of individual freedom and democratic values.[5] Koyasu's revisit to radical intellectuals and activists such as Kotoku Shusui deserves attention, in that it reveals another aspect of twentieth-century Japanese political thought that was overtly opposed to top-down modernization championed by the Japanese state and the Emperor system. This approach, however, does not fully answer an insightful question Katō Shūichi, one of the most preeminent intellectuals in postwar Japan, raised as early as the 1970s. In 1974, Katō problematized the transition from Taisho Japan to wartime Japan and Japan's invasion of northern China in 1931 and the establishment of Manchukuo in the following year fundamentally challenged the topography of Japanese political and social thought.[6] A much bigger task of contriving the logic of rationalizing the position of Japan that was now utterly anti-Western was given to Japanese intellectuals, some of whom had only delved into domestic questions such as state-society relations and class struggle *within* the Japanese economy.

Under these circumstances, Japanese social scientists, and liberal thinkers in particular, found themselves facing a serious challenge in the new context of Japan's hostile relations with the West, given that they had played a pivotal role in promoting and spreading the ideas and values of Western civilization and modernity. As the conflict between Japan and the West became worse, various anti-Western and ultranationalistic discourses flooded academia and the media, both of which had previously provided the intellectual backbone supporting Japan's modernization and the establishment of the Taisho Democracy in the 1920s. Western ideas soon became common targets to be conceptually "overcome," and as a counter theory, Asianism or the emperor-centered Japanism rapidly gained currency among Japanese intellectuals. Paradoxically, the ideas of both chauvinistic Asianists and Japanists in the mid-1930s demonstrated great affinity with the totalitarian and fascist theories originating in "Europe," in that they aimed to restructure domestic politics by overthrowing the existing parliamentary democracy and reforming the capitalist economy.

The early discussions on the subject of regional empire by Japanese intellectuals were led by a newly emerging group of social scientists such as Rōyama Masamichi (1895–1980) and Shinmei Masamichi (1898–1984). Along with other social scientists such as Kada Tetsuji (1895–1964) and Takata Yasuma (1883–1972), they are known as the leading figures who theorized the famous but unexplored and conceptually unpacked notion of the East Asian Cooperative Community (*tōa kyōdōtai*) during the wartime period. In challenging both ultranational fascism and spiritual Pan-Asianism, they represented a "rationalist" intellectual stream, one that sought to construct an idea of East Asian empire in which Japan's regional hegemony could be endorsed by the rest of Asia, and Chinese and other colonial subjects could voluntarily commit to the new empire.

Most of the intellectuals whose work embraced the theory of *kyōdōtai* were trained in the social sciences under the liberal atmosphere of Taisho democracy during the 1920s. Therefore, it is misleading to simply assert that these intellectuals' involvement in supporting imperialist discourse was forced by the fascist government during the wartime period. These Japanese social scientists, including some Marxist intellectuals, subjectively encountered the era of "Europe in crisis" in the post-World War I international order. In doing so, they presented a variety of critiques of liberal democracy and *laissez-faire* capitalism, and Pan-Asianist thinking emerged as an intellectual platform for them to restructure the Japanese empire in the 1930s. At stake is the question of how these *kyōdōtai* social scientists differentiated their ideas from spiritual and Japanist Pan-Asianist discourses and resorted to what they believed to be "rationalist" Pan-Asianism.

The tumultuous 1920s: domestic reforms vs. early Pan-Asian empire

The 1921 work *Critiques of The Modern Nation State* (*gendai kokka hihan*) by Hasegawa Nyozekan (1875–1969), one of the leading intellectuals during the Taisho Period, was a symbolic piece of writing that foregrounded the mentality of Japanese social scientists, liberal intellectuals in particular, in the 1920s. In this book, Hasegawa first observed that the ideal of modern nation-state was to mutually aid and foster each individual in his or her pursuit of real life.[7] However, modern nation-states, he stressed, revealed their limits as they failed to cope with the diversity and complexity required in each sector of their expertise – society, economy, politics and culture. Nyozekan asserted that to get closer to an ideal state, a modern nation-state needed to be organic so that the gap between individuals' real life and the state's execution of political power is reduced. He lamented that the modern nation-state had lost its organic aspect – the spiritual, religious and moral idealism that constituted its internal and external logic.[8]

Hasegawa's critiques of the modern state resonated with a number of Japanese social scientists who shared the observation that the excessive state control of all social sectors and the linear top-down modernization path since 1868 had reached a critical point. It was at this point that the notion of "discovering society (*shakai no hakken*)" captured the attention of Japanese intellectuals. As Hasegawa pointed out in discussing the limits of the modern state, these social scientists tended to first differentiate state from society and conceptualize the latter as a space where cooperation, mutual aid and reforms might occur to protect individuals from incessant conflict and enable them to develop their lives. For this reason, advocates of "discovering society" naturally associated their line of thinking with radical prescriptions that prioritized reducing the state's control over society and individuals, and constructing a new space called society where existing problems such as economic inequality, labor abuse and marginalization of peasants would be solved.[9]

It is misleading to argue that the intellectual trend of discovering society was premised on a naïve theoretical attempt to completely differentiate society from state or that it ended up addressing an unrealistic utopia based on an idealized version of society. To be sure, the concept of society played a crucial role in revealing the shadows of rapid modernization in early twentieth-century Japan and at the same time brought forth the advancement of Japanese social sciences. The emergence of Japanese sociology was concurrent with the notion of "discovering society." However, what mattered more was how, and in what context, they would deal with the intellectual challenges caused by the state being omnipotent. As historian Arima Manabu has argued, the rise of liberal and progressive intellectuals in Taisho Japan ought to be much more broadly considered together with what he termed the internationalization of Japan in the 1920s.[10]

Since these Japanese intellectuals considered themselves as theoretically addressing liberal and progressive reforms within domestic matters, they had to answer growing critiques of Japanese imperialism from the outside, and from European powers in particular. In other words, they also needed to measure to what degree the widely shared perceptions of society and social progress would affect their "locally" focused thinking. Here it is important to note that the "crisis mentality" shared by European intellectuals in the aftermath of the First World War not only pertained to their observation of domestic order in crisis but more importantly, to the limits of a single nation-state framework in the international order which, they believed, would result in another world war. Growing tensions among major powers in post-World War I Europe intensified demands for a new collective security system to operate at an international level, fundamentally questioning the existing League of Nations, a precarious system of diplomatic alliances based on a fluctuating balance of power within the competitive nation-state framework. As Jerry Muller correctly puts it, the European intellectual crisis was about the theoretical impossibility of delineating these radical discussions, as they revolved around the instability of the Euro-centric world order.[11]

While liberal and Marxist intellectuals were centering their academic inquiries over domestic reforms, the sensibility of Japan's position in the international order was rather clearly found in the writings of conservative and "Japanist" intellectuals in the 1920s. They observed that international circumstances surrounding Japan had threatened Japan's position as an imperial power. Anti-Japanese and anti-colonial movements in Korea and China in 1919 required these conservatives to rethink the fundamental logic and structure of Japan's China policy and colonial governance. They were also attentive to demographical changes in Asia. Beginning in the early 1920s, a number of Koreans migrated to Japan proper while Japanese residents found colonial Korea and Manchuria as their new settling down places. Historian Sunil Smith makes a compelling point that China showed a new demographic pattern in the late 1920s, pushing its two million people to Manchuria.[12]

Under these circumstances, conservative Japanese intellectuals quickly responded to the changing topography of the Japanese empire. They paid special attention to the new concept of an empire that embraces Chinese and Korean diaspora by expanding imperial Japan to Manchuria. As early as the mid-1920s, several proposals for an expanded Japanese empire such as the notion of the Mongolian Kingdom or the idea of a Greater Koryo Kingdom were presented by mostly conservative intellectuals.[13] As Ishihara Kanji drafted the Kingly Way in Manchukuo in the 1930s by extracting common religions and philosophical ingredients from Buddhism and Confucianism, these conservative Asianist intellectuals attempted to incorporate Koreans and Chinese. The fact that ancient Mongolia or the Koryo Kingdom in the Korean peninsula (918–1392) appears in their new empire plans clearly reveals their intention to make their ideas of a regional empire sound "inclusive."

To be sure, these early Asianist proposals by Japanese conservatives and ultra-nationalists were not premised on their critiques of Japanese colonialism. It was rather their sense of "victimhood" that intensified in the 1920s. Japan's becoming a rising power in the international order did not clear away this mentality as the Japanese, Japanese immigrants in the United States in particular, were still experiencing overt discrimination from the West. For instance, Japanese immigrant children in San Francisco were forbidden to attend public schools in 1906 based on the fear-mongering that they were the offspring of "dangerous" Mongolians.[14] In other words, Japan's rapid development in the economic and militaristic arenas was not accompanied by fundamental changes in Western perceptions of the Japanese. The constructed images of Japan as part of the Orient that had been discriminated against by the West certainly helped imperial Japan conceal the reality of Japanese colonialism. In that respect, Japanese conservatives' early Pan-Asianist approaches in the 1920s reflect the deceptive and colonialist nature of their internationalist thinking.

However, liberal and progressive social scientists in 1920s Japan did not resonate with growing spiritual Asianist discourses which they might not have considered as the realm of rigid social scientific thinking. This does not mean that they developed critical inquiries on Japan's international position as a regional empire. The notion of "discovering society" was mostly linked to these liberal and progressive social scientists' observation of the urgency of domestic reforms in which colonial issues received little attention. Historian Andrew Gordon has theorized this gap between domestic reforms and colonial reality as imperial democracy, and the absence of critical thinking toward Japanese colonialism was also found in the writings of Japanese social scientists during this time.

Perhaps, it was only a small group of social scientists in the field of colonial policy who articulated their regionalist and internationalist thinking in the 1920s. The renowned economist and often called one of the most conscientious Japanese intellectuals, Yanaihara Tadao (1893–1961) was one who delved into the problem of Japanese colonialism in the 1920s. Influenced by Adam Smith's early colonial theories and the ideas of Nitobe Inazō (1862–1933), a pioneer in the studies of colonial policy in modern Japan, Yanaihara defined colonization as the natural dissemination of civilization from advanced groups to others in his early writings.[15] However, Yanaihara attempted to influence colonial policy in the 1920s and early 1930s by claiming that the colonizer should not simply view the colonized as objects of exploitation, and therefore Japan should implement practical measures to improve the living standards of colonial subjects.[16]

For this reason, it is conceivable that these liberal and progressive intellectuals from a domestic perspective created nuanced voices on the Japanese invasion of Manchuria in 1931 and the creation of Manchukuo in the following year. In 1934, Yanaihara addressed the concept of the "line of sovereignty" in an article he contributed to the journal *Kaizō* shortly after Japan's withdrawal from the League of Nations.[17] This theory, reminiscent of former Prime Minister Yamagata Aritomo's theory of "line of interest," was based on Yanaihara's observation that not all territories in the world can be defined by the modern theory of sovereignty. He stressed that no political sovereignty was established in Manchuria and Mongolia in a modern sense. He then argued that special relationships between these entities and a certain nation-state may occur based on particular interests.[18] Japan's "particular interests" within these territories, according to him, stemmed from her historical and cultural interactions with them and this granted Japan a legitimate right to establish what he called a "Manchu-Mongolian state." Yanaihara's thesis was conceived to differentiate Japan's territorial expansion from the European colonial which, he believed, occupied territories where no special relationships were established.[19] In fact, the notion of Japan's "special interests" in Manchuria had been shared by other liberal intellectuals such as Yoshino Sakuzō (1878–1933) who called for Japan to open its doors to China to ensure that both Japan and China would be protected from Western threats. Unsurprisingly, Yoshino's new diplomatic theory was premised on Japan's special interests in the Manchu and Mongolia area.[20]

Again, one might find innovation in Yanaihara's theory in that he at least did not repeat the victim mentality or the rhetoric of Japan as being marginalized by the West. In fact, he had spoken against Japanese colonial policies, representing the liberalist interpretation of Japanese imperialism in social scientific circles, together with Yoshino Sakuzō. For this reason, it was highly understandable that Yanaihara would not endorse the establishment of Manchukuo as Japan's triumphant achievement. Nor did he take a purely pacifist direction, that is, that Japan should walk out of this imperialist world competition in light of the fact that by that time Japan was engulfed in international criticism, although he argued in 1937 that Japan should consider liberating Korea. His theory of a Manchu-Mongolian state, therefore, can be read as his intellectual endeavor to inject rationality into Japan's invasion of China by addressing the "exceptionalism" or "vacuum" in modern political science in general, and not in the context of Japanese social sciences alone. For this reason, Yanaihara's thinking was a more evolved form of rationalization, compared to the theories of the former generation such as Nitobe Inazō, who outspokenly affirmed colonization as a form of civilization, and from whom Yanaihara himself was taught colonial policy studies. Nitobe Inazō, a pioneer of colonial policy studies as well as a leading liberal economist, suggested that Japan should persuade the world to recognize its civilizing mission in China.[21]

In this way, Yoshino Sakuzō and Yanaihara Tadao, icons of liberal social sciences in the Taisho period strove to draft their own vision of a regional order, partly problematizing the limits of Western social scientific thinking. However, this intellectual journey to break through Japan's diplomatic crisis through presenting an alternative political theory did not receive enough attention in national academia. While rationalist thinking in the social sciences was gradually fading away, Japan's "international" crisis in real politics was easily appropriated as an excuse by right-wing extremists to dismantle the democratic order at home. Surely, the Manchurian Crisis of 1931 changed the topography of Japanese politics. The

United States and Europe were no longer willing to tolerate the emergence of another hegemonic power in East Asia, and diplomatic tensions reached an apex in 1933 as Japan eventually withdrew from the League of Nations. So, while Japan had succeeded in its ambitious territorial expansion, this military success was accompanied by the creation of powerful new diplomatic and political adversities. Under these circumstances, reactionary thinking gradually permeated the mentality of Japanese social scientists. One explicit symptom of this infection was social scientists' rediscovery of the Japanese spirit as a motivating source of social forces. In that respect, it is true that Japanist and ultranationalist writings on Asia prevailed more than the writings of liberal intellectuals on Asia in the early 1930s. In the pages that follow, this study critically revisits these intellectuals' writings on Japan and Asia before exploring rationalist Pan-Asian regional discourses by a group of Japanese social scientists.

The rise of Japanism – a prelude to spiritual pan-Asianism

In 1932, Hijikata Seibi, Professor of Economics at Tokyo Imperial University who later addressed the theory of controlled economy during the wartime period published an article titled "Economic Theories in Crisis (*keizai riron no kiki*)." Hijikata's basic observation was that modern liberal social sciences faced challenges during this era of crisis in the mid-1930s. He asserted that contemporary economic theories based on individuals' rational behavior and the theory of natural balance had failed to explain the existing international crisis.[22] He was equally critical of Marxist economic theory, contending that symptoms of the current economic crisis clearly showed that communism would not be an alternative to the *laissez-faire* system.[23] To him, it was evident that neither liberalism nor communism could explicate the location of contemporary economic crises. His logical conclusion was to give the state an absolute power to control human behavior and eliminate social inconsistencies. Accordingly, he opened fire against liberal democracy as well, insisting that the parliament must be restructured to support the state-controlled economic system.[24]

Hijikata was convinced that the capitalist instinct of human beings would not be controlled through an institutionalized means, that is, the state. Three months later, he contributed another article to the same journal. This time he searched for rational links between the state-controlled economy and what he called Japanese spirit (*nihon seishin*). The individual in capitalism, Hijikata stressed, had been distorted and would thus be destined to collapse. Therefore, what was urgent for him was to redefine the relationship between state and individual.

> The control (*tōsei*) that corresponds to our ethnic spirit (*minzoku seishin*), needless to say, is not a control that limits individuals to a certain category and thus must be one that rejects obstacles oppressing development within individuals. The reason control in contemporary capitalist economies is being condemned is that the pressure of capital suppresses the development of the individual's personality.[25]

Based on this observation, Hijikata continued to argue that insofar as the theory of marginal utility and free competition is enforced, control and balance in the capitalist economy would not be achieved. To resolve this conundrum, he resorted to what he called the Japanese spirit. He claimed that there had been a spirit in Japan that enabled the development of the individual as well as the balance and control of totality.[26] His logic of Japanese spirit and its compatibility with a new state-planned economy, however, was not sufficiently articulated until the mid-1930s. Indeed, it reappeared five years later as a theory of *bun* (given role) in a book titled *The Way of Japanese Economics* (*Nihon keizaigaku no do*). Here, Hijikata sought the sustainability of a total society through the role of an individual's moral behavior. Morality in this book was depicted as a value that could only be accomplished when individuals faithfully follow the roles given to them by the state.[27] In this way, Hijikata intended to rationalize a control economy through terms that were inexplicable from a rational social scientific perspective.

While Hijikata's writings in the mid-1930s show how spiritualism penetrated a social scientific thinking previously epitomized by rationality, Japanism had already obtained a primary discursive status in academic circles. To be sure, the term Japanism (*nihonshugi*) was not a new creation in the 1930s. The notion of Japan as an ideology existed in various forms during the Meiji and Taisho periods. Mori Kiyohito, a leader of The Institute of Japanese Thought (*Nihon shisōkenkyūkai*), categorized Japanism in three different time periods. According to him, early Japanist thinking before the Meiji Restoration was characterized by its adherence to pure Japanese traditional values such as the samurai spirit. This type of Japanism, which Mori termed "conservative Japanism," did not contain concrete discussions of modernization since it appeared in the premodern time period.[28] He then pointed out the emergence of a more aggressive Japanism during the Taisho period. Although so-called Japanists shared spiritual values such as the Japanese spirit (*yamato dasashii*) or *bushido*, Japanism in the Taisho period had to confront the influx of various external ideologies, and socialism and communism in particular. Mori argued that Japanism took the form of defending the capitalist system, as it found socialism the most dangerous ideology opposed to the sustenance of Japanese society.[29] A renowned Marxist intellectual Tosaka Jun observed that Japanism in the 1930s aimed to sustain the so-called Japanese entity by discovering primitive values from traditional Japan in the general crisis of capitalism, while also fighting the spread of communist thinking.[30] By locating premodern Japan as a space where a proper national equilibrium was realized, Tosaka reasoned that these spiritual Japanists depicted a harmonious pre-historical agriculture-oriented society, whereas modernization had produced numerous issues of inequality and imbalance. For this reason, Tosaka cast a dubious eye on the eventual affinity of Japanism with Japanese fascism since both ideologies put forward the elimination of class struggle and social conflicts.[31]

From the perspective of regionalism, the rise of the idea of the Japanist spirit emerged in rapidly changing retroactive political circumstances. European intellectuals' skeptical prescription for liberal democracy and the capitalist economy and the specific political and diplomatic challenges Japan faced both played a pivotal role in accelerating the conservatism of Japanese society, under which a nation-centered spiritualism gained currency. Just as a number of Japanists readily fought socialism and communism as their common enemy, they also shared the belief that the existing international order established right after the end of World War I had represented the interests of European countries. Lacking in this line of thinking was the observation that Japan itself was a major imperial power. For this reason, Japanism in the early 1930s became increasingly chauvinistic and simply reproduced the rhetoric of Japan as victimized.

More importantly, Japanist thinking in the early 1930s was not equipped with any sophisticated ideas of how to position Japan within an Asian regional order. Since Japanist thinking in the early and mid-1930s predominantly focused on intervening in domestic politics within the rhetoric of rejecting Western moderni-zation and returning to traditional Japanese value systems, most spiritual Japanists paid little attention to the issue of how their ideology would appeal to the rest of Asia. To be sure, it is undeniable that spiritual Japanism stemmed from an epis-temology that the Japanese national community had maintained its homogenous entity and thus Japan was superior to the rest of Asia. A pride in a "splendid" national past was often associated with images of Japan as the only successfully modernized nation in Asia. Although Japanist ideologues were generally hostile to modernization as Westernization, their explicit self-esteem and perception of superiority collided with, and conceptually reinforced, Japan's position as an imperial power.

State socialism and ultranationalist Pan-Asianism

As discussed so far, the spread of a crisis mentality continuously challenged lib-eral intellectuals in Japanese academic circles. The reality of Japanese liberal social scientists' being marginalized is traceable to their peculiar intellectual footprints in early-twentieth-century Japan. There was a consensus that liberal social scientists, along with Marxist intellectuals, had brought progress to Japa-nese society by criticizing the state's monopoly of private sectors and expanding autonomous political spaces. In a 1933 book titled, *On Contemporary Tendencies in Japanese Politics*, political scientist Rōyama Masamichi pointedly observed that liberal democracy was being transformed into what he called a parliamentary dictatorship through the rhetoric of "emergency," while *laissez-faire* capitalism was also being replaced by "organized capitalism," that is to say, political power controlled finance, capital and the "free" market.[32] He anticipated that under these circumstances, acute political conflicts would occur between Marxist radicals and rightist nationalists, the latter of whom had already leaned into state-centered totalitarianism and planned economy.[33] Rōyama's analysis indicates that which-ever political standpoint would gain momentum, the sense of democracy and capitalism in crisis would not fade away.

While most liberal social scientists in early 1930s Japan narrowly defined Japan's crisis in terms of its diplomatic conflicts with the West, right-wing extremists usefully appropriated it to reconfigure Japan's domestic structure. However, it is important to note that crisis discourses emanating from Europe were also inseparable from a restructuring of international relations. For European intellectuals, and Germans and Italians in particular, the crisis in the international order was much more closely related to envisioning a paradigm shift in the domestic structure, thereby intensifying hegemony in their own international order. In an effort to overcome the limits of democracy and the *laissez-faire* system, these European intellectuals revisited the liberalist concept of the state and society; as a result, various notions of state-centered social theories appeared in the early 1930s. Totalitarianism and fascism rapidly gained readership in academia and became influential in real politics.

A similar mentality was found in the writings of Japanist and ultranationalist social scientists. They first paid special attention to their political goal to reconstruct domestic society and then gradually moved to the question of sustaining and expanding a Pan-Asian empire under the logic of the Imperial Way. Notably, various political organizations appeared in the early 1930s and produced a wide range of ultranational and Japanese thoughts. While leading Marxist social scientists were preoccupied with the Asiatic Mode of Production debate and liberal social scientists had not presented a new paradigm in Japan's imperial order other than endorsing Manchukuo in the mid-1930s, Japanist discourses quickly permeated not only intellectuals in the field of humanities but importantly, a number of social scientists. Perhaps, state socialism is one of the most politically provocative ideologies that captured the mindset of Japanese social scientists.

The term state socialism itself first appeared in Japanese academic circles before the mid- 1930s. The famous Marxist theoretician Takabatake Motoyuki (1886–1928), who translated Marx's *Das Kapital* into Japanese several times, had already advocated state socialism in the late 1920s.[34] Takabatake contended that social association, political and economic, is based on human beings' social instinct (*shakaiteki honno*), which is nothing but egoism. He went on to argue that human beings' egoism, however, is much more complex than that of other creatures, and for this reason it often generates social conflicts. He was thus convinced that this state of conflict would not be fundamentally resolved unless human beings returned to what might be called the status of primitive society.[35] Interestingly enough, Takabatake's observation bears a striking resemblance to the basic theory of mainstream *laissez-faire* economics that preconditions human beings as profit-oriented animals. However, it did not lead him to endorse capitalism as the most appropriate system for human society. He contended that by transforming a nation into what he called a commodity, the capitalist system constantly reproduces class struggle caused by economic interests. Therefore, Takabatake concluded with confidence that capitalism had failed to produce a nation (*kokumin*) that possessed a quality of patriotism for the state. He was equally critical of Marxism, which refers to the state as simply a "committee" for the bourgeois, and therefore called for the necessity of state-centered socialism.[36]

The early version of state socialism first theorized by Takabatake was followed by more politically motivated intellectuals in the mid-1930s. Various political organizations claimed that their guiding philosophy was state socialism as did a number of social scientists, including those who represented liberal social science during the Taisho period.[37] For instance, Sugimori Kojiro, whose 1919 work on state and society paved the way for the "discovering society" debate in the 1920s, became an advocate of state control over all social sectors.[38] Among them, Waseda University Professor Hayashi Kimio's (1883–1947) writings illuminated the essence of state socialism in early and mid-1930s Japan. Taking the position of secretary in the Academic Association for Japanese State Socialism (*nihonkokkashugi gakumei*), founded at his *alma mater* in April 1932, Hayashi published his first major book on state socialism, titled "The Principles of State Socialism" in the same year. He observed that state socialism first pertained to a state in which all kinds of socio-political, economic and cultural conflicts have been eliminated. Therefore, the concept of the social in his state socialism was indicative of a kind of equilibrium forced by state power.[39] Here, what is most important is how Hayashi produced his totalitarian theory through his harsh critiques of both Western totalitarian and liberal thinking.

It is important to note that the term state socialism did not exist in the West, but it was a Japanized inception of European totalitarian and fascist movements in the mid-1930s. Hayashi was the one who most ardently emphasized the necessity of "Japanizing" Western totalitarianism. However, what he was concerned about was not simply labeling but highlighting theoretical differences between Western totalitarianism and what he would theorize as a Japanese state socialism. His main discontent with Western totalitarianism was about the similarities between Western liberalism and Western totalitarianism. He still viewed European totalitarianism as an extension of state-individual relations in favor of the state and strongly argued that such contract-oriented social theories would not be compatible with the case of Japan, where "pure" statism had been the ultimate principle.[40] Therefore, Hayashi's project of Japanizing Western political theories began with criticizing the concept of the contract-oriented organ theory between state and individual in the West. Here, what captured his attention were the writings of Jeremy Bentham.

Jeremy Bentham, an English philosopher at the end of the eighteenth century, explained the aim of the state as "the greatest happiness of the greatest number," but the idea of "the happiness of the greatest number" is not *integralistic*, but individualistic; for the number is calculated by regarding an individual as its unit, and he considers the State as a *mechanical* group of individuals. This idea is rejected from the integralistic standpoint, which regards the State to be an inseparable organic unity above individuals. . . . In an organic body, what is important is only life as a whole. The individualistic theorists of the State regard individuals – who are mere cells in the State – as the supreme beings.[41]

(emphasis added)

Although utilitarianism advocates the maximization of individuals' happiness, it also recognizes the necessity of social norms and rules to mediate conflicts between individuals' pursuit of happiness and social order. As Bentham's notion of Panopticon well suggests, individuals' act of pursuing happiness can occur only in a closed world where they are always under invisible surveillance. Importantly, the statement above does not reveal that Hayashi was an anti-organ intellectual, but it rather shows his unique understanding of the state organ theory. Given that Hayashi clearly portrayed the state as a unity, it seems evident that he also based his state socialism on a kind of organ theory. But his repugnance for individuals as autonomous subjects within the larger state organ provoked his intentional misreading of the Western state organism idea. Therefore, at the heart of Hayashi's critiques of Western "organ" state theories lay his strong anti-individualism. Such anti-individualism derived from his observation that the amalgam of individuals' happiness would never be realized as the collective good of the totality. This line of thinking was illuminated in his understanding of Italian fascism. The cooperative system between labor and capital in the Italian fascist movement, Hayashi asserted, would further separate that movement from the ideal of state socialism.[42] In other words, Hayashi's state socialism showed a kind of compulsory epistemology against the notion of the political in which individuals' subjective resolution would work for the totality of a society.

Hayashi's theoretical weakness was problematized even by right-wing intellectuals. Minoda Muneki (1894–1946), a famous right-wing critic who was at the forefront of attacking liberal and socialist intellectuals, dismissed Hayashi's state socialism as a work of empty rationalism and ethics that lacked humanity.[43] By presupposing the state as an omnipotent organ that controls the politics, ethics, law and religion of *kokumin*, Minoda argued, the state became a trans-moral institution beyond a scientific analysis. For Minoda, the state apparatus was a mere institution that represented the dignity of the Emperor. Although state socialism gave absolute credit to the Japanese state organ, it could not be a pure reflection of the Japanese spirit in Minoda's view, unless the Emperor and his spirit take the central position in Japanist thinking.

Such critiques reflect internal tensions within conservative and reactionary intellectuals regarding Japanism and state socialism. Hayashi's standpoint represents a new form of Japanese statism in which the emperor is somehow marginalized. Minoda observed, however, that the historicity of the Japanese state organ must derive from the spiritual integration of the Japanese people under the Emperor system.[44] More serious than the problem of temporality was the question of how state socialists positioned the spatiality of their theory. In other words, once the state became an ultimate unit of analytical thinking, state socialism would only operate in the boundary of a single nation-state. Notably, this concern was not fully discussed either in the early state socialism of Takabatake, who died in 1928, nor in Hayashi's theory. What remained unanswered was how a new Japanese statism should define nation (*kokumin*) or national subjects politically and geographically.

Pan-Asianisms in rivalry

It appears that Japanese social scientists did not quite understand the nature of German ethnic nationalism and national movements led by Hitler's National Socialist Party, although most Japanese ultranationalist political organizations and intellectuals were influenced by German fascism in one way or another. The question of the Japanese empire becoming multi-ethnic received little attention from these Japanists, whose focal interests were still concerned with domestic reforms. The rapidly changing demographic configuration of the Japanese empire, the migration boom to Manchukuo in particular, necessitated much more practical policies and theories regarding ethnic governance inside and outside the Japanese empire rather than fantasized Pan-Asian discourses in the 1920s.

In 1932, Akamatsu Katsumarō (1894–1955), a Tokyo Imperial University graduate and a student of political scientist Yoshino Sakuzō, published a book titled "The Basis for a New National Movement." Apparently, his notion of national movement came as new to most state socialists who maintained the firm belief that the state itself was the absolute organ of analysis. Unlike these state socialists, Akamatsu devoted much of his work to envisioning what he called an Asian version of state socialism. He first critically analyzed that internationalism in Marxism is based on the perception that the proletariat in every country is and should be imbued with class struggle consciousness in a monolithic way.[45] If individual differences within the proletariat are ignored, he asserted, this monistic observation of internationality in Marxism is nothing but utopian socialism, which, he believed, became the main reason for the failure of a series of international socialist movements.[46] For him, the most serious problem was racial and ethnic conflicts among the proletariat.[47]

The observation above explains how Akamatsu understood fascism in Europe. He basically viewed it as an economic movement manipulated by financial capital. The state monopolizes financial capital and this necessarily enables the state to control industrial capital. In this process, the fascist state completes the nationalization of the whole economy. Based on this observation, Akamatsu was convinced that the fascist movement would be closely associated with national chauvinism, thus weakening the internationalization of the economy.[48] However, Akamatsu was adamant that this nationalization of the economy would rather reinforce the state-centered capitalist economy and argued that the state manipulates peasants and the working class by propagandizing the fact that they would be liberated from their status as "slave[s] of debt."[49] In short, the nature of fascism in Europe was, for Akamatsu, that of a highly economic and essentially capitalistic movement, and fundamentally different from the idea of state socialism.

It was not simply Akamatsu but also other leading social scientists in Japan who shared the observation that fascist governments in Europe were deceiving destitute peasants and the poor urban working class. But how then did Akamatsu conceptualize the internationality of his state socialism? In a roundtable discussion on the European fascist movements, he first endorsed that in order to protect

Japan from the monopolizing tendency of European powers, it must initiate what might be called single-nation socialism. As for his notion of single-nation social-ism, he referred to the Soviet Union's planned economy as a realistic example.[50] Akamatsu's proposal of the Soviet Union as a model for Japan's economic future, however, soon provoked harsh criticism from other interlocutors, who argued that by focusing on its own people, the Soviet Union's monopolistic economy did not recognize its neighbors as competitive partners, and therefore could hardly serve to support the general good of the proletariat across the world.[51] In defense of his theory, Akamatsu attempted to rationalize his idea of state socialism by pointing to its cosmopolitan ideal. He maintained that the new definition of international-ism must be that inferior ethnic groups form a united front and resist the monopo-lizing interests of superior ethnic groups. To this end, he concluded that a realistic internationalism ought to be based on the guiding spirit that facilitates the equali-zation of the living conditions of various ethnic groups on a world level.[52] Aka-matsu observed that the world was being divided into several politico-economic blocs – the America-Latino bloc, the British Empire bloc and the Russia bloc. However, he was opposed to the idea that Japan's bloc economy system should be based on capitalism. He instead proposed what he called a Greater Asian socialist bloc. He wrote that:

> Greater Asianism in the past was for exploitation. However, it was not based on the principle of the Kingly Way Ideology (*kōdoshugi*). The principle of the Kingly Way Ideology must serve not for exploitation but for the realization of harmony among ethnic groups. To this end, we must construct a socialist Japan that possesses supreme culture. As long as Japan adheres to its capital-istic status, it has neither the qualification for the Asian international, nor the qualification for guiding Manchukuo.[53]

Assuring Japan's leading role in establishing a greater Asian socialist bloc, Aka-matsu believed, would necessitate a fundamental transformation of the domestic structure. Here, he advocated the importance of a national movement. To be sure, his concept of a national movement was different from that of Germany, which he condemned as capitalistic. His notion of a national community instead envisioned the future of Japanese *minzoku*; that is, social and political conflicts would all be eradicated through what he called national spirit (*minzoku seishin*).[54]

Akamatsu was aware that his notion of single-nation socialism had to be regionalized to embrace the rest of Asia. Moreover, he also recognized the neces-sity of the politics of subject formation in his emphasis on a national movement. Therefore, he insisted that a national party be organized to realize what he called Greater Asian socialism. However, the way he intended to infuse subjectivity into the people of East Asia was to return to such transcendental notions as ethnic spirit. In this way, the concept of the political in Akamatsu became increasingly esoteric and as a result, political subjectivity was conceptualized as producing spiritually homogenous subjects, an idea which could not be explained within the perspective of the social sciences.

While state socialists presented various Japanese-style totalitarian theories, liberal and bourgeois social scientists harshly criticized them for being irrational and lacking political subjects within them. In his provocative book, *Critiques of Japanese State Socialism*, Kada Tetsuji (1895–1964), Professor of Sociology at Keio University who later became one of the leading advocates of the East Asia Cooperative Community and a multi-ethnic empire, pointed out the shallowness of state socialism's concept of nation and *minzoku*. He charged that a nation in Hayashi's state socialism is portrayed as a mechanical entity constructed of *minzoku*.[55] Kada observed that the concept of ethnicity or *minzoku* had been conceived of as an intrinsic, blood-oriented homogeneous entity in the writings of most state socialists. This perception, as also found in Hayashi's idea of state socialism, was one that Kada found most problematic. Kada criticized that Hayashi defined *minzoku* in a very intrinsic way, as a group of people sharing the same blood. Kata went on to argue that for this reason, no socio-political explanations can be found in Hayashi's theory regarding why *minzoku* should be transformed into nation. Quite the contrary, Kada emphasized that *minzoku* itself is a socio-political construct formed in the relations of production in capitalism,[56] which was shared by like-minded social scientists of the time. They were grappling with a similar question: how a new concept of ethnicity should be theorized to help envision the political reality of an East Asian community. In this sense, the prevalence of state socialism and fascism in early 1930s Japan, in spite of their theoretical limitations, provides a key to understanding the conceptual directions within the wartime Japanese social sciences. First, Japanese social scientists were preoccupied with the task of contriving a logic of community, national or ethnic, that would serve as a platform for total mobilization as part of Japan's war effort. Second, they believed that by abolishing the distinction between metropole and colony, the East Asia community must achieve regional rationality, thus justifying Japan's role in Asia. Therefore, from a social scientific perspective, the blueprint for the East Asian Cooperative Community had to be at once subjective and objective, national and regional and totalistic and individual.

Tokyo Imperial University political scientist Rōyama Masamichi was one of those who delved into the question of a new direction for the social sciences in the early 1930s. Rōyama nurtured his social scientific scholarship under the instruction of Yoshino Sakuzō at Tokyo Imperial University and traces of Taisho liberalism are deeply mirrored in his early writings. In the mid-1930s, he centered his academic concern with the question of how a new internationalist thinking would replace a single nation-state framework, and thereby overcome the limits of ethnic nationalism. Rōyama observed that the international community in the early twentieth century grew out of modern nationalism and consisted of major European countries, but it was from the beginning embedded also in a context of colonialism and imperialism which gave rise to ethnic nationalism.[57] He, however, analyzed that nationalism as an ideology of the modern nation-state did not meet with the demands of new political communities that had emerged to overcome the limits of national boundaries. Such an observation demonstrates that Rōyama was also influenced by alternative social theories such as European totalitarianism and fascism, although he did not endorse them at face value. He went on to argue that since nationalism was based on the geographical demarcation of national governmental institutions, it was necessary to establish international politics to destroy the obstacles that nationalism had created.[58] Hence, Rōyama's early concept of political science, as many have argued, was primarily concerned with maximizing the potential of what he called international politics beyond the limits of national borders.[59] Rōyama's attention to internationalism turned out to be very timely as Japan was involved in an actual diplomatic crisis. Rōyama began writing extensively on the Great Depression in 1929 and the Manchurian Incident in 1931. However, the contents and directions of his writing changed markedly as he began viewing the world order from a completely new perspective. To begin with, Rōyama insisted that the existing regional order sustained by the League of Nations had already been an old order and thus had come to an end. Like other Japanese intellectuals at the time, he was convinced that European powers could no longer appropriate internationalism by manipulating the League of Nations in order to justify their Euro-centric hegemony. Rōyama also paid attention to new political forces such as the independence movements in India and the Soviet regime in Russia that would not follow white supremacy.[60] In that sense, Rōyama's early writings on internationalism and regionalism were based on the critiques of the Euro-centric order and also showed a tendency to affirm the idea of Japan as victimized. What, then, brought newness to Rōyama's regionalism and made him develop the idea of the East Asian Cooperative Community that emerged as the most powerful regional theory in the late 1930s?

Rōyama first insisted that a new regionalism should be based on "recognizing particular situations that a certain region has in terms of the interrelations between nations or *kokumin*."[61] This logic was linked to his revisiting the Manchurian Incident from a new perspective. The particular situation in Manchuria, he asserted, could not be fully explained in terms of the current international order or existing political theories. Instead, he aimed to redefine this incident as a critical moment in the world order dominated by world capitalism.[62] Beyond the cloistered academic frame, Rōyama also began making strong statements in the "real" political arena. Joining the Japanese Council of the Institute of Pacific Relations,[63] he insisted that Japan had developed "special relations" with Manchuria. Therefore, he believed that the only rational solution for this problem of Manchuria "would seem to lie in the reconsideration of Japan's assertion of a special position" and efforts "to safeguard Japan's substantial interests in Manchuria."[64] He also participated in a special government-led research group whose goal was to find a way to resolve Japan's situation in Manchuria.[65]

On the surface, Rōyama's standpoint reflected the moderate voices of liberal social scientists who attributed Japan's situation to the absurdity of the Euro-centric order. If that is the case, one may wonder how Rōyama differed from other liberal and bourgeois intellectuals such as Yanaihara Tadao or Nitobe Inazō, in that he also intended to rationalize Japan's invasion of China. First and foremost, his notion of internationalism was not simply focused on diplomatic relations with the West. Instead, he placed great emphasis on restructuring both the domestic and the regional political structure to convince both Japanese and colonial subjects to embrace a new order. Nevertheless, he was critical of the existing regionalist theories such as the Japan-Manchuria-China economic bloc system. His critical gaze also targeted the Asia Monroe Doctrine, which, he believed, would function as a mere diplomatic policy, leaving the domestic political system intact.[66] As for the economic bloc system, he asserted, "[T]he term bloc-economy is by all means an artificial term, since no political system exists that connects Japan with China or other Asian countries."[67] He was acutely aware that neither the Asia Monroe Doctrine nor the bloc economy system contained any useful elements to embrace Chinese and other colonial subjects. He was convinced that such theories would only serve Japan's *national* interests rather than the good of a regional community. This statement clearly demonstrates that for Rōyama, his idea of regionalism first pertained to the question of how both a tangible politico-economic structure and its new East Asian subjects should be created, over and beyond the narrow boundary of Japanese national interests.

The "community of destiny"

Rōyama was aware that his new blueprint for an Asian regional order would be a challenging project for any government to undertake, given that a variety of reactionary and totalitarian theories and movements had already encroached on the domestic political scenes. One important task was to differentiate his Asianist perspective from the existing spiritualist literature on Pan-Asianism and state socialism and totalitarianism which shared critiques of Western democracy and capitalism with Rōyama and other social scientists sympathetic to his ideas. In terms of a reactionary state socialism, Rōyama, as a rigid political scientist, insisted from the beginning that his new political theory must go beyond the conventional dimensions of the nation-state in its political concepts and ramifications.[68] He theorized the notion of "constructing a new order" as a political issue to support the obtaining of rationality in people's lives and their action within a community.[69] Here, Rōyama observed that modern political science had served to discover an order in which individual freedom is guaranteed and at the same time individuals' actions must conform to the general interests of the entire society. According to him, the community of a nation-state had been the ultimate political order and the degree of political rationality had been measured through the functionality of liberal democracy and the capitalist economy. This type of what he called "functionalism" in modern political science, he stressed, had already revealed its limits in terms of the general crisis of democracy and capitalism.[70]

Rōyama's inquiries were twofold. First, what kind of a new political form would be ideal for an East Asian regional community if Japan should go beyond the nation-state borders in constructing this new project? Second and more importantly, how would a new political system of East Asian community obtain its rationality in regard to the rest of Asia? To find answers to these questions, as Victor Koschmann notes, Rōyama showed a keen interest in a variety of new political systems from European totalitarianism and the Soviet planned economy to the American New Deal system.[71]

What first captured Rōyama's attention was the German political theoretician Carl Schmitt who concretized German fascism. In a 1931 book, *Der Begriff des Politischen*, later translated as *The Concept of the Political*, Schmitt delineated his notion of politics, as he put it:

> German political science has originally maintained (under the impact of Hegel's philosophy of the state) that the state is qualitatively distinct from society and higher than it. A state standing above society could be called universal but not total, as that term is understood nowadays, namely, as the polemical negation of the neutral state, whose economy and law were in themselves nonpolitical.[72]

Clearly distinguishing totality from universality, Schmitt attempted to denounce the notion of the state as the ultimate destination of modern political science. However, this remark came as no surprise to Japanese social scientists, since many of them were already imbued with the idea that the state merely constitutes part of a total society.[73] What is rather striking in Schmitt's concept of the political was how he defined what he conceptualized as an international order among different states.

> The political entity presupposes the real existence of an enemy and therefore coexistence with another political entity. As long as a state exists, there will thus always be in the world more than just one state. A world state which embraces the entire globe and all of humanity cannot exist. The political world is a pluriverse, not a universe. . . . The political entity cannot by its very nature be universal in the sense of embracing all of humanity and the entire world.[74]

In this way, Schmitt's concept of the political was premised on his conviction that the status of eternal conflicts is inevitable in the world order, and accordingly he defined a political entity, that is to say, a nation-state as recreating itself in its oppositional relation with another political entity. Schmitt's critiques of the functional rationality of modern political science such as the "balance of power" theory were connected to his new notion of political subjectivity. He stressed that political arenas are constituted by both institutional and non-institutional sectors. Political spaces outside the domain of rational political behavior within institutional sectors are defined by Schmitt as the exceptional.[75] It appeared that Schmitt's emphasis on the exceptional in politics stemmed from his diagnosis of Germany in the 1930s as it almost plunged into a national emergency. For this reason, he contended that under these types of situations, the source of alternative political power must come from a political leader who can first determine the state of emergency and present a new set of political norms to comply with such emergency situations. Not surprisingly, Schmitt's political theory in the mid-1930s played a pivotal role in endorsing German totalitarianism and Hitler's dictatorship.[76]

Rōyama's 1935 writing shows his interest in alternative theories of political subjectivity and sovereignty such as Schmitt's. However, Rōyama was also skeptical about the compatibility of Schmitt's theory with the new regional order Japan attempted to construct. Putting aside the issue of the Emperor as a Japanese version of a political dictator in Schmitt's theory, Rōyama centered his concern on the limits of Schmitt's theory for a regional community. Although Schmitt repeatedly denounced the validity of the nation-state framework, his political theory never transcended the border of the state as an analytical unit. More importantly, Schmitt's notion of political leadership in times of national emergency was inseparable from the issue of growing racism in Germany. As I will discuss in detail, Rōyama and like-minded social scientists were well aware that sharing such exclusive racist sentiments had become a driving force for establishing strong political ties between ordinary subjects and dogmatic dictatorial leadership in Germany in the name of a shared community of destiny.

How, then, did Rōyama conceptualize regionalism in his notion of a Pan-Asian community? In the same year Rōyama critically approached Schmitt's political theory, he also considered cooperativism (*kyōdōtaishugi*) in a written article. Once he located the limits within Schmitt's concept of politics and political leadership, Rōyama turned to the eventual question of how a political organization could represent and mediate different interests between different groups toward the goal of engendering collective and moral values. He observed that existing theories in the West were concerned with the process of directing individuals and groups to realize what he called a goal-oriented and self-conscious unification, through coercive institutional means such as law and order. Rōyama called this concept the perception of organizing, borrowing the term from the American political scientist Ernest Barker (1874–1960).[77] However, this perception of organizing, Rōyama argued, neglected the traditional and cultural aspects in a society that take place outside the arena of goal-oriented activities. In other words, the organizing idea as a collective goal at times occurs outside non-organized sectors such as religion, customs and ethnicity. At this point he developed the concept of a cooperative community which could encompass both institutional and non-institutional aspects in human life. Since the exterior of a cooperative community is not simply a political institution, Rōyama redefined politics as the constant process of intervening in various aspects of human life that are not necessarily captured in conventional political systems such as constitutionalism. The ultimate goal of such a cooperative system was to create a community of destiny (*unmeikyōdōtai*) and in this community, political subjectivity is constructed not only by one's participating in political systems but more importantly by sharing common ethical and moral values.[78]

Therefore, Rōyama's concept of cooperative regionalism was premised on the notion of sharing the community of destiny. He first categorized the isolation period of Tokugawa Japan as exclusive regionalism and Japan's encounter with the West as inclusive regionalism. In contrast to the previous two notions of regionalism, which were based on exploitation and imbalance, the principle of cooperative regionalism, Rōyama argued, must be to ensure regional balance and development.[79] To this end, he also postulated the necessity of defining East Asia in a spatial sense.

> A region called East Asia has perpetually existed in a natural and geographical sense since the beginning of the earth. But, if we think about East Asia in a cultural sense, it is possible to say that unlike the West, it has not been considered an entity. A regional cooperative community, in nature, must have something other than natural and perpetual elements or cultural unification . . . The driving force that makes East Asia a regional cooperative community first lies in its *spirit* and mentality. It is generated through the essence of the *regional destiny* (*Raumschicksal*) of its *minzoku* 民族. The destiny that determines the existence of *minzoku* must be produced by the significance of unifying the destiny to certain regions.[80]
>
> (emphasis added)

Importantly, the "spirit" that Rōyama emphasized did not represent something transcendental such as trans-historical Asian spirituality. The regional destiny, he contended, instead occurred through the constant processes of cooperativism. For this reason, East Asia as a region in Rōyama's thinking was not static, nor too was the destiny of the East Asian community. Both East Asia and its destiny must recreate themselves in the subjective and objective logic of cooperativism.

Shinmei Masamichi's concept of *kyōdōtai* in East Asia

Rōyama was not alone in delving into the question of constructing a community of destiny which might transcend the limits of nationalism. Right after the outbreak of the Sino-Japanese War, the concept of the East Asian Community frequently appeared in major academic journals and quickly gained currency among Japanese and colonial intellectuals, Korean social scientists in particular. As Rōyama's conceptual trajectories reveal, this new group of imperial intellectuals had nurtured their common inquiries in rivalry with another group of imperial thinkers who adhered to spiritual Pan-Asianism or state fascism. Advocates of the East Asian community were convinced that the efficacy of governing an empire at the time of total war was contingent on whether an empire could extend an evolved level of rationality to the people at metropole and in the colony. Shinmei Masamichi, Professor of Sociology at Tohoku Imperial University, was one of the main figures of the East Asian Community group who was concerned with creating a rational empire in East Asia. Shinmei and Rōyama, although their academic fields were different, became acquainted with each other at Tokyo Imperial University in the early 1920s. Both joined the famous student activist group, New Man Society (*Shinjinkai*), and were influenced by the liberal and progressive social scientists of the time. Shinmei's mentor was Yoshino Sakuzō, an icon of Taisho Democracy and under Yoshino's instruction, Shinmei first developed his political perspectives until he actually determined to become a sociologist.

Shinmei quickly emerged as one of the nation's leading sociologists and devoted himself to introducing and developing the cutting-edge sociological theories of the time, before gaining an opportunity to study in Germany between 1929 and 1931. He was initially an ardent student of German formal sociology as represented by Georg Simmel, but increasingly found it problematic to explain social phenomena through form alone. He also became critical of the notion of civil society as the most progressive form of social relations, after he witnessed the impossibility of such bourgeois social sciences perspectives in delineating and defusing the crisis in Europe. Like other critical social scientists of the time, Shinmei was acutely aware of the unique gravity of crisis represented by political movements in early 1930s Europe. One of the focal questions that Hilter's National Socialism posited for bourgeois social scientists was the relationship between state and society. Although Shinmei was not sure about how to theorize this new phenomenon, he was at least convinced that the validity of the framework of civil society vis-à-vis state would eventually come to an end in the emergence of a new totalitarian society. On the other hand, he observed that the spread of totalitarianism and chauvinistic nationalism was in large part due to the economic hardship Germany was suffering. Such intellectual inquiries on the rapidly changing socio-political situations in Europe were written in a vivid tone in his correspondence to the famous academic journal *Keizai orai* between 1929 and 1931, later published in a title *Europe in Crisis*.[81] Shinmei paid special attention to the ironic attitude of German fascists toward capitalism and the Jews. He wrote:

> National socialism's attack on capitalism based on its middle-class-oriented ideology is superficial. This is due to the fact that the limits of its middle-class ideology have already been preconditioned. . . . It is certain that the middle class decisively takes a non-negating attitude toward capitalism, compared to that of the proletariat. As long as the ideology of the middle class is *spontaneous*, it would return to the affirmation of capitalism in the end. Because the ideology of national socialism takes nothing but this *natural* sentiment of the middle class, national socialism would hardly be away from affirming capitalism, even if *ideological artificiality* is added to it.[82]

(emphasis added)

Shinmei was convinced that the German fascist movement appealed to the spontaneity of middle-class workers; that is, the middle class is against big businesses by nature. The German fascist government tended to draw support from the middle class by claiming that it would accelerate the nationalization of bourgeois capitalists and big businesses. Shinmei observed, therefore, that fascist movements always resort to nationalist sentiment. This led him to make his second observation about fascist movements; fascism is easily associated with racist politics, something which Rōyama pointed out in similar terms. Shinmei pointed out the paradox that although the German middle class was fascinated by the government policy to nationalize big business and finance capital, they were completely silent about the government's attack on the Jewish middle class.[83]

However, it would be misleading to argue that Shinmei's critiques of fascism and totalitarianism in Europe resulted in his total denouncement of "alternative" theories to liberal democratic capitalism. While showing a keen interest in this new intellectual trend, Shinmei centered his academic concerns on how these radical theories would restructure social scientific thinking, and sociological studies in particular. The phenomenon of Europe in crisis, therefore, was logically connected to Shinmei's observations of social sciences in crisis. His understanding of the social sciences in crisis was twofold. First, as I have discussed, it pertained to the impossibility of explaining current radical political movements with existing social scientific theories, and concepts of democracy and liberal capitalism in particular. Second, he also observed that the wider the distance between theories and practice became, the more intellectuals, and social scientists in particular, would lose their ontological grounds and thus became alienated from society. Therefore, any understanding the nature of European crisis, for Shinmei, could not be separated from rethinking the whole structure of how social scientific knowledge had been produced and obtained its legitimacy as a gateway to understanding social phenomena.

Upon returning from Germany, Shinmei, together with other social scientists, devoted considerable time to introducing and analyzing transformation in social scientific thinking. What struck him most in the early 1930s was the emergence of new disciplines within the social sciences, in particular the sociology of knowledge. The sociology of knowledge as a new discipline was first introduced by German sociologists, and what they problematized was the legitimacy of knowledge as a vehicle through which a social phenomenon and structure is recognized and by which it is judged. In his 1925 work titled, *Problem of the Sociology of Knowledge*, Karl Mannheim presented a provocative thesis that a judgment of the legitimacy of certain knowledge must be made not just by its logical conformity but also by the social conditions under which it was produced.[84] Mannheim continued to develop his thesis and in his famous work *Ideology and Utopia*, he wrote:

> We must see to it that a sociological history of ideas concerns itself with the actual thought of society, and not systems of ideas elaborated within a rigid academic tradition. If erroneous knowledge was formerly checked by appeal to divine sanction, which unfailingly revealed the true and the real or by pure contemplation, in which true ideas were supposedly discovered, at present the criterion of reality is found primarily in an ontology derived from political experience.[85]

Such an epistemological transformation evoked two major questions. First, as Mannheim argued, the myth of historical progress must be challenged, particularly if the historical development of ideas and the myth of historical progress are merely simple reiterations of the assumption that history and human beings will "naturally" make progress. In other words, the notion of progress is relative and by no means absolute, and the unchallenged belief that liberal democratic capitalism was the most advanced human system would no longer be valid. In this respect, the sociology of knowledge first introduced by Karl Mannheim and other German sociologists such as Max Scheler (1874–1928) rapidly gained currency as the sense that democracy and capitalism were in crisis became widespread in the early 1930s. Shinmei was attentive to this new sociological thinking and produced numerous writings on the subject of the sociology of knowledge, publishing *Theories of the Sociology of Knowledge* in 1932.

For Shinmei, the sociology of knowledge was considered a necessary response to the limits of the mainstream sociological studies, particularly as represented by Georg Simmel's formal sociology, something by which Shinmei himself was originally influenced. However, the way social relations and phenomena were explained solely through social forms, Shinmei asserted, could no longer reflect the complexity of social relations. This observation first led him to develop the notion of special sociology (*tokushu shakaigaku*) and general sociology (*sōgō shakaigaku*), the latter idea being closer to the trend of creating scientific theories that contain transcendental causality and compatibility, while the former was more concerned with relative differences at work in each set of social relations.[86] Based on these observations, Shinmei showed interest in the rise of cooperativism in Italy as an alternative to a liberal capitalist economy. A cooperative community essentially arises out of a specific economic demand to overcome the social and class conflicts between labor and capital.[87] At the heart of the cooperative idea was the conviction that the same capitalistic individualism that endorsed an individuals' pursuit of profit could be usefully managed or limited by cooperative organizations that emphasized communal production and distribution. According to Shinmei, the main difference between a cooperative community (*kyōdōtai*) and an association (*kumiai*) lay in the fact that the former functioned as a political organization in itself, while the latter was viewed as an economic organization, with the result that it would have little impact on political issues. In this respect, cooperativism in Italian fascism, Shinmei concluded, emerged in an attempt to replace parliamentary politics.[88] Each cooperative community has different collective goals, at times coming into conflict with other cooperative communities. Therefore, they must belong to a linked grand community, or what might be called a central cooperative bureau. In this way, Shinmei concluded that cooperativism aimed to mediate socio-political conflicts by creating a goal-oriented political space based on organic processes.

It is understandable that Shinmei, who stayed in Germany between 1929 and 1931, and witnessed the strong racist tendency in German National Socialism, was influenced by the Italian fascist movement, which he believed was not based on racism. However, he was also clearly aware that the ideal political totality he advocated faced certain obstacles from the beginning. First, he pointed out that Italian cooperative thought, which was traceable to the 1910s, presupposed the disappearance of class once cooperative communities begin to function effectively. But he observed that powerful class hierarchies still existed even at this stage and this made it harder for cooperative communities to function as media-tors.[89] Second, Italian cooperativism was also premised on the perception that cooperative communities shape horizontal relations both with other communities and with the state. Under this system, individuals become autonomous political subjects, not controlled predominantly by the state. Hence, the emergence of indi-viduals that was emphasized in socialism continues to develop in each cooperative community. Shinmei observed, however, that these hypotheses are barely realized when homogeneous national interests come to the forefront. In this respect, he concluded that Italian cooperativism actually existed as a mere *functional* system for the fascist state, and accordingly, he redefined it as a cooperative state rather than a fully realized cooperativism.[90]

Shinmei's analysis of cooperativism posited two important questions as Japa-nese social scientists were searching for alternative social scientific methodolo-gies. The first question entailed the issue of how a new form of political totality could be represented without resorting to the existing parliamentary system. The Italian version of cooperativism demonstrated that a cooperative community will not function effectively insofar as political leaders' decision making eventually tops all other cooperative processes. Second and more importantly, the political space of cooperativism never exceeds that of the state in reality but rather sustains the state's dominance over all other socio-political sectors. At stake was the issue of whether in the case of imperial Japan, reforming the domestic structure based on state cooperativism was likely to absolutize the Japanese state, thus creating inconsistencies with the regional order beyond the limits of nationalism.

The rise of a *kyōdōtai* group of imperial intellectuals

With growing anti-Japanese nationalism in China in the midst of the Sino-Japanese War, a consensus to concretize a theory of forming a China-Japan cor-porative force was receiving support from Japanese intellectuals and bureaucrats. Even some of the Japanism group of intellectuals now found it imperative to overcome the limits of spiritual Japanism that had maintained a strong nationally exclusive perspective. The 1942 book *The Progress of the Yamato Nation* vividly exemplifies this. Moriyoshi Yoshiteru strove to show that Japanism was not a Japanese exceptionalism, isolating the Japanese people from the rest of the world. He even criticized other fundamental Japanists for their excessive emphasis on the blood-oriented homogeneity of the Japanese imperial state.[91] He was aware that the fixation of Japanism as a Japanese version of racial superiority would isolate Japan from the rest of Asia during the time of total war. He thus vehemently criti-cized Hitler's racist politics, and argued that the Yamato spirit had been, and was, inclusive and anyone who embodied the Japanese spirit could be a citizen of the Japanese nation.[92] Moriyoshi intended to link his "new" Japanist thinking with Japan's modernization, a process that he believed would not be possible without Japan's constant interaction with non-Japanese people. Therefore, a logical con-nection seemed to be created as he concluded that Japanism would contribute to the realization of universal values in the world.[93]

To be sure, this "new" Japanist thinking was hardly received by ultranationalistic Japanists and spiritual Pan-Asianists. However, it clearly illustrates that a political and intellectual atmosphere existed for Asianist and pan-regionalist discourses to flourish and exert an influential power on real politics. Under these circumstances, the notion of the East Asian Community flooded in through books, pamphlets and journal articles, and quickly gained a wide readership beyond academia.[94] The renowned philosopher Miki Kiyoshi's *Principles of the Thought of a New Japan* became a widely received guide to the theory of the East Asian Community. As is well known, Miki was one of the most influential figures in the Showa Institute, a government-funded think-tank in wartime Japan, and this indicates that the vision of an East Asian community exerted an influence on how imperial Japan should carry out its program of total war. Miki shared his observation that a modern world order was characterized by the European imperial powers' constant exploitation of non-Western and economically underdeveloped countries.[95] Miki's critical view of modern world history was followed by his enumeration of eight ideologies to be overcome in constructing a new Asian order. Out of them, nationalism, capitalism and communism rested atop. In short, Miki's draft of an East Asian Cooperative Community was summarized by several streams of analytical thinking. First, Western imperial powers would not give up their ambition to colonize East Asia. Second, a single nation would not prevent this trend and thus, Asian people should construct a regional community of destiny. Third and most importantly, Japan must lead this movement.

Miki's macro drawing of the logic of the East Asia Community was shared by like-minded intellectuals. However, they were also aware that a number of questions remained unanswered. The Keio University Professor of Economics Kada Tetsuji presented a similar viewpoint in his 1939 book *On the East Asian Community*.[96] This shows that this new group of imperial intellectuals aptly turned to the realistic issues of war and empire building from their theoretical speculations on fascism, nationalism and regionalism in the mid-1930s, as best shown in the writings of Rōyama Masamichi and Shinmei Masamichi. Aware that it was crucial to stress the necessity of cooperating China into a Japan-centered East Asian community, these *kyōdōtai* intellectuals increasingly sought platforms beyond the limits of academia and were heavily involved in spreading their theory to the general public and joining various government institutions during the wartime period. This explains why these imperial social scientists concurrently produced both journalistic writing and highly theoretical pieces of work during this period.

Spiritual Pan-Asianists who frequently took an explicit extremist standpoint, often unrealistically criticized the Chinese people for not understanding Japan's will to construct a self-defensive Asian community against Western imperialism and urged them to follow the spirit of the Japanese Emperor. Quite the contrary, most intellectuals in the *kyōdōtai* group understood the historical inevitability of Chinese nationalism. Tracing the history of China's encounter with Western imperial powers, Kada positioned Chinese nationalism as part of a twentieth-century world trend that emerged in the non-Western world as an anti-imperial force.[97] This type of writing reveals the explicit intention to demonstrate to a broad Asian audience just how seriously the empire-colony order had affected the twentieth-century world and dissected the Asian region. Just as liberal and progressive social scientists gained a wider audience within Japan first by sanguinely analyzing the cause of "social problems" and then proposing solutions to them in the 1920s, these imperial intellectuals sought to come closer to China by revealing their understanding of the "China problem," and they believed that such a differentiated and seemingly inclusive gesture to China had already borne fruit to some extent. Shinmei Masamichi, for example, shared his sense of confidence as he argued that Wang Jing Wei, a Chinese leader of the Japanese puppet government in Northern China, fully understood the meaning of the East Asian Community.[98]

However, their seemingly "rational" approach to China and the colony was part of their grand project of rationalizing the Japanese empire through constructing an idea of Pan-Asian community. For this reason, Chinese nationalism must be eventually overcome and Miki defined the beginning of the Sino-Japanese War as a significant world-historical moment toward the deconstruction of the Western empire-colony structure.

Summary

The limits of liberalism during the Taisho period became self-evident as Japan confronted the international crisis in the early 1930s. In an attempt to cope with pressure from the West and at the same time justify Japan's position in China, Japanese social scientists developed various regional discourses. Their responses to the international crisis first demonstrated that the "liberal" notion of developing democracy and capitalism at home and rationalizing colonialism in the name of a civilizing mission during the Taisho period would no longer offer a solution for the international and domestic crises Japan was facing. However, many regional discourses such as the Japan-Manchuria-China bloc economy and the Asia-Monroe Doctrine simply aimed to maintain the status quo without changing the paradoxical dual structure of democracy at home and colonialism abroad. On the other hand, state socialists appropriated the international crisis to overthrow the democratic regime at home and help establish a totalitarian government. However, their state socialism lacked a regional perspective, or a theoretical means as to how subjects outside Japan should be included in their new order and, most importantly, it also lacked any notion of political subjectivity. In their theory, individuals were portrayed as subordinate to the state, without having any political autonomy.

It was under these circumstances that Rōyama Masamichi and Shinmei Masamichi developed regionalist thinking in the mid-1930s. Although they were heavily influenced by the champions of 1920s Japanese social sciences such as Yoshino Sakuzō, they tried to overcome the spatial and theoretical limitations of the Taisho social sciences by contriving a theory of a regional community. Both Rōyama and Shinmei were clearly aware that producing a regional theory and thereby rationalizing Japan's imperialist moves in East Asia must be associated with enabling the creation of new political subjects. To this end, they envisioned a new space called the East Asian Cooperative Community in which the empire-colony power structure was dismantled and transformed into a new form of cooperative identity.

However, such idealized concepts of a new Asia faced theoretical and practical challenges. As Rōyama himself acknowledged, concrete discussions of the cultural, geographical and economic boundaries of the East Asia Community remained unformed. And if the idea of separation by biological race was to be replaced with the notion of a new political subjectivity such as that of the East Asian *minzoku*, did this mean that all discrete traditional and cultural affinities among Asian people should be completely eliminated? Finally, if one grand political identity was to be created, how should the power structure between the Japanese metropole and the wider Asian colony be reconstructed? In confronting these questions, Japanese social scientists continued to produce theories of a Pan-Asian empire and their notion of an East Asian community rapidly gained currency among both Japanese and colonial intellectuals. In the chapters that follow, this book will discuss how these wartime Japanese social scientists were involved in producing the theory and practice of a Pan-Asian community, confronted with various challenges such as ethnic hierarchies within the empire and the economic gap between metropole and colony.

Notes

1 Miki Kiyoshi, "Huan no sishō to sono chokyoku [The Thought of Anxiety and Over-coming It]," *Kaizo* (1933), also available in *Miki Kiyoshi zenshu* 10 [Completed Works of Miki Kiyoshi] (Tokyo: Iwanami Shoten), 285–309.
2 Ibid.
3 Edward Hallett Carr, *The Twenty Years' Crisis 1919–1939* (New York: Harper Torch Books, 1939), 8.
4 Miki Kiyoshi, "Huan no sisho to sono chokyoku," 308.
5 Koyasu Nobukuni, *Taisho wo yomi naosu* [Re-reading Taisho Japan] (Tokyo: Fujiwara Shoten, 2016).
6 Katō Shūichi, "Taisho Democracy as the Pre-Stage for Japanese Militarism," in *Japan in Crisis: Essays on Taishō Democracy*, eds. Bernard Silberman and Harry Harootunian (Princeton: Princeton University Press, 1974), 217–236.
7 Hasegawa Nyozekan, *Gendai kokka hihan* [Critiques of Modern State] (Tokyo: Kōbundō Shobō, 1921), also available in Hasegawa Nyozekan, *Hasegawa Nyozekan senshū* 2 [Selected Works of Hasegawa Nyozekan] (Tokyo: Kurita Shuppankai, 1969–1970), 45.
8 Ibid., 68.
9 Fukuda Tokuzō, *Shakai seisaku to kaikyu toso* [Social Policy and Class Struggle] (Tokyo: Kaizosha, 1922); Sugimori Kojiro, *Shakaijin no tanjō* [The Birth of Social Man] (Tokyo: Ryūbunkan, 1922).
10 Arima Manabu, *Nihon no kindai 4 – kokusaika no nakano teikoku nihon* [Japan's Modernization 4 – Imperial Japan in the Middle of Internationalization] (Tokyo: Chūō Kōron Shinsha, 1999).
11 Jerry Z. Muller, *The Other God That Failed – Hans Freyer and the Deradicalization of German Conservatism* (Princeton: Princeton University Press, 1987), 194.
12 Sunil Smith, *Migration and Diaspora in Modern Asia* (Cambridge: Cambridge University Press, 2011), 52.

13 Hasegawa Yūichi, *Kindai nihon no kokusai ninsiki* [Perceptions of the International in Modern Japan] (Tokyo: Ashishobō, 2016), 61–83.

14 Roger Daniels, *The Politics of Prejudice: The Anti-Japanese Movement in California and the Struggle for Japanese Exclusion* (Berkeley: University of California Press, 1962); Gary Okihiro, *Cane Fires: The Anti-Japanese Movement in Hawaii, 1865–1945* (Philadelphia: Temple University Press, 1991).

15 Yanaihara Tadao, "Shokumin and shokumin seisaku [Colonization and Colonial Policy]," in *Yanaihara Tadao zenshu* 1 [Completed Works of Yanaihara Tadao] (Tokyo: Iwanami Shoten, 1963), 14.

16 For instance, he was critical of Japan's rice exploitation policy toward Korea, arguing that exporting rice from colonial Korea to resolve the rice shortage in Japan proper would greatly aggravate the living conditions of the Korean peasants. Yanaihara Tadao, "Chōsen sanmai josan keikai ni toite [On the Rice Production Increase Plan in Colonial Korea]," *Yanaihara Tadao Zenshu 1*, 692–724. As for Yanaihara's perception of colonialism and Japan's imperialist order, see Ryoko Nakano, *Beyond the Western Liberal Order: Yanaihara Tadao and Empire as Society* (New York: Palgrave MacMillan, 2013); Susan Townsend, *Yanihara Tadao and Japanese Colonial Policy: Redeeming Empire* (London: Routledge Curzon, 2000).

17 Yahaihara Tadao, "Manmoshinkokkaron [On A Manchu-Mongolian State]," *Kaizō* 14, no. 4 (Apr. 1934): 18–29.

18 Ibid., 20.

19 Ibid., 24–26.

20 Fujimura Ichiro, "Yoshino Sakuzō to manmotosshukeniku," in *1920 nendai no nihon no kokusai kankei*, ed. Sugida Yoneyuki (Tokyo: Shunbusha, 2011), 123–165.

21 Nitobe Inazō, "Kokusairenmei ni okeru manshūmondai [The Manchurian Question in the League of Nations]," *Chūōkōron* 47, no. 2 (Feb. 1932): 41–46.

22 Hijikata Seibi, "Keizai riron no kiki [The Crisis of Economic Theories]," *Keizai ōrai* 7, no. 13 (Dec. 1932): 1–11.

23 Ibid., 2.

24 Ibid., 10–11.

25 Hijikata Seibi, "Tōsei keizai to nihon seishin [Controlled Economy and Japanese Spirit]," *Keizai ōrai* 8, no. 3 (Mar. 1933): 7.

26 Ibid., 9–13.

27 Hijikata Seibi, *Nihon keizaigaku no michi* [The Way of Japanese Economics] (Tokyo: Nihonhyōronsha, 1938), 134–158.

28 Mori Kiyohito, *Kagakuteki nihonshugi toha nanizoya* [What Is Scientific Japanism?] (Tokyo: Senshinsha, 1932), 30–33.

29 Ibid., 38–39.

30 Tosaka Jun, *Nihon ideorogi ron* [On Japanese Ideology] (Tokyo: Hakuyosha, 1935), 180–190.

31 Ibid., 190.

32 See Chapter 8, "The Great Depression and Democracy in Crisis," in *Nihon seiji dōkō ron*, ed. Rōyama Masamichi (Tokyo: Kōyō Shoin, 1933), 434–444.

33 Ibid., 419–424.

34 Takabatake translated Marx's *Das Kapital* and published it four times between 1918 and 1928. The most famous one among them was *Shihonron* published by Kaizōsha in 1926–1928.

35 Takabatake Motoyuki, *Kokkashakaishugi taigi* [The Ideal of State Socialism] (Tokyo: Nihon Shakaishugi Kenkyūsho, 1932), 12–17.

36 Ibid., 6–12.

37 About the emergence of state socialist political groups and activists, see Chapter 7 in Fuke Takahiro, *Senkanki nihon no shakai shisō* [Social Thoughts in Interwar Japan] (Tokyo: Jimbun Shoin, 2010), 251–322.

38 Ibid., 253.

39 Hayashi Kimio, *Kokka shakaishugi genri* [Principles of State Socialism] (Tokyo: Shokasha, 1932).
40 Hayashi Kimio, *Seiyō shisō no nihonka* [Japanizing Western Thought] (Tokyo: Nihonhyōronsha, 1932), 1–28.
41 Hayashi Kimio, *The Fundamental Idea of State Socialism* (Tokyo: Maruzen Co., 1936), 25–26.
42 Ibid., 238–242.
43 Minoda Muneki, "Kokka shakaishugi ni taisuru seishinkagakuteki hihan [A Spiritual Critique of State Socialism]," in *Kokka shakaishugi o haigekisu* [Denouncing State Socialism], ed. Wakamiya Unosuke (Tokyo: Sokokukai Shuppanbu, 1934), 71.
44 Ibid., p. 81.
45 Akamatsu Katsumarō, *Shinkokumin undō no kichō* [The Basis for A New National Movement] (Tokyo: Banrikaku, 1932), 30–31.
46 Ibid.
47 Ibid., 48.
48 A roundtable discussion, "Fashizumu hihan [Critiques of Fascism]," *Keizai ōrai* 7, no. 1 (Jan. 1932): 37–68. The other two participants of this roundtable discussion were Sasa Hiroō (1897–1948) and political scientist Rōyama Masamichi.
49 Ibid.
50 A roundtable discussion, "Fashizumu hihan," 44–48.
51 Ibid., 48.
52 Akamatsu Katsumarō, *Shinkokumin undō no kichō*, 48.
53 Ibid., 54.
54 Ibid., 179–196.
55 Kada Tetsuji, *Nihon kokka shakaishugi hihan* [Critiques of Japanese State Socialism] (Tokyo: Shunshusha, 1932), 172.
56 Ibid., 174.
57 Jung Sun Han, *An Imperial Path to Modernity: Yoshino Sakuzō and a New Liberal Order in East Asia, 1905–1937* (Cambridge, MA: Harvard University Asia Center, 2013), 157–158.
58 Rōyama Masamichi, *Kokusai seiji to kokusai gyōsei* [International Politics and International Administration] (Tokyo: Ganshōdō Shoten, 1928), 39.
59 Fujioka Kentarō, "Senkanki nihon chisikijin no higashiajia kokusai jituzoninshiki no kozō [The Structure of Japanese Intellectuals' Understanding of the East Asian International Order in Interwar Japan]," *Kyūshushigaku* 143 (Dec. 2005): 27–51; Kobayashi Keiji, "Senkanki no kokusaichitsujōninshiki to tōa kyōdōtairon no keisei – rōyama masamichi no kokusai seijiron wo chushin toshite [The Concepts of the International Order and the Formation of the East Asian Cooperative Community – With a Focus on Rōyama Masamichi's Theory of International Politics]," *Nihonshi kenkyū* 424 (Dec. 1997): 30–54; Sakai Tetsuya, "<Tōa kyōdōtai> kara <kindaikaron> ē – rōyama masamichi ni okeru chiiki, kaihatsu, nashonarizumu ron no iso [From the East Asian Cooperative Community to Modernization Discourses – Region, Development and Nationalism in Royama Masamichi]," *Nihon gaikō ni okeru ajia shugi – nenpo seijigaku* (Tokyo: Iwanami Shoten, 1998), 109–129.
60 Rōyama Masamichi, "Sekai no saininshiki to chiikiteki kokusai renmei [Reconceptualizing the World and a Regional International Confederation]," *Kokusai chisiki* 13, no. 1 (Jan. 1933), also in *Seikai no henkyoku to nihon no sekai seisaku* [East Asia and the World: Exploring a New Order] (Tokyo: Ganshodo Shoten, 1938), 91–95.
61 Rōyama Masamichi, *Seikai no henkyoku to nihon no sekai seisaku*, 102.
62 Ibid., 3–15.
63 Jung Sun Han, *An Imperial Path to Modernity*, 164–172.
64 Rōyama Masamichi, *Japan's Position in Manchuria* (Tokyo: The Japanese Council Institute of Pacific Relations, 1928), 103. It was the paper written for the third conference of the Institute of Pacific Relations in Kyoto in 1929.

65 In 1932, a year after the outbreak of the Manchurian Crisis, Rōyama wrote an unpublished book titled *Policies for Resolving the Manchurian Problem* (*manshumondai kaiketsuan*)." Rōyama Masamichi, *Manshū mondai kaiketsuan* [Resolutions for the Manchurian Problem] (unpublished) (June 1932).

66 Rōyama Masamichi, "Ajia monrō shugi no ichihihan [A Critique of Asian Monroeism]," *Kokkagakkai zasshi* 46, no. 3 (Mar. 1932): 129–135; Rōyama Masamichi, "Ajia monrō shugi hihan [Critiques of Asian Monroeism]," *Chūōkōron* 47, no. 2 (Feb. 1932): 29–40.

67 Rōyama Masamichi, *Sekai kyōkō to burokku keizai* (*Gendai keizaigaku zenshū* 29) [Economic Recession in the World and Bloc Economy] (Tokyo: Nihonhyōronsha, 1932), 68.

68 Rōyama Masamichi, "Seijiteki tōitsu no sho riron [Theories of Political Integration] (1)," *Kokkagakkaizasshi* 508 (1935): 1–2.

69 Rōyama Masamichi, *Tōa to sekai: shin chistujō e no ronsaku* [East Asia and the World: Exploring a New Order] (Tokyo: Kaizōsha, 1941), 44.

70 Ibid., 42–43.

71 J. Victor Koschmann, "Constructing Destiny: Royama Masamichi and Asian Regionalism in Wartime Japan," in *Pan-Asianism in Modern Japanese History: Colonialism, Regionalism and Borders*, eds. J. Victor Koschmann and Sven Saaler (London: Routledge, 2006), 188.

72 Carl Schmitt, *The Concept of the Political*, trans. George Schwab (Chicago: University of Chicago Press, 1996), 24. Shimizu Ikutarō first translated Schmitt's *Der Begriff des Politischen* together with Max Weber's *Politik als beruf* in 1939. Shimizu Ikutarō, *Seiji no honshitsu* [The Essence of Politics] (Tokyo: Mikasa Shobo, 1939).

73 As I will discuss further in Chapter 2, sociologist Takata Yasuma's theory of state best exemplifies this tendency. See Takata Yasuma, *Shakai to kokka* [Society and State] (Tokyo: Iwanami Shoten, 1922).

74 Carl Schmitt, *The Concept of the Political*, 53.

75 Giorgio Agamben, *State of Exception*, trans. Kevin Attell (Chicago: The University of Chicago Press, 2005).

76 Schmitt argues, "[T]here exists no norm that is applicable to chaos. For a legal order to make sense, a normal situation must exist, and he is sovereign who definitely decides whether this normal situation exists . . . All law is 'situational law.' The sovereign produces and guarantees the situation in its totality. He had the monopoly over this decision. Therein resides the essence of the state's sovereignty, which must be juristically defined correctly, not as the monopoly to coerce or to rule, but as the monopoly to decide. The exception reveals most clearly the essence of the state's authority. The decision parts here from the legal norm, and (to formulate it paradoxically) authority proves that to produce law it need not be based on law." Carl Schmitt, *Political Theology: Four Chapters on the Concept of Sovereignty*, ed. George Schwab (Chicago: University of Chicago Press, 2005), 13.

77 Rōyama Masamichi, "Seijiteki tōitsu no sho riron [Theories of Political Integration] (2)," *Kokkagakkaizasshi* 509 (1935): 31–32.

78 J. Victor Koschmann, "Constructing Destiny: Royama Masamichi and Asian Regionalism in Wartime Japan," 187–192.

79 Rōyama Masamichi, "Tōa shichitsujō kensetsu no riron – tokuni sono chiikiseigenri ni oite [The Theory of a New East Asia Order: With a Focus on Its Regionality]," *Kōgyōkokusaku* 2, no. 4 (1939), in Rōyama Masamichi, *Tōa to sekai*, 145–151.

80 Rōyama Masamichi, "Tōa kyōdōtai no rironteki kiso [A Theoritical Basis for the East Asian Cooperative Community]," in *Azia mondai kōza* 1 (Tokyo: Sōgensha, 1939), also in Rōyama Masamichi, *Tōa to sekai: shin chistujō e no ronsaku*, 156–157.

81 The original title of these articles was *Ōshū tsushin* (Communication from the West) and it appeared in the journal 11 times between February 1930 and January 1931.

82 Shinmei Masamichi, "Doitu fashizumu no ideorogi [Fascist Ideology in Germany]," *Keizai ōrai* 6, no. 7 (July 1931): 8.
83 Ibid., 11–12.
84 Karl Mannheim, *Essays on Sociology and Social Psychology* (London: Routledge, 1953).
85 Karl Mannheim, *Ideology and Utopia* (New York: Harcourt, Brace, 1936), 73.
86 Shinmei Masamichi, *Chisiki Shakaigaku no josho* [Theories of the Sociology of Knowledge] (Tokyo: Jistubunkan, 1932), 28–29.
87 Shinmei Masamichi, "Kyōdōtai kokka no kannen oyobi kikō [The Concept and Structure of a Cooperative State] (1)," *Hōgaku* 3, no. 1 (Jan. 1934): 28–54.
88 Shinmei Masamichi, "Kyōdōtai kokka no kannen oyobi kikō [The Concept and Structure of a Cooperative State] (2)," *Hōgaku* 3, no. 2 (Feb. 1934): 35–77.
89 Ibid., 64–67.
90 Ibid., 59.
91 Moriyoshi Yoshiteru, *Yamato minzoku no zenshin* [The Progress of the Japanese Nation] (Tokyo: Kokusai Hankokyorenmei, 1942).
92 Ibid.
93 Ibid.
94 Shinmei Masamichi, *Tōa kyōdōtai no rishō* [The Ideal of the East Asian Community] (Tokyo: Nihon Seinen Gaikō Kyōkai Shuppanbu, 1939); Kada Tetsuji, *Tōa kyōdōtai ron* [On the East Asia Community] (Tokyo: Nihon Seinen Gaikō Kyōkai Shuppanbu, 1939); Nihon Seinen Gaikō Kyōkai, ed., *Tōa kyōdōtai shisō kenkyū* [A Study of the Thought of the East Asian Community] (Tokyo: Nihon Seinen Gaikō Kyōkai Shuppanbu, 1939); Sugihara Masami, *Tōa kyōdōtai no genri* [Principles of the East Asian Community] (Tokyo: Modan Nihonsha, 1939).
95 Miki Kiyoshi, "Tōa shiso no konkyō," in *Tōa kyōdōtai shisō kenkyu*, ed. Nihon seinen gaikyo kyōkai (Tokyo: Nihon Seinen Gaikō Kyōkai Shuppanbu, 1939), 7–10.
96 Kada Tetsuji, *Tōa kyōdōtairon*.
97 Ibid., 15–29.
98 Shinmei Masamichi, *Tōa kyōdōtai no rishō*, 2–4. Shinmei referred to an interview with Wang Jing Wei which appeared in the October issue of *Nihonhyōron* [Japan Review].

Bibliography

A roundtable discussion. "Fashizumu hihan [Critiques of Fascism]." *Keizai ōrai* 7, no. 1 (Jan. 1932): 37–68.

Agamben, Giorgio. *State of Exception.* Translated by Kevin Attell. Chicago: The University of Chicago Press, 2005.

Akamatsu, Katsumarō. *Shinkokumin undō no kichō* [The Basis for New National Movement]. Tokyo: Banrikaku, 1932.

Arima, Manabu. *Nihon no kindai 4 – kokusaika no nakano teikoku nihon* [Japan's Modernization 4 – Imperial Japan in the Middle of Internationalization]. Tokyo: Chūō Kōron Shinsha, 1999.

Carr, Edward Hallett. *The Twenty Years' Crisis 1919–1939.* New York: Harper Torch Books, 1939.

Daniels, Roger. *Struggle for Japanese Exclusion.* Berkeley: University of California Press, 1962.

———. *The Politics of Prejudice: The Anti-Japanese Movement in California and the Struggle for Japanese Exclusion.* Berkeley: University of California Press, 1962.

Fujimura, Ichiro. "Yoshino Sakuzō to manmotosshukeniku." In *1920 nendai no nihon no kokusai kankei,* edited by Sugida Yoneyuki, 123–165. Tokyo: Shunbusha, 2011.

Fujioka, Kentarō. "Senkanki nihon chisikijin no higashiajia kokusai chituzōninshiki no kozō [The Structure of Japanese Intellectuals' Understanding of the East Asian International Order in Interwar Japan]." *Kyūshushigaku* 143 (Dec. 2005): 27–51.

Fuke, Takahiro. *Senkanki nihon no shakai shisō* [Social Thoughts in Interwar Japan]. Tokyo: Jimbun Shoin, 2010.

Fukuda, Tokuzō. *Shakai seisaku to kaikyu toso* [Social Policy and Class Struggle]. Tokyo: Kaizosha, 1922.

Han, Jung Sun. *An Imperial Path to Modernity: Yoshino Sakuzō and a New Liberal Order in East Asia, 1905–1937.* Cambridge, MA: Harvard University Asia Center, 2013.

Hasegawa, Nyozekan. *Gendai kokka hihan* [Critiques of Modern State]. Tokyo: Kōbundō Shobō, 1921.

Hasegawa, Yūichi. *Kindai nihon no kokusai ninsiki* [Perceptions of the International in Modern Japan]. Tokyo: Ashishobō, 2016.

Hayashi, Kimio. *Kokka shakaishugi genri* [Principles of State Socialism]. Tokyo: Shokasha, 1932.

———. *Seiyō shisō no nihonka* [Japanizing Western Thought]. Tokyo: Nihonhyōronsha, 1932.

———. *The Fundamental Idea of State Socialism.* Tokyo: Maruzen Co., 1936.

Hijikata, Seibi. "Keizai riron no kiki [The Crisis of Economic Theories]." *Keizai ōrai* 7, no. 13 (Dec. 1932): 1–11.

———. *Nihon keizaigaku no michi* [The Way of Japanese Economics]. Tokyo: Nihonhyōronsha, 1938.

———. "Tōsei keizai to nihon seishin [Controlled Economy and Japanese Spirit]." *Keizai ōrai* 8, no. 3 (Mar. 1933): 7–13.

Kada, Tetsuji. *Nihon kokka shakaishugi hihan* [Critiques of Japanese State Socialism]. Tokyo: Shunshusha, 1932.

———. *Tōa kyōdōtai ron* [On the East Asia Community]. Tokyo: Nihon Seinen Gaikō Kyōkai Shuppanbu, 1930.

Katō, Shūichi. "Taisho Democracy as the Pre-Stage for Japanese Militarism." In *Japan in Crisis: Essays on Taishō Democracy*, edited by Bernard Silberman and Harry Harootunian, 217–236. Princeton: Princeton University Press, 1974.

Kobayashi, Keiji. "Senkanki no kokusaichitsujōninshiki to tōa kyōdōtairon no keisei – rōyama masamichi no kokusai seijiron wo chushin toshite [The Concepts of the International Order and the Formation of the East Asian Cooperative Community – With a Focus on Rōyama Masamichi's Theory of International Politics]." *Nihonshi kenkyū* 424 (Dec. 1997): 30–54.

Koschmann, J. Victor. "Constructing Destiny: Rōyama Masamichi and Asian Regionalism in Wartime Japan." In *Pan -Asianism in Modern Japanese History: Colonialism, Regionalism and Borders*, edited by J. Victor Koschmann and Sven Saaler, 185–199. London: Routledge, 2006.

Koyasu, Nobukuni. *Taisho wo yomi naosu* [Re-reading Taisho Japan]. Tokyo: Fujiwara Shoten, 2016.

Mannheim, Karl. *Essays on Sociology and Social Psychology.* London: Routledge, 1953.

———. *Ideology and Utopia.* New York: Harcourt, Brace, 1936.

Miki, Kiyoshi. "Huan no sishō to sono chokyoku [The Thought of Anxiety and Overcoming It]." In *Miki Kiyoshi zenshu* 10 [Completed Works of Miki Kiyoshi], edited by Hyōe Ōuchi, 285–309. Tokyo: Iwanami Shoten.

Minoda, Muneki. "Kokka shakaishugi ni taisuru seishinkagakuteki hihan [A Spiritual Critique of State Socialism]." In *Kokka shakaishugi o haigekisu* [Denouncing State Socialism], edited by Wakamiya Unosuke, 60–83. Tokyo: Sokokukai Shuppanbu, 1934.

Mori, Kiyohito. *Kagakuteki nihonshugi toha nanizoya* [What Is Scientific Japanism?]. Tokyo: Senshinsha, 1932.

Moriyoshi, Yoshiteru. *Yamato minzoku no zenshin* [The Progress of the Japanese Nation]. Tokyo: Kokusai Hankokyorenmei, 1942.

Muller, Jerry Z. *The Other God That Failed – Hans Freyer and the Deradicalization of German Conservatism*. Princeton: Princeton University Press, 1987.

Nakano, Ryoko. *Beyond the Western Liberal Order: Yanaihara Tadao and Empire as Society*. New York: Palgrave MacMillan, 2013.

Nihon Seinen Gaikō Kyōkai, ed. *Tōa kyōdōtai shisō kenkyū* [A Study of the Thought of the East Asian Community]. Tokyo: Nihon Seinen Gaikō Kyōkai Shuppanbu, 1939.

Nitobe, Inazō. "Kokusairenmei ni okeru manshūmondai [The Manchurian Question in the League of Nations]." *Chūōkōron* 47, no. 2 (Feb. 1932): 41–46.

Okihiro, Gary. *Cane Fires: The Anti-Japanese Movement in Hawaii, 1865–1945*. Philadelphia: Temple University Press, 1991.

Rōyama, Masamichi. "Ajia monrō shugi hihan [Critiques of Asian Monroeism]." *Chūōkōron* 47, no. 2 (Feb. 1932): 29–40.

———. "Ajia monrō shugi no ichihihan [A Critique of Asian Monroeism]." *Kokkagakkai zasshi* 46, no. 3 (Mar. 1932): 129–135.

———. *Japan's Position in Manchuria*. Tokyo: The Japanese Council Institute of Pacific Relations, 1928.

———. *Kokusai seiji to kokusai gyōsei* [International Politics and International Administration]. Tokyo: Ganshōdō Shoten, 1928.

———. *Manshū mondai kaiketsuan* [Resolutions for the Manchurian Problem] (unpublished). June 1932.

———. *Nihon seiji dōkō ron* [On the Tendency of Japanese Politics]. Tokyo: Kōyō Shoin, 1933.

———. "Seijiteki tōitsu no sho riron [Theories of Political Integration] (1)." *Kokkagakkaizasshi* 508 (1935): 1–15.

———. "Seijiteki tōitsu no sho riron [Theories of Political Integration] (2)." *Kokkagakkaizasshi* 509 (1935): 30–45.

———. *Sekai kyōkō to burokku keizai* (*Gendai keizaigaku zenshū* 29) [Economic Recession in the World and Bloc Economy]. Tokyo: Nihonhyōronsha, 1932.

———. "Sekai no saininshiki to chiikiteki kokusai renmei [Reconceptualizing the World and a Regional International Confederation]." *Kokusai chisiki* 13, no. 1 (Jan. 1933). In *Seikai no henkyoku to nihon no sekai seisaku* [Changes in World Affairs and Japan's World Policy], edited by Masamichi Rōyama, 91–95. Tokyo: Ganshodo Shoten, 1938.

———. "Tōa kyōdōtai no rironteki kiso [A Theoritical Basis for the East Asian Cooperative Community]." *Azia mondai kōza* 1. Tokyo: Sōgensha, 1939. Also in Rōyama Masamichi. *Tōa to sekai: shin chistujō e no ronsaku* [East Asia and the World: Exploring a New Order]. Tokyo: Kaizōsha, 1941, 152–168.

———. "Tōa shinchitsujō kensetsu no riron – tokuni sono chiikiseigenri ni oite [The Theory of a New East Asia Order: With a Focus on Its Regionality]." *Kōgyōkokusaku* 2, no. 4 (1939). Also in Rōyama Masamichi. *Tōa to sekai: shin chistujō e no ronsaku* [East Asia and the World: Exploring a New Order], 145–151. Tokyo: Kaizōsha, 1941.

———. *Tōa to sekai: shin chistujō e no ronsaku* [East Asia and the World: Exploring a New Order]. Tokyo: Kaizōsha, 1941.

Sakai, Tetsuya. "<Tōa kyōdōtai> kara <kindaikaron> ē – rōyama masamichi ni okeru chiiki, kaihatsu, nashonarizumu ron no iso [From the East Asian Cooperative Community to Modernization Discourses – Region, Development and Nationalism in Rōyama

Masamichi]." In *Nihon gaikō ni okeru ajia shugi – nenpo seijigaku* [Asianism in Japanese Diplomacy], 109–129. Tokyo: Iwanami Shoten, 1998.

Schmitt, Carl and George Schwab, eds. *Political Theology: Four Chapters on the Concept of Sovereignty*. Chicago: University of Chicago Press, 2005.

———. *The Concept of the Political*. Translated by George Schwab. Chicago: University of Chicago Press, 1996.

Shimizu, Ikutarō. *Seiji no honshitsu* [The Essence of Politics]. Tokyo: Mikasa Shobo, 1939.

Shinmei, Masamichi. *Chisiki Shakaigaku no josho* [Theories of the Sociology of Knowledge]. Tokyo: Jistubunkan, 1932.

———. "Doitu fashizumu no ideorogi [Fascist Ideology in Germany]." *Keizai ōrai* 6, no. 7 (July 1931): 1–18.

———. "Kyōdōtai kokka no kannen oyobi kikō [The Concept and Structure of a Cooperative State] (1)." *Hōgaku* 3, no. 1 (Jan. 1934): 28–54.

———. "Kyōdōtai kokka no kannen oyobi kikō [The Concept and Structure of a Cooperative State] (2)." *Hōgaku* 3, no. 2 (Feb. 1934): 35–77.

———. *Tōa kyōdōtai no rishō* [The Ideal of the East Asian Community]. Tokyo: Nihon Seinen Gaikō Kyōkai Shuppanbu, 1939.

Sugihara, Masami. *Tōa kyōdōtai no genri* [Principles of the East Asian Community]. Tokyo: Modan Nihonsha, 1939.

Sugimori, Kojiro. *Shakaijin no tanjō* [The Birth of Social Man]. Tokyo: Ryūbunkan, 1922.

Sunil, Smith. *Migration and Diaspora in Modern Asia*. Cambridge: Cambridge University Press, 2011.

Takabatake, Motoyuki. *Kokkashakaishugi taigi* [The Ideal of State Socialism]. Tokyo: Nihon Shakaishugi Kenkyūsho, 1932.

Takata, Yasuma. *Shakai to kokka* [Society and State]. Tokyo: Iwanami Shoten, 1922.

Tosaka, Jun. *Nihon ideorogi ron* [On Japanese Ideology]. Tokyo: Hakuyosha, 1935.

Townsend, Susan. *Yanihara Tadao and Japanese Colonial Policy: Redeeming Empire*. London: Routledge Curzon, 2000.

Yahaihara, Tadao. "Chōsen sanmai josan keikai ni toite [On the Rice Production Increase Plan in Colonial Korea]." In *Yanaihara Tadao zenshu* 1 [Completed Works of Yanaihara Tadao], 692–724. Tokyo: Iwanami Shoten, 1963.

———. "Manmoshinkokkaron [On a Manchu-Mongolian State]." *Kaizō* 14, no. 4 (Apr. 1934): 18–29.

———. "Shokumin and shokumin seisaku [Colonization and Colonial Policy]." *Yanaihara Tadao zenshu* 1 [Completed Works of Yanaihara Tadao]. Tokyo: Iwanami Shoten, 1963.

2 *Minzoku* and creating a multi-ethnic empire

Nation, *minzoku* and Japanese social sciences

Perhaps, *minzoku* is one of the most controversial terms that have been the center of various scholarly debates in East Asian studies. The term – pronounced "mínzú" in Chinese, "minjok" in Korean, and "minzoku" in Japanese, respectively (hereafter this book uses the Japanese term *minzoku* with no italicization) is often translated into nation. At stake is the widely accepted perception of nation in these countries, that is, a homogeneous ethnic community had existed before each country's encounter with the modern world and this ethnic community – Chinese or Japanese – consists of the symbolic, cultural and political notion of commonness. In many cases, this ethnic commonness even pertains to biological, racial similarities and the primordial sense of cultural unity. This line of thinking has been generally linked to the observation that the modern concept of nation-states – China, Japan and Korea – is indistinguishably associated with the premodern concept of ethnic communities. If this is the case, each country's national history acquires temporal and spatial continuity in which the same ethnic group has resided and developed its own culture, politics and economy in a geographical space that is now called China, Japan and Korea. Precisely for this reason, this conventional concept of minzoku has played a crucial role in constructing ethnic nationalism in all three countries.

As is well known, the master narrative of nationalist history or ethnic nationalism has been criticized for its exclusiveness. Arguably, these intellectuals' critiques of nationalism are in large part indebted to Benedict Anderson's pioneering concept of nation as an "imagined community."[1]

Here, it is important to note that Anderson's work was not originally aimed to critically trace the origin of modern nationalism. To be sure, several major works on studies on the perceptions and politics of nation were presented since the publication of Anderson's book. Ernest Gellner's 1983 work, *Nation and Nationalism*, is characterized by his intriguing thesis that nationalism as an ideology constructs a nation as a community.[2] Arguably, such critical assessments of nations and nationalism were led by scholars whose areas of specialization are European history and colonialism. Over the past decades, this tendency of revisiting ethnic nationalism has been one of the central inquiries that students of East Asian studies have shared. These intellectuals first focused on tracing the trajectories of nation and nationalism in East Asia's encounter with Western modernization and imperialism in the late nineteenth and early twentieth centuries in the broader context of non-white resistant nationalism, Chinese and Korean nationalism in particular. However, this framework has been problematized by recent studies which have emphasized the complexity of early twentieth-century East Asian history. Ironically, the specter of Japanese imperialism, oftentimes conceptualized as anti-Japanese nationalism in China, Korea and Taiwan, gave rise to an urgency of revisiting the whole question of nations and nationalism in early-twentieth-century East Asia.

Introducing the problematic concept of "colonial modernity" in Korea, Gi Wook Shin and Michael Robinson tackle the anti-Japanese nationalist framework: "[K]orean nationalism is always a 'progressive' force deployed first against the corrupt ancient regime and later against 'repressive' Japanese imperialism. . . . Koreans who were successful in the colonial polity, economy, or society 'collaborated' and became non-Koreans, and their constructions of wealth or cultural property are labeled 'anti-national.'"[3] This line of thinking certainly deserves attention and has brought some paradigm shifts to history writing on East Asia. Nonetheless, I also argue that fundamental critiques of nation or nationalism are only possible by exploring how the concept of nation, minzoku in the Japanese context, was first appropriated by imperial powers for ultimate mobilization and colonial violence. In this respect, it was not coincidental that a group of leading social scientists in 1930s Japan were involved in the studies of minzoku, while the ethnic configuration of the Japanese empire, as discussed in the previous chapter, was facing drastic changes. Under these circumstances, the concept of minzoku captured attention from Japanese social scientists in the 1930s and early 1940s. Arguably, the newly contrived minzoku discourses served to rationalize the construction of a multi-ethnic East Asian empire and most importantly, the concept of minzoku became a violent weapon to mobilize Chinese and colonial subjects for Japan's war efforts. Leading Japanese social scientists in the early 1930s turned their attention to this provoking concept of minzoku as they were closely involved in producing various Japan-led East Asian empire-building discourse. Among them, Takata Yasuma (1883–1972) and Shinmei Masamichi (1898–1984) were perhaps the two most renowned social scientists whose prolific writings on minzoku and East Asian nationalism were widely read by both Japanese and colonial intellectuals during the wartime period. Nevertheless, their writings have received little attention from scholars in the field of East Asian intellectual history.

Unquestionably, the notion of minzoku captured the central stage in wartime Japanese identity politics. By the time the wartime government officialized the slogan of the Greater East Asia Co-Prosperity Sphere, journalists and intellectuals responded to this call for new identity formation and published a number of books, newspaper articles and academic papers on minzoku. Unquestionably, wartime identity politics aimed to provide a theoretical basis for optimizing Japanese and colonial subjects' *voluntary* participation in Japan's war. In fact, these intellectuals' theorization of becoming a new imperial subject was widely accepted by both

Japanese and colonial youths. For instance, Ohnuki-Tierney's recent edited work on Japanese kamikaze soldiers includes the story of a Japanese student who found works by the Kyoto School of Philosophy appealing to his decision on becoming a kamikaze pilot.[4]

Importantly, both Takata and Shinmei were already aware that the concept of minzoku would be the key to Japan's Pan-Asian discourses years before imperial Japan launched a full-scale war against China in 1937. While Takata's turn to the concept of minzoku was related to his sociological studies, Shinmei was exposed to the question of imperial borders and identity politics. Born in Taiwan, Shinmei attended a middle school in colonial Korea, an arguably experimental site for Japan's new colonialism. His early experience in Japan's colonies had an impact on developing his social scientific inquiries beyond a nation-stated-oriented conventional set of questions such as state and individual or state and society. His works on a cooperative community (*kyōdōtai*) years before the logic of the East Asian Community (*tōa kyōdōtai*) gained momentum among Japanese social scientists were the outcome of his interest in how social scientific knowledge would serve the formation of a new East Asian imperial subjectivity. In that respect, revisiting wartime Japanese social scientists' writings on minzoku would shed new light on revealing the violent nature of identity politics in the context of inclusion and continuous racial hierarchies in the Japanese empire. For that purpose, this chapter first discusses how the term *minzoku* or the Japanese race was theorized in early-twentieth-century Japan and eventually explores the writings of Takata Yasuma, Shinmei Masamichi and like-minded Japanese social scientists.

Minzoku and the question of the Japanese "race"

In fact, the term *minzoku* was a widely neglected concept by most Japanese intellectuals in the late nineteenth and early twentieth centuries. As many have argued, racist perspectives were not the central part of Japan's early imperialism. Unlike most European imperial powers, which associated their "colonizing mission" with racial superiority, a consensus over the origin of the Japanese race was not even established by Japanese intellectuals in the late nineteenth century. Instead, a number of Japanese intellectuals acknowledged that the Japanese race is not a homogenous one, but a product of mixed races or migrations.[5] For this reason, the early Japanese logic of colonializing its Asian neighborhoods – the Ryukyus, the Ainus, Taiwan and Korea – substantially varied and many advocates of Japan's imperialist moves, Fukuzawa Yukichi in particular, resorted to Japan's "success" in material modernization as their rationale rather than biological or racial superiority.[6] A primordial concept of race as a given blood-oriented community always generated ambiguity in the discussion of the Japanese race which, many believed, was a product of racial interacts.

In 1879, Edward Morse published a monumental piece of writing on the prehistoric origins of the Japanese race. In this work, titled "Traces of an Early Race in Japan," Morse argued that a prehistoric community existed even before the Ainu began settling the northern part of the Japanese archipelago. Based on these observations, he concluded that various cultural differences exist in Japan and that they were due to interactions among different racial groups.[7] Influenced by Morse, who taught anthropology at Tokyo Imperial University in the late 1870s, a group of first-generation Japanese anthropologists also embraced the theory of Japaneseness as a mixed racial construct. Historical sociologist Oguma Eiji has argued that Japanese anthropologists in the late nineteenth and early twentieth centuries, although their research methodology was amateurish by today's standard, made it clear that the Japanese nation consists of heterogeneous racial communities.[8] Even the renowned philosopher Inoue Tetsujirō (1856–1944) discussed the heterogeneousness of the Japanese race. He argued that the Japanese race was heterogeneously formed by the arrival of different minzoku (nation) groups from all over East Asia. He wrote: "In the Japanese *race* (*jinshu*), there exists a *minzoku* that came from the Korean peninsula in ancient times, and there exists the southern *minzoku* that came from the Southern Seas. The Ainu have been mixed with the Japanese race and the Chinese have migrated to Japan."[9]

Whether or not the Japanese people could be said, from an academic perspective, to have heterogeneous origins, the political necessity of framing the superiority of the Japanese minzoku over other Asian ethnic communities greatly intensified as Japan annexed colonial territories. First, the superiority of the Japanese minzoku had to be proven scientifically to convince the rest of Asia that Japan's leading role in the continent corresponded to the social evolutionist theory. To do this, Japanese intellectuals, and anthropologists in particular, initially showed keen interest in the forms of scientific racism that had originated in Europe and later developed in the United States. Scientific racism was closely related to the emergence of new disciplines – physiognomy, phrenology and craniology – that first served to discover differences among racial groups and eventually intensified the belief system of white supremacy.[10] As Etienne Balibar and Immanuel Wallerstein have correctly argued, scientific racism played an important role in producing and circulating the popular "universal" belief throughout the twentieth century that rationalized the homogeneity and superiority of the modern nation-state, as comprised of a single racial community in relation to other distinct racial groups.[11]

For this reason, creating the narrative of a superior Japanese race is inseparable from the task of disconnecting the Japanese race from other racial groups in Asia, the Chinese in particular. As is well known, Fukuzawa's notion of "de-Asianization" was already turned into political action as early as the 1870s, as Japan began colonizing the Ainu, and Ryukyu and eventually attempted to annex Korea. However, the concept of all Asian races as part of the Chinese and thus underdeveloped was a dominant idea on the part of Western intellectuals, although some white intellectuals produced writings that described the Japanese in a much more favorable way as compared to the Chinese.[12] In fact, the notion of racial similarities was actively promoted by the Japanese empire, and Torri Ryuzo's theory of Japanese and Koreans as having the same ancestors clearly exemplifies one facet of racial politics in the Japanese empire.

Receiving financial support from the Japanese government, Torri made several field trips to Korea and Taiwan in 1895 and 1910 respectively.[13] Based on his empirical research, he produced numerous writings that focused on the similarity among Asian races and the heterogeneousness of the Japanese race. His theory of *nissendōsoron*, that is, the Japanese and Korean races stemmed from the same biological and cultural ancestor, was the apex of Torri's discussion of racial similarity. While growing anti-Japanese sentiment in Korea (which culminated in 1919, the year of the March 1st Independence Movement) prevented Torri from further research trips to support his work, he never withdrew his theory of *nissendōsoron*.[14] This theory of racial similarity was, however, certainly not proposed to recognize independence movements in Japan's colonies, but explicitly targeted Korean nationalist intellectuals. In this regard, the broad dispersion of the theory of *nissendōsoron* was officially supported in order to reduce ethnic nationalism in post-1919 Korea.

The logic of racial similarities or early versions of Pan-Asian discourses was frequently revisited by Japanese intellectuals since it was hardly reflected in actual colonial policies. In addition, while racial mixture was not yet a major phenomenon in 1920s East Asia, racial discourses based on Asian commonness did not directly affect the mindset of the Japanese in Japan proper. For this reason, the notion of Asian commonness was also adopted in 1920s Japan by ultranationalists who firmly believed in the superiority of the Japanese race under the Emperor. Mitsukawa Kametarō's 1924 book, *Historical Perspectives of Racial Conflicts Between the East and the West*, published right after the passage of the 1924 Immigration Act, well shows how the politics of Asian commonness, rather than racial differences among Asians, was appropriated even by ultranationalists to rationalize the Japanese colonial empire. Mitsukawa, the leader of a fascist organization at that time, maintained that in its political interests Japan must return to Asia to protect the continent from Western imperialism.[15]

However, race and the concept of minzoku emerged as one of the central aspects of Japan's colonial governance in the early 1930s. The establishment of Manchukuo and the slogan *gozoku kyowa* (harmony of five races) epitomized imperial Japan's new approach to colonial racial politics. To be sure, the significance of developing new ethnic discourses was shared only by the small number of Japanese intellectuals who were envisioning an East Asian regional community as imperial Japan's ultimate stance in East Asia. This small group of Japanese social scientists, however, soon became pioneering imperial intellectuals who spearheaded Japan's imperial ambitions to become a regional hegemonic power which aimed to turn anti-Japanese sentiments into dynamic energies to construct an East Asian community.

Takata Yasuma and the question of minzoku in 1930s Japan

Takata Yasuma was already a renowned sociologist years before he emerged as a leading intellectual in wartime discourses on minzoku and nationalism. Born in 1883, Takata was exposed to sociology at Kyoto Imperial University, a newly emerging discipline in early- twentieth-century Japan. His 1922 book, *Introduction to Sociology*, is often considered a pioneering work that introduced the most sophisticated sociological theories of the time to the Japanese academia. In the 1920s and early 1930s, he was a prolific writer who authored more than ten monographs on various social issues such as poverty, population and class. Takata's encounter with the concept of minzoku needs to be carefully examined, since his early works in sociology show the trend of Japanese social sciences in the Taisho Democracy period that focused on domestic social problems. As is well known, the renowned political scientist Ishida Takeshi once made the point that Japanese social sciences during the Taisho period were characterized by their thinking pattern, that is, first diagnosing social issues and then setting up social problems and finally providing solutions for them.[16] Perhaps, Takata was also one of these liberal and progressive Japanese social scientists, although he was never involved in radical academic activities.

Takata developed his own regionalist and transnational visions as early as the 1920s, while most Japanese social scientists focused their inquiries on domestic issues. However, Takata's encounter with transnational questions, unlike Rōyama Mamasmichi who developed his regionalist mindset through the newly emerging field of international politics, in large part stemmed from his peculiar nativist worldview. Takata basically observed that ethnic and international conflicts caused by economic imbalance would be greatly reduced by retrieving the primordial distribution and production system in *Gemeinschaft*, a sociological concept of community first introduced by the German sociologist Ferdinand Tönnies.[17] He, however, did not show keen interest in the so-called communitarian fascism that was on the rise in Germany, Italy and Japan. Nor was he satisfied with formal sociology by Georg Simmel who became one of the most influential sociologists in the early twentieth century. In a reaction to communitarian sociological trends such as the popularity of Tönnies' notion of *Gemeinschaft*, Simmel presented a methodological shift in sociological thinking, often called formal sociology.[18] Although Simmel's formal sociology had an impact on a number of first-generation Japanese sociologists in the 1920s, community-oriented discourses on the making of the Japanese empire gradually gained momentum in late 1920s and early 1930s Japan. As Harootunian has argued, a number of Japanese intellectuals in folklore studies, ethnology and philosophy developed the nativist concept of a community in their support of Japan's imperialist moves as if this would bring an equilibrium to Asia, which, they believed, had been stained by the Western-style capitalist system.[19] A group of romance school (*roman-ha*) literary intellectuals also developed similar visions of a new imperial society.[20] Apparently, Takata's social scientific inquiry adhered to the notion of *Gemeinschaft*; however, he never put it forward as an ultimate solution for capitalist problems. This peculiar stance was in large part due to Takata's firm belief that all social phenomena would be basically conceptualized as relational. Takata was convinced that human beings desire gregariousness; that is to say, desired coexistence (*Gewelltes Zusammenleben*). These notions shape the core concepts of Takata's early sociology; that is, human society constantly searches for communitarian modes of life, but these cannot be extracted from intrinsic and primordial elements precisely because every phenomenon is socially constructed.[21]

Based on these observations, Takata also developed his early concepts of minzoku and nationalism. In a 1920 article titled, "An Individual Opinion on Racial Problems," he observed, as did many Japanese social scientists at the time, that racial problems were basically an issue between white and colored people.[22] Therefore, Takata too, intentionally or unintentionally, tended to conflate the issue of racism with the problem of discrimination between Europeans and Asians in the early 1920s, thus avoiding mention of Japan's racial oppression in the colony. However, unique in Takata's understanding of race was his tendency to approach it not as an issue of a single nation-state, but as a broader issue involving a world society.

Beginning in the early 1930s, Takata became increasingly involved in ethno studies from a social scientific perspective. Here, it would be worthwhile to examine his 1935 book *The Problem of Nation*. Again, this 1935 publication first shows how seriously Takata found the whole question of minzoku years before both the Japanese wartime government and intellectuals became conscious about incorporating Chinese and colonial subjects for Japan's empire building. In translating the following text and the following pages, this book will adhere to the term minzoku with no italicization rather than ethnicity or nation to minimize any conceptual confusion:

> What is minzoku? Minzoku is a group of people who recognize themselves as a minzoku. This, by all means, sounds like a circular definition. Nonetheless, it articulates that the locus of minzoku does not reside in external characteristics such as blood and physical similarities, but in the consciousness of its members. The fact that minzoku consciousness is not induced by minzoku, but minzoku *is induced by* minzoku consciousness is, irrespective of its somewhat insufficient manifestation, a truth that can hardly be refuted.[23]
>
> (emphasis added)

As early as the mid-1930s, a few years before the outbreak of the Asia-Pacific War, Takata was already making a subtle but very compelling argument about the concept of ethnicity. Not only did he completely denounce race as irrelevant to minzoku, but he also argued that ethnic consciousness precedes the existence of an ethnic group. Therefore, for Takata, minzoku as a collective consciousness was not a given community but a social construct by its nature, and this reconfirms the location of the term minzoku as an object of social scientific study. He then moved to the issue of the relationship between minzoku and nation (*kokumin*). Here, Takata raises some conceptual questions:

> First, some discomfort occurs when the term *kokumin* is translated into the word nation. The word *kokumin* includes in its meaning all members of a nation-state and it is often considered to be identical to the nation-state in dimension. However, nation corresponds only in exceptional cases to the nation-state in its dimensions. Second, nation has often been translated as minzoku. Since the term nation has been commonly used in expressions such

as minzoku problems, minzoku autonomy and *minzokushugi* (nationalism),
I believe that calling nation *kokumin* would create a great many difficulties
and this tendency would not change. . . . For this reason, I have decided to
call nation minzoku.[24]

Although he chooses minzoku as the translation for nation, Takata does not
acknowledge that it has the same definition as nation in terms of a nation-state
or in terms of formal nationality. This clearly indicates that instead of a Japanese word, Takata adhered to the English word "nation" in the original text. For
Takata, the term minzoku, therefore, is highly equivocal, and he thus affirmed its
limited similarity to the concept of nation-state. Theoretically, Takata's hesitation
to equate minzoku with nation-state is directly concerned with his whole sociological concept of partial (部分) and integral (全体) society. Takata stressed that
the dimensions of an integral society are determined based on its degree of self-
sufficiency.[25] For him, the tendency for a nation-state to be considered as ultimate
integral society and its members the *subjects* of an integral society did not indicate
that a nation-state is in itself a self-sufficient society. More importantly, this logic,
Takata argued, neither explains the hybridity of one's becoming a subject in com-
plicated social interactions, nor does it provide practical solutions for the crisis in
the modern nation-state.

Takata maintained that the combination of Koreans and Taiwanese with Japanese minzoku itself does not constitute a nation-state as a self-sufficient integral society. Therefore, he contended that the boundary of a nation (*kokumin*)
does not become the boundary of an integral society.[26] In other words, he was
strongly opposed to the idea that minzoku as a form of nation is itself either an
integral society or a constituent of an element of an integral society, the nation-
state in particular. Such a radical interpretation of the term minzoku tells us that
Takata was painstakingly searching for a new logic of subjectivity formation in
his observation of the limitations of the nation-state framework. Just as giving
formal nationality to colonial subjects does not guarantee that they *subjectively*
belong to the empire, Takata was opposed to the notion of constructing an East
Asian empire by mechanically consolidating different ethnic groups. Here, he
reconfirmed that minzoku itself does not constitute an integral society, nor a
nation-state:

> Minzoku is not an integral society. Needless to say, various partial groups are
> included in an integral society, but these partial groups are not included in
> minzoku. Minzoku is also nothing but a partial society and the reason it has
> a particular meaning among partial societies is only because it is extended to
> the broad dimension of people's lives. On the one hand, the combination of
> an integral society includes the combination of minzoku as its most important
> part, but an integral society is constituted by various combinations and mix-
> tures. Therefore, the combination of minzoku at times positions itself against
> (the general combination of) an integral society; that is, an integral society
> even includes the combination of a group [minzoku] against it.[27]

Although minzoku, among other social groups, constitutes part of an integral society, it is extended to people's lives to a greater degree. This first explains why Takata placed an enormous emphasis on it in his vision of an East Asian empire. Second, it is a dynamic element in society itself; that is, minzoku is not a given and static creature. It always negates and recreates itself and it is in this very process that a new form of subjectivity necessary for a grand community emerges. To this end, Takata had to debunk any possible links between transcendental, primordial, and thus nonscientific elements of society such as race, blood and land. In other words, Takata shed new light on the possibility of the concept of minzoku as voluntarily incorporating Chinese and colonial subjects into a new Japanese empire which he believed to be constructed.

Politics of anti-racism in 1930s Japan

Takata was not the only Japanese social scientist who developed a seemingly radical vision of minzoku and nation-state. In the late 1930s, a group of Japanese social scientists produced numerous writings about the concept of minzoku, ethnicity and nation-state. Needless to say, their ultimate question was how to contrive new forms of subject formation as Japan would attempt to construct an East Asian empire. Fujitani's recent trans-Asia-Pacific study on wartime racism also shows how the rhetoric and practice of anti-racism laid the foundation for minority subjects' voluntary participation in imperial wars.[28]

In October 1938, a year after the outbreak of the Sino-Japanese War, Kada Tetsuji, who was taking sociology and economics lectures at Keio University, a prestigious Japanese private university, published *Race, Nation and War*, which soon became a best-seller.[29] Not surprisingly, Kada reiterated the thesis that the Japanese race had mixed heritages, as already demonstrated in anthropologists' ethnographic studies from the 1910s and the 1920s. Carrying this previous concept of race a step further, he asserted that the existing situation of white supremacy was merely a reflection of the capitalistic development that dominated Western Europe. Kada maintained that Western capitalism, historically speaking, had little to do with "superior" physiological characteristics of any kind within the white races.[30] He was equally critical of the conventional concept of minzoku, which he viewed as a mere extension of blood-centered essentialism. Under this extremely narrow conceptual understanding of the term minzoku, it is natural that Kada, who had been writing extensively on the issue of nationalism, internationalism and cosmopolitanism since the early 1930s, could not find any potential for a regional community through any blood-centered identities. This is why he called for "minzoku's development beyond the conventional definition minzoku."[31]

Given that not only Kada but also many other wartime Japanese social scientists rejected racism and racial science, Kada's somewhat heated critiques of racist thinking were not surprising. However, important in Kada's discussion of racism is the fact that not only was he aware of the irrationality of Western racism but he was also attentive to the way both racist and anti-racist discourses in Japan were appropriated in real politics in a very complex way, thereby producing another form of racism. With these observations in mind, Kada discussed the genealogy of racial thinking in modern Japan. For him, racial science in the West was deeply flawed in the fact that it served as a theoretical tool for demonstrating the superiority of white Europeans in modern civilization.[32] Interestingly, he was outspoken when he argued that modernization is not a one-dimensional, linear process, and that even industrialized societies continue to need agriculture and other not-yet-industrialized sectors.[33] He then argued that Japanese social scientists had focused on scientifically proving that the Japanese race also had genetically dominant characteristics as Europeans tried to prove about themselves. For example, he discussed Taguchi Yukichi's notion of the Japanese race which emphasized its similarity to European races in Taguchi's refutation of the "yellow peril" theory.[34] Kada problematized this "orientalist" version of racial theory put forth by Japanese social scientists, asserting even anti-Western racism in Japan was in fact a replica of Western racism, in that it had paradoxically repeated the logic of Western racism. He pointed out the irony in the fact that advocates of anti-Western racism in Japan firmly believed in Japan's glorious modernization as proof that the Japanese race was as inherently superior as white races.

Takata, Kada and like-minded Japanese social scientists observed that Japanese racial discourses seemingly emphasized a Pan-Asianist unity among Asian races but never denied the superiority of the Japanese race. Needless to say, this distorted racist thinking by Japanists actually played a role in their concealing of Japan's colonization of its neighboring countries. Therefore, the discontent of social scientists was centered on the observation that any kind of politicized racial discourses, even if seemingly "anti-racist," would give way to a far more essentialized racism. Kada was thus adamant in his denunciation of racial studies as fundamentally unscientific:

> The reality of racial theories in our time becomes evident when we think of the problem of racial conflict between white races and colored races. However, the differences between them lie in the question of whether we should think about it from the standpoint of Western imperialism or from Japan's standpoint. Racial theories, as I have discussed, do not contain elements as a hard science. Therefore, their validity as social science is different (from other disciplines).[35]

As a social scientist, Kada clearly explains in this comment why racial theories continued to resurge both in Japan and in the West, although they do not have social scientific rationality. To him, therefore, racial studies became the dark side of modern social science. Distinguishing social science from racial theories, however, did not preclude racism from being politically appropriated for propagandistic purposes. Nor did it provide a practical solution for the problem of ethnic conflicts within the Japanese empire. Theoretically speaking, Kada's critical approach to the concept of race clearly exemplifies Japanese social scientists' tendency to avoid racial and ethnic discourses that originated in Germany. However, it also left much room for further discussion on what ought to be a driving force for creating a theory of a multi-ethnic empire.

Shinmei Masamichi: neither Hilter nor Mussolini

The writings of Takada and other Japanese social scientists on minzoku seem to tell us that they were armed with a reformist mindset in order to change the empire-colony racial structure. However, it is misleading that their writings on a multi-ethnic empire and involvement in actual policy making – Takata was appointed as the director of the Ethnic Research Institute in January 1943 – were intended to construct a racially liberated regional community. Instead, they were grappling with a much more evolved question of maximizing the voluntary participation of Chinese and colonial subjects for Japan's war efforts through their ethno studies. In this regard, one thing most of these social scientists commonly observed was the incompatibility of the German or Italian ethnic nation theory with the Japanese case, although these three "fascist" countries maintained close diplomatic and militaristic alliances until the end of the Second World War. Again, their anti-racist stance did not emerge in the mid- and late 1930s to fight racism as such. For this reason, their critiques of German racism and the Western images of Asia functioned as a tool for contriving an alternative logic of integrating the Chinese and ethnic minorities for the optimization of Japan's war efforts.

While Takata was producing a set of pioneering works on the concept of minzoku, Shinmei Masamichi, who appears in the previous chapter of this book, more aggressively approached ethnic discourses in Germany and Italy. In 1929, the year of the Great Depression, he embarked on a trip to Germany, where he studied German sociology until his return to Japan in 1931. Given that he already had taken a professorship at one of the leading imperial universities, his stay in Germany was not aimed at obtaining a professional degree. Moreover, he was not fortunate enough to enjoy the strength of the yen currency which had enabled many Japanese students to rush to Germany in the late 1920s.[36] Instead, the Great Depression did make him experience economic hardships, but his being at the center of the most radical social changes in Europe had an enormous impact on his later sociology and his encounter with the concept of minzoku.

While maintaining his ties to Japanese intellectual circles by writing brief monthly reports on German society and politics in the famous journal *Keizai ōrai*, Shinmei witnessed the rise of the fascist movement in Germany.[37] Upon his return to Japan, he became one of the most sophisticated writers in Japanese intellectual circles on this new political current, and produced numerous articles on fascism in various journals. Not surprisingly, he was aware that Japanese social sciences, arguably the icon of progressive scholarship in the 1920s, faced an ontological crisis with the emergence of this reactionary and conservative political movement. However, what captured his attention from a social scientific perspective was that German social scientists, sociologists in particular, became gradually involved in real politics, redefining the principle of the social sciences. Sociologist Hans von

Freyer was one of the German social scientists who captured Shinmei's special attention.

Author of the seminal book *Soziologie als Wirklichkeitswissenschaft* (Sociology as a science of reality), published in 1929, Freyer advocated a methodological transformation in sociology in his emphasis on a structuralist approach to building a national community and his debunking of Simmel's formal sociology.[38] Not surprisingly, Freyer's engagement with real politics as a sociologist received attention from Shinmei, who spent a long time developing a politico-sociological perspective. As a result, Shinmei's 1935 book *Sociology of National Revolution* was actually an interpretation of Freyer's sociology.[39] Freyer denounced Simmel's formal sociology as *Logoswissenschaft* (science of logos), which had only concentrated on constructing a world of abstraction in which, Freyer believed, the historicity of sociological objects was completely ignored. He instead insisted that contemporary sociology must be a science of *ethos*. To put this another way, sociology like Simmel's, Freyer argued, had merely enumerated social phenomena through various social forms, but it did not provide a way to totalize social activities in a concrete structure, and as a result, society was deprived of its historicity.

Freyer's critiques of social science, however, were not simply an attempt to endorse a return to what might be called conventional structuralism. He observed that Hegel's idealism conceptualized the state as a synthesis of people's collective freedom and cognitive personality in a community. However, he maintained that the state itself had been dominated by powerful social classes. For this reason, in order to conceptualize a total society, he contended, social scientists must pay attention to real power dynamics and structural changes that occur to the state.[40] As the German sociologist Franz Oppenheimer put it, "[S]ociology is a science that studies totality as totality. It consolidates various social principles and therefore it is *universalwissenschaft* (universal science)."[41] Freyer thus redefined sociology as a discipline of discovering universal totality in the web of social and political phenomena.

It was Freyer's logic of totality that Shinmei drew special attention to in *Sociology of National Revolution*. Arguing that industrial society had been overwhelmed by economic interests, Freyer emphasized the necessity of its revolutionary transformation. However, he rejected both Marxist class struggle and civil society theories because they all marginalized the state as a by-product of social conflict. Instead, he contended that by creating a trans-class subject in society, the state of perpetual class struggle and crisis in the capitalist system could be overcome. He defined this new subject as *nation* and a conservative national revolution would have to be accomplished by these cooperative national subjects.[42]

Although Freyer did not use the term cooperative community in his discussion of national subjects, the concepts of cooperativism and cooperative subject were already gaining currency among European intellectuals. Shinmei also showed keen interest in these new political theories, and in 1934, he contributed two articles to *Legal Studies*, the college journal of Tohoku Imperial University, that explicitly touched on the issue of cooperativism. In these articles, titled "The Concept and Structure of the Cooperative State," he defined the cooperative state as a new type of state in which social subjects are incorporated into national subjects and the state accordingly eradicates all kinds of social and class conflicts through establishing a cooperative order.[43] He was aware, of course, that this unprecedented political phenomenon in Western Europe, Germany and Italy in particular, was basically a totalitarian movement. However, Shinmei was less concerned with fundamental violence and coercion in fascist movements than with the observation that advocates of national socialism were mainly targeting peasant and urban workers, promising that they would be emancipated from the status of "debt slave." Acutely aware that the identity politics of incorporating marginalized groups into national subjects became a driving force for the fascist state, Shinmei was also convinced that this rosy picture of eradicating socio-political hierarchies would never be realized. As Shinmei himself emphasized, both Hitler and the Italian fascists were heavily dependent on the industrial bourgeoisies, and more importantly, the formation of national subjects in Hitler's Germany was in fact excluding those who they considered to be racial minorities, the Jews in particular.[44]

Therefore, it is misleading to assume that Shinmei accepted the logic of European fascist movements at face value after his return from Germany. As a matter of fact, he was a most ardent critic of the German and Italian fascist movements. More important than evaluating how he viewed fascism is the question of how Shinmei attempted to theorize a new concept of subjectivity in his critical analysis of totalitarian movements in Europe. To be sure, German totalitarianism and Italian fascism, in spite of their theoretical limits, came as a new form of subject formation to Shinmei and like-minded Japanese social scientists. The popularity of totalitarian theories in Japan was also closely related to the dismal status-quo Japanese sociology was facing in the early 1930s. As the young sociologist Shimizu Ikutarō lamented in a 1934 article in *The Central Review*, sociologists' tendency to view civil society as the most advanced framework precludes sociological theories from developing further.[45] Under these circumstances, reactionary and community-oriented social theories such as Tönnies' *gemeinschaft* were quickly gaining momentum among Japanese social scientists.

In summary, Shinmei's sociology experienced a few detours before he engaged himself in ethnographic studies in the late 1930s. His search for a total society beyond Simmel's formal sociology led him to directly confront European social theories. Yet it was through Shinmei's stay in Germany and his exposure to fascist movements that he developed critical perspectives toward European social sciences and faced the challenge of creating a new paradigm for subject formation and a multi-ethnic empire in Japan. Thus, Shinmei developed his ethnographic studies in the late 1930s and early 1940s as he confronted the tension between state as a total society and minzoku as part of it. In contrast to Shinmei, Takata took an idealistic approach to the term minzoku that constantly distanced itself from the boundary of the nation-state. How, then, did these seemingly different paths of theorizing racial and ethnic issues shape mainstream ethnographic studies during wartime Japan? How did Japanese social scientists face the eventual challenge of rationalizing a multi-ethnic empire through their social scientific research?

Takata's *grand nationalism* and the question of capitalism

Shinmei's observation of European fascism in the mid-1930s tells us what major theoretical questions Japanese social scientists were grappling with. As I have argued, the notion of racism based on the superiority of the Japanese race was conceptually rejected by them, but anti-racism itself did not provide any alternative logic of a regional community. This is why Shinmei, in spite of his eventual disapproval of German fascism and Italian cooperativism, showed keen interest in the theory of national community as the platform for integrating various ethnic subjects within East Asia. Shinmei was aware that the German notion of the national community was not only a racist approach but also, perhaps more importantly, it would be operating in a single nation-state, since it pertained to a single racial group. For this reason, Shinmei's encounter with European fascism explained why he later developed the theory of an East Asian League (*tōa renmei*), a late 1930s version of the United States of East Asia.

Takata basically embraced the ideas of like-minded Japanese social scientists at the time as he also presented his own vision of East Asian minzoku, a collective and grand ethnic identity that would extend beyond the nation-state border. However, he showed considerable disagreement over the question of how to construct a new imperial economy through this new politics of ethnic identity formation. Takata was a sociologist as well as a scholar of economics who taught core courses on economics – history of economic thought and principles of economics – at Tokyo University of Commerce (present-day Hitotsubashi University), Kyushu Imperial University and Kyoto Imperial University. Unlike many Marxist social scientists whose analyses of the Japanese economy were based on the class struggle theory, Takata showed a sort of nativist view of economic changes. Echoing cutting-edge theories of population growth introduced by Thomas Malthus in the 1920s, Takata observed that economic domination by a leading ethnic group or a nation-state would ultimately end or constant physical war would have to take place to secure resources for uncontrollable population growth.[46] Takata's observation first indicates that the scope of his economic inquiries certainly exceeded the nation-state framework,[47] which set a theoretical platform for his notion of the East Asian community in the late 1930s and early 1940s.

Nonetheless, Takata's observation of the limits of the capitalist economy and his perceptions of imperialism did not come from his critical understanding of Japanese colonial policies in Korea, Taiwan and northern China and the economic imbalances between metropole and colony. As I will discuss later, Takata's somewhat naïve understanding of colonial reality became the target of acute criticism by social scientists in the East Asian community group such as Rōyama Masamichi. Not surprisingly, Japanese Marxist social scientists accused Takata of concealing the exploitative nature of Japanese capitalism. While facing criticism, however, Takata hardly modified his economic perspectives in the 1930s and early 1940s. He even wrote several academic and non-academic works in which he praised poverty as an ideal and minimalized form of life and expressed romanticized views on the nativist and primordial notion of economic communities as the status of equilibrium and non-economic conflicts.[48]

Takata's critical approach to class struggle theory shed new light on the complex relationship between nationalism and capitalism. Class consciousness in the capitalistic mode of production, he maintained, is often associated with ethnic consciousness, and those two factors reinforce each other. This relationship becomes all the more complex in a society with multi-ethnic groups. At the early stage of capitalism, Takata contended, national interests appropriate capital in order to reinforce their influence, and the development of capitalism thus becomes a passive means of realizing the demands of nationalism.[49] Takata argued that the nation-state, appropriating the power of capital in the form of "nationalistic demands," attempted to increase its profit at its highest stage of development.[50]

According to German sociologist Ferdinand Tönnies' theory of *Gemeinschaft* and *Gesellschaft* (Community and Civil Society), the spread of goal-oriented activities by human beings comes about because of complex social relations. Further, the development of productivity and technologies necessarily gives rise to the prevalence of capitalism. Takata was exquisitely aware of Tönnies' logic and acknowledged that nationalism as a form of community and capitalism are diametrically opposed to each other in *theory*. This explains why he described nationalism as "centripetal," that is, an individual is represented as part of a total self, whereas capitalism is "centrifugal," in that an individual always pursues a sense of superiority and a relationship of dominance.[51]

The problem here is that unlike Tönnies' somewhat simplistic analysis of *gesellschaft*, the proliferation of profit-oriented relationships in modern society does not necessarily mean that a community-centered society would come to an end. As Žižek has correctly argued, the elementary feature of capitalism is its circularity, so that capital's constant production of surplus value would not allow it to find equilibrium. According to Žižek, capitalism could not exist without its "inherent structural imbalance."[52] Takata observed that under this mechanism, capital must constantly increase its surplus value to limit social and economic inequality. He concluded that this is precisely the means by which a modern nation-state achieved development in the name of material civilization. He also pointed out that precisely for this reason, modern nation-states are not immune from all sorts of conflicts that are engendered by hierarchy and unevenness from a sociological perspective.[53]

Takata's analysis of modern warfare and his somewhat pessimistic view of modern capitalism were in fact based on his understanding of *gesellschaft*. To peacefully increase capital and surplus value, he stressed, a modern nation-state strives to develop modern technologies and expand the capitalist market. To this end, it must subordinate the selfish desires of individuals to the collective good of the community by establishing an authoritative but highly rational state institution. This modern nation-state system, Takata acknowledged, does not necessarily generate conflicts between nation-states, as he noted in the examples of Sweden,

Belgium and the Netherlands, all of which had achieved a certain level of capitalist development.[54] However, the ostensible status created by the peaceful accumulation of capital would not last forever, unless a modern nation-state permanently maintains what might be called an autarchy system. In an attempt to realize self-sufficiency and minimize the potential risks of conflict, Takata observed, a modern nation-state with many ethnic groups is often divided into several independent ethnic nation-states.[55] He maintains that this differentiation, however, would never fundamentally resolve ethnic conflicts that are intertwined with the capitalistic mode of production in such an overdetermined society as modern society.[56]

Takata's zeal for a new society beyond the limits of *gemeinschaft* and *gesellschaft*, therefore, is closely connected to his phenomenological discovery that nationalism and capitalism are essentially reciprocal. In this respect, he, like other wartime Japanese social scientists, paid attention to the necessity of creating a broad nation-state through which a higher level of communitarian integration might be realized. Importantly, Takata's project of constructing a grand communal body was not intended to eliminate socio-political elements that cause conflict and inequality. As Žižek has argued, the corporatist temptation, often called a fascist fantasy, aims to create a community by way of eradicating those social and economic elements that give rise to structural imbalance and social antagonism. A totalitarian state, therefore, often strives to create a homogeneous means of forming subjectivity, in which profit-oriented, selfish individualism must be subordinated to the communitarian good. Precisely for this reason, these anti-social and anti-harmonious elements are explicitly imputed to groups and matters outside society, that is, racism.[57] Žižek therefore conceptualizes the desire of eliminating unevenness in modern society as "capitalism without capitalism."[58]

Takata was keenly aware of the structural risks inherent in the capitalist system. He too unmasked his "corporatist" vision of a grand communal body. However, it should be emphasized that Takata's notion of cooperative community was not centered on creating an omnipotent creature such as the Master that would realize social balance, as was described in Žižek's analysis of German fascism. Nor was it based on institutional and thus highly rationalized faith: specifically, that the bigger and stronger a nation-state was, the more effectively it could control social and economic inequality. Inherent in Takata's logic of community was regionality beyond the limits of a single nation-state. This explains why Takata, citing the writings of Alfred Rosenberg, a symbolic figure in the racist theory of Nazi Germany, somehow expressed sympathy with his general idea of creating a *regional* community.[59] Takata's interest in Rosenberg, however, was nothing more than academic and superficial. To be sure, he was keenly aware of Rosenberg's extremely racist orientation, as his main argument was to spread the trans-historical superiority of the Aryan race, which he himself "discovered" in the myths of Northern Europe.[60]

Importantly, the problem Takata found in Rosenberg's theory was the issue of the distorted relationship between German nationalism and the German nation-state. He observed that Nazi Germany's ultimate destiny was to establish a regional political community in Europe by expanding a German nation-state. What Takata found problematic in this process was that German nationalism was presented as the principle of the integration of subjects in Germany's political community.[61] He stressed, however, that German nationalism was based on two unchangeable myths: (1) one was a faith in the superiority of the German minzoku, and (2) the other, based on this faith, was that the German minzoku had always been creative and thus contributed to the development of world culture.[62] Most problematic in this theory was that the German minzoku itself is always portrayed as a given and thus trans-historical, lacking the dynamics of subject formation.

Takata was adamant that a number of Japanese social scientists were recklessly replicating this one-dimensional and scientifically inconsistent thinking in their vision of the East Asian Community, particularly regarding the East Asian economic bloc theory. To put it another way, there is no absolute minzoku, as Nazi Germany attempted to postulate about German nationalism. Takata strove to establish his theory of an East Asian nation as a grand minzoku and at the same time to rationalize it by reconfirming that his theory of nation was actually a product of his long-standing sociological speculation that he had been developing since the 1920s.[63]

Toward an East Asian empire: contesting theories of a multi-ethnic community

Apparently, Takata and like-minded social scientists hardly resonated with any radical voices such as Marxist movements in late 1930s Japan as a feasible way of constructing a Japan-led East Asian empire. Takata hardly shared any radical notion of resistance by the lower class against capitalists and the state, nor was he interested in accepting the Marxist power-production relation theory as the most determinant invariable for class struggle. As early as the 1920s, Takata developed the so-called "third historical viewpoint" through which he intended to overcome the existing two master narratives of historical changes – the material view of history by Marxism and abstract universal historical development theory.[64] As a sociologist, he contended that social relations, including the class structure, were determined by a much more complex web of systems and institutions such as ideology, politics and law, and the quantitative and qualitative structure of each society is built on these various social relations, not predominantly determined by the Marxist power-production relation theory.[65] At stake was the question of how he predicted the historical future of this much sophisticated and stratified modern society. Again, Takata, unlike many of his colleagues who endeavored to provide solutions for problems caused by modern capitalism, resorted to the notion of gemeinschaft and showed little interest in a "futuristic notion" of developing both domestic and colonial economies as a way of reducing economic gaps and eventually maximizing production power for Japan's war efforts.

On the other hand, a call for a changed ethnic policy in China and the colony was being frequently made by Japanese intellectuals and bureaucrats since the outbreak of the Sino-Japanese War in 1937. While anti-Japanese sentiments were growing more rapidly than ever before in China, a concern for Japanese being the target of ethnic violence in China and Manchukuo, if it sounds ironic, also grew in Japan proper. In a 1939 book titled *Nation and Culture*, Komatsu Kentarō (1894–1959), one of the most influential sociologists in prewar and postwar Japan, wrote:

> For example, one elite young Japanese man who does not have a sense of ethnic identity happens to go to work for a trading company near the Yangtze River upon graduation. If this young man is condemned, lynched and robbed of his belongings by a man from a certain country for no reason other than because he is Japanese, he will naturally feel that his ethnicity has been insulted. If his wife is violated on the street for no reason, he will feel the same way. In these cases, irrespective of his Japanese consciousness, he becomes Japanese as a natural man.[66]

To be sure, this statement by itself does not allow us to assess the intellectual depth of Komatsu's discussion of ethnicity. However, one might observe from it that the problem of ethnic conflict in the Japanese empire became so complex that leading social scientists like Komatsu indirectly disclosed their fear of ethnically motivated reprisals against the Japanese in Japan's occupied territories. This book does not intend to make the preposterous argument that fear of ethnic and racial discrimination against the Japanese was equivalent to that suffered by Japan's colonial subjects. Komatsu's seemingly naïve statement nonetheless shows how anxiety over the prospect of ethnic revolts within the Japanese empire gradually permeated the mindset of Japanese social scientists. The above statement also confirms that Japanese intellectuals were in a position of having to contrive convincing Pan-Asian discourses that would be appealing to both Chinese and colonial subjects.

In this respect, Takata's discusson of mizoku, in spite of its pioneering theoretical role in challenging the blood-oriented concept of ethnic community, showed its conceptual limits as it was applied to actual policy making, and more importantly appealed to the colony. Apparently, Takata's early alternative historical thinking that rejected a West-centered narrative of historical development continued to dominate his mindset in the late 1930s and early 1940s. One more thing that had impact on Takata's wartime writings on minzoku and capitalism was the presence of the Kyoto School of Philosophy. In 1938, Takata was appointed as the chair of the Economics Department at Kyoto Imperial University after giving a series of lectures in Japan and Manchukuo. As is well known, it was around the late 1930s when a group of philosophers including Miki Kiyoshi (1897–1945), Tanabe Hajime (1885–1962) and Kōyama Iwao (1905–1993), most of them affiliated with Kyoto Imperial University, attempted to present a new interpretation of world history as their commitment to the Japanese empire.

Stressing that the 1937 Marco Polo Bridge Incident in China was a "world-historical moment," Miki insisted in this 27-page pamphlet, titled "Principles of Thought for a New Japan," that "abstract modern ideologies" should be overcome in order to establish "East Asian thought" and complete an "East Asian Cooperative Community."[67] Interestingly, among some eight ideologies to be sublated,

Miki's first target was nationalism.[68] Needless to say, his somewhat extravagant charge against nationalism reflects the concern of Japanese intellectuals' with growing Chinese nationalism. Miki wrote:

> With respect to Chinese nationalism, just as all of the world's countries moved from feudal societies to modern states through nationalism, China is experiencing nationalism in the same way; thus, it is important to recognize *the historical necessity of Chinese nationalism*. Japan should not interrupt China's national unification; rather, it is important for the true establishment of the East Asian Community that China acquires *individuality through national unity*. But at the same time, China, in order to enter the new world, must go beyond nationalism.[69]

(emphasis added)

Miki's call for overcoming a single ethnic nation-state-oriented nationalism and his critiques of Western ideologies, if they were abstract, including individualism, capitalism and communism, resonated with Takata's zeal for an alternative historical narrative. Miki also showed keen interest in the possibility that the notion of ethnicity (minzoku) might replace the logic of nationalism and nation in terms of formal nationality.[70]

Takata's writings in the early 1940s show that he encountered the Kyoto School of Philosophy as they both called for overcoming capitalism and a West-centered historical developmental path. On the other hand, both Takata and Kyoto School intellectuals pointed to their philosophy's limits due to its lack of practical approaches to restructuring the empire-colony power structure, economic imbalances in particular. The notion of overcoming capitalism was widely shared by both Japanese and colonial intellectuals in the name of the "overcoming modernity (*Kindai no chōkoku*)" debate. To be sure, the Kyoto School of Philosophy also criticized the rise of fascist movements in Europe in the 1930s. However, this does not indicate that, as Naoki Sakai has pointedly argued, these philosophers' anti-fascist activities gave them the status of progressive intellectuals.[71] Instead, they came at the forefront of contriving the most metaphysical logic of supporting Japan's imperialism in the early 1940s. Miki, for instance, theorized the 1937 outbreak of the Sino-Japanese war as a world-historical moment to change the West-centered international order.[72] However, missing in the overcoming modernity discussion by the Kyoto School was how to actually engage colonial subjects for Japan's continuing war efforts. Takata's anti-capitalism and anti-communism revealed similar limits in spite of his highly sophisticated theoretical discussion of minzoku. It was at this point that Takata's wartime writings on the East Asian community showed discrepancies from the writings of his colleagues.

Among various doctrines presented in a series of discourses on the East Asia Cooperative Community, Takata primarily criticized the notion of the community of destiny. Importantly, he also recognized the reality that Western imperialism necessitated the self-defense of East Asia to some extent. However, he was reluctant to accept the logic that the presence of the West would bind East Asia from a regional perspective, and that it would guarantee the historicity of the notion of the community of destiny, as best described in political scientist Rōyama Masamichi's theory of the East Asian Cooperative Community. Takata's critiques were twofold. He argued that insofar as East Asian regionalism was associated with the theory of the "destiny" of East Asia, it would create a geography-centered and thus highly oversimplified epistemology of the East and the West.[73] Therefore, his second observation was that the problem of people of yellow color was not whether they belonged to East Asia in a regional sense, but rather whether they have an awareness of ethnically belonging to Asian minzoku:

> The cooperation of regional destiny has actually become the destiny of *common regions* that have been oppressed by Western powers. However, I must raise this question. . . . Is this destiny regional in nature? Was it yellow people who experienced the oppression of Western powers, in particular imperialistic oppression by white people in the West? White people in Hong Kong and Shanghai live and breathe in East Asia, but they never experience oppression, but all the people of color residing in East Asia experience it. Minzoku in East Asia is exposed to a common destiny, since we yellow people live in the region of East Asia. *This is not so much a spatial destiny but rather minzoku.* The so-called cooperation of regional destiny is in fact nothing but the cooperation of the destiny of minzoku. (For this reason), is regionalism no more than a form of nationalism?[74]

(emphasis added)

The subtle but significant difference between Takata and other advocates of East Asian regionalism is telling in many ways. Specifically, Takata emphasized the importance of nationalism in envisioning a new Asia. In doing so, he also reconfirmed that one's sense of belonging to a certain ethnic group is not concerned as much with geographical and blood-related realities as it is with the dynamics of subjectivity formation. More importantly, by casting a critical eye on any sort of regionalism, Takata prevented his theory from being reduced to a regional logic of universality and particularity. He rejected the notion that the world is geographically constituted by the West as universal and the East as particular and oppressed.

Rōyama also resonated with Takata's critiques of the notion of the "community of destiny" by making the point that an East Asian region itself should not be the preconditioned constructive invariable of an East Asian community.[75] Nonetheless, Rōyama raised a practical question in realizing a Japan-led East Asian empire. An East Asian regional community, Rōyama stressed, would not be a feasible opinion without dealing with growing anti-Japanese nationalism in China. Under these circumstances, the concept of the "community of destiny" was presented by Rōyama and like-minded Japanese social scientists to appeal to the Chinese. For this reason, Rōyama found Tataka's belief skeptical that China's misleading anti-Japanese nationalist would be corrected by emphasizing cultural and blood-oriented commonness between the two countries.[76] In other words,

Rōyama contended that practical prescriptions for anti-Japanese nationalism in China and Japan's colony should be provided rather than reiterating cultural and racial commonness among Asian nations. It was at this point that Takata's theory of minzoku faced real challenges in policy making.

Criticizing the notion of the "community of destiny," Takata presented his famous concept of Grand Nationalism (*kō-minzokushugi*) and East Asian Nation (*tōa minzoku*), in which he attempted to embrace each country's nationalism and postulate a new process of identity formation of East Asia that is constantly self-changing. With regard to ethnic nationalism in China and the colony, Takata was primarily faced with two contradictory realties. The first was that each ethnic group constitutes a community based on ethnic nationalism, and tends to be exclusive in nature. Second, plural nationalisms in each ethnic group nonetheless have to accept the nationalism of East Asian minzoku in a broader sense, which he called "Grand Nationalism," or East Asian nationalism.[77] In order to scientifically rationalize this seemingly impossible logic, Takata proposed that the nature of East Asian nationalism is as follows:

> Above all, nationalism as a demand for an essential minzoku is neither subordinated to East Asian nationalism, nor does the former serve as a means to the latter. To take this further, I do not argue that essential minzoku integrated with one another and constituted an East Asian minzoku. Each individual belongs to an essential minzoku and at the same time he belongs to a minzoku with a wider range. The two (nationalisms) have separate meanings in a sense. The question of how these two nationalisms have their own content and to what degree they integrate their members is primarily concerned with how they manage to effectively function in two different stages. Insofar as the maintenance and development of its members is only possible through the power of an essential minzoku, essential nationalism would be dominant. According to the degree to which essential nationalism recognizes and frees itself for nationalism in a broader sense, it [East Asian nationalism] might occur.[78]

Clearly, the question Takata found to be most urgent was how he could theorize Chinese nationalism in his scientific approach to minzoku. To be sure, he never naively denounced Chinese nationalism as such. As he emphasized in *On the East Asian Nation*, he was convinced that the capitalist system of *gesellschaft* and ethnic consciousness as a form of *gemeinschaft* could coexist. For him, this coexistence was necessary to create a modern subject as well. Therefore, capitalist development and the rise of ethnic nationalism in China were viewed by Takata as "necessary" steps toward an East Asian minzoku. However, this does not mean that he accepted discourses on Chinese nationalism produced by Chinese intellectuals at face value. In particular, Takata was critical of Sun Yat-sen's Three Principles of People. Citing the renowned philosopher Funayama Shinichi's (1907–1994) work on Sun Yat-sen, Takata dismissed Sun's theory of democracy and nationalism as "atomistic."[79]

Of course, the notion of "atomism" that Takata appropriated to devalue Chinese nationalism was not Takata's original work. In the mid-nineteenth century, Hegel conceptualized atomism by explaining civil society as a state of *atomon* where particularized individuals with multiple personalities form a society without an absolute unity.[80] Individuals in civil society, Hegel argued, constantly attempt to compel the realization of their own interests over those of others, and the very impossibility of realizing the goals of individuals without interacting with others generates social relations. Therefore, everyone in civil society forms a network of inter-dependency and this network itself becomes the goal and means of human life.[81] Hegel conceptualized this as a state of "anti-ethics," and proposed the state as an absolute and universal unity for synthesizing the particularity of individuals. Although Takata seemed to accept the Hegelian logic of atomism, his extension of this logic to nationalism was quite distinctive. Takata observed that the relation between individual and minzoku, especially in modern (Chinese) nationalism, isolates individuals within the narrow confines of a single minzoku, thus prohibiting individuals from forming subjectivity beyond ethnic nationalism.

Takata contended, the "establishment of a new order in East Asia" would be extremely difficult without asking for the "destruction of China's atomistic nationalism" and the "complete negation of the basic principles of Sun-Yat Sen's theory."[82] However, this logic created two problems. First, as Takata himself acknowledged, one could not completely eradicate atomistic thought in the structure of *gesellschaft* such as Chinese society. More importantly, if atomism pertains to the subordination of individuals to a totality, as described in Takata's critiques of Chinese nationalism, how could East Asian nationalism overcome atomism as the legacy of modern nationalism? As a social scientist, Takata was faced with the question of how this theory of subjectivity formation could explain real problems, in particular the relations between different ethnic groups. To be sure, Takata also reiterated throughout *On the East Asian Nation* that the relationship between ethnic groups must be based on reciprocity, and that becoming part of an East Asian minzoku did not mean that one had to sacrifice his essential ethnicity.[83]

This idealistic approach to East Asian minzoku, however, clashed with both Takata's basic concept of sociology and the actual hierarchical relation between ethnic groups. The boundaries of society were always fluid in Takata's view because interactions between social actors and between integral and partial societies constantly create new forms of society. In this respect, the dialectics of self-negation between total and part, and between objectivity and subjectivity, seem to correspond with Takata's theory of society. Yet it is important to note that Takata's understanding of dialectics did not necessarily presuppose the equal status of social actors and groups. In other words, he acknowledged social divisions in class, culture, religion and ethnicity, and in this respect his sociology was not intended to eliminate these social hierarchies. However, most advocates of a new East Asian order emphasized anti-hierarchical and anti-discriminatory relations among ethnic groups as an ideal goal for the East Asian Community. Conceivably, this gesture was intended to hide the real imbalance in power relations, and at the same time to project a utopian and messianic perception of the East Asian Community in the future.

Caught between idealism and a fragmented reality, Takata once again returned to what he called scientific thinking. He first acknowledged the reality of an uneven configuration between minzoku groups. Minzoku groups that are superior in population, culture and politics, Takata stressed, have become leading ethnic groups in human civilization, whereas inferior minzoku groups, or the middle ground as he called it, have naturally disappeared in world history.[84] He conceptualized this as a theory of circulative minzoku. This thinking seems not to be a simple replica of the Comtean or Spencerian social organism, reminiscent of the logic of the "survival of the fittest." Takata argued that the relationship between majority and minority ethnic groups is not one of "winner takes all." Relatively inferior ethnic groups such as Indians in North America, he contended, would also survive, being surrounded by stronger ethnic groups. At stake is the fact that these non-mainstream ethnic groups could not develop enough to become a mainstream ethnic group in world history.[85] Therefore, a "world-historical moment" for Takata occurs when a certain ethnic group emerges as a world-leading minzoku.

Takata's observation clearly shows that he not only affirmed capitalistic development and the rise of nationalism in China as its result, but he recognized these phenomena as what the Kyoto School philosophers referred to as a "world-historical moment."[86] Since he did not take the one-dimensional worldview of the "survival of the fittest," the rise of Chinese nationalism did not mean that minority ethnic groups such as the Ainu, the Ryukyu and the Koreans would disappear. He was open to the possibility that these minor groups would take the position of a leading ethnic group through social interaction. Through interaction with Japan, Takata was convinced that Korean agriculture had developed significantly, and he called this process "rationalization."[87] He went on to argue that rationalization in East Asian minzoku must take the form of organizations in each ethnic group functioning to serve their own interests without exploitation and oppression. In so doing, he also tried to rationalize the role of a leading minzoku like the Japanese who, he believed, could bring about a world-historical moment.[88]

East Asian empire and the "community of destiny"

The ostensibly "rational" and even "rosy" future for Asian people predicted by Takata, however, reached an impasse as he faced the difficulty of having to endorse Japan's leading role in the current situation. To begin with, Takata had to explain why ethnic groups in East Asia had to be united in order to logically apply his theory of circulative minzoku to a new East Asian empire. He did not attempt to solve this problem by framing it in terms of Western imperialism versus Asianism; that is, Asian people were destined to be united, otherwise they would be colonized by the West.

Other social scientists such as Rōyama Masamichi, Ezawa Jōji and Moritani Katsumi faced a similar dilemma and attempted to find a rationale for this unification by emphasizing futurity in their so-called developmentalist Pan-Asian discourses. In other words, Asian people who had experienced different paths to subject formation could find a sense of common destiny by projecting their present into a new future, as yet to be constructed. Based on this observation, these social scientists were convinced that economic development in China and the colony would first reduce the imbalances between metropole and colony. More importantly, by accepting the futuristic vision of reconstructing a new and developed Asia, they stressed, Asian subjects would be able to share in the new identity, which Shinmei Masamichi termed the "United States of East Asia." Unquestionably, their ultimate goal was to turn Asian subjects' developmentalist passion into an optimized structure for Japan's total war. Therefore, Rōyama and Ezawa argued for the necessity of the unity of Asian people less from the perspective of a historical past characterized by sharing the same ancestry than from the standpoint of an unknown but dynamic future that could be realized through the "community of destiny."[89]

Takata's critiques of these "future-oriented" social scientists centered primarily on their excessive emphasis on the notion of spatiality. If either construction or development of the future were to play a central role in realizing the East Asian Cooperative Community, he argued, it would be geographically limited to East Asia, where the Japanese nation-state could exert direct political and economic control, thereby marginalizing Southeast Asia and other areas where people who are conscious of being "East Asian" resided.[90] Takata, however, became increasingly engaged with arguments that were apparently neither scientific nor rational in order to rationally refute these social scientists. Presenting ancestry, region and culture as three key elements in unifying East Asia, he endorsed *historical* similarities inherent in Asian people because they share Asian blood and culture.[91] To be sure, he was reluctant to accept the theory that Japan was messianically destined to unify East Asia in response to the West's invasion of Asia. The necessity of an East Asian union was, for Takata, theorized by the national fate of Asian people, rather than by its spatial configuration that included Japan, China and Korea in relation to the West.[92]

Arguably, Takata's endorsement of blood and culture should not simply be equated with that of so-called nativists who argued for the pureness and eternity of the Japanese race. To be sure, he was heavily influenced by the Kyoto School philosophers whose thinking about subject formation was characterized by the co-figuration of self-negation and creation. In this respect, Takata's preoccupation with envisioning an East Asian Community that would extend beyond the regional boundary of China, Japan and Korea was inseparable from his zeal for a world society whose outlines he had been developing since the 1920s. However, his vision of a world society never included the notion of a cosmopolitan subject, as best described in Miki Kiyoshi's wartime philosophy.[93] According to Miki, Asian minzoku is defined as a dialectic object to be negated, recreated and eventually become part of a cosmopolitan society. However, Takata observed that there are no objective and irrefutable truths in Miki's philosophy through which Japan might rationalize its leading role in East Asia. To resolve this dilemma, Takata's notion of East Asian minzoku was destined to return to *History*, where he could find what he believed were objective realities such as blood and culture, while at the same time he had to present his vision of minorities' becoming a majority *within* the Asian community.

Takata's logic of East Asian minzoku, therefore, employed several theoretical orientations that are seemingly irreconcilable in one theory. To highlight the potential that minority ethnic groups might become a majority, he appropriated the philosophy of Miki Kiyoshi and Funayama Shinichi. Through the process of negating the self and creating a totality, Takata maintained that a minority ethnic group in the present could become a leading ethnic group of a new East Asian minzoku in the future. In this respect, his theory of East Asian nationalism apparently spoke to the future and this logic was intended to mobilize colonial subjects to the project of building an East Asian empire. Takata constantly tried to distance himself from the specter of the nation-state, and from the faith that a new nation-state would become a "buffer-zone" for existing ethnic conflicts as it incorporated colonial subjects.

However, he returned to history to conceal the irrational reality he was facing in the present. Takata was acutely aware that Japan's past and present as an imperial colonizer must be rationalized in order to accomplish a Japan-centered empire-building project for the future. To this end, he immersed himself in the fantasy of culture and blood. It was precisely for this reason that he asserted that Japan's annexation of Korea was not an imperial colonization but the dissemination of culture and advanced technologies between two nations [minzoku] that had shared cultural similarities in history.[94] Such a naive view of colonization might not be expected from a social scientist like Takata, who was meticulous in his contemplation and writing.

Notably, Takata never touched upon issues relating to individual colonies other than Chinese nationalism in his writings. By not taking on the colonial problem as a particular issue, Takata could become a universalist. But I argue that it was Takata's "performative" choice of refusing to directly address colonial problems in reality that created a paradoxical and very powerful discursive space between colonial and imperial intellectuals. Colonial subjects could internalize imperial discourses like Takata's in their hidden desire to directly project themselves into a universal and cosmopolitan world beyond the inconsistencies between empire and colony. For this reason, colonial intellectuals' failure to find any recounting of the colony in the writings of imperial intellectuals did not in fact disappoint them, nor did it detach them from the project of establishing a universal empire. Rather, it reinforced the desire of colonial intellectuals to be universalists. Takata's writings demonstrate this paradox clearly.[95]

In contrast to Takata, who did not position the nation-state as a central organization for the East Asian Community, Shinmei attempted to find through the nation-state the middle ground for resolving problems caused by an ethnic hierarchy. One focal question he posited was how the notion of a multi-ethnic nation-state would be different from the previous one, which had already failed to incorporate colonial intellectuals. To begin with, Shinmei divided ethnic groups into two subcategories, grand minzoku and small and medium-sized minzoku. He observed that so-called ethnic spirit is inversely proportional to the size of each ethnic group; that is, small and medium-size ethnic groups often show much stronger nationalist sentiment than large-size ethnic groups do.[96] Therefore, he maintained that a serious problem would occur when these small-size ethnic groups with strong passions create a nation-state and protest against nation-states made up of grand ethnic groups.

> As we witness the establishment of strong nation-states based on grand ethnic groups, it is very problematic that small and medium size ethnic groups form nation-states based on nationalism and continue to resist against strong nation- states. The success of nationalism by these ethnic groups is eventually possible only when they receive support from grand nation-states. In getting through this difficulty, small and medium size ethnic groups can only think of one direction. . . . That is not a nationalism that has the notion of one minzoku and one nation as its content. That is a form of *kō-kuminshugi*, in that it affirms the formation of multi-ethnicity and a single nation. However, although the content of *kokumin* is multi-ethnic, it has the possibility of forming a single grand minzoku, insofar as there exist affinities in blood, region and culture.[97]

Shinmei attempted to separate his concept of *kokumin* from what he called the "modern" concept of nation in terms of formal nationality. According to him, modern national society is characterized by the integration of national subjects based on administrative, financial and military measures.[98] However, modern national society, he contended, had collapsed with the general crisis in democracy and liberal capitalism, and for this reason, he emphasized the importance of "restructuring national subjects" based on a new way of thinking. In delving into this highly philosophical question of subjectivity, Shinmei, like Takata, showed keen interest in the theories of Miki Kiyoshi and Funayama Shinichi. To be sure, Shinmei's encounter with their philosophical perspectives deeply influenced his vision for a new East Asia, but on the other hand he did not hesitate to express harsh criticism of their ideas.

Shinmei's main criticism against Miki and Funayama focused on their philosophical perspective to see all variables as non-static. In other words, for Shinmei, the principle of cooperativism as espoused by these philosophers lay in the perception that the relationship between total and part is spiral, always creating a new form of total and part which will be self-negated again. For this reason, the cooperativism of Miki and Funayama, he observed, regarded minzoku as part of these social variables to be self-negated and recreated.[99] Shinmei's discontent with these philosophers focused on the excessiveness and impracticality of their metaphysical understanding of society. For Shinmei, the dynamism between total and part, which Miki and Funayama theorized as the dialectics of self-negation and creation, was conceivable insofar as a visible totality is recognized in a society.

Not surprisingly, Shinmei reiterated that minzoku is a basic organization, but at the same time it constitutes in itself a general society as reality.[100] Therefore,

Shinmei stressed that leaning too much on the logic of metaphysics to link min-zoku to philosophical cooperativism would result in cosmopolitanism, which can be a characteristic of any human society, but (precisely for this reason) cannot be a leading social theory in reality.[101] The theoretical distance between Shinmei and these philosophers also explains some fundamental differences between Takata and Shinmei. As I have discussed, Takata's concept of minzoku, which to some extent contains essentialism such as blood and culture, was not theorized in a binary relation to the state from the beginning. Therefore, Takata attempted to draw the spatiality of his East Asian nationalism vis-à-vis a world society as the universal. However, the spatiality of Shinmei's notion of minzoku was confined, as sociologist Seino Masayoshi has argued, to the realm of the nation-state.[102]

Just as Takata emphasized that his East Asian nationalism is a continuation of his sociological thinking from the early 1920s onward, Shinmei's notion of minzoku and the East Asian Cooperative Community is traceable to his obsession with the state as a universal totality. The question was, then, how a new East Asian nation-state as a universal totality would overcome the limits of ethnic conflicts and the decadence of democracy and capitalism shown in the modern nation-state. To this end, Shinmei stressed that a new cooperative state should not simply be identified with *gesellschaft* based on goal-oriented activities. Of course, he was clearly aware that Tönnies' logic of *gemeinschaft* as a form of community would hardly be compatible with the multi-ethnic formation of the Japanese empire.

For this reason, what was stressed in Shinmei's logic of the East Asian Community is the concept of artificial rationality. According to him, *gemeinschaft* is a conventional form of community based on what he called natural and emotional associations. Shinmei maintained that either cooperation or association in the cooperative community must take the form of organic thought.[103] In this sense, the term artificial rationality was presented as a vehicle for accomplishing "profit-oriented integrality," which Shinmei envisioned as a form through which the inconsistencies between community and civil society could be transcended.

However, it is at this point that Shinmei's faith in rationalization came to an impasse. At the center of his logic of artificial rationality and organic thought was the nation-state. The state, he argued, transforms certain types of cultural similarities into the political and social will of a subject.[104] Without a nation-state, a certain ethnic group, he emphasized, would never form a community in a real sense, simply because their cultural similarities could be neither politicized nor socialized, and therefore they could never create subjectivity. For this reason, he went so far as to argue, "In the case of multi-ethnic formations, there must be a nation-state that lacks cultural commonness."[105] However, Shinmei's rosy picture of an Asian nation-state never offered a sophisticated discussion of how these different ethnic identities could be incorporated into a nation-state.

Moreover, this seemingly extreme rationalist approach to the notion of community, which eliminated primordial and natural elements inherent in ethnicity, does not explain why ethnic groups in Asia had to be united under the banner of the East Asian Cooperative Community. If blood-oriented similarities in ethnic communities were to be transcended in a cooperative community in the end, why should it be geographically limited to East Asia? As I have discussed, Takata attempted to avoid this question by directly projecting his theory of minzoku into a world society. Shinmei's notion of ethnicity, however, could not avoid this trap, since the spatial dimension of his theory was confined to a nation-state. For this reason, he also returned to commonness in blood-centered relations and culture as a precondition to rationalize the necessity of constructing an East Asian empire led by Japan. In other words, like Takata, he was also trapped in the irony that the more he stressed the state as the ultimate rationalized future of East Asia, the more he had to resort to blood, nature and culture, all of which he could not explicate through social scientific thinking.

Conclusion

Wartime Japanese social scientists exposed their messianic and universalist zeal for an East Asian empire through their involvement in ethnographic studies. Of course, their thinking started with the realistic observation that ethnic conflicts and discriminatory hierarchies both in the colony and at the metropole would create instability in the empire. To provide a practical solution for a complex web of socio-political imbalances and unevenness in the highly capitalist empire, they paid attention to the newness of the term minzoku and tried to extract from it a new logic of community and wartime participation.

The multi-ethnic vision of an Asian empire emphasized an organic dynamism in which subjects belong to the East Asian Community while retaining their ethnicity. This vision also retained subjects' goal-oriented desires in society. Theoretically speaking, this logic was nothing more than the reflection of social scientists' desire to overcome the limits of capitalism and civil society. Unsurprisingly, Takata Yasuma and Shinmei Masamichi envisioned a community in which a certain kind of socio-political equilibrium is realized. Ostensibly, this balance and harmony also guaranteed a higher degree of social mobility. Other social scientists such as Kada Tetsuji, in spite of their theoretical differences, all emphasized that this new form of community would overcome the imbalance and inequality in the present system. Their futuristic logic clearly explains why their voices shaped such powerful discursive spaces among colonial intellectuals, although they never grappled with colonial problems in detail.

In this way, Takata's "radical" approach to the term minzoku and Shinmei's logic of a multi-ethnic nation-state temporarily concealed colonial problems, and presented a theoretical platform to further mobilize colonial subjects for the sake of the Japanese empire. However, their attempts to rationalize the empire by way of the term minzoku vividly show their distorted desires for a universal social science. Their theories did not offer a fundamental critique of colonialism. In order to avoid colonial reality, they constantly subordinated it to the specter of universal community. However, their vision of community was by no means free from colonial violence and this clearly demonstrates that social scientists served the empire in the name of a multi-ethnic regional community.

Notes

1 Benedict Anderson, *Imagined Communities: Reflections on the Origin and Spread of Nationalism* (London: Verso, 1983, reprinted 1991 and 2006).

2 Ernest Gellner, *Nations and Nationalism* (Ithaca: Cornell University Press, 1983, reprinted 2009).

3 Gi Wook Shin and Michale Robinson, eds., *Colonial Modernity in Korea* (Cambridge, MA: Harvard University Asia Center, 1999), 13.

4 Emiko Ohnuki-Tierney, *Kamikaze Diaries: Reflections of Japanese Student Soldiers* (Chicago: University of Chicago Press, 2007), 46–47.

5 Oguma Eiji, *The Genealogy of Japanese Self-Images* (Melbourne: Trans Pacific Press, 2002), 31–51.

6 As for Fukuzawa's notion of modernization, refer to Fukuzawa Yukichi, "On De-Asianization," in *Meiji Japan Through Contemporary Sources III*, ed. Center for East Asian Cultural Studies (Tokyo: Center for East Asian Cultural Studies, 1973), 129–133.

7 Edward Morse, "Traces of an Early Race in Japan," *The Popular Science Monthly* 14 (1879): 257–266. Morse's article was based on his discovery of shell mounds in the Omori area during his self-funded research trip to Japan. These ruins were later called the *Omori kaizuka* (大森貝塚) and have been considered of monumental importance in explaining the origins of the Japanese people.

8 Oguma Eiji, *The Genealogy of Japanese Self-Images*, 53–63.

9 Inoue Tetsujirō, *Tetsugaku to shūkyō* [Philosophy and Religion] (Tokyo: Kōdōkan, 1915), 785.

10 As for the historical development of scientific racism, see John S. Haller, *Outcasts from Evolution: Scientific Attitudes of Racial Inferiority, 1859–1900* (Carbondale: Southern Illinois University Press, 1995), first published in 1971 by the University of Illinois Press); Samuel J. Redman, *Bone Rooms: From Scientific Racism to Human Prehistory in Museums* (Cambridge: Harvard University Press, 2016).

11 Etienne Balibar and Immanuel Wallerstein, *Race, Nation, Class: Ambiguous Identities* (London and New York: Verso, 1991), 15–68.

12 Rotem Kowner, "Lighter than Yellow, but Not Enough: Western Discourse on the Japanese Race, 1854–1904," *The History Journal* 43, no. 1 (2000): 113–118.

13 For Torri's research trips to Taiwan and Korea, see Torri Ryūzō, *Kanpan ni kizamareta sekai: torri ryūzō no mita ajia* [The World Engraved On a Plate: Torri Ryūzō's Asia] (Tokyo: Tokyo Daigaku Sōgō Kenkyū Shiryōkan, 1991), 8–10.

14 He wrote, "Koreans are not racially different from Japanese (*naichijin*) and they are the same *minzoku* and thus must be included in the same category. *This is an anthropological and linguistic truth that cannot be changed.*" Torri Ryūzō, "Nichisenjin wa 『dōgen』 nari [Japan and Korea as Having the Same Origin]," *Dōgen* 1 (1920), *Torri ryūzō zenshū* 12 (Tokyo: Asahi Shibunsha, 1976), 538.

15 Mitsukawa Kametarō, *Tōzai jinshu tōsō shikan* [A Historical View on Racial Conflicts Between the East and the West] (Tokyo: Tōyō Kyōkai Shuppanbu, 1924).

16 About the discovery of the concept of society and social scientists' encounter with social problems, see Chapter 2 in *Nihon no shakai kagaku* [The Social Sciences in Modern Japan], ed. Ishida Takeshi (Tokyo: Tokyo Daigaku Shuppankai, 1984).

17 Ferdinand Tönnies, *Community and Civil Society* (Cambridge: Cambridge University Press, 2001).

18 According to Simmel, society is an amalgam of social interactions. Therefore, the duty of sociologists is to find similar forms (形式) – collaboration, conflict and competition – in a variety of social interactions and to examine the essential meanings of these forms in different social contexts. For Georg Simmel's formal sociology, see Georg Simmel, *Georg Simmel 1858–1918: A Collection of Essays*, trans. Howard Becker (Columbus: Ohio State University Press, 1959).

19 Harry Harootunian, *Overcome by Modernity: History, Culture and Community in Interwar Japan* (Princeton: Princeton University Press, 2000), 294–328; Kim Brandt, *Kingdom of Beauty: Mingei and the Politics of Folk Art in Imperial Japan* (Durham: Duke University Press, 2007), 124–135.

20 Kevin Doak, *Dreams of Difference: The Japanese Romantic School and the Crisis of Modernity* (Berkeley: University of California Press, 1994).

21 Takata Yasuma, *Shakaigaku gairon* [An Introduction to Sociology] (Tokyo: Iwanami Shoten, 1922), 102.

22 Takata Yasuma, *Gendai shakai no so kenkyū* [A Study of Modern Society] (Tokyo: Iwanami Shoten, 1920), 179–199.

23 Takata Yasuma, *Minzoku no mondai* [The Problem of Nation] (Tokyo: Nihonhyōronsha, 1935), 193.

24 Ibid., 238.

25 Takata Yasuma, *Shakai to kokka* [Society and State] (Tokyo: Iwanami Shoten, 1922), 17.

26 Ibid., 16–17.

27 Takata Yasuma, *Minzokuron* [On Nation] (Tokyo: Iwanami Shoten, 1942), 28.

28 Takashi Fujitani, *Race for Empire: Koreans as Japanese and Japanese as Americans during World War II* (Berkeley: University of California Press, 2013).

29 Kada Tetsuji, *Jinshu, minzoku, sensō* [Race, Nation and War] (Tokyo: Keio Shobo, 1938). The 15th printing of this book appeared in 1942.

30 Ibid., 8–9.

31 Ibid., 70. For Kada's writings on nationalism and internationalism see Kada Tetsuji, *Kokuminshugi to kokusaishugi* [Nationalism and Internationalism] (Tokyo: Dobunkanjōhan, 1932); Kada Tetsuji, *Kokuminshugi* [Nationalism] (Tokyo: Shunshusha, 1932); *Nihon kokkashugi no hatten* [The Development of Statism in Japan] (Tokyo: Keioshobo, 1938).

32 Kada Tetsuji, *Jinshu, minzoku, sensō*, 55.

33 Ibid.

34 Ibid., 63.

35 Ibid., 64–65.

36 Yamamoto Shizuō and Tonosaki Akiko, eds., *Shinmei shakaigaku no kenkyū: ronko to shiryō* [A Study of Shinmei Masamichi's Sociology: Works and Materials] (Tokyo: Shinchosha, 1996), 192–196.

37 The original title of these articles was *Ōshū tsūshin* (Communication from the West) and these articles appeared in the journal 11 times between February 1930 and January 1931.

38 Hans von Freyer, *Soziologie als Wirklichkeitswissenschaft: Logische Grundlegung des Systems der Soziologie* (Leipzig: Hirschfeld, 1929); its Japanese translation first appeared in 1944. Fukadake Tadashi, *Genjitukagaku toshite shakaigaku* [Sociology as Science of Reality] (Tokyo: Nikkōshoin, 1944).

39 Shinmei Masamichi, *Kokumin kakumei no shakaigaku* [The Sociology of National Revolution] (Tokyo: Kōbundō Shoten, 1935).

40 Ibid., 112–115.

41 Ibid., 124.

42 Ibid., 195. For Freyer's theory of revolution from the right, see Jerry Z. Muller, *The Other God That Failed: Hans Freyer and The Deradicalization of German Conservatism* (Princeton: Princeton University Press, 1987), 186–266.

43 Shinmei Masamichi, "Kyōdōtaikokka no kannen oyobi kikō [The Concept and Structure of a Cooperative State] (1)," *Hōgaku* 3, no. 1 (Jan. 1934): 26–39; "Kyōdōtaikokka no kannen oyobi kikō [The Concept and Structure of a Cooperative State] (2)," *Hōgaku* 3, no. 2 (Feb. 1934): 35–77.

44 Shinmei Masamichi, "Kyōdōtaikokka no kannen oyobi kikō (2)," 184–995. Shinmei Masamichi, *Fashizumu no shakaikan* [Social Views in Fascism] (Tokyo: Iwanami Shoten, 1936), 141–195.
45 Shimizu Ikutarō, "Shakaigaku no higeki [The Tragedy of Sociology]," *Chūōkōron* 555 (Jan. 1934): 60–61.
46 Takata Yasuma, *Jinko to hinko* [Population and Poverty] (Tokyo: Nihonhyōronsha, 1925).
47 Takata Yasuma, *Minzoku Taibo* [The Austerity of Nation] (Tokyo: Kocho Shorin, 1942), 33–49.
48 Takata Yasuma, *Hinja hisshō* [The Poor Must Win] (Tokyo: Chikura Shobo, 1935); *Minzoku Taibo*, 175–206.
49 Takata Yasuma, *Minzokuron*, 129.
50 Ibid., 130.
51 Ibid., 131.
52 Slavoj Zizek, *Tarrying with the Negative* (Durham: Duke University Press, 1993), 209.
53 Takata Yasuma, *Minzokuron*, 135.
54 Ibid., 132.
55 Ibid., 135.
56 Ibid.
57 Slavoj Zizek, *Tarrying with the Negative*, 210.
58 Ibid., 205–211.
59 Takata Yasuma, *Minzokuron*, 142–143.
60 Alfred Rosenberg's preoccupation with the superiority of the Aryan race culminated in 1930, when he published the book *Der Mythus des 20. Jahrhunderts*. See Vivian Bird, trans., *The Myth of the Twentieth Century: An Evaluation of The Spiritual-Intellectual Confrontations of Our Age* (Torrance, CA: Noontide Press, 1982). Its Japanese translation first appeared in 1938 from *Chūōkōronsha*. Suita Junsuke and Kamimura Kiyonobu, *Nijisseiki no shinwa: gendai no shinreiteki seishinteki na kachi tōsō ni taisuru hitotsu no hyōka* [The Myth of the 20th Century: An Evaluation on the Conflicts of Spiritual and Psychological Values in the Modern World] (Tokyo: Chūōkōronsha, 1938).
61 Takata Yasuma, *Minzokuron*, 143.
62 Takata Yasuma, *Minzoku to keizai* 2 [Nation and Economy] (Tokyo: Yuihaigaku, 1940), 67.
63 Takata Yasuma, *Minzokuron*, 145. Takata stressed, "[T]he logic of a grand minzoku (廣民族主義, grand-nationalism) is by no means a theory I developed out of the current situation in East Asia or Germany's domination (in Europe). It [grand-nationalism] is simply a theory that is derived from the article 'The Law of Expansion and Reduction in Basic Society,' which I wrote twenty-five years ago."
64 Kawamura Nozomu, *Takata Yasuma no shakaigaku* [The Sociology of Takata Yasuma] (Tokyo: Inaho Shobo, 1992), 98–99.
65 Ibid., 106–107.
66 Komatsu Kentarō, *Minzoku to bunka* [Nation and Culture] (Tokyo: Rishōsha, 1939), 45.
67 Miki Kiyoshi, *Shin nihon no shisō genri* [Principles of a New Japan] (Tokyo: Showa Kenkyūkai Jimukyōku, 1939); also in *Miki kiyoshi zenshū* 17 (Tokyo: Iwanami Shoten, 1968), 505–533.
68 The eight modern ideologies were nationalism, totalitarianism, familism, communism, liberalism, internationalism, Sun Yat-sen's Three Principle of People, and Japanism.
69 Miki Kiyoshi, *Shin nihon no shisō genri*, trans. Lewis Harrington, *Principles of Thought for a New Japan* (unpublished), 6.

70 Miki Kiyoshi, "Gendai minzoku ron no kadai [An Analysis of Modern Discourses on Nation]," in *Miki kiyoshi zenshū* 19 (Tokyo: Iwanami Shoten, 1966–1968), 806–824.

71 Naoki Sakai, "Imperial Nationalisms and the Comparative Perspective," *Positions: East Asian Cultures Critique* 17, no. 1 (2009): 196.

72 As for Miki's concept of the "world historical moment," see Takeshi Kimoto, "Antinomies of Total War," *Positions: East Asian Cultural Critiques* 17, no. 1 (2008): 97–125.

73 Takata, *Minzoku to keizai* 1, 268–269.

74 Ibid., 272.

75 Rōyama Masamichi, *Toa to sekai*, 160–161.

76 Ibid., 163.

77 Takata Yasuma, *Minzokuron*, 11–12.

78 Ibid., 12.

79 Ibid., 18. Takata's writings were based on his reading of Funayama Shinichi's *Sanminshugi no shisoteki seikaku* (Intellectual characteristics of the three principles of people).

80 Friedrich Hegel, *The Philosophy of Right*, trans., T. M. Knox (Chicago: Encyclopedia Britanica, 1952), 64–80. In the book, Hegel presented three categories of civil society: (A) The mediation of need and one man's satisfaction through his work and the satisfaction of the needs of all others – the System of Needs. (B) The actuality of the universal principle of freedom therein contained – the protection of property through the Administration of Justice. (C) Provision against contingencies still lurking in systems (A) and (B), and care for particular interests as a common interest, by means of the Police and the Corporation. Ibid., 65.

81 Ibid.

82 Ibid.

83 Ibid., 25.

84 Takata Yasuma, *Minzokuron*, 199–200.

85 Ibid., 199.

86 About the notion of "world history" and an East Asian new order by the Kyoto School of Philosophy, see a roundtable discussion, "Sekashiteki tachiba to nihon [The World-Historical Standpoint and Japan]," *Chūōkōron* 57, no. 1 (Jan. 1942): 159–192.

87 Takata Yasuma, *Minzokuron*, 37–38.

88 Ibid., 38.

89 For a discussion of the community of destiny in the writings of Rōyama Masamichi and Ezawa Jōji, refer to Chapter 3 of this book.

90 Takata Yasuma, "Tōa to minzoku genri," in *Minzoku to keizai* 1, 237–239.

91 Ibid., 267–268.

92 Ibid., 272.

93 For Miki's cosmopolitanism, see John Namjun Kim, "The Temporality of Empire: The Imperial Cosmopolitanism of Miki Kiyoshi and Tanabe Hajime," in *Pan-Asianism in Modern Japanese History: Colonialism, Regionalism and Borders*, eds. Sven Saaler and J. Victor Koschmann (London: Routledge, 2006), 151–167.

94 Takata never dealt with the Korea problem in detail in his wartime writings. But he discovered in a number of places that Korea had already become part of Japan and it was by no means imperial colonization. Takata Yasuma, *Minzokuron*, 96–120.

95 I will examine the issue of colonial intellectuals' subjective responses to imperial discourses in detail in Chapter 5, focusing on the writings of In Jeong-Sik, who was one of the most influential Marxist intellectuals in colonial Korea.

96 Shinmei Masamichi, *Minzoku shakaigaku no kōso* [The Concept of the Sociology of Nation] (Tokyo: Mikasa Shobo, 1942), 41. For your information, most of Shinmei's writings on the East Asian Cooperative Community and East Asian nationalism during the wartime period are not included in *Selected Works of Shinmei Masamichi*.

97 Ibid., 42–43.

98 Shinmei Masamichi, *Tōa kyōdōtai no rishō* [The Ideal of the East Asian Community] (Tokyo: Nihon Seinen Gaikō Kyōkai Shuppansha, 1939), 143–144.
99 Ibid., 177–179.
100 Ibid., 180.
101 Ibid., 187.
102 Seino Masayoshi, "Senjika no minzoku kenkyū (2) – takata yasuma to shinmei masamichi no baai [Ethno Studies in Wartime Japan: The Case of Takata Yasuma and Shinmei Masamichi]," *Ritsumeikan sangyōshakai ronshū* 30, no. 2 (Sep. 1994): 30–31.
103 Shinmei Masamichi, *Tōa kyōdōtai no rishō*, 205–208.
104 Shinmei Masamichi, *Minzoku shakaigaku no kōso*, 13.
105 Ibid.

Bibliography

A roundtable discussion. "Sekashiteki tachiba to nihon [The World-Historical Standpoint and Japan]." *Chūōkōron* 57, no. 1 (Jan. 1942): 159–192.

Anderson, Benedict. *Imagined Communities: Reflections on the Origin and Spread of Nationalism*. London: Verso, 1983, reprinted 1991 and 2006.

Balibar, Etienne and Immanuel Wallerstein. *Race, Nation, Class: Ambiguous Identities*. London and New York: Verso, 1991.

Brandt, Kim. *Kingdom of Beauty: Mingei and the Politics of Folk Art in Imperial Japan*. Durham: Duke University Press, 2007.

Doak, Kevin. *Dreams of Difference: The Japanese Romantic School and the Crisis of Modernity*. Berkeley: University of California Press, 1994.

Freyer, Hans von. *Soziologie als Wirklichkeitswissenschaft: Logische Grundlegung des Systems der Soziologie*. Leipzig: Hirschfeld, 1929.

Fujitani, Takashi. *Race for Empire: Koreans as Japanese and Japanese as Americans during World War II*. Berkeley: University of California Press, 2013.

Fukadake Tadashi, trans. *Genjitukagaku toshite shakaigaku* [Sociology as Science of Reality]. Tokyo: Nikkōshoin, 1944.

Fukuzawa Yukichi, "On De-Asianization." In *Meiji Japan Through Contemporary Sources III*, edited by Center for East Asian Cultural Studies, 129–133. Tokyo: Center for East Asian Cultural Studies, 1973.

Gellner, Ernest. *Nations and Nationalism*. Ithaca: Cornell University Press, 1983, reprinted 2009.

Gi Wook, Shin and Michael Robinson, eds. *Colonial Modernity in Korea*. Cambridge, MA: Harvard University Asia Center, 1999.

Haller, John S. *Outcasts from Evolution: Scientific Attitudes of Racial Inferiority, 1859–1900*. Carbondale: Southern Illinois University Press, 1995.

Harootunian, Harry. *Overcome by Modernity: History, Culture and Community in Interwar Japan*. Princeton: Princeton University Press, 2000.

Hegel, Friedrich. *The Philosophy of Right*. Translated by T. M. Knox. Chicago: Encyclopedia Britanica, 1952.

Inoue, Tetsujirō. *Tetsugaku to shūkyō* [Philosophy and Religion]. Tokyo: Kōdōkan, 1915.

Ishida, Takeshi. *Nihon no shakai kagaku* [The Social Sciences in Modern Japan]. Tokyo: Tokyo Daigaku Shuppankai, 1984.

Kada, Tetsuji. *Jinshu, minzoku, sensō* [Race, Nation and War]. Tokyo: Keio Shobo, 1938.

———. *Kokuminshugi* [Nationalism]. Tokyo: Shunshusha, 1932.

————. *Kokuminshugi to kokusaishugi* [Nationalism and Internationalism]. Tokyo: Dobunkanjōhan, 1932.

————. *Nihon kokkashugi no hatten* [The Development of Statism in Japan]. Tokyo: Keio-shobo, 1938.

Kametarō, Mitsukawa. *Tōzai jinshu tōsō shikan* [A Historical View on Racial Conflicts Between the East and the West]. Tokyo: Tōyō Kyōkai Shuppanbu, 1924.

Kawamura Nozomu. *Takata Yasuma no shakaigaku* [The Sociology of Takata Yasuma]. Tokyo: Inaho Shobo, 1992.

Kim, John Namjun. "The Temporality of Empire: The Imperial Cosmopolitanism of Miki Kiyoshi and Tanabe Hajime." In *Pan-Asianism in Modern Japanese History: Colonialism, Regionalism and Borders*, edited by Svan Saaler and J. Victor Koschmann, 151–167. London: Routledge, 2006.

Kimoto, Takeshi. "Antinomies of Total War." *Positions: East Asian Cultural Critiques* 17, no. 1 (2008): 97–125.

Komatsu Kentarō. *Minzoku to bunka* [Nation and Culture]. Tokyo: Rishōsha, 1939.

Kowner, Rotem. "Lighter Than Yellow, But Not Enough: Western Discourse on the Japanese Race, 1854–1904." *The History Journal* 43, no. 1 (2000): 103–131.

Miki, Kiyoshi. "Gendai minzoku ron no kadai [An Analysis of Modern Discourses on Nation]." In *Miki kiyoshi zenshū* 19 [Completed Works of Miki Kiyoshi], edited by Hyōe Ōuchi, 806–824. Tokyo: Iwanami Shoten, 1966–1968.

————. *Shin nihon no shisō genri* [Principles of a New Japan]. Tokyo: Showa kenkyūkai jimukyōku, 1939. Also in *Miki kiyoshi zenshū* 17 [Completed Works of Miki Kiyoshi], edited by Hyōe Ōuchi, 507–533. Tokyo: Iwanami Shoten, 1968.

Morse, Edward. "Traces of an Early Race in Japan." *The Popular Science Monthly* 14 (1879): 257–266.

Muller, Jerry Z. *The Other God That Failed: Hans Freyer and The Deradicalization of German Conservatism*. Princeton: Princeton University Press, 1987.

Oguma Eiji. *The Geneology of Japanese Self-Images*. Melbourne: Trans Pacific Press, 2002.

Ohnuki-Tierney, Emiko. *Kamikaze Diaries: Reflections of Japanese Student Soldiers*. Chicago: University of Chicago Press, 2007.

Redman, Samuel J. *Bone Rooms: From Scientific Racism to Human Prehistory in Museums*. Cambridge: Harvard University Press, 2016.

Sakai, Naoki. "Imperial Nationalisms and the Comparative Perspective." *Positions: East Asian Cultures Critique* 17, no. 1 (2009): 159–205.

Seino, Masayoshi. "Senjika no minzoku kenkyū (2) – takata yasuma to shinmei masamichi no baai [Ethno Studies in Wartime Japan: The Case of Takata Yasuma and Shinmei Masamichi]." *Ritsumeikan sangyōshakai ronshū* 30, no. 2 (Sep. 1994): 23–40.

Shimizu, Ikutarō. "Shakaigaku no higeki [The Tragedy of Sociology]." *Chūōkōron* 555 (Jan. 1934): 58–70.

Shinmei, Masamichi. *Fashizumu no shakaikan* [Social Views in Fascism]. Tokyo: Iwanami Shoten, 1936.

————. *Kokumin kakumei no shakaigaku* [The Sociology of National Revolution]. Tokyo: Kōbundō Shoten, 1935.

————. "Kyōdōtaikokka no kannen oyobi kikō [The Concept and Structure of a Cooperative State] (1)." *Hōgaku* 3, no. 1 (Jan. 1934): 26–39.

————. "Kyōdōtaikokka no kannen oyobi kikō [The Concept and Structure of a Cooperative State] (2)." *Hōgaku* 3, no. 2 (Feb. 1934): 35–77.

————. *Minzoku shakaigaku no kōso* [The Concept of the Sociology of Nation]. Tokyo: Mikasa Shobo, 1942.

————. *Tōa kyōdōtai no rishō* [The Ideal of the East Asian Community]. Tokyo: Nihon Seinen Gaikō Kyōkai Shuppansha, 1939.

Simmel, Georg. *Georg Simmel 1858–1918: A Collection of Essays*. Translated by Howard Becker. Columbus: Ohio State University Press, 1959.

Suita, Junsuke and Kamimura Kiyonobu, trans. *Nijisseiki no shinwa: gendai no shinreiteki seishinteki na kachi tōsō ni taisuru hitotsu no hyōka* [The Myth of the Twentieth Century: An Evaluation on the Conflicts of Spiritual and Psychological Values in the Modern World]. Tokyo: Chūōkōronsha, 1938.

Takata, Yasuma. *Gendai shakai no so kenkyū* [A Study of Modern Society]. Tokyo: Iwanami Shoten, 1920.

————. *Hinja hisshō* [The Poor Must Win]. Tokyo: Chikura Shobo, 1935.

————. *Jinko to hinko* [Population and Poverty]. Tokyo: Nihonhyōronsha, 1925.

————. *Minzoku no mondai* [The Problem of Nation]. Tokyo: Nihonhyōronsha, 1935.

————. *Minzoku Taibo* [The Austerity of Nation]. Tokyo: Kocho Shorin, 1942.

————. *Minzoku to keizai* 2 [Nation and Economy]. Tokyo: Yuihaigaku, 1940.

————. *Minzokuron* [On Nation]. Tokyo: Iwanami Shoten, 1942.

————. *Shakai to kokka* [Society and State]. Tokyo: Iwanami Shoten, 1922.

————. *Shakaigaku gairon* [An Introduction to Sociology]. Tokyo: Iwanami Shoten, 1922.

Tönnies, Ferdinand Jose Harris, ed. *Community and Civil Society*. Cambridge: Cambridge University Press, 2001.

Torri, Ryūzō. *Kanpan ni kizamareta sekai: torri ryūzō no mita ajia* [The World Engraved on a Plate: Torri Ryūzō's Asia]. Tokyo: Tokyo Daigaku Sōgō Kenkyū Shiryōkan, 1991.

————. "Nichisenjin wa 『dōgen』 nari [Japan and Korea as Having the Same Origin]." *Dōgen* 1 (1920), *Torri ryūzō zenshū* 12. Tokyo: Asahi Shibunsha, 1976.

Vivian, Bird, trans. *The Myth of the Twentieth Century: An Evaluation of the Spiritual-Intellectual Confrontations of Our Age*. Torrance, CA: Noontide Press, 1982.

Yamamoto, Shizuō and Tonosaki Akiko, eds. *Shinmei shakaigaku no kenkyū: ronko to shiryō* [A Study of Shinmei Masamichi's Sociology: Works and Materials]. Tokyo: Shinchosha, 1996.

Žižek, Slavoj. *Tarrying with the Negative*. Durham: Duke University Press, 1993.

3 Constructing Greater East Asian space

Geopolitics and the question of imperial modernization

The "Greater East Asian space"

In 1938, a year after the outbreak of the Sino-Japanese war, Prime Minister Konoe Fumimarō made a series of announcements about a new order in East Asia, which eventually became officialized in the early 1940s as the Greater East Asia Co-Prosperity Sphere. As the term "sphere" signifies well, Japan's Pan-Asian discourses during the wartime period were aimed at creating a spatial regionalism. Under these circumstances, the question of how to rationally and scientifically conceptualize East Asian space quickly emerged as a main concern in East Asian discourses.

In *Principles of Constructing a Greater East Asia*, published in 1943,[1] Murayama Michiō (1902–1981), Secretary of the Planning Bureau, provided three main principles for constructing a new Asia: Imperial Spirit, Co-prosperity based on the *Way*, and Japan's leading role in a new order. In Murayama's vision of a new East Asia, the concept of East Asian space was not simply represented as a given geographical unity vis-à-vis the West. Referring to the geopolitics of Karl Haushofer (1869–1946), a renowned German thinker and politician who will be one of the main figures in this chapter, Murayama outlined his concept of a new East Asian space as part of overcoming the artificial geographical and political constitution of the world which was improperly divided by Western powers.[2] In his seminal book *Geopolitik des Pazifischen Ozeans* (Geopolitics of the Pacific Ocean), Haushofer argued that the population of Ireland decreased from 8 million to 4.5 million, while Korea's population increased from 11 million to 20 million under Japan's rule. Reading this as Haushofer's recognition of the superiority of Japan's colonial policy over that of Europe, Murayama attempted to link the construction of a greater East Asia to Japan's glorious spiritual culture.[3] Therefore, mapping East Asian space went beyond geographical borders which, for Murayama, were a highly ideological issue. Given that Murayama's book was a kind of official governmental guide for the Greater East Asia Co-Prosperity Sphere, one could understand the extent to which geopolitical thinking was influential in shaping the spatial concept of East Asian discourses by both Japanese intellectuals and bureaucrats.

Beginning in the early 1930s, a group of Japanese social scientists grappled with the question of restructuring East Asian space in their commitment to the

Japanese empire.[4] To be sure, geopolitics drew the attention of these intellectuals since it first provided favorable intellectual ground for them through its somewhat messianic endorsement of the rise of a Japan-led Asia and the demise of the West. Not surprisingly, these Japanese social scientists who were involved in geography and geopolitics showed keen interest in emerging discussions of minzoku and the East Asian community. Rōyama Masamichi's writings, for example, touched on various issues ranging from the ideological concept of the East Asian community to the theories of minzoku and geopolitics. In that regard, the spread of spatial consciousness in late 1930s and early 1940s Japan shows a facet of how existing social scientific disciplines were engaged in new methodologies to contrive a synthesizing logic of a Japan-led East Asian empire.

Importantly, these intellectuals in the field of geography and geopolitics could not simply avoid the issue of the economic imbalance between metropole and colony. The notion of creating a new East Asian space was often associated with the task of remapping and restructuring the geographical configuration of Japan's empire, which intended to serve for Japan's war efforts to locate and mobilize human and material resources. Due to this nature, geopolitics and spatial discourses in wartime Japan were deeply linked to actual colonial policies and this gave birth to a group of imperial and colonial intellectuals who recognized the gravity of the issue of economic imbalance between Japan and the colony. For this reason, they showed keen interest in a developmentalist-oriented blueprint for a new East Asia. Regional planning, agricultural reforms and national land planning, all these ideas were premised on the observation that capitalistic economic development was urgent in the colony to integrate colonial subjects into the Japanese empire.[5] As was reiterated in the previous chapters, one of the important theoretical aspects of wartime East Asian discourses was to denounce a capitalist direction and emphasize the cooperative vision of a multi-ethnic empire. This abstract and utopian anti-capitalist direction, however, created tension as its incapability of dealing with colonial problems became increasingly clear. Japanese social scientists who produced wartime spatial discourses concretized the developmentalist perspective within geopolitics and prioritized economic development in the colony. This seemingly "rational" notion of social science aimed at convincing colonial subjects that by joining the project of industrializing the colonial economy and modernizing agriculture, they would eventually belong to the "community of destiny" in Japan's empire building. As recent studies of colonial and postcolonial developmentalism in East Asia have shown, the developmental aspect of wartime spatial discourses provided visible blueprints for Japan's East Asian discourse that were predominantly theoretical.[6] In that respect, geopolitical discourses were one important field within wartime Japanese social sciences that first rationalized Japan's imperial expansion and more importantly attracted colonial intellectuals.

Space and politics in post-World War I Europe

World War I has often been described as Germany's collapse and the rise of the America-centered international order, but its impacts on European society were much more profound than its political aftermath. In a geographical sense, Europe experienced a full-scale war not in the colonies but on its own soil for the first time in modern history. The impact of the "war in Europe" played a major role in establishing the League of Nations, the first international political organization in modern times. On the other hand, the sense that such an international organization was inevitable clearly reflected European intellectuals' skepticism toward their longstanding belief in what might be called the "balance of power" theory, namely that the major powers in Europe had successfully maintained political stability at home as well as European hegemony abroad. Interestingly, this observation of the limits of existing political theory was logically connected to European intellectuals' fundamental reexaminations of democracy itself. In the 1919 book *Democratic Ideals and Reality*, published one year after the end of World War I, Halford Mackinder, a British geographer and political scientist, vehemently argued as follows:

> Democracy refuses to think strategically unless and until compelled to do so for purposes of defense. That, of course, does not prevent democracy from declaring war for an ideal, as was seen during the French Revolution. One of the inconsistencies of our pacifists today is that they so often urge intervention in the affairs of other nations.[7]

Given that Britain as a member of the Entente Powers reconfirmed its hegemony in its victory over the Central Powers represented by Germany in World War I, Mackinder's statement above leaves much room for further discussion. Why did a renowned British intellectual come up with the idea that democracy, unquestionably the fruit of British political thought, was no longer compatible with maintaining peace in the international order?

Mackinder's insights on the limits of democracy were in large part grounded in his observation that the existing political ideology could no longer correspond to the rapidly changing geopolitical constitution of nation-states. To put it another way, he viewed nation-states as what he called a "Going Concern," by which he theorized that the state as an organic unity was destined to expand its territory.[8] Therefore, he argued that in order for democracy as a political theory to correspond to this new geopolitical configuration of the nation-state, a whole new spatial perspective was needed to replace the old-fashioned notion of democracy as a static political theory. What he offered as an alternative to the geopolitical constitution was "heartland theory." Contending that the world consists of a few "heartlands," Mackinder predicted that nation-states which could occupy these heartlands would take political hegemony in the international order, and he also pointed out that "Eurasia" would become the most important heartland in the world.[9] Just as Haushofer's geopolitical writings ostensibly endorsed Japan's role in East Asia, Mackinder's heartland theory contained a prediction that Asia would rise in the post-World War I geographical reconfiguration of the world order. Unquestionably, European intellectuals' turn to the East shaped the favorable ground for geopolitics to be well accepted by Japanese intellectuals.

If new geopolitical thinking could be conceived of as a kind of political sug-
gestion from the side of British intellectuals, geopolitics had a much stronger
potential to be directly connected to national policies in Germany, where the sense
of loss was endemic throughout the country in the aftermath of World War I.
Friedrich Ratzel's seminal book of 1897, *Politische Geographie* (Political Geography), and his theory of *Lebensraum* (Living Space) attracted attention in 1920s
Germany,[10] and the geopolitical theory of the Swedish political scientist Rudolf
Kjellen (1864–1922), who has often been regarded as the first to conceptualize
geopolitics, also became popular among German intellectuals. Ratzel's theory of
Lebensraum, based on the state-organ theory, emphasized that a nation-state must
ensure that it has enough living space for its people, and in this respect his geopolitical conceptualization of a nation-state in his famous phrase, "expand or perish"
was a vivid example of how an organist perspective became increasingly popular
among post-World War I European intellectuals. German intellectuals' engagement with geopolitical thinking culminated in the emergence of political scientist
and politician Karl Haushofer as a leading figure both in German academic circles
and in Hitler's Nazi Germany. Defining geopolitics as a "science to understand
political living forms in natural living space in terms of geographical restrictions
and historical movement," Haushofer contended that geography as a discipline
providing knowledge about the surface of the earth should now serve as a branch
of policy studies for the territorial expansion of the nation-state.[11]

Despite its potential to overcome the spatial limits of democracy and its theoretical justification of a fascist nation-state based on the organist notion, geopolitics never became a dominant social theory in Europe except in the case of
Germany. Interestingly, it was in wartime Japan that this Western-originated spatial discourse rapidly gained currency among intellectuals and eventually played
an important role in the making of the East Asian Community and the Greater East
Asian Co-Prosperity Sphere during the wartime period.

Japanese intellectuals' encounter with geopolitics

The first encounter of Japanese geography with geopolitical thinking took place
in 1925 and 1926, when Tokyo Imperial University geographer Iimoto Nobuyuki
(1895–1989) contributed three articles to *The Geographical Review* titled "The
Reality of Racial Control and Its Geopolitical Analysis."[12] Basically accepting
Friedrich Ratzel's concept of living space (*Lebensraum*), Iimoto argued that conflicts surrounding living space mainly take a form of racial conflict.[13] Iimoto's
early encounter with geopolitical thinking appeared in a more sophisticated form
in his 1928 essay "The Concept of So-called Geopolitics."[14] Introducing the general stream of Western geopolitics, he paid special attention to how geographers,
who he believed belonged to natural science, exerted academic influence over
state theories and thus gradually remapped the scope of social science. More
importantly, Iimoto's conceptualization of geopolitics was grounded in the geographical configuration of the world based on racial constitution. However, his
understanding of race was not concerned with simply acknowledging physical

and social differences among races. He instead argued that geopolitics based on Western racism had served to constitute and justify the geography of white supremacy. Devoting more than half of the articles to analyzing various forms of Western racist ideologies,[15] Iimoto emphasized that Western powers had discriminated against both the Chinese and Japanese people.[16] In other words, while Western geographers, German intellectuals in particular, were developing geopolitical thinking to criticize the existing world order dominated by "liberal democratic" powers within Europe, Iimoto's approach to geopolitics in fact took on the schematic form of a dichotomy between the West as a victimizer and the East as the victimized. Iimoto's theorization of geopolitics clearly shows how this new spatial discourse would be appropriated by Japanese intellectuals. In other words, the anti-white-supremacy aspect of geopolitics would be easily associated with other Pan-Asianist theories such as East Asian minzoku.

As examined in the previous chapter, a close affinity between geopolitics and the West's racial prejudice over Asians did not simply stem from Japanese intellectuals' imagination. The "yellow peril" mentality was already contagious to a considerable degree in the West, the United States in particular, and it was clearly reflected in the 1924 Immigration Act which precluded Asian migrants from becoming American citizens. Not just Iimoto but a number of Japanese intellectuals took this "opportunity" to highlight Western racial prejudice over Asians in general, thereby addressing the Pan-Asiastic rhetoric that emphasized Japan's position, along with the rest of Asia, as the victimized. Unquestionably, such an epistemology shows the mentality of Japanese intellectuals who intended to hide the reality of Japan as an imperial power colonizing its fellow Asian countries.

In this way, Japanese intellectuals' early encounter with geopolitical thinking shows how this spatial theory provided the political basis for rationalizing Japan's hegemonic power in the East. In the aftermath of the May 4th and March 1st Independence Movements in China and colonial Korea respectively, both of which mainly targeted Japanese imperialism, Japan was searching for a new theory to justify its imperialism in Asia. Under these circumstances, many Japanese intellectuals resorted to spiritual Pan-Asianism that was premised on intrinsic and biological affinities among Asian people. Their easy target was Western racism and by emphasizing the fact that the West had unconditionally discriminated against Asian people, these Japanese intellectuals attempted to nullify the differences between Japan as a colonizer and the rest of Asia as the colonized. Right after the notorious 1924 Immigration Act was passed in the United States, the right-wing intellectual Mitsukawa Kametarō published a book titled *Historical Perspectives on Racial Conflicts Between the East and the West*. His main thesis was that the long-standing racial prejudice over Asians by white Americans had aggravated, and therefore Japan must represent Asia to fight, Western racism. In this way, Mitsukawa attempted to endorse Japan's status of a hegemonic power in Asia. Notably, Mitsukawa was one of the leading fascist leaders who constantly challenged the spread of democracy and the capitalist economy during the Taisho period.[17] At stake was the validity of geopolitical thinking that provided theoretical depth and political context for a manifesto-like Pan-Asian idea like that of Mistukawa. In fact, similar geopolitical thinking was shared by minority intellectuals on the other part of the globe as a gateway to transcend the Euro-centric world order. Halford Mackinder's heartland theory, for instance, influenced W.E.B. Du Bois, one of the leading African-American intellectuals who supported Japan's Pan-Asianism.[18]

While geographical thinking just began attracting Japanese geographers in a highly political manner, the field of geography itself was developing both qualitatively and quantitatively. The geography lecture at Kyoto University, which was first separated from the Department of History in 1907, gained status as an independent department in 1917. Professor Ogawa Takuji (1870–1941), one of the founding members of the geography lecture, went on to establish the Geology and Mineralogy Lecture in the School of Natural Science in 1921.[19] With the establishment of the department, geography studies at Kyoto Imperial University were led by Ishibashi Gorō (1877–1946) and his human geographical approach. Ishibashi, together with graduates of the history department, organized a research group, *Shigaku-chirigaku dōsōkai* (Association of History and Geography Studies), in 1915 and published the journal *History and Geography* (*rekishi to chiri*) and in 1932, the Kyoto geography department began publishing its major journal, *Journal of Geography*.[20]

At Tokyo Imperial University, geography was first launched as an independent discipline in 1919, two years after the department of geography at Kyoto University was formed, but the speed and scale of its expansion was comparable to that of the Kyoto geography department. In addition to the general trend that geography was gradually obtaining the status of an independent academic department, Tokyo had another reason to intensify its geography research. The Great Kanto Earthquake of 1923 fueled the idea that thorough geography studies could contribute to the "physical" stability of the Japanese nation-state.[21] On the other hand, while Kyoto's geography department was focusing on establishing its own scholarship, independent of the influence of the geography studies at Tokyo, Tokyo's geography studies focused on representing Japanese geography as a whole. Yamazaki Naokata (1870–1929), Professor of Geography at Tokyo Imperial University and often called the father of modern Japanese geography, organized a research group, *Chiri dōsōkai* (Club of Geography) and in 1923, the year of the Kanto Earthquake, founded and became president of a nation-wide research association, *Association for Japanese Geographers* (hereafter AJG).[22]

The development of geography studies in both Tokyo and Kyoto fostered the spread of the geopolitical thinking that would come later, but it is important to note that there existed regional as well as theoretical tension between the two leading institutions. A glimpse at the process of the establishment of the AJG shows the degree of tension between Kyoto and Tokyo. Although the Association for Japanese Geographers, as its name signifies, was aimed at representing geography studies in Japan, its cadre of researchers was from the beginning "geographically" limited to the Kanto area. Of the 49 founding members of the AJG, most members were geography researchers at universities or high school teachers whose regional base was the Tokyo area. As a matter of fact, the division of geography studies in the 1920s was already accepted as a *fait accompli* by Tokyo-based geographers.

According to the 50th anniversary publication of the AJG in 1975, the establishment of the AJG and its own journal, *The Geographical Review*, was a result of competition between the two institutions. Geographers in the Tokyo area had in common the sense that in order to compete with the geography studies at Kyoto, which was on the rise and already publishing its own journal in the mid-1920s, it was necessary to found a sizable research organization as well as an academic journal in Tokyo.[23] Since the mid-1920s, the AJG gradually extended its membership and academic influence in Japanese geography, but there was little intellectual exchange between Kyoto and Tokyo aside from a few articles contributed to *The Geographical Review* by Professor Ishibashi Goro (1876–1946), who was teaching at Kyoto but was a graduate of Tokyo Imperial University.[24]

The tension increased as both institutions started directing their research toward the realm of geopolitics. The influx of geopolitical thinking on the one hand played a role in creating a social scientific approach for geography, which had long been conceived of as part of the humanities, but in the case of the Tokyo and Kyoto geography departments, geopolitics, intentionally or unintentionally, became a barometer that now revealed the differences in their research. The Kyoto geography department's endeavors to establish its own scholarship marked a turning point as Komaki Saneshige (1898–1990), Kyoto's own Professor of Geography, rapidly directed the department's research from the field of geopolitics in the mid-1930s.[25]

Around the same time, geopolitical thinking was gradually gaining currency for social scientists in Tokyo, but Komaki made it clear from the beginning that Kyoto's geopolitics was fundamentally different from either Tokyo's or Western geopolitics. This difference was due in large part to the academic trend surrounding a social organist perspective. Geopolitical thinking itself was heavily influenced by the institutionalist notion of viewing space, people and most importantly the state as a social construct, and this notion of geopolitics did not come as something new to social scientists in Tokyo. Iizuka Kōji (1906–1970), an economist and Tokyo University Professor of Geography, contended in his 1942 and 1943 articles in *Journal of Economics* (*Keizaigaku ronshū*) that the distinction between geography and geopolitics lay in whether or not researchers would accept the institutional theory.[26]

As is well known, at Tokyo Imperial University the "organ theory" as it is often called, not only became increasingly popular among geographers but had already been widely accepted by social scientists as a major social and political theory. Minobe Tasukichi (1873–1948), a legal scholar and Professor of Law at Tokyo University, introduced the famous *tennokikansetu* (Emperor as an organ) as early as the 1910s and boldly attempted to redefine the emperor system as part of the state organ system. Not surprisingly, his institutionalist perspective was criticized by other social scientists and ultranationalist activists, and he was forced to resign from the House of Peers in 1936, when this ultra-rightist movement reached its apex with the outbreak of the February 26 Incident.[27] However, these fierce responses to Minobe's organ theory paradoxically showed that an organist perspective was at least widely accepted in academia. In contrast, geographers at

Kyoto University were heavily influenced by the Imperial Way, which showed salient differences from the organist approach. In short, the regional and theoretical differences between the leading geography institutions failed to find a middle ground, and this lack of a compromise was important in the formation of multiple approaches to the mapping and constructing of East Asian space during the wartime period.

In spite of the seemingly irreconcilable differences between the two leading geography institutions in their developing geopolitical thought, Japan's rapidly changing position in the international order called for the birth of a new spatial thinking. Japan's contradictory position in the League of Nations as the third largest country in naval power, which, at the same time, constantly represented itself as belonging to the "have-not" nations was reaching a dead end.[28] With the outbreak of the 1931 Manchurian Incident, Japan made it clear that it would continue territorial expansion in mainland China. Under severe criticism by major European powers in the League of Nations for this premeditated violence, Japan finally withdrew its membership from the League of Nations in 1933. Japan's withdrawal from the most powerful international organization was passionately welcomed by both the masses and the media in Japan proper. On the other hand, it bestowed on Japanese intellectuals an enduring task to contrive an alternative theory of the international order, overcoming both the "have" and "have-not" frameworks and the Pan-Asiatic rhetoric. Importantly, the lack of dominating theories in mid-1930s Japan explains why new social scientific thinking such as geopolitics became popular among Japanese social scientists. At the center of such an intellectual fashion was one German intellectual, Karl Haushofer.

Karl Haushofer and the rise of Japanese geopolitics

Geopolitical thinking, once introduced to Japan by several geographers in the 1920s but ironically utilized with a view toward criticizing Western racism toward Asian races, started gaining attention now from different perspectives by Japanese scholars. Not only intellectuals but also the government came to the forefront in introducing geopolitical thinking. Many works on geography and geopolitics translated into Japanese were financially and institutionally supported by the Japanese government,[29] and among a number of Western specialists in geopolitics, the presence of the German geographer and politician Karl Haushofer (1869–1946) became especially important in Japanese academia beginning in the late 1930s. The somewhat overheated interest in Haushofer's geopolitics by Japanese intellectuals and the government leaves much room for further discussion. A glimpse at the successive translations of Haushofer's major works gives us a picture of how rapidly he emerged as an influential scholar in Japanese academia.[30] In particular, his seminal book *Geopolitik des Pazifischen Ozeans* (Geopolitics of the Pacific Ocean) was translated and introduced in three different versions in 1940, 1942 and 1944 respectively.[31] Most works on geopolitics produced by Japanese intellectuals commonly placed Haushofer as a symbolic figure who upgraded geopolitics from a subfield of geography or political science to an independent academic discipline. However, Haushofer was not simply content to reiterate the statement that geopolitics also belongs to the social sciences. For him, geopolitics was an intellectual weapon by which he could redefine the basic concepts of the social sciences so that social scientists were able to produce imperial knowledge in a more scientific and systematic way. Therefore, it is important to explore the impacts of geopolitics on the social scientific thinking system and how it was practically applied to Japan's blueprint for an East Asian community.

How did Haushofer obtain the title of the father of geopolitics, challenging the previous generation of geographers and political scientists such as Rudolf Kjellen and Friedrich Ratzel? More broadly, given that his geopolitical thinking was expanding its influence beyond the border of geography, what made his social scientific approach so distinct as to penetrate the mindset of Japanese intellectuals? The following statement, if not complete, would supply us with an important clue in understanding the structure of his social scientific thinking:

> Politics can be, as it were, broadly defined as conflict about the exchange, acquisition and maintenance of power surrounding the surface of the world. Politics has the meaning that it has been created in a humanistic sense. . . . At the same time, it is tacitly accompanied by *techne*, that is to say, technology in politics. To be sure, as the example of *geo* (land) succinctly shows, things accumulated (either scientifically or practically) by knowledge on land and soil must be prepared for the preconditions for *political technology*.[32]
>
> (emphasis added)

Haushofer here makes a provocative statement regarding how the social sciences should cope with the crisis in the modern international system. He first attempted to differentiate political science from political technology and argued that the latter responded to the demands for a new political thinking. However, what was more striking in his new approach to the social sciences was that the notion of *techne*, or technology in a broader sense, was not accompanied by the notion of objectivity as it had been for most social scientists. The importance and necessity of political technology, Haushofer contended, lay in its highly subjective nature. He asserted that "[T]hings necessary for people who are eager to develop geopolitics are not just knowledge related to it but *superiority* in human nature"(emphasis added).[33] Accordingly, his geopolitics was now newly defined as a discipline not just to deal with spatial knowledge in a political sense but also to challenge the essential question of objectivity in the social sciences. His overthrow of the existing thinking in the social sciences through geopolitics reached its apex when he remarked on the temporality of geopolitics:

> The scientific policies of the Allies, history, international law and eventually law, all these things should not be limited to merely elucidating the past. (a number of political geographers were limited to this) These things must

strive to construct a *spiritual structure* (= geopolitics) in order to contribute to the courage of *going forward and venturing toward the future.*[34]

(emphasis added)

Futurity, as Haushofer emphasized, emerges as the locus for consolidating space and temporality in social scientific thinking. It is of course true that the existing social scientific disciplines did not neglect the notion of temporality. However, Haushofer contended that temporality in what he called scientific knowledge is no more than the representation of the past, and it therefore lacks insight into both where we exist spatially now and how we can predict the future. For this reason, geopolitics could and should be, according to Haushofer, a spiritual structure to restore the integrity of space and temporality in social scientific thinking. Yet it is important to keep in mind that futurity in geopolitics is not determined only by scientific knowledge, but rests on human beings' subjective resolution through political technology.

It is not surprising that not all Japanese social scientists endorsed Haushofer's bifurcation between subjectivity and objectivity in the social sciences. Unquestionably, Japanese social scientists in the 1920s and early 1930s had a firm belief in the objectivity of social scientific thinking. However, Haushofer's perception also paved the way for Japanese intellectuals who had been overwhelmed by the perception that "Western" social sciences were characterized by scientific objectivity. It had a tremendous impact on intellectuals who were grappling with the question of how to theorize and rationalize East Asian Space, keeping a distance from Euro-centric scholarship. In this respect, the coming of rationalist geopolitics to Japan was not just a strategic acceptance of a strain of anti-Euro-centric thinking within Europe, but was also an example of how and in what context Japanese social scientists were dominated by an oversimplification of objectivity and were directly facing the long-standing question of the West as universal and Japan or the East as particularistic.[35]

In addition to his application of scientific knowledge to the world, Haushofer had one more distinction that made him stand out in Japan among other Western geopolitical thinkers. Together with his geopolitical research, what captured the attention of Japanese intellectuals was his extensive understanding of Japanese history and culture. The degree of Haushofer's understanding of Japan simply surpassed that of other Western scholars and this was largely due to his 18-month stay in East Asia between 1909 and 1910.[36] Interestingly, his first book-length publication *Greater Japan (Dainihon)* as well as his doctoral dissertation in 1914 were not works about geopolitics but works on Japan.[37] This meant that his later interest in Japan and the Pacific Ocean was not just a mechanical application of Euro-centric theories to a case study of Asia, as was much of the Western scholarship at this time.[38] This was the main reason for the popularity and extensive translation of Haushofer's books in Japan.[39]

Haushofer's observations of Japan and his later writings basically viewed Japan as a country with great potential for development in a geopolitical sense. What made Haushofer's encounter with Japan distinct was his peculiar emphasis on

Japan's spiritual side. He explained Japan's successful modernization in terms of its balance between technology and spirit. He also argued that precisely because of the presence of the Imperial Spirit, Japan could maintain distance from what he called the flooding of individualism and liberalism that he believed was destroying European society.[40] To be sure, many Western intellectuals showed interest in Japan's "modern achievements." However, their interpretation of Japan's emergence in the international order was mainly concerned with how faithfully Japan had accepted Western knowledge and technologies. In contrast, Haushofer paid attention to the spiritual aspect of Japanese culture and importantly, this notion corresponded to his later work on geopolitics, which emphasized a spiritual structure. For this reason, it is not hard to understand why Haushofer's presence was essential in wartime Japanese geopolitics as well as in cementing diplomatic relations between Japan and Germany during the wartime period.[41]

Presumably Haushofer's peculiar interest in Japan paved the way for Japanese intellectuals' willingness to accept his geopolitical thinking. Nonetheless, it does not fully answer the question of how his geopolitics could be transformed into "Asian" geopolitics, or "Japanese" geopolitics. This inquiry becomes even more complex considering that most of his writings on Japan were first published in German in the 1910s and 1920s, and strategically translated into Japanese in the wartime period. This difference of some 20 years could be understood as the typical gap between the production of knowledge in the West and its introduction to Japan.[42] However, in the case of Haushofer, that would be an oversimplification, since geopolitical thinking started to gain currency in Japan in the 1930s, when Japan invaded northern China and withdrew from the League of Nations. In spite of his in-depth understanding of Japanese history and culture, Haushofer's geopolitics had some theoretical characteristics that were not compatible with Japan's geopolitical position. Most of all, since Haushofer's geopolitics developed in Germany, where the nation-state simply consisted of a single German minzoku, it was hardly possible to find in his geopolitics any theoretical speculations on the relationship between the state and nation (*minzoku*). To put it another way, he was more concerned with how the state should mobilize people from an organist perspective than with whether or not the association between the state and nation *could* be possible through geopolitical thinking.

More importantly, these Japanese social scientists who found Haushofer's writings path breaking were not necessarily influenced by his endorsement of the Japanese spirit, the Imperial Way in particular. It was a group of geographers at Kyoto Imperial University who put forward the concept of Imperial-Way geopolitics. Ironically, the Kyoto School of Geography was adamantly opposed to Western geopolitics in any form, including that of Karl Haushofer. On the contrary, Tokyo-based social scientists showed keen interest in Haushofer's writings but the newness of his geopolitics mainly came from his notion of subjectivity in social science and the question of how it could serve for remapping East Asian space. In summary, without regard to the presence of Haushofer and Western geopolitical thinking, an impending question was unfolded to Japanese social scientists and it pertained to contriving a spatial theory that rationalizes the creation of an East Asian community and at the same time provides an intellectual basis for regional development, economic development in particular. It was the Kyoto School of Geography who first responded to this question.

The Kyoto school of geography

The origin of modern geographical and spatial discourses at Kyoto Imperial University is traceable to the early twentieth century, and as a matter of fact, it was not just the Department of Geography at Kyoto that was grappling with the notion of an "Asianized" spatial discourse. Some philosophers at Kyoto, later called the Kyoto School of Philosophy, were also focusing their attention on this issue. For instance, Watsuji Tetsurō (1889–1960), one of the founding members of the Kyoto School of Philosophy, and his 1935 book *Fūdo* (Climate) directly touched on the question of how space and human beings living in space should be defined.[43] Watsuji's philosophical approach to the notion of spatiality was based on his observation that the ontological question of what it means to be a human being is not only a matter of social and historical concern but, more importantly, is a matter of geographical and environmental import. In other words, Watsuji's search for subjectivity as a philosopher marked a turning point in his encounter with the notion of spatiality and his discovery of East Asia as an ontological space vis-à-vis the West.[44]

Kyoto geographers' bold move in the process of developing Japanese geopolitics began with the appointment of Komaki Saneshige, one of the first of Kyoto's own doctor of philosophy in geography, as an assistant professor in the Department of Geography in 1931.[45] Komaki's joining the Department of Geography symbolizes the launching of Kyoto University's own geography program, yet his emergence also foreshadowed the ever-present tension between the Tokyo and Kyoto geography departments. Originally trained in both human geography and geology under the instruction of Ishibashi Gorō, who obtained a PhD at Tokyo University and resigned from his professorship at Kyoto shortly after Komaki was appointed as a professor, Komaki accelerated his move toward the world of geopolitics. Clearly aware of the tension between his position at Kyoto and its rival Tokyo University, Komaki's engagement with geopolitics began with a criticism of Western geopolitics and an association of his geopolitical theory with the Imperial Way:

> German geopolitics started by defining the state as an acting power. Insofar as it was created in the West, it is not strange for us to witness from this the manifestation of Western imperialism. For this reason, it is natural that such scholarship cannot permanently satisfy us. Our eventual purpose is to declare the Imperial Way in the world and to realize the spirit of the *Hakkō ichiu* (Eight Corners of the World Under One Roof) in Japan's world.[46]

Komaki's audacious attack against what he called Western geopolitics was in fact part of his gradual thinking processes that eventually resulted in his self-conviction that Tokyo-based geopolitics is a simple replica of the West and thus should not represent Japanese geopolitics. However, simply charging geopolitics in Tokyo with being a poor imitator of Western geopolitics does not elucidate the real academic theoretical tensions between the two geography institutions in serious rivalry. Furthermore, as discussed so far, it is a mistake to characterize the encounter of Japanese social scientists with Western geography as parasitic on Western scholarship. Komaki himself wrote an interesting piece of work on Karl Haushofer, the icon of German geopolitics. In a 1941 article, "On Karl Haushofer," Komaki first gave credits to Haushofer whose intellectual trajectories showed an in-depth appreciation of not only Japan but the Japanese spirit, which one may not easily find from Western scholars.[47] Haushofer's exceptional understanding of the Imperial spirit, Komaki stressed, came to an impasse in the mid-1930s as Haushofer's geopolitics came to terms with the Nazi ideology which degraded geopolitics as an instrument to pursue national interests. Based on these observations, Komaki concluded that the guiding principles of German geopolitics would not resonate with Japan's imperial geopolitics whose guiding principles were to spread the spirit of the *Hakkō ichiu*.[48]

Kyoto geographers' own answers to the question of the Japanese spirit can be found in *Introduction to East Asian Geopolitics*, written by Yonekura Jirō, Komaki's own student and one of the main members of the Kyoto School of Geography. In the book, Yonekura provided an interesting definition of geography, that is, geography is a science to examine the world where the society of *species* spatially coexists.[49] In addition to being the statement of a geographer who unquestionably regarded geography as a "science," what was more striking in this comment was Yonekura's peculiar introduction of the notion of species in geography. If geographical studies had already been redefined as a "social science" by Kyoto geographers, how, then, did the concept of species play an important role in shaping their politicized spatial discourses?

For Yonekura, the ultimate issue of geography must be the question of how geography could and should respond to the question of the unity between space and human beings.[50] In order to respond to this question, however, Yonekura did not turn to the determinist perspective in viewing space as a given and the human being as a passive actor in relation to space. He instead paid special attention to the notion of dialectics. By focusing on the interplay between space and human beings, Yonekura attempted to redefine space in terms of objectivity and subjectivity.[51] Needless to say, his dialectics and the configuration of subjectivity and objectivity did not operate based on a simple schema that equated space with objectivity and individuals with subjectivity. Yonekura contended that as Hegel's dialectics vividly showed, dialectic thinking in the Western philosophical tradition had often resulted in neglecting the importance of space in its excessive dependence on the state both as the reason and as a medium between subjectivity and objectivity.[52] In contrast to Western dialectics, Yonekura's concepts of space and spatial dialectics were centered on redefining space as a sphere where the interplay and interrelation between space and human beings can take place. Space was on the one hand characterized by its objective nature against each individual, but insofar as space was a representation of each human being's life, Yonekura argued, it should also be understood as an amalgam of multiple subjectivities.[53] Therefore, the notion of the unity between space and human beings was naturally redefined, for Yonekura and other Kyoto geographers, as the question of how to resolve the conundrum of subjectivity and objectivity in human society. Here, Yonekura encountered the notion of species. He argued:

> Species as a superior concept of nation [minzoku] is a broader concept of race including various nations. For example, in the case of what we call Asian races or European races, species as groups of nations preconditions Asian or European races that have Asia or Europe as their spatial ground. In addition, species have in common relatively similar characteristics through the proximity and similarity of residence and environment; therefore, they share a common destiny to cooperate and co-prosper.[54]

As the statement above clearly shows, Yonekura's search for spatial dialectics between human beings and nature bestowed the status of a medium between subjectivity and objectivity on the concept of species. Yonekura's account of species is reminiscent of the theory of species developed by the Kyoto School of Philosophy, Tanabe Hajime (1885–1962) in particular. Not surprisingly, Yonekura acknowledged that his notion of dialectic space was formulated from his close readings of Tanabe and other Kyoto philosophers.[55] It also implied that for Kyoto-based geographers, the schema of space was essential to their search for absolute dialectics, as Tanabe and the Kyoto School of Philosophy were grappling with the same question.[56]

Anti-modern and imperial way geopolitics

As Komaki's engagement with geopolitics intensified, the Department of Geography at Kyoto itself also emerged as a new center for geopolitical studies. After becoming a full professor in 1938, Komaki started to organize a research group focusing on geopolitics and another Kyoto School, the Kyoto School of Geography, was brought into being. With the confidence that came from being the leader of a school that included some 15 researchers and graduate students,[57] Komaki boldly declared that the Kyoto School's geopolitics was the only pure geopolitics that could realize the Imperial Spirit.[58] Given that Kyoto's geopolitics had been heavily influenced by the Kyoto School of Philosophy and had accordingly established a clear-cut binary formation of the East and the West, it was highly understandable that Komaki would turn to the notion of the Imperial Way.

However, it was not a simple distinction between the East and the West that constituted the backbone of Kyoto's geopolitics. Komaki was convinced that by situating his Kyoto geopolitics within the spiritual arena of the Imperial Way, he could avoid the problem of social science becoming the slave of policy studies, or in Haushofer's term, political *techne*.[59] Importantly, while both Komaki and Haushofer emphasized spiritualism in their geopolitics, their understandings of spirit or the Imperial Spirit were quite different from one another. While spiritualism in Haushofer's geopolitics was logically associated with the search for a subjective social science that would overcome the myth of objectivity in scientific thinking, Komaki's turn to the Imperial Way was connected to a kind of essentialism, that is, to rescue the purity of Japan from the influx of tainted Western knowledge.

Just as he saw the Imperial Way as the locus of East Asian geographies with which species in East Asia could be spiritually united, Komaki also paid attention to scientifically demonstrating that East Asian geographies in a physical sense were superior to the West and had the potential to integrate the East Asian people. Here it is important to note that Komaki did not simply attempt to search for an East Asian space by leaning on the conventional geo-environmental determinist notion that had attributed the creation of race to its geographical factors.[60] Being conscious that human beings are creative creatures, Komaki redirected his question of spatial unity in East Asia as follows: How could people living in East Asia where there exist so many geographical dynamics eventually be united under the leadership of the Imperial Way?

Interestingly, according to this epistemological underpinning, the fact that East Asia was full of geographical dynamics that could be scientifically discovered did not became an obstacle to Komaki's search for a dialectic unity in East Asia. Rather, he believed that the diversity of environmental and racial constitutions could explain why East Asian space was superior to the West in a geographical and ethnic sense. In that sense Komaki was not most concerned with declaring that East Asia had existed in a form of perfect unification, rather, in accordance with the spirit of the Imperial Way, he focused on scientifically discovering a medium that could integrate such geographical diversity. He argued that the presence of the Pacific Ocean and its currents played an important role in integrating geographical characteristics and people in East Asia.[61] Simply put, since the Pacific Ocean mediates the diverse characteristics of East Asian geographies, Komaki was concerned that East Asia as a spatial unit had the capability to embrace geographical differences and at the same time integrate them under the aegis of the Imperial Spirit.

One of the major concerns for the Kyoto School of Geography was theorizing East Asian geographies with a view toward shaping the scientific framework in East Asia for the precondition of a Greater East Asian Co-Prosperity space. Therefore, its next task was necessarily to discover the conditions for integrating people residing in East Asian space. However, the response to this search for an absolute dialectics between East Asian space and East Asian people had to be sought outside such inherent characteristics as blood and skin. Komaki himself reiterated in many of his writings that minzoku could not be created by simply sharing the same blood.[62] If species is a superior concept of minzoku as well as a medium of unifying space and individuals, how could the concept of East Asian people be established in Komaki's geopolitics? It is at this point that Komaki's Greater East Asian geopolitics showed its fundamental difference from the so-called rationalist geopolitics or Haushofer's geopolitics. As examined so far, Haushofer called for an epistemological and methodological transformation by bringing a new notion of temporality to the social sciences. In other words, instead of leaning on a formula-laden future that is explicable as well as predictable in terms of social scientific objectivity, Haushofer paid special attention to the unpredictability of the future and the role of subjective political technologies in driving people toward a common destiny. Komaki's geopolitics also gave attention to the notion of temporality, but in exactly the opposite manner. What captured Komaki's attention was *History*. However, his notion of history was characteristic in that whereas history in a general sense signifies the accumulation of time, in Komaki's theory of geopolitics, it was particularly concerned with how people had responded to challenges pertaining to space. Komaki believed that the issue of temporality and space could be the locus to differentiate East Asian space from Western space.

Both Komaki and Yonekura were convinced that the crisis in civilization was primarily responsible for destroying the possibilities for the unification of space and humans. To put it another way, by exerting too much artificial power over nature, Yonekura argued, European civilization had lost its spirit.[63] Komaki also remarked "Europe's discovery and colonization since the eighteenth century is in no way different from this tendency (toward spiritual destruction), and the development of science in Europe in fact has served for this."[64] Borrowing this time from the observations of Nishitani Keiji (1900–1990), a scholar of religion in the Kyoto School of Philosophy, Yonekura adamantly argued that the spiritual crisis caused by modernization could only be cured by restoring what he called three spirits – Nature, Reason and Religion.[65]

Yonekura's encounter with Nishitani's historical analysis of European civilization came as no surprise, given that the philosophical base of the Kyoto geographers was derived mostly from their fellow Kyoto philosophers. Yet looking at their criticism toward Western civilization from a geopolitical perspective, one could find that their Imperial Way geopolitics was now attempting to juxtapose East Asian space with the West in the realm of modernization. The following remark by Komaki seems to give us the clearest sense of how Kyoto's geopolitical strategies of contrast operated:

> [However] Asian minzoku has neither disobeyed nor resisted against nature. Rather, it has adored and been in accordance with nature. It has neither analyzed nor anatomized nature. Asian minzoku has never tried to overcome nature, but tried to make it alive. This is the *spirit of Asia*.[66] (emphasis added)

Needless to say, the "spirit" that Komaki is praising for Asia minzoku's loyalty to nature could only be realized and maximized by being subordinated to the spirit of the Emperor, as demonstrated by Japan's capability for restoring its national polity since the nineteenth century following Europe's exploitative invasion into East Asian space. Therefore, China and the Southern Seas were geopolitically redefined as a strategic area where Europe's exploitive spirit and Asia's Imperial spirit would collide.[67] Interestingly, Komaki's analysis is reminiscent of the notion of *Lebensraum* (Living space), which is the core concept of Western geopolitics. However, while *Lebensraum* in Western geopolitics was a concept that justified a nation's territorial expansion into the future, Komaki's East Asian space was constantly conceptualized as a return to the past. His bold "declaration" of Japanese geopolitics in 1940 was repeated in 1942, yet this time with a new manifesto, Greater Asia's Declaration of Restoration.[68]

Once Asian space as well as Asian minzoku gained an independent and nature-friendly status in contrast to Western civilization and imperialism, how did the Kyoto School of Geography envision the economy of East Asian space? Komaki's restorative (or reactionary) geopolitics now attempted to offer a spatial community in the Greater East Asia Co-Prosperity sphere. Imperative in Komaki's observation of East Asian space was to create a self-sufficient economy.[69] Here his Imperial Way geopolitics was closely associated with the traditional family system in East Asia.

> In looking at the occupational constitution of the people of Greater East Asia, more than 50 percent of the Japanese, 60–70 percent of the Chinese, and over 90 percent of people in the rest of Asia are working in agriculture. In addition, due to environmental factors, agriculture in Greater East Asia is mostly irrigation agriculture. Without cooperation from family or village, managing this [irrigation agriculture] would be difficult. *Society in Asia is based on the family system and it is for this reason that Asian society has permanently maintained a self-sufficient economy benefiting each ethnic group.*[70]
>
> (emphasis added)

East Asian space, minzoku, and the Imperial Spirit, Komaki believed, could be most gloriously realized when they were combined with the family system and agriculture as its economic base. Completely missing in Komaki's pursuit of Asian commonness through its traditional family system and agricultural economy was the question of how to resolve the issue of economic and cultural imbalance between metropole and colony. As examined in Chapter 1, Komaki's notion of a self-sufficient economy bore a striking resemblance to the Japan-Manchuria-China economic bloc theory in which Japan's colonies such as Korea and China are conceived of as agricultural bases or at best spaces for raw materials. Such a hierarchal configuration of East Asian space explains why Kyoto geographers did not join the discussion of national land planning (*kokudo keikaku*) mainly organized by bureaucrats, economists and geographers in the Tokyo area. As I shall discuss later in this chapter, one of the integral questions that advocates of national land planning projects shared was to restructure the colonial economy as well as Japan's domestic economy to optimize imperial Japan for its prolonged total war. Instead, the recently discovered footprints of Kyoto geographers' commitment to the Japanese empire lead us to rethink the role of intellectuals.

Kyoto geopolitics' involvement in total war

Just like a number of Japanese social scientists who were involved in various think-tanks and imperial institutions during the war, Komaki Saneshige and the

Kyoto School of Geography also came at the forefront in producing and propagandizing wartime imperial knowledge. To begin with, Komaki deeply involved himself in the processes of propagandizing his Imperial Way geopolitics through media and roundtable discussions.[71] He was in a favorable position to lead what might be called the "thought war" (*shisōsen*). Koyama Iwao, a Kyoto School philosopher, focused on the necessity of "thought war" in various writings,[72] and this peculiar intellectual trend was easily accepted by Komaki and the Kyoto geographers who were already familiar with the Kyoto School philosophers.[73] However, Komaki and Kyoto geopolitics were not content with this somewhat "traditional way" of encountering the world outside the university.

The extended commitment of Komaki and his students to imperial Japan was traceable to their peculiar relations with the army. The Kyoto School of Geopolitics established special ties with the army from an early stage in their geopolitics studies. Their collaboration is traceable to late 1937, when Komaki had just launched geopolitical studies at Kyoto Imperial University.[74] In response to a request from the Imperial Army, Komaki established a secret geopolitics research group later called "The Yoshida Group (*Yoshida no kai*)." This research group, whose real name is General Research Group of Geography, was actually established under the financial and political guidance of the Institute of National Defense.[75] Renting a private house near Kyoto Imperial University, Komaki and the Imperial Army continued this secret meeting and shared strategic geographic information on battlefields and the colonies until the end of the war.[76]

Kyoto geopolitics' collaboration with the Imperial Army is a perfect example that Komaki's criticism of Karl Haushofer's theory of geopolitics as a branch of policy studies was no more than meaningless rhetoric. More importantly, Kyoto geopolitics' wartime studies of Asia and Southeast Asia as area studies became increasingly systematic and organized through their collaboration with the Imperial Army. Since the primary purpose of the "Yoshida Group" was to provide information on a region of interest to the army on a weekly or biweekly basis, Komaki and his research group were accordingly reorganized so that each member would focus on one or two specific regions. Their first collective work of 1943, titled *A New Discourse on East Asian Geopolitics*, clearly showed that Komaki's geopolitics studies operated under a highly organized division of research.[77] Although there were changes in the composition of the researcher team, this basic division of research remained intact until 1945.[78]

In tracing the trajectories of Kyoto geographers' involvement in Japan's total war, one may wonder why they built special ties with the Army rather than the Navy. Komaki emphasized the Pacific Ocean, which, he stressed, physically separates Asian space from that of Europe. Moreover, Komaki's Imperial Way geopolitics was unquestionably closer to the thinking of the Navy, which emphasized the Imperial Way more than the Army. Moreover, it has been widely accepted that the Kyoto School of Philosophy, by which Kyoto geopolitics was heavily influenced, was closely connected to the Navy.[79] I argue that Kyoto geopolitics' collaboration with the Army that came in late 1938, when a full-scale war against China was in progress and, accordingly, the Kwantung Army was exerting a much more powerful influence than the Navy. This could partly explain the conditions and reasons for Komaki's relationship with the Army. Finally, their somewhat peculiar "honeymoon" terminated when the Army made its last request, which was to predict where the US Air Force would bombard in Tokyo in 1945.[80]

Rationalist geopolitics

While geographers at Kyoto University were advocating a spirit-oriented geopolitics based on the Imperial Way, in what context was geopolitical thinking being developed by social scientists in the Tokyo area? More importantly, how did Japanese social scientists attempt to create a new geopolitical perspective of their own, overcoming the influence of Western geopolitics characterized by Karl Haushofer?

From a quantitative standpoint, geopolitics in early 1940s Japan had already been widely accepted as a major social theory. As many as 20 articles on geopolitics by various social scientists appeared between 1937 and 1945 in *Kaizō* alone.[81] Moreover, as the translation of Haushofer's works exemplifies, the wartime Japanese government financially supported the spread of this spatial theory. However, the quantitative expansion of geopolitics in Japan did not necessarily mean that geography studies, once divided into two camps regarding geopolitics, eventually found a middle ground. Komaki contributed a few articles to *Kaizō*, but other Kyoto School geographers hardly participated in this journal.[82]

This spread of the new spatial discourse eventually resulted in the establishment of both an independent geopolitics research group as well as a research journal. In November 1941, the Japanese Association of Geopolitics (hereafter JAG) was founded, led by Iimoto Nobuyuki, who had first introduced geopolitics to Japanese academia in the 1920s. While the JAG did not have a direct impact on the Association of Japanese Geographers, the existing national geography association, the rise of the JAG implied that geopolitics had now become a powerful ideological and theoretical weapon, accepted not only by geographers but also by social scientists in general. It also started publishing its own journal, *Geopolitics* (地政学), beginning in January 1942, one month after the Pearl Harbor attack. The membership numbers of the JAG varied from year to year but around 50 people remained active until 1945. What was more conspicuous was its composition. College professors, high school teachers, researchers at government-funded institutions such as *Tōa kenkyūsho* (東亜研究所), and generals and officers from the Army and the Navy alike were all involved in this new academic association, but no one from Komaki's Kyoto school joined.[83]

However, the fact that geopolitics was becoming a widespread and commonly discussed theory in wartime Japan makes it much harder to accurately determine the characteristics of what might be called Tokyo geopolitics. Komaki denounced it as rationalist-centered and thus a mere imitation of Western geopolitics. However, it remains unclear how rationalism became so closely intertwined with geopolitics. More importantly, it should not be overlooked that irrespective of the different intellectual camps in geopolitics, the notion of the Greater East Asia

Co-Prosperity sphere was universally espoused and eventually each and every work on geopolitics was aiming at realizing a co-prosperity space in Asia, which was most vividly depicted in Komaki's Imperial Way geopolitics. Based on these observations, I will examine the work of economic geographer Ezawa Jōji (1907–1975), whose geopolitical thought can be seen as the locus of a rationalist extreme.

Born in 1907, Ezawa Jōji attended Tokyo University of Commerce (present-day Hitotsubashi University), where the famous neo-Kantian philosopher Sōda Kiichirō (1881–1927) was teaching economic philosophy. After spending nearly 10 years in Germany, Sōda introduced the concept of culture [*kultur*] to Japanese academia. Among the many issues in connection with which the so-called neo-Kantian philosophers studied, Sōda was particularly interested in how intellectuals should cope with the crisis of culture triggered by rapid industrialization. For this reason, culture was reconceptualized by Sōda not as a value parallel to politics and economics, but as a fundamental spirit that one must nurture in order to maintain independence from the state.[84] Hence, "culturalism" was for Sōda a series of activities to develop *kyōyō* (*bildung*) for each individual.

Heavily influenced by Sōda's thought, which had shaped a mainstream perspective in economic philosophy at Tokyo University of Commerce, Ezawa began writing about German philosophy and culture in the 1930s. Just as Sōda pointed out the dominance of industrialized nation-states over individual freedom and values, Ezawa vehemently criticized the notion that reason and rationalism had served only in the formation of a despotic nation-state. He pointed out that reason in the European intellectual tradition took precedence over an individual's various experiences with things.[85] In other words, he contended that in the European philosophical tradition, individuals' judgment of things is determined not by the images of their direct experiences with things but by the pure sense that already exists before experiences.[86] He went on to argue that the state and the aristocratic class had defined reason and forced ordinary people to acknowledge its primacy, this highly abstract and exclusive process which he called rationalization seemingly provided a common value that everyone could share in the name of freedom and equality. However, it actually resulted in subordinating people's social experiences with things to the narrow and standardized space called the "nation-state."[87] Ezawa's observation later played an important role in developing his geopolitical thinking in relation to individuals' experiences of subjectivity in space.

Ezawa's highly "interdisciplinary" early writings on Western philosophy focused on the question of how he could make this theoretical framework more sophisticated in his later encounters with economic geography and eventually geopolitics. Rather than directly discussing geopolitics, Ezawa showed special interest in the field of economic geography, which had become popular among European intellectuals. Ezawa's 1935 book *Theory of Economic Location* was his first work in which he associated the economic philosophy that Sōda introduced to Japan with geographical thinking. Ezawa's primary concern centered on the question of how a new form of objectivity can be achieved if, as I have discussed, reason or rationality is merely a construct that the ruling class created to justify its political power.

How, then, did the concept of space and geography provide Ezawa with an alternative way of contemplating rationality and objectivity? In *Theory of Economic Location*, Ezawa first expounded his views on human beings' relationship with nature. According to him, conflicts and collaboration between human beings and relationship form the basis of their interaction. Unlike Komatsu, who attempted to associate the primitiveness of Asian nature with the Imperial Way, Ezawa boldly argued that human beings' efforts to obtain objectivity against nature as *a priori* could be realized by conceptualizing nature as an object of negation.[88] It is through this conjunction that Ezawa shed a new light on the theory of economic location. In fact, the location theory of industry was first introduced by German economic geographer Alfred Weber, the younger brother of sociologist Max Weber. Translating Weber's books into Japanese, Ezawa first interpreted Weber's thought as seeking for economic rationalization, that is, how human beings could maximize economic profits by determining geographic locations that maximize the economic effects of capital, raw materials, labor and transportation.[89] However, Ezawa was not simply content with this new theory but carried it a step further to criticize the notion of living space (*Lebensraum*), the core concept of German geopolitics, which he believed to essentialize nature as a space where human beings are restricted to nature's predominating power. Ezawa argued:

> The concept of living form (*Lebensform*) is a living that human beings experience in reality and it is preconditioned as an essential "meaning" before it is regarded as an object. Insofar as it is understood as such, it cannot be said that it is an object of geopolitics. That it [living form] could be objectively represented as a living form is premised on the assumption that it conflicts with or resists against the other, or it is resisted by the other. In this case, *conflict, challenge and resistance become elements of negation in order for a living form to be objectified.*
>
> (emphasis added)[90]

The above statement clearly shows that Ezawa basically conceptualized space as a place (*basho*), where both experiences and the interaction of experiences take place. According to this observation, national territory was also conceptualized as the space where a group of people living in the state have shared their experiences. However, Ezawa argued that living within the same territorial boundary does not guarantee that people in the state have the same "objective" experiences.[91] For this reason, he redefined the object of geopolitics as transforming these experiences into objectifying experiences. In this respect, Ezawa's spatial thought presents a striking contrast to that of Komaki Saneshige, who searched for a middle ground between space and human beings in the spiritual mediation of the Imperial Way.

Furthermore, Ezawa's observations of human beings as actors in space were substantially different from Komaki's positioning of *minzoku* or *species* in space. In Ezawa's notion of objectifying experiences within common geographical spaces, minzoku or race is not conceived of as a medium between nature and human beings. Ezawa instead insisted that minzoku cannot be objectified within a given space since minzoku is not necessarily restricted to a certain territorial border and the concept of minzoku pertains to the spatial as well as the temporal, the latter of which cannot be simply objectified. Ezawa held that in order to eventually comprehend the relationship between geography and history, which Haushofer himself termed a subfield of geopolitics, geopolitics should not simply be limited to the realm of objectification.[92] In short, the main issue in Ezawa's spatial theory was how to redirect the relationship between space and human beings in a futuristic sense rather than how to prove that a certain minzoku or species has an objectified spatial experience by returning to history as suggested by Komaki and Yonekura's notion of species. Evidently, this question was not separable from the question of how to spatially conceptualize the "community of destiny" among different ethnic groups.

Ezawa's understanding of minzoku and temporality was a turning point where he attempted to redirect geopolitics from the realm of objectivity to subjectivity. Ironic as it may sound, obtaining objectivity through spatial experiences, he stressed, is only possible when a diversity of subjective experiences is transformed into commonness. Through this logic, Ezawa intended to redefine the imperial rhetoric of the "community of destiny" in his own light. Borrowing Haushofer's statement that the aim of geopolitics is to *predict* the tendency of each group in the future and therefore it is not only an academic discipline but also a *technology*, Ezawa asserted that geopolitics enters the realm of "performative intuition" through a de-objectification process, and that this is how geopolitics encounters the future as the mediator of the community of destiny. Such an observation was also shared by other Japanese social scientists and among them, the political scientist Rōyama Masamichi elaborated on the nature of geopolitics as subjective social science. Rōyama wrote:

> The historical movement that shapes historical phenomena such as nation and *minzoku* has been the focus of a geopolitical approach [. . .] Since historical examination is accompanied by value judgment, it has been said that there exists no objective reality in geopolitics. However, in contrast to the existing social sciences that have advocated objectivity and represented reality through formulation and fixation, it is interesting that geopolitics (in the social sciences) for the first time acknowledges subjectivity and also its characteristics as policy studies.[93]

Ezawa and Rōyama's somewhat coincidental observations of geopolitics as a subjective social science entail several important questions. First, why is the notion of subjectivity such an important issue in examining the Greater East Asia Co-Prosperity sphere? Second, what role did the notion of subjectivity play in the making of Greater East Asian space? One possible answer might be that by emphasizing subjectivity and intuition in conceiving East Asian space, both Ezawa and Rōyama could dislocate East Asian space from the binary formation of the East vs. the West which is invariably associated with geographical determinism. For this reason, both Ezawa and Rōyama could not simply resort to the concept of Asian space as intrinsic and given, and this tells us the paradoxical deconstructive aspect of the so-called rationalist geopolitics in imperial Japan which rendered East Asian space into the realm of uncertainty and ambiguity. Rōyama never negated the problem of abstraction inherent in East Asian discourses as he indicated, "[T]he notion of the Greater East Asia Co-Prosperity Sphere is still ambiguous in its grounds and content, and it is difficult to understand its origins."[94] However, the impossibility of demarcating the geographical border between the East and the rest of the world through objective social science ironically opened up new possibilities of subjectivity, thereby allowing geopolitics to emerge as an intellectual weapon for envisioning a new East Asian order.

Developing space, constructing the community of destiny

Henri Lefebvre has theorized space in his concept of spatial practice. According to him, space, a social construct, "embraces production and reproduction." He observes that through this process of production and reproduction, some degree of cohesion between space and each member in a society takes place.[95] To put it another way, the relationship between space and human beings is by no means static, and the capitalistic mode of production constantly intervenes in the process of human beings' becoming spatial subjects. Notably, the logic of capitalist development was one of the main targets for wartime Japanese intellectuals as they accused individualism and capitalism of being the two wheels of Western imperialism. While the intellectual fashion of overcoming the West never faded away, solving the issue of the economic gap between metropole and colony also emerged as a central theme to convince colonial subjects of the historical necessity of creating a Japan-centered East Asian empire. The problem of economic imbalance was closely connected to the question of how spaces in the colony should be restructured and thus become a social space, where "some degree of cohesion" between metropole and colony takes place.

Just like Lefebvre stressed the process of production in space, Ezawa questioned the conventional threefold relationship of the state, national territory and people (*minzoku*). National territory, he observed, functions as a spatial basis for people's common experiences.[96] In this respect, he called national territory as *basho* and observed that in *basho* the notion of commonness predominantly occurred through the process of sharing the same past in the same territory.[97] At stake was the question of whether simply consolidating different national territories, Chinese or Korean territories for instance, into the Japanese empire would give rise to East Asian commonness or the community of destiny which constitutes the spiritual part of the East Asian Community. He was quite skeptical about such a mechanical annexation of territories, labeling it a greater East Asian "sphere." Instead, he insisted that a "sphere" be where the constant relationships between subjects and living forms (*Lebensform*) take place.[98] Based on these observations, Ezawa contended that creating a co-prosperity sphere would only be possible when people living in the "sphere" had a "stream of experiences" that pointed to the future. In order for this concept of a "sphere" to operate constantly in the process of creating the stream of experiences, Ezawa observed that the conventional concept of space (*Lebensraum*) should be substituted for a new geopolitical concept.

What attracted Ezawa's attention was the notion of reconstructing space (*Raumordnung*).[99] Surely, the German term *Raumordnung*, often translated as "spatial planning" or "spatial development," was first conceptualized in German geopolitics. As the term clearly suggests, German social scientists paid attention to actual policies that would realize a secured German living space in the midst of the Second World War. In tandem with the fashion of geopolitical thinking, a journal *Raumforschung und Raumordnung* (Spatial Research and Spatial Planning) was published in 1936. Ezawa, however, did not simply confine the concept of *Raumordnung* to the realm of policy studies. Reiterating Kjellen's famous concept of the "community of soul" (*seelengemeinschaft*) and revisiting Haushofer's pioneering work on geopolitics, Ezawa intended to contrive a Japanese version of rational geopolitics. Among a number of research agendas Haushofer called for into further consideration, Ezawa grappled with the questions of the relationship between ideology and living space and the notion of living as a variable of the formation and division of race and class.[100]

Such observations led Ezawa to further explore the difference between Europe, Germany in particular and Imperial Japan. First of all, he adamantly rejected the idea of a bloc economy, which aimed at consolidating East Asian space in the clear schematic division of Japan (Heavy Industry), Korea and Manchukuo (Agriculture and Heavy Industry) and Southeast Asia and the Southern Seas (Raw Materials). Criticizing this kind of geographical division of Asia as a lopsided production, he argued:

> In terms of the co-prosperity sphere in the Southern Seas, the one-sided viewpoint by the leading powers based on the theory of location, that is, the notion of lopsided production, on the one hand destroys the self-sufficient power of indigenous people and on the other hand causes the maldistribution of population.[101]

As the above statement clearly shows, the theoretical origins of Ezawa's discontent with the mainstream discourses of a Japan-Manchuria-China bloc economy are traceable to his critiques of the industrial location theory by Alfred Weber who Ezawa himself first introduced to Japanese academia in the mid-1930s. However, he was now convinced that the theory of finding the optimized location for reducing cost and maximizing economic margins would not fit into the task of restructuring East Asian space Japan was facing. Arguing that the bloc economy system would eventually destroy the ethnicity of people living in the colonies,[102] Ezawa stressed that the East Asian economic sphere should not be constructed based on hierarchal relations between ethnic groups.

It is widely accepted that the notion of a Japan-Manchuria-China economic bloc was premised on the conviction that a self-sufficient economy must be established to protect Asia from "Western imperialism" that had exploited Asia as suppliers of raw materials and cheap labors. In addition to the rhetoric of saving Asia from

Western threats, the bloc economy theory was constantly revisited by Japanese social scientists in a hyperbolic way. They aspired to approach Chinese intellectuals and appeal to Chinese nationalism by emphasizing the ideological similarity between the notion of self-sufficiency in traditional Chinese Confucian philosophy and the twentieth-century version of Asian self-sufficiency. Ezawa, however, acutely pointed out that the bloc economy system Imperial Japan attempted to construct bears striking resemblance to European imperialism. The expansion of an East Asian economic bloc to a Greater East Asian Co-Prosperity Sphere by adding Southeast Asia and Southern Seas right after the Pearl Harbor attack, he stressed, rather made it clear that Japan only viewed these Southern spaces as a supplier of raw materials. Ezawa charged that the phenomenon of lopsided production and lopsided raw materials usually takes place when authentic spaces for a certain minzoku were destroyed by external powers and contended that Southeast Asia had been historically the game of such spatial destruction.[103] In this way he attempted to challenge the mainstream but highly hierarchal notion of the Greater East Asia Co-Prosperity Sphere and redefine it as an economic sphere upheld by the common ethnic sentiment and will of Asian people.[104]

National land planning and the question of capitalist development

Just as a group of Japanese social scientists sophisticated their notion of an East Asian community, Ezawa also paid particular attention to the concept of autarky. If we loosely interpret this term to mean an economically self-sufficient nation or sphere, we can see that it was not just Ezawa who explicitly advocated an autarky. Komaki Saneshige's Imperial Way geopolitics ultimately targeted a self-sufficient East Asian Co-Prosperity sphere, and the ultimate goal of the "bloc economy" system in Komaki's geopolitics was no doubt to establish a self-sufficient anti-Western economic order. However, Ezawa's notion of autarky seemed to be concerned with restructuring ethnic and economic borders of Greater East Asian space, rather than with assuring territorial expansion to the West. Ezawa contended that the previous and existing theories of European geopolitics simply emphasized territorial expansion based on the perception that solving the problem of limited resources in living space was only possible by politically occupying another space. For him, Britain's colonization of India was a clear example of this resource-centered geopolitical concept of space.[105]

Instead of advocating constant territorial expansion by the leading powers, Ezawa's spatial theory, associated with the theory of marginal utility, focused on a "retrospective" approach to natural resources.[106] Ezawa believed that the division of space through the distribution of raw materials could be an easy way for a leading power to temporarily obtain economic self-sufficiency, but he also maintained that this mechanical division of space would inevitably create political hierarchies within a certain spatial community and would not reach the level of sharing a common destiny. Precisely for this reason, for Ezawa the concept of autarky did not mean continuing to conquer unexplored space, but rather to economically develop "marginal" spaces so that people in these spaces could have a new set of experiences. In short, autarky as the final destination of the Greater East Asia Co-Prosperity sphere was also the ultimate end of Ezawa's geopolitical thinking, which emphasized the processes by which human beings negate natural space as given and construct a new space, constructing their own identity through this schema of negation and construction.

In terms of envisioning industrialization in the underdeveloped region of Greater East Asia, Ezawa's idea might be seen as one of the most imperialized economic approaches for Japan's war efforts. Even Yanaihara Tadao, Professor of Economics at Tokyo Imperial University and a leader among progressive intellectuals during the wartime period,[107] relentlessly argued that oppressive and violent measures should be taken in ruling "uncivilized" people in Southeast Asia.[108] Instead, Ezawa's geopolitics became closely associated with developmentalist modernization, and geopolitics' encounter with modernization was also found in Rōyama's notion of regional development. Criticizing both commercial investment and the notion of a bloc economy, Rōyama asserted that the final aim of an East Asian Cooperative Community should take the form of regional development.[109]

To turn his theory of space into a realistic force for colonial economic development, Ezawa showed keen interest in the notion of national land planning. This idea rapidly gained currency among bureaucrats and intellectuals as Japan conducted its war against China, and it was highly likely that Japan would declare a total war against the United States. As the notion of total war clearly suggests, these intellectuals observed that both human and material resources must be mobilized for Japan's war efforts. Central to this logic lay the question of how marginal utility should be maximized under the condition of limited resources. Therefore, advocates of national land planning naturally focused their concern on restructuring spaces in the Japanese empire for the sake of wartime mobilization.

After the Committee for National Land Planning was established in Japan in 1939, national land planning became an important issue in the colony as well. In 1940, the Committee for National Land Planning was established in colonial Korea and it was filled with top-ranking officials in the Governor General's Office and leading intellectuals at universities in colonial Korea. Between 1940 and 1942, a number of articles on national land planning appeared in major journals in Korea. Importantly, their discussion of national land planning varied substantially based on these authors' political positions. For example, the converted Korean Marxist intellectual In Jeong-Sik interpreted it as part of a state-centered controlled economy that would replace the laissez-faire system based on individualism.[110] Inherent in In's observation was the thinking of a colonial intellectual that the economic gap between Japan and colonial Korea might be lessened by Korea's voluntary participation in national land planning, which would result in the development of the Korean economy. But most Japanese intellectuals viewed it as merely part of the wartime total mobilization policies to exploit resources in the colonies. To this end, they emphasized the necessity of scientifically measuring the location of raw materials and effectively utilizing them in colonial Korea. For this reason, their discussion of and writings on national land planning took the form of geography-centered area studies to accumulate knowledge and information about raw materials in the colony. However, completely missing in their observation was how people in the colony should become the subjects of a politically reconstructed and economically "developed" East Asian empire.

Ezawa was clearly aware of such limitations of national land planning when it was applied to the colony as a means to exploit resources. He was also equally critical of the economics-centered interpretation of such planning, which was that national land planning was primarily concerned with increasing productivity and marginal utility, or in other words, maximizing exploitation. Interestingly, he critically revisited Alfred Weber's theory of industrial location, which Ezawa himself introduced to Japan in the mid-1930s, arguing that it is premised on the perception that economic conditions are naturally given. To put it another way, establishing plants or factories as part of national land planning where the total cost of labor, production and transportation is lower might contribute to increasing productivity and effectiveness. However, he contended that it would not change the political constitution of people's lives.[111] In *Basic Theories of National Land Planning*, Ezawa theorized the notion of economic development in national land planning as a logic of subject formation.

> In order to completely realize national land planning, it must encompass all aspects of human life. For this reason, it should not only restructure population, the economy and transportation, but should also reach the political, administrative, legal and customary order of minzoku. It is insufficient to manage labor in industries and construct cities and villages, and build new railroads, national roadways and waterways that are necessary for development. . . . To put it another way, true national land planning is to take into consideration various representations, customs, blood-centered sentiments and religions in people's lives in rural villages. *We should be able to anticipate that through the reorganization of (national land), what kind of effects the interplay of minzoku would bring out to a new order.*[112]
>
> (emphasis added)

Ezawa's understanding of national land planning and economic development clearly showed how he appropriated modernization as a driving force for constructing a new order. To be sure, he was also aware that capitalism had constantly caused economic inequality, and that this gap became the major reason for imperialism and colonialism. Therefore, modernization in a Japan-centered new order needed to be associated with restructuring the discriminatory political hierarchy between metropole and colony. Accordingly, his geopolitical approach to Southeast Asia concentrated on the question of how rapidly national land planning could restructure Southeast Asia into a modern space, and this was no doubt the same question that the general economic plan of imperial Japan had to confront. Criticizing Europe's exploitative imperialist economy in Southeast Asia, Ezawa argued:

> In order for Japan to construct a mutually unified relationship in Southeast Asia, it is imperative that Japan change the allocation and distribution of

raw materials and at the same time change the transportation relations of these raw materials. . . . *To discuss industrialization in Southeast Asia presumably means to correct the existing relationships* [in Southeast Asia], *and at the same time, the reconstruction of the existing relationships is essential in restructuring Japan's economic structure itself from a new perspective.*[113]

(emphasis added)

Consequently, the so-called rationalist geopolitics developed by both Ezawa and Rōyama ironically was associated with the concept of developmentalist modernization, which had long been believed to be the fruit of the Western social scientific tradition. However, their notion of modernization leaves much room for further discussion. How could subjects in East Asia share the sense of the "community of destiny" while experiencing different stages of economic development? How could the notion of geopolitics and national land development constitute the realistic content of the Co-Prosperity sphere, without simply "objectifying" colonial subjects as a means of exploitation for Japan's war efforts?

Conclusion

Geopolitical thinking gained currency in interwar Japan as "Asia" emerged as a spatial concept challenging and replacing the West as universal in the international order. Yet it should not be overlooked that this rapid spread of spatial discourse unequivocally reflected the double mindset of Japanese intellectuals who on the one hand were advocating "overcoming the modern," and "overcoming the West," but who were also searching for scientific and rational ways to justify Japan's spatial hegemony over the rest of Asia.

Nowhere were the seeds of geopolitics stronger than in the social sciences in wartime Japan. Various Pan-Asian discourses produced by Japanese social scientists during the wartime period aimed at distinguishing themselves from the previous Pan-Asianism, which had been characterized by its particularistic and culturalist orientations. Rationalizing the East in a social scientific manner and theorizing East Asian space were unquestionably among the most imperative problems that Japanese social scientists were confronted with. In that respect geopolitics played an important role in providing intellectual grounds for this very fundamental and important question.

This argues that the notion of geopolitics in wartime Japan went beyond a temporary intellectual fashion. Geopolitics provided a new space for other disciplines that had not been conceived of as social sciences. In this process, the fixed border of "objectivity" in the social sciences was gradually deconstructed. This did not mean that a certain departmental unit, geography for example, was newly included in the realm of social sciences. Instead, as the geopolitical thinking of Ezawa and Rōyama shows, these two social scientists tried to redefine the objectivity-centered framework of social scientific thinking by engaging with new concepts such as spatiality and futurity.

Notes

1 Murayama Michiō, *Daitōa kenseturon* [On Constructing a Greater East Asia] (Tokyo: Shōkō Gyōseisha, 1943), 6.
2 Ibid., 3–4.
3 Ibid.; 4. Karl Haushofer, *Geopolitik des Pazifischen Ozeans*, trans. Taiheiyō Kyōkai, *Taiheiyō chisegaku* [Geopolitics of the Pacific Ocean] (Tokyo: Iwanami Shoten, 1942), 244.
4 A brief list of recent studies on East Asian space in wartime East Asian discourses is as follows: Shibata Yōichi, *Teikoku nihon no chiseigaku: Ajia, Taiheiyō Sensōki ni okeru chiri gakusha no shisō to jissen* (Osaka: Seibundō, 2016); Yamamurō Shinichi, "Koku-minteikoku, nihon no keisei to kūkanchi [The Construction of the Japanese Empire and Knowledge on Space]," in *Teikoku nihon no gakuchi* 8 [The Academy and Knowledge of Imperial Japan], eds. Yamamurō Shinichi, Sakai Tetuya, et al. (Tokyo: Iwanami Sho-ten, 2006), 21–66; Fukuma Yoshiki, " 'Daitōa' kūkan no seisan- Chiseigakune okeru kūkan ninshiki no doutaiseto nashonarizumu no zaikochiku [Producing Greater Asian Space] (1)," *Seijikeizaishigaku* 441 (May 2005): 1–23; Fukuma Yoshiki, " 'Daitōa' kūkan no seisan- Chiseigakune okeru kūkan ninshiki no doutaiseto,nashonarizumu no zaikochiku [Producing Greater Asian Space] (2)," *Seijikeizaishigaku* 442 (June 2005): 15–31; Christian Spang, "Karu haushofar to nihonno chiseigaku-daiichiji seikaitaisen-gono nichidokukankei no nakade [Karl Haushofer and Japanese Geopolitics: German-Japanese Relations after the Great War]," trans. Ishi Shokai, *Kūkan, shakai, chirishisō* 6 (2001): 2–21; Hisatake Tetsuya, "Hawaiha chisana manshukoku- nihonchiseigakuno kaihō [Hawaii is a small Manchukuo – The Liberation of Japanese Geopolitics]," *Gendaishisō* 27, no. 13 (Dec. 1999): 196–203; Takeuchi Keiichi, "The Japanese Impe-rial Tradition, Western Imperialism and Modern Japanese Geography," in *Geography and Empire*, eds. Anne Godlewska and Neil Smith (Oxford: Blackwell Publishers, 1994), 188–206; Takeuchi Keiichi, "Geopolitikuno hukatuto seijichirigakuno atarashii tenkai- geopolitikuhutatabi kangae [The Revival of Geopolitics and the New Trends in Political Geography]," *Hitotsubashironsō* 96 (1986): 523–546.
5 As for developmentalism in wartime East Asia, see Hiromi Mizuno, Aaron Moore and John DiMoia, eds., *Engineering Asia- Technology, Colonial Development, and the Cold War Order* (London: Bloomsbury, 2018).
6 Aaron Moore, *Constructing East Asia: Technology, Ideology and Empire in Japan's Wartime Era, 1931–1945* (Stanford: Stanford University Press, 2013).
7 Halford J. Mackinder, *Democratic Ideals and Reality: A Study in the Politics of Recon-struction* (London: Constable and Company, 1919), 31.
8 Ibid., 147–190. For a detailed analysis of Mackinder's notion of "Going Concern" and "heartland theory," R. Mayhew, "Halford Mackinder's 'New' Political Geography and the Geographical Tradition," *Political Geography* 19 (2000): 771–791; see also Chapter 3 in Mark Polelle, *Raising Cartographic Consciousness: The Social and For-eign Policy Vision of Geopolitics in the Twentieth Century* (Lanham, MD: Lexington Books, 1999).
9 Ibid., 191–235. Mackinder wrote a famous phrase on his Heartland theory,
   "Who rules East Europe commands the Heartland:
   Who rules the Heartland commands the World-Island:
   Who rules the World-Island commands the World,"
   ibid., 194.
10 Friedrich Ratzel, *Politische Geographie* [Political Geography] (München und Leipzig: R. Oldenbourg, 1897).
11 Karl Haushofer, *Bausteine zur Geopolitik, von Karl Haushofer, Erich Obst, Hermann Lautensach, Otto Maull; hrsg. der Zeitschrift fur Geopolitik. Mit 20 Skizzen* (Berlin-Grunewald: Kurt Vowinckel, 1928), trans. Tamaki Hajime, *Chiseijigaku kiso riron* [Basic Theories of Geopolitics] (Tokyo: Kagakushugikōgyōsha, 1941), 27.

12 Iimoto Nobuyuki, "Jinshutōsei no jijitu to chiseigakuteki kōsatu [The Reality of Racial Control and Its Geopolitical Approach] (1)" *Chirigaku hyōron* 1, no. 9 (Sep. 1925): 16–37; "Jinshutōsei no jijitu to chiseigakuteki kōsatu [The Reality of Racial Control and Its Geopolitical Approach] (2)," *Chirigaku hyōron* 1, no. 10 (Oct. 1925): 955–967; "Jinshutōsei no jijitu to chiseigakuteki kōsatu [The Reality of Racial Control and Its Geopolitical Approach] (3)," *Chirigaku hyōron* 2, no. 1 (Jan. 1926): 47–60.

13 Iimoto Nobuyuki, "Jinshutōsei no jijitu to chiseigakuteki kōsatu (1)," 21–23.

14 Iimoto Nobuyuki, "Iwayuru chiseigaku no gainen [The Concept of Geopolitics]," *Chirigaku hyōron* 4, no. 1 (Jan. 1928): 76–99.

15 It is highly conceivable that Iimoto's understanding of geopolitics was nurtured by the general social and political trend of 1920s Japan, when the issue of racism emerged as an important topic both in real politics and in academia. The year 1925, when Iimoto's articles were published, was a year after the Immigration Act to restrict Japanese immigration to the United States was passed by the US government.

16 Iimoto Nobuyuki, "Jinshutōsei no jijitu to chiseigakuteki kōsatu (1)," 30–37. Iimoto actually contributed three articles in 1925 and 1926. He briefly analyzed Western geopolitics and political geography in the first article and focused on criticizing Western racism against Asian races in the second and third articles.

17 For Mitsukawa's Pan-Asianism and ultra-nationalism, see Christopher W. A. Szpilman, "Between Pan-Asianism and Nationalism: Mitsukawa Kametarō and His Campaign to Reform Japan and Liberate Asia," in *Pan-Asianism in Modern Japanese History*, eds. Sven Saaler and J. Victor Koschmann (London: Routledge, 2006), 85–100.

18 W.E.B. Du Bois, "A Chronicle of Race Relations," *Phylon* 3, no. 4 (1942): 412.

19 Kyoto daigaku hyakunenshi henshū iinkai, ed., *Kyoto daigaku hyakunenshi bukyōkushi hen* [The 100-Year History of Geography at Kyoto University] (Kyoto-Shi: Kyoto Daigaku Kōenhai, 1997), 174.

20 Ibid.

21 Ishida Ryūjirō, "Meiji-taishōkino nihon no chirigakkainoshisōtekidōkō [The Intellectual Trend of Japanese Geographers during the Meiji and Taisho Periods]," *Chirigaku hyōron* 44, no. 8 (Aug. 1971): 545. The 1919 Tokyo Imperial University Act stated reasons for establishing an independent geography department: (1) Geography can vividly show the international order and its applied fields are not small. (2) Geography in Western universities has already been producing its own students, therefore it is imperative that Japan also produces geography specialists. Tokyo daigaku hyakunenshi henshu iinkai, ed., *Tokyo daigaku hyakunenshi* 5 [The 100-Year History of the University of Tokyo] (Tokyo: Tokyo Daigaku Shuppankai, 1984), 604.

22 It seems to be correct to translate *Nihon chiri gakkai* into the Association of Japanese Geography, but I follow the official English title provided by the association.

23 Nihon chiri gakkai, ed., *Nihon chiri gakkai gojū nenshi* [The 50-Year History of the Japanese Association for Geography] (Tokyo: Kōkon Shoin, 1975), 6.

24 Ibid., 19.

25 Kyoto daigaku hyakunenshi henshū iinkai, ed., *Kyoto daigaku hyakunenshi bukyōkushi hen* [The Hundred-Year History of Kyoto University: Departments and Bureaus] (Kyoto-Shi: Kyoto Daigaku Koenhai, 1997), 174.

26 Iizuka Kōji, "Geopolitikuno kihontekiseigaku [The Fundamental Nature of Geopolitics] (1)," *Keizaigaku Ronshū* 12, no. 8 (Aug. 1942): 56–84. Iizuka's articles were published in three parts. The second and third part of his articles appeared in *Keizaigaku Ronshū* 13, no. 3 (Mar. 1943) and *Keizaigaku Ronshū* 13, no. 5 (May 1943), respectively.

27 Minobe finally resigned from the House of Peers in 1936, when his organist perspective was severely attacked by ultra-rightists who attempted to restore the Emperor as the central political authority. As Andrew Gordon correctly points out, the purge of Minobe and his "conservative" political theory symbolized Japan's rapid move

toward a fascist society. See Andrew Gordon, *A Modern History of Japan: From Toku-gawa Times to the Present* (London and New York: Oxford University Press, 2003), 198–199.

28 Japan's position as the third largest country in naval power was the result of the Wash-ington Naval Conference held from November 12, 1921 to February 6, 1922. The main purpose of the conference was to restrict the leading countries' naval power, which emerged as the main threat to international peace during World War I. As a result, it was determined that the US, Britain and Japan were allowed to maintain battleships in a ratio of 5:5:3 tons respectively. The Washington conference was followed by a series of naval conferences in the 1920s, at which Japanese military leaders asked for equal status with the US, arguing Japan's "have-not" position in the international order. See Sadao Asada, "From Washington to London: The Imperial Japanese Navy and the Politics of Naval Limitation, 1921–1930," in *The Washington Conference 1921–1922: Naval Rivalry, East Asian Stability and the Road to Pearl Harbor*, eds. Erik Goldstein and John Maurer (Ilford: Frank Cass, 1994), 147–191.

29 The publication of a twelve-volume work titled *An Outline of New Germany* (*Shin doitsu kokka taikei*) best exemplifies the massive influx of German state theories into Japan. Importantly, one chapter in Volume 3 was dedicated to introducing Karl Haush-ofer's geopolitics. Satō Hiroshi, Professor of Economics at Tokyo University of Com-merce, and Ezawa Jōji, Lecturer at Tokyo University of Commerce, participated in this project. See, Satō Hiroshi and Ezawa Jōji, "Chiseigakuteki kite," in *Shin Doitsu kokka taikei; dai 3 seiji hen*, ed. Futara Yoshinori (Tokyo: Nihonhyōronsha, 1939), 335–417.

30 The Japanese translation of Haushofer's works was concentrated between 1940 and 1944. The following are Japanese titles of Haushofer's works on geopolitics and Japan: *Taiheiyō no Chiseigaku* [Geopolitics of the Pacific Ocean] (1940, 1942); *Gen-dai Eikokuron* [A Study on Modern Britain] (1940); *Chisejigaku no kiso riron* [Basic Theories of Geopolitics] (1941); *Chiseijigaku nyūmon* [An Introduction to Geopoli-tics] (1941); *Semeiken to Sekaikan* [Life and Living Sphere] (1942); *Nihon* [Japan] (1942); *Tairiku seiji to kaiyō seiji* [Land Politics and Sea Politics] (1943); *Dainihon* [A Greater Japan] (1943); *Nihon no kokka kensetsu* [Japan's Nation Building] (1943).

31 Haushofer's *Geopolitik des Pazifischen Ozeans* was first published in Germany in 1924 and republished in 1938. Its first Japanese translation appeared in 1940 by Nihon Seinen Gaikō Kyōkai titled *Taiheiyō Chiseijigaku* (2 vols.), and was followed by the translation of Taiheiyō Kyōkai with a slightly different title, *Taiheiyō Chiseigaku*, in 1942. The third version, in 1944, was not a direct translation but an introductory book to Haushofer's *Geopolitik des Pazifischen Ozean*. See Nihon Seinen Gaikō Kyōkai, *Taiheiyō Chiseijigaku: Chiri rekishi sōgō kankei no kenkyū* [Geopolitics of the Pacific Ocean: A Study on the General Relations between Geography and History] (Tokyo: Nihon Seinen Gaikō Kyōkai, 1940), 2 vols; Taiheiyō Kyōkai, trans., *Taiheiyō Chisei-gaku* [Geopolitics of the Pacific Ocean] (Tokyo: Iwanami Shoten, 1942); Sato Sōichirō, *Haushofarno taiheiyō chiseigaku kaisetu* [An Introduction to Karl Haushofer's *Geo-politics of the Pacific Ocean*] (Tokyo: Taiheiyō Gakkai Rokkoshuppanbu, 1944).

32 Karl Haushofer, Erich Obst, Hermann Lautensach and Otto Maull, *Bausteine zur Geopolitik, 1. Ueber die historische Entwicklung des Begriffs Geopolitik* (Berlin-Grunewald, Kurt Vowinckel, 1928), trans. Tamaki Hajime, *Chiseijigaku no kiso riron* [Basic Theories of Geopolitics] (Tokyo: Kagakushugikōgyōsha, 1941), 61–62.

33 Ibid., p. 54. Notably, the notion of technology in thinking about the dialectics between material and human beings' labor and between subjectivity and objectivity was gaining attention from Japanese intellectuals. For example, Aikawa Haruki, a leading Koza-faction Marxist, and Tosaka Jun were developing debates on technology. For an exten-sive study of discourses on technology in wartime Japan, Aaron Moore, *Constructing East Asia*.

34 Karl Haushofer, *Chiseijigaku no kiso riron*, trans. Tamaki Hajime, 63.

35 For a discussion of wartime Japanese intellectuals' concept of subjectivity and objectivity, see J. Victor Koschmann, "Constructing Destiny: Royama Masamichi and Asian Regionalism in Wartime Japan," in *Pan-Asianism in Modern Japanese History: Colonialism, Regionalism and Borders*, eds. Sven Saaler and J. Victor Koschmann (New York: Routledge, 2007), 185–189.

36 Haushofer travelled to Japan, Korea and Manchuria as a military observer of the Bavarian Army. Christian Spang, "Karl Haushofer Reexamined: Geopolitics as a Factor of Japanese-German Rapprochement in the Inter-war Years," in *Japanese-German Relations, 1895–1945 War and Diplomacy*, eds. Christian Spang and Rolf Harald Wippich (London: Routledge, 2006), 139–140.

37 Karl Haushofer, *Dai Nihon; Betrachtungen über Gross-Japans Wehrkraft, Weltstellung und Zukunft* (Berlin: E. S. Mittler und Sohn, 1913). This book was translated into Japanese in 1942. Wakai Rinichi, *Dai Nihon* [The Greater Japan] (Tokyo: Rakuyō Shōin, 1942).

38 Alfred Mahan's writings on East Asia are one example of how Western geographers viewed and situated Asia in their geopolitical thinking. Mahan predicted that Japan, together with Russia, would threaten American hegemony. Mahan's analysis was based on his famous geopolitical theory of sea power and land power. According to him, countries that acquired sea power first would take the initiative in the world order, and Japan was one of the nations which had geographical access to sea power. But Mahan's writings on East Asia were highly strategic and observational, not based on actual and empirical knowledge. See Alfred Mahan, *The Problem of Asia and Its Effect on International Polices* (Boston: Little, Brown and Company, 1900).

39 A complete list of Haushofer's writings on Japan can be found in Christian Spang, "Karuhaushofarto nihon no chiseigaku: daiichijisekai daisengo no nichitokukankei no nakade [Karl Haushofer and Japanese Geopolitics: German-Japanese Relations after the Great War]," trans. Ishi Shokai, *Kūkan, shakai, chirishisō* 6 (2001): 2–21.

40 Karl Haushofer, *Dai Nihon*, trans., Wakai Rinichi, 167–228.

41 "Karuhaushofarto nihonno chiseigaku: daiichijisekai daisengo no nichitokukankeino nakade," *Kūkan, shakai, chirishisō* 6 (2001): 2–21.

42 For a quantitative study of Japanese students' study in Germany in the 1920s and 1930s, see Kato Tetsurō, "Personal Contacts in Japanese-German Cultural Relations during the 1920s and Early 1930s," in *Japanese-German Relations, 1895–1945 War and Diplomacy*, eds. Christian Spang and Rolf Harald Wippich (London: Routledge, 2006), 119–138.

43 Watsuji Tetsurō, *Fūdo: ningenteki kosatsu* [Climate: A Humanistic Approach] (Tokyo: Iwanami Shōten, 1935).

44 For Watsuji's turn to spatiality and East Asian space, Naoki Sakai argues as follows:
   Imitating the restorationist move in the West toward Eurocentricity, which was to a great extent motivated by an anxiety concerning the putative loss of the West's superiority over the non-West in the 1930s and which found its cumulative expression in the obsessive emphasis on the idea of the distinctiveness of the West and on the separationist distinction of "we the West" from the rest of the world, Watsuji seemed to produce an equally ethnocentric move toward the East.
   Naoki Sakai, *Translation and Subjectivity: On "Japan" and Cultural Nationalism* (Minneapolis: University of Minnesota Press, 1997), 91.

45 Kyoto daigaku chirigaku kyōshitsu, *Chirigaku kyoto no hyakunen* [The 100-Year History of Geography at Kyoto University] (Kyoto: Nakanishiya Shuppan, 2008), 80–83.

46 Komaki Saneshige, *Nihonchiseigaku sengen* [A Declaration of Japanese Geopolitics] (Tokyo: Kōbundō, 1940). The actual citation is from its second publication in 1942 by Hakuyōsha. Komaki Saneshige, *Nihonchiseigaku sengen* (Tokyo: Hakuyōsha, 1942), 69.

47 Kamaki Saneshige, "Karu haushofar ron [On Karl Haushofer]," *Kokumin hyoron* 15, no. 4 (1941): 3.

48 Ibid., 8–9.
49 Yonekura Jirō, *Tōa chiseigaku josetsu* [An Introduction to East Asian Geopolitics] (Tokyo: Seikatsusha, 1941), 23.
50 Ibid.
51 Ibid., 21.
52 Ibid., 22.
53 Ibid., 20.
54 Ibid., 25.
55 Ibid.
56 For Tanabe Hajime's theory of species, see Naoki Sakai, "Ethnicity and Species: On the Philosophy of the Multi-ethnic State in Japanese Imperialism," *Radical Philosophy* 95 (May/June 1999): 33–45; Naoki Sakai, "Subject and Substratum: On Japanese Imperial Nationalism," *Cultural Studies* 14, no. 3 (2000): 463–530.
57 Although the exact number of researchers in the Kyoto School of Geography was not revealed, it can be estimated at approximately 15 researchers including Komaki himself. This number is based on the number of geographers who participated in a government-supported secret research group, the Yoshida Group, founded by Komaki Saneshige. See, Mizuuchi Toshio, "Tsusho 'Yoshidano kai' ni yoru chiseigaku kanren shiryō [Historical Materials on the Geopolitics of the 'Yoshida' Group]," *Kūkan, shakai, chirishisō* 6 (Osaka: Osaka Siritu Daigakko, 2001): 59–112.
58 Komaki Saneshige, *Nihon chiseigaku sengen*, 75–80.
59 Ibid., 78–79.
60 Komaki clearly differentiated race (*jinshu*) from nation (*minzoku*). While race is more subject to environmental and geographical factors, he contended that race just represents the geographical and inherent part in the creation of minzoku. Thus, he emphasized the necessity of minzoku geography rather than racial geography. Komaki Saneshige, *Minzoku chiri* [Ethnic Geography] (Tokyo: Chijinshōkan, 1937), 1–13.
61 Komaki Saneshige, *Chiseigakujōyori mitaru daitōa* [A Greater Asia from a Geopolitical Perspective] (Tokyo: Nihon Hōsō Shuppansha, 1939), 20.
62 Ibid., 28–29.
63 Komaki Saneshige, *Tōa chiseigaku josetsu*, 12.
64 Komaki Saneshige, *Chiseigakujōyori mitaru daitōa*, 38.
65 Komaki Saneshige, *Tōa chiseigaku josetsu*, 12.
66 Komaki Saneshige, *Chiseigakujōyori mitaru daitōa*, 36.
67 Ibid.
68 Komaki Saneshige, "*Dai azia no hukō ishin sengen* [A Declaration of the Restoration of The Greater Asia]," *Gendai* 23, no. 3 (Mar. 1942): 5–22.
69 Komaki Saneshige, *Nihon chiseigaku oboegaku* [A Statement of Japanese Geopolitics] (Osaka: Akita, 1944), 25–27.
70 Komaki Saneshige, *Chiseigakujōyori mitaru daitōa*, 51.
71 Komaki's *Chiseigakujōyori mitaru daitōa* was actually a compilation of his lectures to a Kyoto radio station between February 23, 1942 and February 28, 1942. Komaki Saneshige, *Chiseigakujōyori mitaru daitōa*, 3. Komaki also actively engaged in the publication of books concerning the so-called thought war. See Komaki Saneshige, "Dai tōa no rinen [The Ideals of a Greater East Asia]," in *Seikaikan no tatakai* [A War on Worldviews], ed. Dainihon genron hōkoku kyōkai (Tokyo: Dōmei Tushinsha, 1944), 204–233.
72 Koyama Iwao, "Sōryōkusen to shisōsen, [Total War and Thought War]" *Chuōkōron* 58, no. 3 (Mar. 1943): 2–28.
73 For example, Koyama's article "Shinchitujō no dogisei" was also included along with Komaki's in *Seikaikan no tatakai*.
74 Mizuuchi Toshio, "Tsushō 'yoshidano kai' ni yoru chiseigaku kanren shiryō [Historical Materials on the Geopolitics of the 'Yoshino' Group]," *Kūkan, shakai, chirishisō* 6 (Osaka: Osaka siritu daigakkō, 2001): 59–112.

75 Shibata Yōichi, "Ajia taiheiyōsensoki no senryakukenkyū ni okeru chirigakushano yakuwari- sōgōchirikenkyūkai to rikukunsanbohonbu [The Role of Geographers in Strategic Research During the Asia-Pacific War – The General Geographical Study Group and the General Staff Office]," *Rekishichirigaku* 49, no. 5 (Dec. 2007): 3–5. According to Shibata's research, the "Yoshida Group" received financial support from two different sources. One is *Kōsenkai* (The Imperial War Group) that officers in the Imperial Army constructed and a private company, the Showa Trade Company, was another. Also see Shibata Yōichi, *Teikoku Nihon to chiseigaku: Ajia, Taiheiyō Sensōki ni okeru chiri gakusha no shisō to jissen* [Geopolitics of the Japanese Empire: Thoughts and Practice of Japanese Geographers in the Asia-Pacific War] (Osaka: Seibundo, 2016).

76 Through the financial aids provided by the Imperial Army, Komaki and his students were able to accumulate books on geography and geopolitics and their volumes outnumbered those of the university library. Shibata Yōichi, "Ajia taiheiyōsensoki no senryakukenkyuni okeru chirigakushano yakuwari- sōgōchirikenkyūkai to rikukunsanbohonbu," 6–7.

77 Komaki Saneshige, ed., *Daitōa chiseigaku shinron* [A New Theory of Geopolitics in Greater East Asia] (Kyoto: Hoshino Shoten, 1943). In this volume, except for Komaki's introductory article, each contributor wrote an article on every region in East and Southeast Asia.

78 Shibata Yōichi, "Ajia taiheiyōsensoki no senryakukenkyū ni okeru chirigakusha no yakuwari- sōgōchirikenkyūkai to rikukunsanbohonbu," 7–11.

79 Ohashi Ryosuku, *Kyōto gakuha to Nihon Kaigun: shinshiryō oshima memo" o megutte* [The Kyoto School of Philosophy and the Japanese Navy: On the Oshima Memo Materials] (Tokyo: PHP Kenkyūjo, 2001). However, Ohashi interprets Kyoto philosophers' secret meetings with the navy as an "anti-governmental" collaboration instead of their unconditional support of Japan's total war. About a critical reevaluation of the relationship between the Kyoto School of Philosophy and the Imperial Navy, see Takeshi Kimoto, "Antinomies of Total War," *Positions: East Asian Cultural Critiques* 17, no. 1 (2008): 97–125.

80 Ōtake Tetsuya, "Heiyōchiri chōsa kenkyūkai ni tsuite," in *Kūkan, shakai, chirishisō* 4: *gaisetsuhen* [On the Research Institute of the Pacific Ocean] (Osaka: Osaka Siritu Daigakko, 1999), 14.

81 Takagi Akihiko, "An Essay on Geopolitical Writings in the Magazine *Kaizō* during the Asia-Pacific War in Japan," in *Critical and Radical Geographies of the Social, the Spatial and the Political*, ed. Toshio Mizuuchi (Osaka: Osaka City University Department of Geography Urban Research Plaza, 2006), 51–58.

82 Ibid., 54. Komaki's three articles appeared in 1942, 1943 and 1944.

83 It is noteworthy that officers from both the Navy and the Army participated in the JAG. Vice Admiral Ueda Yoshiki of the Imperial Army became president of the association, but a few high-ranking officers from the Navy also joined it. More importantly, the JAG clearly stipulated in the "Mission of the Japanese Association of Geopolitics" that it should recognize the seas as the basis for the development of the Japanese nation, a position which bears a striking resemblance to Komaki's emphasis on the Pacific Ocean. See "Sengei," *Chiseigaku* 1, no. 1 (Jan. 1941).

84 Sōda Kiichirō, *Keizai tetsugaku no sho mondai* [Key Issues in Economic Philosophy] (Tokyo: Iwanami Shoten, 1917).

85 Ezawa Jōji, "Doitsuteki ideorogitoshite kantō [Immanuel Kant as a German Ideologue]," *Shisō* 150 (Nov. 1934): 679.

86 Ezawa Jōji, "Keimōteki sensei [Enlightening Dictatorship]," *Shisō* 138 (Nov. 1933): 606–607.

87 Ibid., 608.

88 Ezawa Jōji, *Keizaichirigaku* [Economic Geography] (Tokyo: Kawade Shobo, 1935), 1–12.

89 Ezawa Jōji, "Kaidai [Introduction]," in *Kōgyōbunburon* [Theories of Industrial Location], ed. Alfred Weber, trans. Ezawa Jōji (Tokyo: Kaizōsha, 1938), 3. Ezawa published another book introducing Alfred Weber's economic geography in the same year. Ezawa Jōji, *Keizai chirigaku no kiso riron: shizen, gijutsu, keizai* [The Basic Theories of Economic Geography] (Tokyo: Nankōsha, 1938).

90 Ezawa Jōji, "Chiseigakujono kihonmondai [Basic Problems in Geopolitics]," *Kagaku pen* 6, no. 9 (Sep. 1941), also in Ezawa Jōji, *Chiseigaku kenkyū* [A Study on Geopolitics] (Tokyo: Nihonhyōronsha, 1942), 31.

91 Ezawa Jōji, *Chiseigaku kenkyū*, 32.

92 Ibid., 34.

93 Rōyama Masamichi, "Daitōa kyōeiken no chiseigakugteki kosatsu [A Geopolitical Approach to the Greater East Asian Co-Prosperity Sphere]," in *Tōa to sekai: shin chitsujō e no ronsaku* (Tokyo: Kaizōsha, 1941), 366–367.

94 Ibid., 363.

95 Henri Lefebvre, *The Production of Space*, trans. Donald Nicholson Smith (Oxford: Blackwell Publishers, 1991), 33.

96 Ezawa Jōji, *Kokudo keikaku no kisoriron* [The Basic Theories of National Land Planning] (Tokyo: Nihonhyōronsha, 1941), 6–10.

97 Ibid., 8.

98 Ibid., 6.

99 Ibid., 4.

100 Ibid., 10.

101 Ibid., 149.

102 Ibid., 146.

103 Ezawa Jōji, *Nanpō seijiron* [On Politics in the Southern Seas] (Tokyo: Chikura Shobo, 1943), 154–155.

104 Ezawa Jōji, "Kyōeiken to kokudo keikaku [The Co-Prosperity Sphere and National Land Planning]," *Chiseigaku* 2, no. 3 (Mar. 1941): 34.

105 Ezawa Jōji, "Shinjitujō no rinen toshiteno ōutarki [Autarky as a New Order Theory]," in *Kokudo to minzoku* (Tokyo: Meguro Shoten, 1945), 209–210.

106 Ibid.

107 Yanaihara was deprived of his professorship at Tokyo Imperial University for his provocative article "Kokka no rishō [The Ideals of the State]," criticizing Japan's invasion of China, in *Chūō kōron* in 1937.

108 Yanaihara Tadao, "Nanpō rōdō seisaku no kichō [The Basis of Labor Policy in the Southern Seas]," *Shakai seisaku jihō* 260 (May 1942): 148–161.

109 Rōyama Masamichi, "Tōa kyōdōtai no riron [Theories of the East Asian Community]," *Kaizō* 20, no. 11 (Nov. 1938): 21. Unlike Ezawa's geopolitics and modernization theory, several works are available for Rōyama's idea of modernization in his theory of an East Asian Cooperative Community. See J. Victor Koschmann, "Constructing Destiny: Royama Masamichi and Asian Regionalism in Wartime Japan," in *Pan-Asianism in Modern Japanese History: Colonialism, Regionalism and Borders*, eds. Sven Saaler and J. Victor Koschmann (London: Routledge, 2007), 185–199; Han Jung Sun, "Rationalizing the Orient: The East Asia Cooperative Community in Prewar Japan," *Monumenta Nipponnica* 60, no. 4 (Winter 2005): 481–513; Sakai Tetsuya, "Tōa kyōdōtairon kara 'kindairaron' e: rōyama masamichi ni okeru chiiki-kaihatsu nashonarizumuron no iso [From the East Asian Community to the Theory of Modernization]," in *Nihon gaikō ni okeru ajia shugi nenpō seijigaku 1998*, ed. Nihon seiji gakkai (Tokyo: Iwanami Shoten, 1999), 109–129.

110 In Jeong-Sik, "Chosun nongop kwa sikryang kwa kuk'tokyehoek [Agriculture, Food and National Land Planning in Colonial Korea]," *Samcholl'i* 13, no. 6 (June 1941): 113.

111 Ezawa Jōji, *Kokudo keikaku no kisoriron*, 13–28.

112 Ibid., 45.

113 Ezawa Jōji, *Nanpō seijiron*, 192.

Bibliography

Asada, Sadao. "From Washington to London: The Imperial Japanese Navy and the Politics of Naval Limitation, 1921–1930." In *The Washington Conference 1921–1922: Naval Rivalry, East Asian Stability and the Road to Pearl Harbor*, edited by Erik Goldstein and John Maurer, 147–191. Ilford: Frank Cass, 1994.

Christopher, W. A. "Between Pan-Asianism and Nationalism: Mitsukawa Kametarō and his Campaign to Reform Japan and Liberate Asia." In *Pan-Asianism in Modern Japanese History,* edited by Sven Saaler and J. Victor Koschmann, 85–100. London: Routledge, 2006.

Du Bois, W.E.B. "A Chronicle of Race Relations." *Phylon* 3, no. 4 (1942): 417–434.

Ezawa, Jōji. *Chiseigaku kenkyū* [A Study on Geopolitics]. Tokyo: Nihonhyōronsha, 1942.

———. "Doitsuteki ideorogitoshite kantō [Immanuel Kant as a German Ideologue]." *Shisō* 150 (Nov. 1934): 65–77.

———. "Keimōteki sensei [Enlightening Dictatorship]." *Shisō* 138 (Nov. 1933): 62–76.

———. *Keizai chirigaku no kiso riron: shizen, gijutsu, keizai* [The Basic Theories of Economic Geography]. Tokyo: Nankōsha, 1938.

———. *Keizaichirigaku* [Economic Geography]. Tokyo: Kawade Shobo, 1935.

———. *Kōgyōbunburon* [Theories of Industrial Location]. Tokyo: Kaizōsha, 1938.

———. *Kokudo keikaku no kisoriron* [The Basic Theories of National Land Planning]. Tokyo: Nihonhyōronsha, 1941.

———. "Kyōeiken to kokudo keikaku [The Co-Prosperity Sphere and National Land Planning]." *Chiseigaku* 2, no. 3 (Mar. 1941): 30–42.

———. *Nanpō seijiron* [On Politics in the Southern Seas]. Tokyo: Chikura Shobo, 1943.

———. "Shinjitujō no rinen toshiteno ōutarki [Autarky as a New Order Theory]." *Kokudo to minzoku.* Tokyo: Meguro Shoten, 1945.

Fukuma, Yoshiki. "'Daitōa' kūkan no seisan- Chiseigakune okeru kūkan ninshiki no doutaiseto nashonarizumu no zaikochiku (1) [Producing Greater Asian Space]." *Seijikeizaishigaku* 441 (May 2005): 1–23.

———. "'Daitōa' kūkan no seisan- Chiseigakune okeru kūkan ninshiki no doutaiseto nashonarizumu no zaikochiku (2) [Producing Greater Asian Space]." *Seijikeizaishigaku* 442 (June 2005): 15–31.

Gordon, Andrew. *A Modern History of Japan: From Tokugawa Times to the Present.* New York: Oxford University Press, 2003.

Han, Jung Sun. "Rationalizing the Orient: The East Asia Cooperative Community in Prewar Japan." *Monumenta Nipponnica* 60, no. 4 (Winter 2005): 481–513.

Haushofer, Karl, Erich Obst, Hermann Lautensach and Otto Maull. *Bausteine zur Geopolitik, 1. Ueber die historische Entwicklung des Begriffs Geopolitik.* Berlin-Grunewald: Kurt Vowinckel, 1928. Trans. Hajime, Tamaki. *Chiseijigaku no kiso riron* [Basic Theories of Geopolitics]. Tokyo: Kagakushugikōgyōsha, 1941.

———. *Chiseijigaku nyūmon* [An Introduction to Geopolitics]. Translated by Hikikata Teiichi and Tokumatsu Sakamoto. Tokyo: Ikuseisha, 1941.

———. *Dai Nihon; Betrachtungen über Gross-Japans Wehrkraft, Weltstellung und Zukunft.* Berlin: E. S. Mittler und Sohn, 1913. Trans. Rinichi, Wakai. *Dai Nihon* [The Greater Japan]. Tokyo: Rakuyō Shōin, 1942.

———. *Gendai Eikokuron* [A Study on Modern Britain]. Tokyo: Tōkō Shoin, 1940.

———. *Geopolitik des Pazifischen Ozeans* [Geopolitics of the Pacific Ocean]. Trans. Nihon Seinen Gaikō Kyōkai. *Taiheiyō Chiseijigaku: Chiri rekishi sōgō kankei no kenkyū* [Geopolitics of the Pacific Ocean: A Study on the General Relations between Geography and History]. Tokyo: Nihon Seinen Gaikō Kyōkai, 1940, 2 vols; trans. Taiheiyō, Kyōkai. [Geopolitics of the Pacific Ocean]. Tokyo: Iwanami Shoten, 1942.

———. *Nihon no kokka kensetsu* [Japan's Nation Building]. Translated by Shinji Umezawa. Tokyo: Ryūginsha, 1943.

———. *Semeiken to Sekaikan* [Living Space and Worldview]. Translated by Wakai Rin'ichi. Tokyo: Hakubunkan, 1942.

———. *Tairiku seiji to kaiyō seiji* [Land Politics and Ocean Politics]. Translated by Yoshimichi Kuboi. Tokyo: Taihosha, 1943.

Hisatake, Tetsuya. "Hawaiha chisana manshukoku- nihonchiseigakuno kaihō [Hawaii Is a Small Manchukuo – The Liberation of Japanese Geopolitics]." *Gendaishisō* 27, no. 13 (Dec. 1999): 196–203.

Iimoto, Nobuyuki. "Iwayuru chiseigaku no gainen [The Concept of Geopolitics]." *Chirigaku hyōron* 4, no. 1 (Jan. 1928): 76–99.

———. "Jinshutōsei no jijitu to chiseigakuteki kōsatu [The Reality of Racial Control and Its Geopolitical Approach] (1)." *Chirigaku hyōron* 1, no. 9 (Sep. 1925): 16–37.

———. "Jinshutōsei no jijitu to chiseigakuteki kōsatu" [The Reality of Racial Control and Its Geopolitical Approach] (2)." *Chirigaku hyōron* 1, no. 10 (Oct. 1925): 955–967.

———. "Jinshutōsei no jijitu to chiseigakuteki kōsatu [The Reality of Racial Control and Its Geopolitical Approach] (3)." *Chirigaku hyōron* 2, no. 1 (Jan. 1926): 47–60.

Iizuka, Kōji. "Geopolitikuno kihontekiseigaku (1) [The Fundamental Nature of Geopolitics]." *Keizaigaku Ronshū* 12, no. 8 (Aug. 1942): 56–84.

In, Jeong Sik. "Chosun nongop kwa sikryang kwa kuk'tokyehoek [Agriculture, Food and National Land Planning in Colonial Korea]." *Samcholl'i* 1 & 3, no. 6 (June 1941): 112–120.

Ishida, Ryūjirō. "Meiji-taishōkino nihon no chirigakkainoshisōtekidōkō [The Intellectual Trend of Japanese Geographers during the Meiji and Taisho Periods]." *Chirigaku hyōron* 44, no. 8 (Aug. 1971): 532–551.

Kato, Tetsurō. "Personal Contacts in Japanese-German Cultural Relations during the 1920s and Early 1930s." In *Japanese-German Relations, 1895–1945 War and Diplomacy*, edited by Christian Spang and Rolf Harald Wippich, 119–138. London: Routledge, 2006.

Komaki, Saneshige, ed. *Chiseigakujōyori mitaru daitōa* [A Greater Asia from a Geopolitical Perspective]. Tokyo: Nihon hōsō shuppansha, 1939.

———. "Dai azia no hukō ishin sengen [A Declaration of the Restoration of the Greater Asia]." *Gendai* 23, no. 3 (Mar. 1942): 5–22.

———. "Dai tōa no rinen [The Ideals of a Greater East Asia]." In *Seikaikan no tatakai* [A War on Worldviews], edited by Dainihon genron hōkoku kyōkai, 204–233. Tokyo: Dōmei Tushinsha, 1944.

———. *Daitōa chiseigaku shinron* [A New Theory of Geopolitics in Greater East Asia]. Kyoto: Hoshino Shoten, 1943.

———. "Karu haushofar ron [On Karl Haushofer]." *Kokumin hyoron* 15, no. 4 (1941).

———. *Minzoku chiri* [Ethnic Geography]. Tokyo: Chijinshōkan, 1937.

———. *Nihon chiseigaku oboegaku* [A Statement of Japanese Geopolitics]. Osaka: Akita, 1944.

———. *Nihonchiseigaku sengen* [A Declaration of Japanese Geopolitics]. Tokyo: Hakuyōsha, 1942.

Koschmann, J. Victor. "Constructing Destiny: Rōyama Masamichi and Asian Regionalism in Wartime Japan." In *Pan-Asianism in Modern Japanese History: Colonialism, Regionalism and Borders*, edited by Sven Saaler and J. Victor Koschmann, 185–199. London: Routledge, 2007.

Koyama, Iwao. "Sōryōkusen to shisōsen [Total War and Thought War]." *Chuōkōron* 58, no. 3 (Mar. 1943): 2–28.

Kyoto daigaku chirigaku kyōshitsu. *Chirigaku kyoto no hyakunen* [The 100-Year History of Geography at Kyoto University]. Kyoto: Nakanishiya Shuppan, 2008.

Kyoto daigaku hyakunenshi henshū iinkai, ed. *Kyoto daigaku hyakunenshi bukyōkushi hen* [The Hundred-Year History of Kyoto University: Departments and Bureaus]. Kyoto-Shi: Kyoto daigaku kōenhai, 1997.

Lefebvre, Henri. *The Production of Space*. Translated by Donald Nicholson Smith. Oxford: Blackwell Publishers, 1991.

Mackinder, Halford. *Democratic Ideals and Reality: A Study in the Politics of Reconstruction*. London: Constable and Company, 1919.

Mahan, Alfred. *The Problem of Asia and Its Effect on International Polices*. Boston: Little, Brown and Company, 1900.

Mayhew, Robert. "Halford Mackinder's 'New' Political Geography and the Geographical Tradition." *Political Geography* 19 (2000): 771–791.

Mizuno, Hiromi, Aaron Moore and John DiMoia, eds. *Engineering Asia: Technology, Colonial Development and the Cold War*. London: Bloomsbury, 2018.

Mizuuchi, Toshio. "Tsusho 'Yoshidano kai' ni yoru chiseigaku kanren shiryō [Historical Materials on the Geopolitics of the 'Yoshino' Group]." In *Kūkan, shakai, chirishisō* 6, 59–112. Osaka: Osaka Siritu Daigakko, 2001.

Moore, Aaron. *Constructing East Asia: Technology, Ideology and Empire in Japan's Wartime Era, 1931–1945*. Stanford: Stanford University Press, 2013.

Murayama, Michiō. *Daitōa kenseturon* [On Constructing a Greater East Asia]. Tokyo: Shōkō Gyōseisha, 1943.

Naoki, Sakai. "Ethnicity and Species: On the Philosophy of the Multi-Ethnic State in Japanese Imperialism." *Radical Philosophy* 95 (May/June 1999): 33–45.

———. "Subject and Substratum: On Japanese Imperial Nationalism." *Cultural Studies* 14, no. 3 (2000): 463–530.

———. *Translation and Subjectivity: On "Japan" and Cultural Nationalism*. Minneapolis: University of Minnesota Press, 1997.

Nihon chiri gakkai, ed. *Nihon chiri gakkai gojū Nenshi* [The 50-Year History of the Japanese Association for Geography]. Tokyo: Kōkon Shoin, 1975.

Ohashi, Ryosuku. *Kyōto gakuha to Nihon Kaigun: shinshiryō oshima memo" o megutte* [The Kyoto School of Philosophy and the Japanese Navy: On the Oshima Memo Materials]. Tokyo: PHP Kenkyūjo, 2001.

Ōtake, Tetsuya. "Heiyōchiri chōsa kenkyūkai ni tsuite [On the Research Institute of the Pacific Ocean]." *Kūkan, shakai, chirishisō* 4: *gaisetsuhen*, 5–19. Osaka: Osaka Siritu Daigakko, 1999.

Polelle, Mark. *Raising Cartographic Consciousness: The Social and Foreign Policy Vision of Geopolitics in the Twentieth Century*. Lanham, MD: Lexington Books, 1999.

Ratzel, Friedrich. *Politische Geographie*. München und Leipzig: R. Oldenbourg, 1897.

Rōyama, Masamichi. "Daitōa kyōeiken no chiseigakugteki kosatsu [A Geopolitical Approach to the Greater East Asian Co-Prosperity Sphere]." In *Tōa to sekai: shin chitsujō e no ronsaku*, 360–381. Tokyo: Kaizōsha, 1941.

———. "Tōa kyōdōtai no riron [Theories of the East Asian Community]." *Kaizō* 20, no. 11 (Nov. 1938): 6–27.

Sakai, Tetsuya. "Tōa kyōdōtairon kara 'kindairaron' e: rōyama masamichi ni okeru chiiki-kaihatsu nashonarizumuron no iso [From the East Asian Community to the Theory of

Modernization]." In *Nihon gaikō ni okeru ajia shugi nenpō seijigaku 1998*, edited by Nihon seiji gakkai, 109–129. Tokyo: Iwanami Shoten, 1999.

Satō, Hiroshi and Ezawa Jōji. "Chiseigakuteki kite." In *Shin Doitsu kokka taikei; dai 3 seiji hen* [The National Structure of a New Germany: Politics], edited by Futara Yoshinori, 335–417. Tokyo: Nihonhyōronsha, 1939.

Sato, Sōichirō. *Haushofarno taiheiyō chiseigaku kaisetu* [An Introduction to Karl Haushofer's *Geopolitics of the Pacific Ocean*]. Tokyo: Taiheiyō Gakkai Rokkoshuppanbu, 1944.

Shibata Yōichi. "Ajia taiheiyōsensoki no senryakukenkyū ni okeru chirigakushano yakuwari- sōgōchirikenkyūkai to rikukunsanbohonbu [The Role of Geographers in Strategic Research During the Asia-Pacific War – The General Geographical Study Group and the General Staff Office]." *Rekishichirigaku* 49, no. 5 (Dec. 2007): 1–31.

———. *Teikoku nihon no chiseigaku: Ajia, Taiheiyō Sensōki ni okeru chiri gakusha no shisō to jissen* [Geopolitics of the Japanese Empire: Thoughts and Practice of Japanese Geographers in the Asia-Pacific War]. Osaka: Seibundō, 2016.

Sōda, Kiichirō. *Keizai tetsugaku no sho mondai*. Tokyo: Iwanami Shoten, 1917.

Spang, Christian. "Karu haushofer to nihonno chiseigaku-daiichiji seikaitaisengono nichidokukankei no nakade [Karl Haushofer and Japanese Geopolitics: German-Japanese Relations after the Great War]." Trans. Shokai, Ishi. *Kūkan, shakai, chirishisō* 6 (2001): 2–21.

Takagi, Akihiko. "An Essay on Geopolitical Writings in the Magazine *Kaizō* during the Asia-Pacific War in Japan." In *Critical and Radical Geographies of the Social, the Spatial and the Political*, edited by Toshio Mizuuchi, 51–58. Osaka: Osaka City University Department of Geography Urban Research Plaza, 2006.

Takeshi, Kimoto. "Antinomies of Total War." *Positions: East Asian Cultural Critiques* 17, no. 1 (2008): 97–125.

Takeuchi, Keiichi. "Geopolitikuno hukatuto seijichirigakuno atarashii tenkai- geopolitikuhutatabi kangae [The Revival of Geopolitics and the New Trends in Political Geography]." *Hitotsubashironsō* 96, no. 5 (1986): 523–546.

———. "The Japanese Imperial Tradition, Western Imperialism and Modern Japanese Geography." In *Geography and Empire*, edited by Anne Godlewska and Neil Smith, 188–206. Oxford: Blackwell Publishers, 1994.

Tokyo daigaku hyakunenshi henshu iinkai, ed. *Tokyo daigaku hyakunenshi* 5 [The 100-Year History of the University of Tokyo]. Tokyo: Tokyo Daigaku Shuppankai, 1984.

Watsuji, Tetsurō. *Fūdo: ningenteki kosatsu* [Climate: A Humanistic Approach]. Tokyo: Iwanami Shōten, 1935.

Weber, Alfred. *Kōgyōbunburon*. Translated by Ezawa Jōji. Tokyo: Kaizōsha, 1938.

Yamamurō, Shinichi. "Kokuminteikoku, nihon no keisei to kūkanchi [The Construction of the Japanese Empire and Knowledge on Space]." In *Teikoku nihon no gakuchi* 8 [The Academy and Knowledge of Imperial Japan], edited by Yamamurō Shinichi and Sakai Tetsuya, 21–66. Tokyo: Iwanami Shōten, 2006.

Yanaihara, Tadao. "Nanpō rōdō seisaku no kichō [The Basis of Labor Policy in the Southern Seas]." *Shakai seisaku jihō* 260 (May 1942): 148–161.

Yonekura, Jirō. *Tōa chiseigaku josetsu* [An Introduction to East Asian Geopolitics]. Tokyo: Seikatsusha, 1941.

Part II
The Korea question

4 Moritani Katsumi and reconstructing colonial Korea

Between theory and practice: locating colonial Korea

In the 1930s and early 1940s, Japanese social scientists were largely focused on contriving theoretical frameworks in order to rationalize Japan's new empire building. One may then wonder how these newly developed ideas of governance and organization addressed practical issues in the colony, and more importantly, how colonial intellectuals responded to this imperial knowledge. Arguably, colonial Korea became a laboratory of imperial knowledge – knowledge created in the name of what this book conceptualizes as a "colonial social science."

To be sure, it was not only during the wartime period that colonial Korea received attention from Japanese intellectuals who were involved in a variety of imperial institutions and think-tanks. From the moment Japan annexed Korea in 1910, a large number of Japanese intellectuals and bureaucrats came to colonial Korea for professional opportunity. Many Japanese bureaucrats spent a substantial amount of time in colonial Korea in order to accumulate "field experience," and this enabled them to return to Japan with the guarantee of a more promising future. For instance, the Governor-General in colonial Korea was considered a position one must take to be promoted as prime minister in Japan proper. Not surprisingly, the ivory tower of academia was no different from the professional political and bureaucratic arenas. Kyungsung Imperial University (present-day Seoul National University) was Japan's 6th Imperial University, established in 1924 several years after the March 1st Independence Movement. In quick succession as many as 70 professors were all recruited from Japan proper, and many of them would soon return to imperial and private universities in Japan.[1]

The establishment of Kyungsung Imperial University changed the topography of the entire academic world in colonial Korea. First and foremost, imperial Japan made it clear that it aimed to instill in colonial youths the legitimacy of Japanese colonialism, and also produce pro-Japanese human resources that would be utilized for colonial governance. To this end, it was vital to establish a curriculum that was optimized for the production and reproduction of colonial knowledge in the name of objective and empirical science. In so doing, Imperial Japan intended to create a form of cultural and intellectual power that would regulate the mindset of elite Koreans.[2] There is no doubt that Kyungsung Imperial University soon faced challenges by Korean intellectuals who attempted to present alternative anti-colonial and nationalistic narratives in the 1920s and 1930s.[3] Under these circumstances, Kyungsung Imperial University remained a tensional space in the late 1920s and 1930s in guiding the direction of Japanese colonial governance, and many of its faculty members, first trained in imperial universities in Japan proper, were involved in producing a body of practical knowledge about colonial Korea.

Perhaps the academic trajectories of Moritani Katsumi provide a valuable example through which to investigate the question of how colonial knowledge was produced in Japan proper and was applied to colonial Korea as Japan aimed to create a multi-ethnic empire in the 1930s and early 1940s. Immediately after graduating from Tokyo Imperial University, Moritani was appointed as a teaching associate in charge of the Social Policy Lectures at Kyungsung Imperial University in 1927. In April 1929, he was promoted to an assistant professor, but this was to be the last change in his status during his 19-year tenure in colonial Korea. Trained in a Marxist approach to social science under the instruction of Hirano Yoshitarō, an ideological leader of prewar Japanese Marxism, Moritani maintained his teacher's radical perspective. His adherence to Marxism partly explains his peculiar position within Kyungsung Imperial University, and he even received special attention from the colonial police for his radical thinking and possible ties with anti-colonial activists in Korea.[4] Due to his irregular personal history, Moritani remains a largely unearthed figure among students of intellectual history in East Asia. However, he was a prolific writer and an influential Marxist social scientist. And in the mid-1930s and early 1940s, Moritani was deeply engaged with major academic debates over the role of a Marxist social science in both Japan and colonial Korea. He was particularly interested in the debates over the Asiatic Mode of Production and the discussion of an "Asiatic society," the latter triggered by the introduction of German socio-economic historian Karl Wittfogel's provocative writings on China. Moritani emerged as one of the most influential Japanese intellectuals residing in colonial Korea during the wartime period through his writings on an East Asian empire, and his actual commitment to policy-making processes. His perspectives resonated with and at the same time offered a unique critique of Japan's empire-building project, and he utilized colonial Korea as a platform to test the feasibility of emergent ideas toward the construction of the new East Asian empire. He was acutely aware that his encounter with wartime colonial Korea should not be separated from the rationalist notion of the "East Asian Community," first theorized by social scientists such as such as Rōyama Masamichi, Kada Tetsuji and Shinmei Masamichi.

Since he was deeply involved in the production of colonial knowledge and putting it into practice, Moritani centered his inquiries on the question of how the seemingly innovative logic of a multi-ethnic empire could be realized in the colony. For this reason, his rare position as a Japanese social scientist trained in radical Marxist theory and an in-depth understanding of the colonial situation provides us with an opportunity to examine how radical social science was converted into an imperialist regional idea in rivalry with intrinsic and ultranationalist Pan-Asian thought. Just like Rōyama and Kada advocated a developmentalist prescription to colonial problems, Moritani incessantly argued that economic development was the key to convincing colonial subjects to commit to Japan's empire-building project. This developmental perspective was echoed by Korean social scientists who hoped to utilize the momentum of the wartime period to promote the economic and political status of Korea. For instance, Moritani had a significant impact on the writing of In Jeong Sik, a prominent Korean intellectual who positively identified the notion of the East Asian Community and considered economic development as crucial to the restructuring of Korea. Moritani's professional trajectory exemplifies precisely how imperial knowledge generated by social scientists in Japan proper was accepted, criticized and modified, through the practice of social science in the colony itself, and the intellectual gap between the metropole and colony was bridged by the emergence of colonial social science. In the pages that follow, this chapter will critically examine how Moritani became engaged with the rebuilding of colonial Korea as an epitome of Japan's Pan-Asian empire project, coping with several intellectual challenges among his fellow Japanese Marxist social scientists as well as Korean intellectuals.

Colonial Korea and Moritani's early internationalist thinking

The fact that Moritani was in this colonial setting carrying a Marxist perspective played an important role in shaping his early scholarship. What discerned him from other Japanese Marxist social scientists at the time was his propensity to think beyond the dominant monolithic ideological milieu of the Japanese state. Most Japanese Marxists in Japan proper were preoccupied with exploring and explaining only *Japan*'s economic development based on Marx's idea of historical materialism, and unquestionably their common goal was to conceptually liberate Japan from the specter of underdevelopment and stagnation ingrained in the Western Marxist notion of Asia, exemplified by the Asiatic Mode of Production debate. Instead, Moritani's Marxist writing looked beyond the framework of the nation-state. He continued to maintain a regional perspective and refigured his social scientific inquiries in the global context of what he called "oriental studies," a purview that certainly included China and Korea. The following statement from his 1937 book, a collection of essays on the Asiatic Mode of Production in the mid-1930s, clearly reveals his perception of Asia as a collective academic unit.

> In a nutshell, the Asiatic mode of production is not a social relation that only exists in the orient, but it is a world-historical category. Nor does it mean a dominant mode of production that penetrates the entire oriental society. Therefore, students of oriental society, needless to say, should not metaphysically fix the *contemporary* oriental society through the Asiatic mode of production but conduct detailed research on the Orient through this world-historical category.
>
> (emphasis added)[5]

The "international" mindset of Moritani's Marxist thinking and its application to Asian matters were both visible within his early writing in colonial Korea. In

1929, he contributed a 40-page article titled "A Thought About the Problem of Nation in Social Democracy" to *A Study of the Korean Economy*, a compilation of articles by Kyungsung Imperial University professors and students. In this article, Moritani revisited the famous debate on nation (*minzoku*) by two prominent Western theoreticians, Otto Bauer (1881–1938) and Karl Kautsky (1854–1938). Moritani first investigated the validity of Kautsky's notion of the community of national language. Arguing that nationality is constituted by social relations, Kautsky asserted that "nation (*minzoku*) came into being with the development of the capitalist commodity economy."[6] Kautsky's definition of nation, reminiscent of Benedict Anderson's notion of "imagined community," indicates that he clearly differentiated the concept of race from that of the modern nation. Otto Bauer also reconfirmed that modern capitalism gave rise to the nation as a social construct and this indicates that Moritani was aware of the latest discussions surrounding the idea of minzoku while a number of intellectuals in Japan proper were still preoccupied with the idea of nation as an institutional formation based on biological race. However, Moritani was not satisfied with the simple idea of nation (minzoku) as a product only of capitalist relations, existing outside of any racial determination. Since the national context exerted a much more profound influence on individuals' patterns of behavior and belief system than any other ideological form or force, Moritani wondered how Marxism might explain why the idea of nation binds people so powerfully. Here, he found an important disagreement between Bauer and Kautsky on national language and culture. Kautsky stressed that a certain national group would not exist without having an independent national language. For him, the material condition of nation is a language. In response, Bauer contended that national language alone was insufficient to form a modern nation as various groups in premodern times spoke the same language and different national groups occasionally shared one language.[7] Instead, Bauer stressed that national character (*minzokuteki seikaku*) distinguished one nation from another, and cultural commonality as a major national character played a decisive role in determining one's belongingness to a certain national group.[8]

To be sure, the Kautsky-Bauer debate did not answer the many challenging questions surrounding the concept of nation. However, it played an important role in extending the temporality and spatiality of Moritani's scholarship beyond a nation-state framework. Through the article, Moritani showed a keen interest in the term "community of destiny," used in the discussion of nation by Bauer and Kautsky. Its literal meaning referred to a belief system that people in a given "national" group often share the notion of a common future bound together. However, Moritani found compelling Bauer's argument that the notion of the "community of destiny" had been conceived of as a "community of blood (*blutsgemeinschaft*)."[9] Based on these observations, Bauer went on to argue that such a communal national consciousness served to disguise the class struggle and economic imbalance in real politics, as if all members in a nation-state belonged to an even homogeneous national community. Bauer wrote "the workers do not see the positive aspect of the nation-state – they do not perceive it as the *natural state*, as the external organization of the power of an internal community,"[10] and he in response theorized internationalism led by proletarian workers. A few years later, Moritani revisited the concept of the "community of destiny" in light of his own concerns. Specifically, he articulated, like Bauer did at the turn of the twentieth century, his own vision of internationalism based on the notion of the East Asian Community. And immediately after, Moritani went on to immerse himself in the raging waves of the Asiatic Mode of Production debate that swept away most Japanese Marxist social scientists in the mid-1930s.

First intellectual challenge: the Asiatic Mode of Production Debate

Beginning in the late 1920s, a group of the Soviet and Western Marxist social scientists launched a series of theoretical debates over the historical stages of economic development in Asia, often called the Asiatic Mode of Production (hereafter AMP) debate. This argument would continue to ideologically haunt Asian intellectuals, and radical intellectuals in particular, during the next decade. The debate was ignited by Marx's statement on Asian economic development in relation to Western imperialism. In contrast to his incessant attacks on the exploitative nature of the capitalist economy, Marx's writing on the role of the West in the Orient was far less critical. He basically viewed the colonization of India by the British empire as a historical necessity.[11]

Unquestionably, Marx's statement offers an endorsement of the inevitability of Western intervention in "underdeveloped" areas. From the perspective of Marxism as an ideology of political movements, such an evaluation can be paraphrased like this: If the backwardness and underdevelopment in Asiatic society was geographically determined, how could immanent forces for a revolution be theorized within Asia? Arguably it was impossible to conclude that Marx's concept of Asia was simply a single disappointing facet of his otherwise useful radical philosophy. Instead, Marx himself, in concert with other Western intellectuals such as Adam Smith, James Mill and Friedrich Hegel, offered up a closed perception of Asian society as stagnant and lacking any internal force of revolutionary development. From this, one can infer that for Asian Marxist social scientists, their problematization of the AMP was not a mere passing concern but a fundamental problem, one with the power to change the destiny of Marxist scholarship in the context of Asia.[12]

The unsophisticated ambiguity of the AMP concept within Western Marxist scholarship resulted in the idea being unable to address the fundamental questions facing the Asian economy in the 1930s. For instance, Marx himself never provided a concrete explanation of how and why Asian society, China and India in particular, had experienced a unique path to development in comparison to his neat five-stage developmental path that most European countries had apparently demonstrated. Although one can logically assume that Marx cast a skeptical eye on the organization of the Indian economy under British rule in his own time, his definition of the AMP was confined to a peculiar time period that preceded the ancient mode of production. As is well known, the ancient mode of production in

Marx's historical materialism is characterized by the early accumulation of capital and thereby the birth of a class that possesses surplus value. Therefore, the emergence of slavery in Marx's periodization of developmental stages epitomizes the classification of human society, which later gave rise to more evolved modes of production. In 1859, Marx published his epoch-making work, *Foundations of the Critiques of Political Economy* and in this book, he offered four different modes of production in historical development – Asiatic, ancient, feudal and modern bourgeois.[13] In *Foundations of the Critiques of Political Economy*, Marx presented three forms of production and possession that existed before capitalism – the Hebrew, Germanic and Asiatic forms. In contrast to the Germanic form, in which individuals possess property independent of community, Marx argued, "[T]he individual's property can in fact be realized solely through communal labor." Therefore, the (village) community in the Orient was conceptualized by Marx as the "presupposition of *property* in land and soil."[14] Marx's early writings on Asiatic society were based on his observation that private ownership did not emerge in the Orient. However, Marx did not articulate further on how this mode of production in the Orient should be positioned in his general theory of historical materialism. These ambiguities in Marx's own writings caused a number of different interpretations of Asiatic society by Western Marxist theoreticians.

Ludvig Mad'iar, for example, presented an in-depth analysis of Marx's discussion of Oriental society. According to him, the dismantlement of the blood-centered primitive community in ancient society must be followed by a slavery system, but this universal path did not take place in China.[15] Chinese society, Mad'iar maintained, instead sustained a unique state-centered land ownership system, which resulted in the absence of private land ownership necessary for the advent of the feudalistic mode of production.[16] In this way, he concluded that Chinese society represented four *unique* elements distinct from feudalism in Europe – (1) absence of private land ownership; (2) artificial irrigation and state-centered huge irrigation projects; (3) village communities; and (4) despotic politics.[17] Echoing Marx's writings on China and India, Mad'iar observed that these "Asiatic" characteristics are essentially related to unique geographical conditions in China.

How then did the broad conceptual current of the AMP first enunciated by Western social scientists change the intellectual topography of Marxist academic circles in Japan? Before moving to Moritani's discussion of the AMP, let us examine how Marxists in Japan proper responded to this Marxist theory of an Asian particularity that so clearly pointed to economic stagnation in Asia. Although the Comintern and Russian and German Marxists focused on Chinese agriculture in the AMP debate in the early 1930s, Japanese Marxists had developed their own interpretations of economic transformation in Japan and Asia and actively plunged into the AMP debate in the mid-1930s. Notably, academic discrepancies over notions of the historical economic path Japan had undergone gave rise to two distinctive Marxist schools in Japan – later called the *Koza-ha* (the Lecturer's faction) and the *Rono-ha* (the Peasants-Workers faction). The *Koza-ha* Marxists positioned the Japanese economy as semi-feudal in nature and observed that due to the remnants of the feudal modes of production, and peasant-landlord relations in particular, a bourgeois democratic revolution would be necessary instead of a direct socialist revolution.[18] On the contrary, the *Rono-ha* Marxists contended that the Japanese economy had already entered the stage of bourgeois democratic revolution and therefore the time had come to forge a direct socialist revolution. Although such stark disagreements over the nature of the Japanese economy were premised on their different perspectives of Japanese economic history, they were not free from the broad question of how Asia should be located in Marxist thinking. At stake were Western Marxist theoreticians' negative conceptions of historical development in Asia based on Asia's fundamental geo-cultural obstacles and Asian evolutionary stagnation preventing continental progression onto the universal pathway of communist revolution. They pointed out that peculiar features of Asian society – the despotic political system, self-sufficient village community and Confucianism – had been the major causes that held off the rise of a commercial economy and industrialization, both of which took place in Europe in the late-medieval and early modern periods. The depth and degree of the debates over the precise current developmental stage of the Japanese economy were intense. For Japanese Marxist social scientists, the issue was not so much a disagreement over the proper time to forge a socialist revolution as a more fundamental question of how, or where, to locate Japan within an ongoing discussion of Asian underdevelopment and stagnation.

The easiest solution to this conundrum was to completely differentiate Japan from the rest of Asia. In other words, some Japanese Marxists – mostly *Rono-ha* and some *Koza-ha* Marxists – concentrated their focus on conceptually detaching Japanese economic and social history from the previously mentioned negative features of a typical Marxist idea of Asian society. For *Rono-ha* Marxists, this standpoint served to endorse Japan's universal development as equivalent to that of the West. While such a perspective did not produce any internal inconsistencies, affirming the presence of stagnating semi-feudal remnants and at the same time distancing Japan from Asia necessitated large amounts of profound writing by *Koza-ha* Marxists. More importantly, limiting Asian underdevelopment and stagnation to the cases of China, India and Korea would result in a political dissociation and dislocation between *Koza-ha* Marxists and colonial Marxists. *Koza-ha* Marxists' acute criticism of Japanese imperialism and the emperor system had inspired colonial Marxists, especially Korean Marxists, who believed that the empire-colony power structure would be destroyed through Marxist revolution. If Japan had experienced a completely different path to modernization than its colonies, the shared radical dream between *Koza-ha* and colonial Marxists would be diffused. For this reason, the AMP debate was actually a litmus paper that would test the colonial consciousness of Japanese Marxist social scientists. In this respect, it was not surprising that those *Koza-ha* Marxists who extensively wrote on Japan's exceptionality within Asia were gradually subjugated by the perception of Japanese superiority over Asia and eventually endorsed Imperial-Way fascism during the wartime period in the name of *tenko* (conversion).

In a 1933 article, Aikawa Haruki (1909–1953) first problematized the particularistic interpretation of the Asiatic mode of production. Vehemently criticizing the stagnation-oriented analysis of Mad'iar and Vargas, he defined the Asiatic mode of production as "the first hostile form in the process of social production," which existed between primitive community and ancient slavery.[19] According to him, a hostile form in social production was indicative of the advent of class society. Therefore, for Aikawa, the ancient slavery system demonstrated that class relations first came into play in human relations, and slave-ownership took on the form of private property in Marx's periodization of historical development. However, Aikawa paid special attention to Marx's 1859 article "Foundations of the Critiques of Political Economy," in which Marx himself divided the modes of production before capitalism into three categories. Carrying this notion a step further, Aikawa attempted to theorize the Asiatic mode of production as an offshoot of slavery. At this stage, primitive communities were drastically deconstructed, but the conflict between slaves and slave owners still took on a communitarian form. To put it another way, Aikawa contended that slaves were a "commonly shared private property" in ancient Asiatic society, but the system could still be regarded as a form of ancient slavery.[20]

Aikawa held that this mode of production existed not only in Asia but in other parts of the world. This observation led him to fundamentally reject the so-called geographic determinism that was mentioned by Marx and had constantly reemerged in the writings of Mad'iar and Varga. He was discontented with Godes' theory as well. Although Godes rejected geographic determinism, Godes' theory was distinctive from that of Aikawa in that Godes understood the Asiatic mode of production as a "unique feudal system" that existed only in Asia. Since Aikawa viewed it as a "transitional" system between primitive community and ancient slavery, it was neither a unique nor a particularistic form of *feudalism*, nor a mode of production that existed only in Asia.

It is not difficult to see Aikawa's intention in his harsh critique of Godes' analysis of the Asiatic mode of production. By preventing it from being discussed in relation to feudalism, Aikawa aimed to minimize the impact of the notion of the Asiatic society in relation to contemporary Japanese society. He was clearly aware that any logical connection being established between the Asiatic mode of production and feudalism in Japan would eventually result in extending to contemporary Japanese society the same images of stagnation and underdevelopment that had been consistently applied to China and India. Therefore, it is highly understandable that Aikawa strongly emphasized the fact that Marx himself had acknowledged the presence of feudalism in Japan.[21]

To be sure, Aikawa's viewpoint represented one stream regarding the *Koza-ha* Marxist social scientists' discussion of the Asiatic mode of production. In contrast, Hayakawa Jirō (1906–1937), who introduced the perspectives of Godes and the Leningrad Conference regarding the Asia problem into Japanese academic circles, attempted to get through this challenge by defining the Asiatic mode of production as a unique "tribute system."[22] He acknowledged that, as Lenin articulated, there must be slavery between the primitive and feudal modes of production.[23] Central to this observation of Japanese history was the problem that the transitory period between these two modes of production was very complex. According to him, primitive communities began to collapse as external powers conquered them and this very process of conquering and being conquered represented the development of productivity and the emergence of class relations. However, this transition, he argued, did not necessarily result in the coming of a new mode of production. The development of a productive power had to create class relations and gradually dismantle primitive communities in theory. Hayakawa argued, however, that the leaders of the conquered primitive communities formed communal relations with the conqueror to sustain their power. This unique relationship between a new ruler and the conquered community was therefore referred to as the tribute system.[24] Based on these observations, Hayakawa concluded that Asian societies entered the stage of feudalism without experiencing slavery.

Hayakawa acknowledged that the tribute system would represent a form of stagnation in historical terms, but he was also adamant that it was "by no means an independent social relation."[25] Therefore, for him the lack of a slavery system did not imply that Asian society had not taken the universal path of economic development. Three months later, he reconfirmed this view in a new article, which contended that Asian society had experienced what he called a "slavery economic system," not the social constitution by slave-owners that appeared in the West.[26] Consequently, Hayakawa argued that Asia had simply "passed by" the slave-ownership stage and had taken normal development stages afterwards.

Although Aikawa and Hayakawa differed slightly in their understanding of the Asiatic mode of production, their notion of Asia and the orient is still telling in many ways. To begin with, both attempted to *historicize* the Asiatic mode of production. By staging it between the primitive community and the feudal system, they aimed to minimize its contemporaneity and claimed that it existed for a "short and transitory period of time" in *ancient* history. To be sure, this argument did not completely refute the fact that feudal remnants still functioned as a decisive factor in the mode of production in Japan. However, one can clearly recognize their intention to historicize the Asiatic mode of production and so preclude it from being used to deterministically prove that no social forces for a socialist revolution could be found in Japan.

But more importantly, the historicization of the Asiatic mode of production entailed addressing the more profound theoretical problems inherent in *Koza-ha* Marxist social scientists' perception of Asia. As Aikawa boldly argued, "[T]he term 'Asia' itself is inappropriate in discussing the Asiatic mode of production since this phenomenon existed in other parts of the world as well."[27] However, his attempt to remove the idea of Asia from the yoke of a deficient particularism paradoxically produced a highly abstract concept of Asia. First and foremost, Aikawa's and Hayakawa's strategy to overcome the limits of the Asiatic mode of production focused on demonstrating that *Japanese* society had already passed through the stage of Asiatic and thus stagnant primitive society. Both argued that the class struggle took place as primitive communities were dismantled. Such an approach was in no way illogical since Marx's concept of Asiatic society, if not precisely articulated so, was primarily concerned with the commune, that is, the idea of primitive forms of community in Asia.

Unlike these interpretations of the AMP produced in Japan proper, Moritani did not center his inquiry on rescuing *Japan* from the specter of Asian stagnation. Instead, he was more inclined to challenge the concept of Asian particularity inherent in the AMP that would eventually intensify the civilizational configuration of the world, in terms of the "advanced" West versus the East as "stagnated." Moritani's adherence to the concept of Asia played a significant role in forming his early perceptions of China and Korea, and more importantly, his active involvement in Asian discourses during the wartime period. Another point that deserves attention in Moritani's writings on the AMP was that he aimed to differentiate the term stagnation from the perception of underdevelopment. For him, the former designates the primordial and irreversible conditions of a certain mode of society which necessitate change through external forces, while the latter pertains to structural and institutional issues that cause a relatively low degree of development.

Based on these observations, Moritani revisited Marx's early writings and reasoned that Marx's theory of the AMP was based on factors of "stagnating despotism" in Asia and the "village community," both of which, Marx observed, prevented the emergence of a surplus-value-oriented economy.[28] It seemed that Moritani understood the gravity of Marx's choice of words like "stagnation." And he highlighted that these negative perceptions of Asia were not present in the ideas of Marx prior to the publication of *A Critique of Political Economy*.[29] Moritani then analyzed that Marx's critical approaches to Asia were theoretically influenced by Hegel's writings on Asia. However, Moritani also pointed out that the term Asiatic mode of production was described in Marx's work as one of the stages of economic development that preceded the ancient modes of production. For this reason, Moritani took a very cautious stance and argued that as long as the AMP was periodized as a developmental stage in Marx's thinking, it would be misleading to conclude that the existing perceptions of stagnant Asia directly stemmed from Marx's concept of Asia as *particular*. That is, Asia is from the beginning positioned outside the universal path to economic development.[30] Moritani's interpretation of Marx's work provided a certain break to the vicious circle of the AMP, as the previous notions of Asian particularity and Asian underdevelopment had reinforced each other. By reducing the historical temporality of the Asiatic mode of production to a limited time period, Moritani attempted to reverse the perception that the geographical and historical dimension of the Asiatic mode of production encompassed Asia in its entirety, as well as its history from antiquity to the present.[31]

In this way, Moritani intended to overcome the negative connotations attached to the Asiatic mode of production, and he considered that his interpretation of Marx's concept of the AMP was the most orthodox. Moritani's positioning within the AMP debate was not unrelated to his personal circumstance as a scholar teaching at a colonial institution. His concern was to defend Asia from two distinctive challenges: on the one hand, from the Western thinkers who argued that the Asiatic mode of production characterized Asia's inferiority to the West *throughout* history, and on the other, from Japanese Marxist social scientists who tended to avoid this question entirely. They instead argued that the Asiatic mode of production itself did not exist in Japan, but only in China, India and Korea, a position which logically endorsed Japan's colonization of the rest of Asia.

However, his ideas were not welcomed by his academic peers in Japan and Korea. Critiques of Moritani's understanding of the AMP centered on the absence of any analytical thinking in his writing. Whether or not they agreed with Moritani's method to overcome the challenge of the Asiatic mode of production debate, they observed that a more detailed scientific approach was necessary to confront the question of the Asiatic mode of production or Asiatic society. Since Moritani adhered strongly to the perspective that the Asia-related debate was concerned only with interpretive differences regarding the writings of Marx, he was disinterested in analyzing what actually constituted modes of production in each time period, in each part of Asia. In that respect, Moritani's critiques of the Asiatic mode of production lacked any convincing social scientific explanation as to what modes of production existed in each part of Asia and how they would be situated in the universal trajectory of historical materialism. Instead, Moritani maintained that the Asiatic mode of production was simply a description of a transitory village style community. This Marx and other Western Marxists had problematized as the epitome of Asian underdevelopment, but the actual mode of production had also existed in Europe in a similar way. For this reason, Moritani's essential intent, the need to defend the oriental from the shadow of inferiority, was not even recognized by Korean Marxist social scientists.

Lee Chung Won, a Korean *Koza-ha* Marxist, was one such critic. He attacked Moritani's understanding of Asian society for its obscure relevance to the current state of affairs.[32] According to Lee, Marx's notion of Asiatic society and the contemporary debate over the Asiatic mode of production were two different things and the gravity of Asia-related discussions lay in the latter since it directly targeted contemporary Asian society, while Marx predominantly discussed premodern times.[33] Lee contended that a mode of production must accompany visible systems and the power relations that determined the social-political structure of a certain society. In that respect, Lee maintained that there are as many as seven characteristics of the Asiatic mode of production which he defined as a "variant form of Western feudalism."[34] He went on to argue that according to these categories, a socio-economic relation called the Asiatic mode of production had existed in Korea from the unified Silla Kingdom period (AD 676-) onwards.[35] Ostensibly, Lee's analysis of the AMP and Korean society sounded more scientific and specifically critical than that of Moritani. Lee without hesitation affirmed the continuation of stagnating elements in Korean society. For him, the village community in traditional Korea was nothing but a feeder trough that provided the material basis for the despotic central government.[36] Lee might have believed that a Marxist intellectual must remain objective and acknowledge that his or her own country contained aspects of stagnation. Perhaps such objectivity gave him the confidence to evaluate that Moritani and other Japanese Marxist intellectuals had not nurtured any functional understanding of historical materialism.[37] However, Lee himself could not solve the issue of how it was that Chosun Korea (1392–1910) overcame these elements of the Asiatic mode of production and entered onto the stage of capitalism. In contrast to his acute analysis of premodern Asian and Chosun Korea, he simply concluded in passing that commercialization and industrialization had taken place in Chosen Korea, without providing any tangible historical evidence in support of why or how.[38]

In the meantime, the perception that the Japanese developmental path was commensurate with the universal Western one had gradually gained currency among Japanese Marxist social scientists. Unquestionably, the ultimate destination of this course was to completely remove any historical elements of stagnation in Japanese society in order to prove that Japan had successfully undertaken universal development, and should be considered in the same regard as the nations of Western Europe. This methodological turn had a profound impact on *Koza-ha* Marxists who had argued that a bourgeois democratic revolution, as opposed to a direct socialist revolution, was essential in Japan due to the pervasive social remnants of semi-feudal relations of production. A leading *Koza-ha* Marixst Hirano Yoshitarō's 1934 book, *The Constitution of Japanese Capitalist Society*, clearly demonstrated this tendency. In this work, Hirano, who taught Moritani Katsumi Marxist economics at Tokyo Imperial University, emphasized that Japanese peasants still existed under conditions of what he called "half-slavery." According to him, the oppressive Meiji government and landlords had emerged as new exploitative powers and as a result, most peasants in Japan cultivated land on a small scale and became "fractured and isolated."[39] However, Hirano's description of the Japanese peasantry as fractured and isolated shaped conspicuously different images of Japanese agriculture in relation to other Asian countries, and China in particular. This was because the dispersion and isolation of the Japanese peasants was portrayed by Hirano as the absence of the *communal* labor that was considered as an essential element in the Chinese village community. For this reason, the problems with Japanese agriculture could now be characterized not in terms of the static Asian village community but through those of an immature capitalist mode of production.[40] Therefore, Hirano's critiques of Japanese agriculture confirmed the general *Koza-ha* Marxists view that Japan had already passed through the stage of the village community, and that a proper capitalist mode of production would occur as soon as the "isolated" but "liberated-from-the-village-community" of contemporary peasantry had absorbed modern technology and nurtured a political awareness.

Second challenge: Karl Wittfogel and the specter of Asian particularity

As examined so far, the AMP debate was a "weak point" for Asian Marxist social scientists. It linked the concept of "stagnation" or "underdevelopment" to the epistemology of Asian particularity vis-à-vis Western universality. More importantly, the ways in which Japanese Marxist intellectuals responded to this intellectual challenge created a profound rift among Asian Marxists. The more the notion of "Japanese exceptionalism" (Japan as the only Asian country to experience the universal path to capitalist development) was popularly shared by Japanese Marxist social scientists, the dimmer their critiques of Japanese imperialism became. Just as Marx himself conceived of British imperial rule in India as inevitable, these Japanese Marxists gradually accepted Japan's colonial rule in Asia as a *fait accompli*. In this way, Japanese Marxist social scientists' inquiries as to the regressive nature of Asian society served to dilute any critical Marxist perspective that might support the liberation of Asia from both its feudal remnants and imperial oppression.

The notion of Japan as separate from the rest of Asia in terms of its developmental stages gave rise to another important conceptual tendency in Japanese Marxist circles of the mid-1930s. Universalizing Japan's past necessitated the historical particularization of other Asian countries. The primary object of this particularization was China, and the rise of this sinocentric concern among Japanese Marxist intellectuals was often termed "scientific" China studies. Hirano's 20-page-long introductory article of 1934 titled "Two Ways in China Studies (*Shina kenkyū ni taisuru hutatsu no michi*)" epitomized the epistemological view that Japanese Marxist intellectuals, and *Koza-ha* Marxists in particular, held regarding Chinese history.[41] Hirano began this article with the bold statement that China studies in Japan thus far should not be termed "scientific studies" due to its chauvinistic nature, and orientation toward matters of policy studies.[42] He argued that China studies in Japan had been primarily concerned with the issue of how socio-political changes in China would affect the Japanese economy or *vice versa*. He claimed that this approach lacked the analytical perspective to account for how China had taken the initial steps toward immanent social development.[43] For Hirano, the only methodological approach that might constructively address this question was Marx's historical materialism. The beginning of the article read like a manifesto and established the author's continuing ideological adherence to Marxism.

Hirano's proclamation presaged one constant feature of the wartime social sciences, by particularizing China and the other colonial territories, and providing a logical rationale to justify Japan's imperial mission, to save its stagnated Asian neighbors from Western colonialism. Notably, Hirano advocated this new idea of an academic field of China studies years before his official conversion to Japanese imperialism. As such, it appeared that he maintained a Marxist perspective to represent the oppressed, through identifying structural and institutional violence against them. For instance, in an article published in 1934, Hirano made it clear that the Asiatic mode of production had bound Chinese peasants within an oppressive landlord-peasant relationship, and as a result had prevented civil society from emerging in China.[44] However, it was at this point that Hirano and other Japanese Marxist social scientists faced a cleavage between scientific thinking and reality, and their inquiry was repositioned to address how Japanese Marxists might imagine the immanent and radical transformation of the modes of production in a country where Marx's theory of historical materialism could not be neatly applied. But what if this "scientific" pursuit of objective knowledge led them to the conclusion that particularistic and stagnating elements were deeply ingrained within Chinese society?

Another perspective might be that imperialism and colonialism in Asia were irrelevant to the positive transformation of the Asiatic mode of production. Hani Goro, a Marxist historian, took this stance. He observed that under the state's monopoly over land ownership, surplus value was not transformed into commercial capital but was absorbed predominantly by bureaucrats as land taxes. This precluded the capitalist mode of production from taking place in urban areas. Surplus labor in the village community was not absorbed by industrial and commercial sectors in the city either, a factor which worsened the overpopulation and impoverishment of the rural peasantry.[45] Hani believed that this situation also explained the underdevelopment of commercial capital and urban areas in China. Thus, the Asiatic mode of production in China was redefined by him as the question of how this "vicious circle" should be destroyed. And he was fundamentally opposed to the idea that the arrival of external powers would solve the problem:

> Under the despotic ruling system in China, where the feudal relationships of production and possession are centered on the state level, the deconstruction of feudal relationships trapped in this circulation in Chinese society must lead to a complete emergence of the new relationship of production. Therefore, it is to destroy feudal forms in the class relations of production by realizing the capitalist relations of production. . . . However, the fact that China actually has been colonized and is forced to become a supplier of commodities and cheap labor power for foreign capital undoubtedly makes much more complex the problem of searching for liberation through collapsing the old relations of production and possession.[46]

Hani did not believe that imperialist expansion in underdeveloped countries would stimulate the collapse of feudal relations, as Marx had argued regarding the impact of British imperialism on India. He instead emphasized that colonial powers had also exploited Chinese peasants and as a result, the vicious circle continued. Paradoxical as it may sound, this acute and critical analysis of Western imperialism and foreign capital in Asian society marked a point of departure, as Hani envisioned that only the peasant masses could induce a bourgeois democratic revolution in Asia. Hani asserted that irrespective of the village community, and concurrent stagnation and underdevelopment, the capitalist economy in the Orient was a *historical necessity*.[47] And he continued to argue that on behalf of the immature bourgeois class, the Chinese peasant masses might provide an organizing revolutionary force against both colonialism and imperialism.[48]

However, Hani's optimistic projection of bourgeois revolutionary potential into the hands of the Chinese peasantry did nothing but reveal the inconsistency of his argument. Since they had not been exposed to any new modes of production, and were marginalized within overpopulated village communities, it was unreasonable to expect these peasant masses to become revolutionary subjects with a functional Marxist political and class awareness. In these terms, Hani had only imposed his abstract belief in the natural unstoppable progress of oriental society on the Asian peasantry, who were not equipped to realize bourgeois revolution in the terms of Marx's historical and dialectic materialism.

The theoretical incapability of rationalizing a bourgeois socialist revolution in "stagnated" Asia outside Japan, and the growing trend of Japanese Marxist social scientists' ideological conversion (*tenko*) to the cause of the Japanese empire shaped the ground for the direction of a colonial social science in the coming wartime period. Under these circumstances, Karl Wittfogel, the German socio-economic historian, captured the attention of Japanese social scientists. In fact, Hirano's draft of "Two Ways in China Studies" was heavily influenced by Wittfogel's writing on China. Wittfogel is well known in the English-speaking world for his epochal 1957 work, *Oriental Despotism*. Given the prevalent harsh anticommunist atmosphere in US political and social arenas, Wittfogel's work was accepted by American intellectuals as an answer to the question of why despotic society in traditional China continued in Mao's dictatorship in modern China.[49] The way in which Wittfogel was read in American intellectual circles was influenced by an ideological value judgment during the Cold War period that China was doomed to suffer underdevelopment, stagnation and despotism, when measured against the universal current of Western historical progress. And in a similar fashion, a number of wartime Japanese intellectuals 20 years earlier would also reproduce their own desires of national superiority in reading and analyzing Wittfogel.

Importantly, Hirano was not alone in welcoming Karl Wittfogel as an influential figure within Japanese Marxist circles of the 1930s. A number of Japanese Marxist social scientists shared the notion that Wittfogel's ideas would instill a real scientific basis to the incipient field of China studies.[50] Moritani Katsumi was another intellectual deeply involved in introducing Wittfogel's work. Wittfogel published his seminal work *Wirtschaft und Gesellschaft Chinas* (Economy and Society in China) in 1931 and Hirano soon began the massive project of translating it into Japanese. This nearly 900+ page two-volume translation finally came out in 1934 with the Japanese title *Kaitai katei ni aru Shina no keizai to shakai* (Chinese Economy and Society in the Process of Dismantlement, hereafter *Shina no keizai to shakai*).[51] Given that the 4th edition was published in 1939, *Shina no keizai to shakai* seemed to be well accepted by the Japanese audience in spite of its substantial volume. Hirano was in charge of supervising the whole translation project, but three other Japanese intellectuals actually translated it, and among them Moritani took the second part of the first volume, which was about 270 pages.[52]

Wittfogel's writing on China had a significant impact on Japanese Marxist scholarship in the mid-1930s, and this influence was not limited to those who were involved in translating his works. At first Wittfogel's appearance in Japanese Marxist circles was relatively subtle, and his works were only intensively translated into Japanese around 1934 and 1935, as social scientists became increasingly preoccupied with what might be called Japanese exceptionalism. That is to say, Japan should not be categorized as part of the Orient in the Asiatic mode of production debate. To complete this task, they had to address the question of Japan's place on the universal path to capitalist development, and the idea of the Chinese economy as the epitome of Asiatic stagnation. Importantly, Wittfogel did not explicitly reiterate Western Marxist theoreticians' existing value-laden thesis and instead used the term "underdevelopment" to describe the nature of the Chinese feudal system. His primary interest was to explain why the Chinese agricultural system had given rise to a particular governing structure, which he later conceptualized as "oriental despotism." Here, he contrived the famous theory of a "hydraulic society," which prioritized the usage and management of water resources in a geographic area with excessive and unpredictable flood and drought. He reasoned that the Chinese government absolutized its power to help control these geographical conditions. This irrigation-oriented agricultural crisis management system, he stressed, precluded guild-types of commercial groups from emerging under feudalism that are essential in the rise of the capitalist economy.[53] Driven by a massive amount of data and historical evidence, Wittfogel's "scientific" study of China quickly made him the champion of a "scientific and objective" China studies in 1930s Japan. At the same time, his work left great room for its subjective interpretation by Japanese Marxist social scientists. And their ideas could no longer be simply confined to the academic world. Given that the Sino-Japanese war began in 1937, these Japanese Marxist social scientists' perceptions of China certainly affected their attitudes toward Japan's war and imperialism. All in all, the boom of Karl Wittfogel in the name of "scientific China studies" played an important role in determining Japanese Marxist intellectuals' standpoint in real political terms, within a rapidly changing context of war.

Wittfogel's writings illustrated another facet of Western scholarship on Asia in the 1930s, one that would lead him to offer a challenge to the shadow of universalism and geographical determinism inherent in the Marxist conception of the Asian mode of production. Instead of simply repeating Marx's concept of the Asiatic society, Wittfogel's early writing was more concerned with demonstrating his peculiar understanding of dialectical materialism in relation to space and geography. Wittfogel maintained that dialectical materialism was predicated on its notion of geography being a completely separate issue from the human being's power of social production.[54] He went on to contend that neither nature, nor geography, nor human beings' own acquired production power normatively explained the stages of certain economies.[55] While it might seem that Wittfogel's overarching perspective was similar to Marx's concept of nature, Wittfogel's view was that the traditional Marxist notion of nature focused more on how nature determined human social behavior, rather than on how it might provide different *possibilities* for revolution.[56] For this reason, Wittfogel never denied the validity of nature's impact on human activity, but he also tried to avoid a somewhat deterministic conclusion that natural restrictions would provide the rational reason for the developmental stage of any given geographically determined economy, as Marx had conceptualized in his theory of the Asiatic mode of production.

In his 1933 book, *A Critique of Geography*, Wittfogel further elaborated on his spatial theory.[57] Here, Wittfogel's critiques targeted Marx's concept of nature as well as the idea of a political geography, the latter of which had rapidly gained currency in post-World War I Europe. Wittfogel's concept of nature was premised on the perception that the world is not divided into universal spaces and particular spaces, as Marx's concept of geography put forth. Criticizing Karl Haushofer's geopolitical analysis of Asian society, Wittfogel argued that geopolitics does not provide a scientific analysis for why peasants in China, India and Japan developed particular socio-economic activities.[58] In other words, for Wittfogel, the issue of particularity in Asia was not a problem that should be explained according to geographical characteristics, but more in terms of how people in Asia had engaged in certain social, economic and political activities in their specific geographical circumstances. Based on these observations, Wittfogel refined his concept of scientific study and constantly reflected on it through the lens of China. The following remark best illustrates his stance on the idea of scientific study and China. Wittfogel wrote:

> A *Scientific attitude* was, in terms of its fundamental configuration, based on the conviction that although Chinese civilization exists along with a variety of Western civilizations, the former is the same as the latter to some extent. For this reason, many social scientists think that categories that apply to the development of Western civilization can also be applicable to Chinese studies. The validity of this notion is obvious; that is, it enabled the introduction of scientific methods [to Chinese studies]. Since various characteristics of agricultural society are similar, a certain kind of mechanical identification is applied and this produces *objective truth* to some degree. But this accomplishment does not transcend this level. A number of theoretical and practical misunderstandings and failures take place, and presumably these problems are, most of all, due to the lack of consciousness on what kind of society China is in its basic sense.[59]

(emphasis added)

As the statement above indicates, Wittfogel's concept of both nature and China as scientific object(s) was not premised on the assumption that the West represented the universal in social scientific research and the East the particular. Rather, for Wittfogel, particular circumstances of each society, as illustrated by the case of Asian society in particular, were scientific variables that enabled social scientists to consider in retrospect the limits of the universality of the social scientific method. Moritani was aware of the underlying theoretical dimensions of Wittfogel's social scientific study and he took a very cautious stance as he applied Wittfogel's theory to China and colonial Korea. For instance, the footprints of Wittfogel's critical understanding of geographical determinism were also found in Moritani's wartime writings on the natural conditions of Chosun Korea. In a 1934 article titled "Natural Environment and Chosun Korea," which was published shortly after his own translation of Wittfogel's *Shina no keizai to shakai*, Moritani basically reiterated Wittfogel's point, arguing that geographical materialism and determinism could be considered as unavoidably bound up with a narrow-minded nationalism.[60]

However, what most powerfully appealed to Japanese Marxist social scientists in the 1930s was the way that Wittfogel's masterful empirical study of China scientifically determined the state of Chinese society. The 1934 translation of *Shina no shakai to keizai* played a pivotal role in furnishing Japanese Marxist intellectuals with the conviction that Wittfogel had finally provided rigid evidence for China's stagnation theory. In this work Wittfogel concretized his famous theory of hydraulic society. Agriculture in China, Wittfogel argued, had been greatly influenced by water resources. Since floods and drought frequently occurred in China, these geographical conditions necessitated massive state-sponsored irrigation projects.[61] Thus explained Wittfogel, the state directly intervened in the process of agricultural production, which was characterized by the state's dominant ownership of arable lands. This observation by Wittfogel led him to conclude that these geographical and structural conditions were not conducive to the Western form of a landlord-peasant relationship. Instead, the peasants were directly bound to the state and this unique production relationship lasted until external powers arrived in China.[62] Through Wittfogel's theory of hydraulic society, Hirano and like-minded Japanese Marxist social scientists observed that development and social changes in China were only concerned with the question of how foreign powers had transformed China into a new society, not with how China's immanent social dynamics had brought about any independent development. Hirano's "Two Ways in China Studies" symbolized this perspective. He drove attention to the issue of how *foreign power* had transformed China from a semi-feudal to a capitalist society.[63] The Japanese Marxist appropriation of Wittfogel's writing to underpin stagnation-driven interpretations of Chinese society was exemplified in the following statement of his, one which became a guiding principle for Japanese Marxists. In reconfirming the thesis of China as a particular case, Wittfogel answered his own question as to why no independent development towards industrial capitalism existed in China:

> The oriental state and its representatives . . . arrogate to themselves the bulk of the land revenue, whereas Western (and *Japanese*) absolutism conceded a great part of the land rent to the feudal lords. . . . The development of Western industrial capitalism accordingly occurred because there a peculiarly decentralized structure of the agricultural productive power permitted – economically, sociologically and politically – the commencement of capital accumulation, *while the centralized structure of the highly productive oriental agrarian order worked in the opposite direction, namely toward the reproduction of the existing order, toward its stagnation.*

> (emphasis added)[64]

As Wittfogel became accepted as the "terminator" of debates over the nature of the Chinese economy, the next question Japanese Marxists had in mind was to reconfirm via Wittfogel that Japan's path to modernity was substantially different from that of China. Interestingly, Wittfogel visited Japan in 1935 as a part of commemoration of the translation of *Shina no keizai to shakai* into Japanese.[65] At a meeting with Japanese Marxist intellectuals, Wittfogel was asked four major questions, two of which were about the differences between Chinese Confucianism and Japanese Confucianism, and the difference between the Chinese family system and the Japanese family system.[66] Wittfogel had written in a clear tone in the foreword of *Shina no keizai to shakai* that Japan had undergone a quite different process of economic development from China.[67] This short remark provided Japanese Marxist social scientists with a powerful basis for their claim that Japan had already passed through the stage of the Asian village community, characterized by stagnation and the despotic political structure. However, such seemingly purely academic approaches marked a turning point as Japan turned its imperial ambition into a full-fledged war against China. At this point, Wittfogel's writing, along with other works on China, served to scientifically rationalize why Japan should lead China to liberate it from the status of underdevelopment.

Moritani's response: "The Orient still exists"

How then did Moritani, who introduced some of Wittfogel's major works to Japan, find this new methodology relevant to his understanding of China and Asia? It appeared that he could not prevent Wittfogel from having a profound impact on his perception of Chinese society, while Moritani took a very critical stance over the extension of Marx's notion of the Asiatic mode of production to cover the entirety of Asia. Moritani's 1934 work *Socio-Economic History of China* best demonstrates Wittfogel's considerable influence in his scholarship. Describing the historical period of ancient China as an "immature feudal system" and explaining the Ming and Qing period (fourteenth to nineteenth centuries) through the concept of the centralized bureaucratic feudal system, Moritani provided a narrative of Chinese history which held a striking resemblance to Wittfogel's depiction.[68] This unchanging society, Moritani observed, was now experiencing massive transformations, and the concept of "old society in dismantlement" was tacitly borrowed from Wittfogel.

Moritani's early writing on Korean history was also linked to Wittfogel's inspiration. Beginning with the condition that the socio-economic constitution of Korean society was similar to that of China, Moritani argued that as Korean society's central bureaucratic system was being dismantled, so was China's.[69] Since Wittfogel never mentioned Korea in his China-centered research, Moritani attempted to borrow Wittfogel's "grand theory" of Asiatic society to interpret Korean history and filled the missing content by introducing some existing works on Korean history which, he believed, might correspond to Wittfogel's general framework. Moritani's 1934 article titled "Old Korean society that entered the era of dismantlement" illuminates the level of Moritani's understanding of Korean history and society. In this article, he basically referred to Fukuda Tokuzō's writing on the Korean economy in the early twentieth century. In this work, Fukuda ruthlessly concluded that the economic status of late-nineteenth- and early-twentieth- century Korean society was commensurate with Japan in the eleventh to thirteenth centuries, due to Korea's failure to constitute a modern national economy.[70] Fukuda's scholarship on Korean history illustrates how even radical intellectuals in Japan proper were preoccupied by their own version of Asian stagnation excluding Japan, leading them to endorse the Japanese colonization of Asia in the name of an inevitable external intervention. One could easily infer that Wittfogel's theory of Asiatic society and static bureaucratic feudalism, intended or unintended, had become a timely source to theoretically underpin the legitimacy of Japanese colonial rule in Asia. Although Moritani was hesitant to acknowledge the notion of Japanese exceptionalism either in the AMP or Wittfogel's theory of Asiatic society, he failed to develop his own understanding of Korean or Chinese society beyond borrowing from existing literature, much of which eventually converged to the point of stagnation theory vis-à-vis an "advanced Japan."

Nonetheless, what differentiated Moritani from other Japanese Marxist social scientists of the time was his peculiar concept of the Orient. Moritani never provided an alternative narrative to the perception of a static Korean society in his somewhat naïve reception of the previous value-laden scholarship on Korea. However, he never agreed that the contemporary economic gap was persuasive evidence of fundamental civilizational differences between Japan and the rest of Asia. Instead, Moritani maintained the standpoint that the relative underdevelopment apparent in early-twentieth-century China and Korea should be attributed to an *institutional* failure, that is, its feudal system never functioned rationally, and this prevented any systematic evolution from a feudal to a capitalist economy in these national contexts. For this reason, he believed that the fact that the "Orient exists" could not be denounced simply due to visible economic gaps between Asian countries. In a similar vein, he was opposed to the conservative notion of Chinese civilization, as characterized by its difference from Japanese society. For instance, Tsuda Sōkichi, a prominent historian of ancient Japan and East Asia, presented a provocative thesis that something analogous to the idea of "the Orient" never existed in the mid-1930s. Unquestionably, he problematized the position of China as he addressed the question of the Orient, and attempted to minimize China's cultural and political influence on Japan. However, his aim was to denigrate the cultural capacity of what he called the "Chinese thinking system" as an ideological force of influence in establishing the modern idea of Japanese national thought (*kokumin shisō*), arguing instead that Japan could find the basis for such a national thought from within her own ancient historical texts. Importantly, Tsuda never resisted Japan's expanded war in China proper, but he redefined Japan's conflicts against China in his famous 1938 work *Chinese Thought and Japan* as an inevitable clash between one civilization that had stagnated and another that had made progress in universal terms.[71] Tsuda's notion was reminiscent of Samuel Huntington's much debated notion of the clash of civilizations,[72] however, it was not endorsed by most Japanese intellectuals, not least as the necessity of incorporating the Chinese people into Japan's empire- building project grew in the late 1930s. Referring to Tsuda's work, Moritani was constantly critical of such a cultural approach to Asia, when designed to highlight the supposed difference between Japan and China.[73] Moritani pointed out that Tsuda's notion of Japan's irrelevance with China and its detachment from Oriental culture was based on the fundamental perception that climate and geographic conditions produce different *ethnic* cultures.[74] Picking up individual differences in the living things (*seikatsu sono mono*), Moritani stressed, Tsuda tended to link them to the intrinsic nature of each cultural unit.[75] Therefore, Moritani observed that nationality in Tsuda's theory always ends up reconfirming one's homogeneousness by rendering *the past* into the present. In addition, Moritani went on to argue that the validity of Tsuda's concept of each particular cultural national community could not be appreciated unless he elaborated as to why and how these *Japanese* things could be differentiated from those of the West and the rest of Asia.[76]

Second, he rejected the idea of the Orient as a counter concept to the idea of the West. In other words, the Orient, Moritani stressed, existed in the northeastern area of the "old world" in a geographic sense, particularly within the Western Christian tradition based on the bible. Here, the "old world" refers to the Greek-Roman world and thus the area present-day called West Asia was designated as the Orient in ancient times.[77] What Moritani intended to present was that the concept of the Orient had been shaped as a counter area to the West politically and culturally, not as a natural geographical unit. However, he contended that the Orient had maintained its own cultural self-sufficiency and thus the world map of civilization must be drawn by recognizing three spheres of living spaces along with the Anglo Saxon and the European spheres.[78] In this respect, the Orient, Moritani argued, was now transforming itself into the Greater East Asia Co-Prosperity sphere, the official slogan of imperial Japan during the Asia-Pacific War. Needless to say, he, like other Japanese intellectuals, endorsed imperial Japan's Pan-Asian rhetoric, and he seemed to be influenced by German geopolitics as he introduced the concept of an oriental "living-space" (*lebensraum*) and published a full-length book with the same title. To be sure, Moritani adopted in his wartime writing common rhetorical expressions such as the *Hakkō ichiu* (Eight Corners of the World, indicating the entire world under the Japanese emperor, or the Imperial Way). He also acknowledged that Japan did not follow the same "oriental path" as traditional China, but he also stressed that the differences between Japan and China would not be sufficient to place Japan as part of the universal West. More importantly, he was convinced that Japan had shared several important similar elements with the rest of Asia such as irrigation-oriented agriculture, the village community and patriarchy.[79] For this reason, Japan's "uniqueness" or ostensible advancement, Moritani observed, only came from what he termed "adaptive renovation," that is, modern Japan institutionally modified its traditional values to fit the trend toward modernization effectively.[80] In this way, Moritani intended to avoid both the intrinsic or geographically determined discussion of the Orient and Japan's exceptionalism vis-à-vis the rest of Asia and instead advocated the logic of constructivism, that is, how contemporary East Asia can and should be structurally recreated in the service of a new idea of Asia.

Turning colonial Korea into an East Asian community

As discussed so far, Moritani's encounter with an East Asian Empire in the late 1930s was decorated by his somewhat peculiar understanding of Asian space and its historical and cultural constitution. However, his logic of the Orient was not premised on any epistemological ideal of rehabilitating Asian traditional value systems, something which often served as a cultural and spiritual vehicle for an idea of Asian unity under Japanese leadership against Western colonialism. Instead, he took a different route, and pursued a developmentalist perspective which stressed Japan's realistic role in developing the Asian region. To this end, he had to historicize and endorse Japan's successful modernization as tangible evidence of the value of renovation from within, and support the expansion of the Japanese way to the rest of Asia. Therefore, tracing the trajectory of Japan's colonization of Korea emerged as an important issue through which Japan's capability for the inspirational "renovating" of the rest of Asia could be tested. In doing so, Moritani intended to create discursive spaces within the intellectual arena of an East Asian imperial order. This position certainly resulted in the increase of Moritani's influence among Korean intellectuals, many of whom were concerned with the marginalization of colonial Korea with the dominance of the "China problem," amid the background of the ongoing Sino-Japanese War.

However, Moritani's intention to revisit Korea was accompanied by several intellectual and political challenges. For the most part, he had to overcome the trap of stagnation which had engulfed most Japanese Marxist social scientists. Again, Moritani did not produce an alternative narrative to the perception of stagnated Korea and China until the mid-1930s. How, then, did he respond to these questions? A short article he contributed to the *Newspaper of Kyungsung Imperial University* a year after the outbreak of the Sino-Japanese War indicates his new standpoint toward the Korea problem. In this article titled, "The so-called Asiatic mode of production and Chosun Korea," Moritani first acknowledged that major elements of what Karl Wittfogel pointed out as Asiatic characteristics existed in colonial Korea. Referring to Wittfogel's theory of hydraulic society, Moritani contended that the difficulty in obtaining water for agriculture due to erratic precipitation and unpredictable drought and flood patterns had determined the nature of Korean agriculture. As a result, controlling the water supply and managing irrigation projects emerged as one of the most important tasks for the Chosun government.[81] Moritani was, however, aware that the logic of this explanation was in sync with the popular social scientific notion of Japanese superiority, and inconsistent with his argument that "the Orient exists."

The next year, he published an article that contained a more detailed discussion of how the problem of Asian stagnation presented by Wittfogel might be solved in colonial Korea. The title of this article – "The position of Korean agriculture in East Asian agriculture" – suggests Moritani's intention to indicate the general direction of Japan's agricultural policy as regards the rest of Asia by specifically discussing the Korean case. Moritani began with a strong argument that the Asiatic mode of production in Korea remained in place due to the *institutional* failure

of the Chosun government, not because of any intrinsic geographical characteristics of Korean agriculture, or any other fundamentally irreversible problems.[82]
This statement was logically linked to Moritani's assessment of the success of
Japan's industrialization as an example of "adaptive renovation." He intended to
render the future of Chosun Korea within the problem of governmental effectiveness. Accordingly, Moritani had no hesitation to celebrate Japan's colonization of
Korea as a successful example of governance. He argued that Korean agriculture
and industry had significantly developed since 1910,[83] although there remained a
number of tasks to be completed before it could be considered as paradigmatic of
a progressive new Asian Imperial order.

Perhaps the most explicit prescription for the Korea problem during the wartime period was *naisenittai* (Japan and Korea as one body). Although the context
of re-making Koreans as Japanese subjects varied depending on who addressed
the issue, it was premised on the epistemological position that colonial Korea
had completely become part of imperial Japan politically and culturally. On
the other hand, Japanese social scientists put forward the wider notion of the
East Asian community, and this idea rapidly gained currency in Japan proper.
Moritani observed that *naisenittairon* must be redefined and armed with realistic
policy changes in order to be considered as linked to the vision of an East Asian
community by the Korean people. To this end, he contended that each nationalist perspective, including Korean ethnic nationalism, must be recognized within
Japan's new order, but he also argued that not every form of nationalism would
always result in the completion of a nation-state project.[84] Ironic as it may sound,
he criticized Chinese nationalism for being associated with "imperialism" and
asserted that it was only Japan that had achieved nationalism in a true sense.[85]
Moritani's perception of the East Asian Cooperative Community indicated that
he, like other imperial intellectuals, took it for granted that Japan must lead other
ethnic groups in Asia. However, he was also aware that the socio-economic
gap between metropole and colony would eventually hinder the incorporation
of colonial subjects into the East Asian community. Therefore, he believed that
naiseittairon, a Koreanized version of the East Asian Cooperative Community, must be associated with the "epoch-making development of the status of
underdeveloped Chosun."[86] To find solutions for the "Korea problem," Moritani
became increasingly involved in realistic issues such as the problem of agriculture, social policy and national land planning in Chosun Korea, all of which were
closely related to "social problems" (*shakai mondai*), but all requiring solutions
at a governmental level.

While reconstructing Korean agriculture drew special attention from Moritani,
it was not just Moritani who found agricultural issues in colonial Korea and China
one of the most important challenges to realize within the remit of the new East
Asian community. Coincidentally, the great drought of 1939 became a turning
point in Japan's wartime agricultural policy. The production of rice decreased by
46 percent in comparison with the previous year, which raised a serious red signal
for Japan's initial project of a self-sufficient East Asian empire in which colonial Korea was certainly defined as a place of massive agricultural production.

Accordingly, the dramatic shortage of rice in 1939 ironically led Japanese intellectuals and bureaucrats to reconsider the importance of Korean agriculture. Not surprisingly, their discussion focused on increasing the production power of Korean agriculture, while normalizing the devastated Japanese agricultural sector at the same time. As a result, the notion of "reconstructing agriculture" proliferated in both Korea and Japan between 1939 and the early 1940s. A particularly large number of theories and policies were produced in 1941, so the year 1941 was often referred to as the year of the boom of reconstructing agriculture. The main issue in these discourses was the question of where the main problems of many within Korean agricultural production were actually to be located.

In a 1941 roundtable discussion hosted by *Ryokki Renmei*, Moritani pointed to irrigation and the landlord-peasant relationship as the two main problems in Korean agriculture.[87] These issues had already been discussed in full in Moritani's prewar writings on Asian agriculture. In order to manage hydraulic issues, the state also emerged as a great landlord and most peasants were tenant farmers. This unique landlord-peasant relationship did not change in twentieth-century Korea. Most peasants were still tenant farmers cultivating extremely small plots of land. Moritani described this characteristic of the Asiatic mode of production as intensive agriculture; that is, cultivation greatly depended on laborers who possessed small plots of land.[88] Once peasant revolution was no longer the preferred prescription for the feudal system, how did imperial intellectuals like Moritani attempt to solve this issue and envision a new type of productive social community in colonial Korea? Here, it is vitally important to note that Japanese intellectuals and bureaucrats had a strong tendency to reduce the *political* nature of the tenant-landlord relationship to the issue of an excessive supply of labor. In other words, intensive labor-power-oriented agriculture in colonial Korea, they argued, resulted in overpopulation in rural areas and inefficiency in production. Therefore, they observed that Korean agriculture could not meet the demand for rice in Japan proper, if these problems persisted. Moreover, as Japan waged a total war against the United States, a shortage of manpower emerged as a major issue in relation to securing human resources on the battlefield as well as for the war industry. For this reason, discourses on restructuring agriculture in colonial Korea turned to increasing production power without destroying the feudal peasant-landlord relations. Although reshaping the landlord-peasant relationship was closely intertwined with the mode of production itself, many of these landlords were Japanese residents and pro-Japanese Koreans. Depriving them of their socio-economic privileges might result in destroying the backbone of the colonial structure. Instead, the terms "productivity" or "production power" within the existing agricultural structure took the central position in their discussion. In this way, ironic as it may sound, these imperial intellectuals were envisioning a community filled with a highly capitalist productivist spirit, but a community in equilibrium with neither class struggle nor economic inequalities.

Hirano Yoshitarō, Moritani's colleague, was one of these converted social scientists who dreamed of an Asian agricultural utopia. To theorize it, he rediscovered the value of the Asian, or more correctly, the Chinese village system in Asia.

After leading a massive fieldwork research project in China under the auspices of the East Asia Institute, perhaps the biggest think-tank of the wartime Japanese government, Hirano began reinterpreting village community structure in China and Southeast Asia. Among the characteristics of everyday life in the village community, he paid special attention to how the space of autonomous governance should be created. Hirano aimed to link this question to critiques of the modern legal system in the West, and to theorize moral codes in the Chinese village community as noninstitutional but rather a highly effective self-sufficient system. He initially vehemently argued that the modern legal system in the West was characterized by its noninvolvement in an individual's economic life in the name of liberalism, utilitarianism, individualism and self-responsibility. He pointed out, however, that unless equality before the law was guaranteed, or if there was anything undefined by the law in one's life, the principle of nonintervention in an individual's private life was not respected.[89] Based on these observations, Hirano asserted that the Western law system precluded the relationship of metropole and colony from being transformed into a jointly prosperous cooperative community.[90] He wrote:

> National policy is based on the ideology of co-prosperity – autonomism and cooperativism and recognizes and acknowledges the life and tradition of indigenous society. Since it [cooperativism] aims to develop indigenous society toward its own direction, it is opposed to the lopsidedness of assimilation policy and takes the form of the individual and the particular. The national policy (*minzoku seisaku*) of Japan, a member of the co-prosperity sphere, that has led and protected national groups in East Asia is a cooperativism that has gone beyond Europe's cooperativism originating from the aspect of economic profit.[91]

> (emphasis added)

What, then, did Hirano suggest as the principle of a cooperative community to replace profit-oriented European imperialism? Among other aspects of the Chinese village community that interested him, what particularly captured his attention was the concept of national morality inherent in Chinese villages. He observed that national morality had controlled and enabled the cooperative life of Chinese village communities.[92] In contrast to Europe's legal system in which magistrates or administrators regulated the community, national morality, Hirano argued, constituted a system of law that permitted townspeople to mediate, regulate and integrate socio-economic activities with the everyday life of the community. Hirano showed an especially keen interest in the Chinese tradition of keeping moral ledgers (*Gong guo Ge*). *Gong guo Ge* was a kind of everyday life manual that recorded the bad and good deeds and also provided townspeople with a way to compensate for misbehaviors by doing good deeds. In this way, Hirano believed that the indigenous legal system of *Gong guo Ge* created a political space where individuals in the community were given the autonomy to evaluate and criticize themselves, but their individual activities contributed to the general good of the community.[93] Hirano further argued that the Chinese village functioned as a space for negotiation and mediation in which elderly people minimized internal conflict and sustained the autonomy of the community.[94] Hirano held that this decision-making process, in spite of the fact that it had paradoxically isolated townspeople within the limited spatial boundary of the village community and prevented them from protesting against the despotic state, enabled them to live with minimal inter-class conflict.[95]

Lacking in Hirano's spiritual approach to Asian agriculture was the blueprint for reconstructing agricultural systems. Unlike Hirano, Moritani took a substantially different standpoint and called for mechanization and industrialization. In addition, he believed that all these impending tasks for Korean agriculture would be completed by the government's "organized intervention" instead of relying on autonomous decision-making processes in the village communities Hirano so highly evaluated.[96] Moritani believed that if mechanization and efficiency reached a certain degree through institutional reforms, it would push superfluous rural labor powers to the city, where they could fill jobs in the war industries. In this way, he drew on the picture of an East Asian economic co-prosperity sphere, and accordingly defined the relationship between metropole and colony:

> The intensification of *gaichi* (colonial Korea) as a military base or a stronghold in Japan's conducting of radical policies in East Asia must be accomplished by facilitating industrialization, once agriculture has been improved to a certain degree. . . . In the aftermath of the Manchurian Crisis, industrial policy in Chosun Korea has changed from rice-cultivation-oriented agriculture to the uniform advancement of agriculture and industry.[97]

On the surface, Moritani's discussion of economic policy bore resemblance to the notion of the controlled economy promulgated by Japanese economists and bureaucrats in the name of the Japan-Manchuria-China economic bloc. In an attempt to overcome the capitalist system and control individuals' profit-oriented desires, these intellectuals insisted that major industries should be nationalized, and turned to spiritualism as a means to bind individuals to the state. Putting forth the Imperial Way, these intellectuals intended to create homogeneous subjects who functioned organically under the leadership of the state.[98]

The imperial state organ: social policy and national land planning in colonial Korea

While taking charge of the Social Policy Lecture program at Kyungsung Imperial University, Moritani did not explicitly reveal his identity as a social policy expert in the mid- and late 1930s. Considering that social policy had long been regarded as a practical means of intervention by the state to relegate social problems, Moritani's social policy lecture at Kyungsung Imperial University might have at least functioned to dilute his Marxist ideology. Beginning in the 1940s, Moritani, however, began advocating social policy and attempted to construct his realist vision of creating a new Chosun Korea within the Japanese empire, along with other projects such as rehabilitating Korean agriculture and reorganizing Korean land.

A close look at his postwar memoir shows us why Moritani revisited social policy and other forms of socio-political engineering as important steps to create an East Asian community in colonial Korea. He wrote:

> First, I believed that I had maintained an acute critical viewpoint that the minzoku problem in East Asia is the problem of the nation of colonization. However, after settling for the present as an employee at Kyungsung Imperial University, I was influenced by the atmosphere so much as to consider that *existence somehow determined meaning*. Therefore, I could no longer critically think that the colonial problem of Chosun minzoku was to liberate it from the home country of imperialism, that is, Japan. . . . As long as Chosun Korea was part of Imperial Japan, I could not help thinking about the direction of promoting the status of colonial Korea to that of the Japanese people. In this way, instead of looking at the problem of colonial Korea from the principle theory of liberating it from Japanese imperialism, I naturally transformed my viewpoint into the ways in which the *contemporary* problems of Chosun Korea are speculated with a view to promote the status of Chosun minzoku *within* Imperial Japan.
>
> (emphasis added)[99]

Writing two decades after the end of the Asia-Pacific War, Moritani frankly acknowledged that he had lost his critical standpoint toward Japanese imperialism soon *after* Japan had begun to conduct its imperial war. The above statement also contains a highly nuanced evaluation of Moritani's wartime writings and political activities in colonial Korea. Instead of negating a positive involvement in Japanese imperialism, Moritani justified his wartime commitment through the notion of "promoting the status of the Korean people," a perspective naturally aimed to engender a new Asian order led by Japan. Such a thinking process eventually led him to observe contemporary socio-political issues in colonial Korea from a different angle. In other words, social problems (*shakai mondai*) in Chosun Korea must also be resolved in the same way as Japanese social scientists, liberal and progressive intellectuals in particular, endeavored to solve social problems in the 1920s and early 1930s. While Japanese intellectuals during the Taisho period appropriated the issue of "social problems" as a way to challenge the dominance of the state over society, Moritani's involvement in contemporary colonial Korea took the opposite path. He contended that new political spaces ought to be created between individuals and the state and this could only happen through the involvement of the state in individual sectors.[100] It is at this point that Moritani came to terms with the logic of state-oriented economic development and the necessity of social engineering to promote the living standards of the Korean people. In this respect, it was natural that he revisited the discipline of social policy as an important force to integrate Korean subjects into the Japanese empire.

At stake is the question of how the concept of social policy would shed a new light on changing the empire-colony relations, given that the political dimension of social policy was often confined to a single nation-state. In two articles contributed to the Legal Studies Association at Kyungsung Imperial University in 1942 and 1944 respectively, Moritani first defined social policy as a discipline that "problematizes the balance of the social configuration of a nation (min-zoku) within the state."[101] However, his seemingly conventional understanding of social policy as the state's intervention in people's lives drastically changed as he encountered the contemporaneity of imperial war. Moritani articulated that the conventional notion of social policy would not correspond with imperial Japan's empire-building project. At first, it was Mori Kojiro's (1895–1962) *Introduction to Social Policy* that Moritani labeled "conventional." Moritani observed that Mori had narrowly defined social policy as the state's political intervention to resolve distribution problems caused by the capitalist-oriented bourgeois economy.[102] Professor of Economics at Kyushu Imperial University and a leading scholar in the field of social policy, Mori's academic career was unique compared to other social scientists. Studying classical economists such as David Ricardo and Adam Smith in Europe and the United States, he showed a keen interest in bourgeois economic theories and social policy as a means to create a buffer-zone between capitalists and workers. In this respect, labor became the primary concern of Mori's social policy; how to prevent labor exploitation, guarantee a reasonable working wage and institutionalize a minimum wage.[103]

What Moritani found more compatible with the circumstance of wartime conditions was the new concept of social policy presented by Okochi Kazuo who was teaching social policy and economics at Tokyo Imperial University. Beginning in the 1940s, Okochi wrote extensively on the necessity of redefining Japan's social policy and called for attention to be paid to the logic of productivity (*seisansei*). According to him, social policy is no longer a set of policies to protect workers from exploitation within the capitalist economy. On the contrary, Okochi stressed that as the capitalist economy increased both in its external size and at its internal technological level, the problem of configuring labor powers based on the advancement of the entire economy emerged as a main issue. Okochi maintained that in this frame "it became important for workers to voluntarily nurture themselves to cope with rapid technological developments and socially cultivate capabilities that subjectively understand these technologies."[104] Through this process, he believed that the state would increase the level of production and reproduction to its highest potential, and for this reason Okochi emphasized that the primary focus of social policy must be transformed from simply protecting labor powers into productively configuring or arranging them.

Okochi's concept of social policy reveals one important facet of wartime Japanese social sciences. Not content to just endorse imperial Japan's Pan-Asian rhetoric, social scientists also endeavored to contrive theory that would serve the purpose of total mobilization. Needless to say, Okochi intended to maximize the power and efficiency of wartime production by nurturing a next generation of laborers who could subjectively absorb technological development and turn it into enhanced productivity for Japan's war efforts. If such new approaches to social policy reflected the highly advanced level of the Japanese capitalist economy, the question remained as to how Moritani would bring them into the reality of colonial Korea, given that he aimed to promote the living standards of the Korean people to the same level as that of the Japanese. Toward this challenge, Moritani seemed to be aware of the imbalance between metropole and colony. While he also fully agreed with Okochi's call for increasing labor productivity through a new social policy, Moritani observed that colonial Korea would not be an ideal place to put such cutting-edge social theories into practice. In a 1940 article, Moritani basically reiterated this standpoint. Accusing Nazi Germany's theory of an Aryan national community of subordinating all other aspects of society to the state, Moritani advocated that social policy in Chosun Korea must work for the acknowledgment of a national community by the Korean people and necessary steps should be made to develop social policy in Korea.[105]

Geographically speaking, Okochi's and other Japanese social scientists' discussion of social policy predominantly focused on Japan proper. While catching up with latest social theories produced in Japan, Moritani was at the same time concerned with finding common value systems in East Asia from within the perspective of a social policy. What captured his attention was the historical trajectory of social policy in China. As examined so far in this chapter, Karl Wittfogel's notion of the ancient Chinese state as despotic prevailed in the writings of converted Japanese Marxist social scientists. Moritani, however, constantly attempted to find alternative historical evidence that might challenge Wittfogel's linear historical perspective. Based on this, Moritani critically revisited two reformist politicians in traditional China, Wang Mang (BC 45- AD 23) and Wang An Shi (1021–1086). Both are known for their strong state-driven reform policies within traditional China during periods of national crisis. Citing Hu Shih, often called the father of Chinese literary modernization, Moritani evaluated Wang Mang's reform policy during the Shin period (a new empire between former Han and later Han, BC 45 to BC 25) as the first evidence of state socialism in world history.[106] In the same vein, Wang An Shi's reform during the Song period was positively interpreted as expanding social mobility.[107] As is well known, both Wang Mang and Wang An Shi were upholders of so-called statecraft, that is, that a reformed bureaucracy would bring impoverished and socially marginalized peasants back under the control of the state by providing for them basic economic means of survival. In this respect, Moritani's keen interest in these Chinese reformers clearly shows that he had made the diagnosis that the living conditions of destitute Korean peasants had already reached a critical point and immediate state involvement was required.

Such seemingly "forward-looking" stances in Moritani's diagnosis of the problems of colonial Korea played an important role in differentiating him from other Japanese intellectuals, many of whom simply resorted to spiritual and Imperial-Way Pan-Asianism. Another example of Moritani's state-oriented approach to colonial Korea was his involvement in the National Land Planning project in the late 1930s and early 1940s. The concept of national land planning emerged as one important stream for the construction of East Asia within Japanese academia and the government. Eventually, a review committee for national land planning was established in Japan proper in 1939 under the direct control of the Planning Bureau, and it was followed by the launching of the National Land Planning Committee in colonial Korea in October 1940. Moritani was appointed as an external committee member in December 1940,[108] and his involvement in the Governor General's Office continued until 1945, when he was appointed as a member of the Research Committee for Resources.[109]

While Japanese social scientists' discussion of national land planning focused on redesigning Japan proper, Moritani was from the beginning concerned with examining its validity and urgency within the grand plan of creating an East Asian regional sphere. Revisiting two previous examples of national land planning, the German and Russian cases respectively, Moritani took a very cautious stance to extract only positive aspects from them. Interestingly, he was more critical of the German way. According to him, Germany's national land planning was strikingly different from what Japan would pursue, since Germany was already an established industrialized country by the time national land planning was mapped out.[110] He observed that Germany's plan basically targeted industrial sectors that shared more than 40 percent of the whole industry, while marginalizing agricultural sectors that were less than 30 percent of the German economy.[111] For Moritani, the Russian case seemed to be much closer to and compatible with colonial Korea and Manchukuo, given that Russia's national land plan aimed to transform its agricultural economy into an industrial one. However, he did not consider it suitable to follow Russia's national socialist direction in Chosun Korea, although he emphasized the colonial government's leading role in reorganizing Korea's geography and economy.[112] If one removes the shadow of socialism from Russia's state-centered planned economy, Moritani's affinity with the Russian case would be far more conspicuous. Notably, Moritani was the person who translated the former Frankfrut School neo-Marxist economist Friedrich Pollock's study of the Soviet-controlled economy, and he continued to meticulously examine the legacy of the socialist-controlled economy even before he finally discarded Marxism in the late 1930s.[113]

Moritani also problematized the theory of industrial location, formulated by the German economist Alfred Weber, younger brother of sociologist Max Weber. According to Weber, an industry had to be located where the transaction cost of raw materials, labor and transportation was minimized. Moritani found this theory suitable for the case of colonial Korea, where the Governor General's Office was supposed to construct basic infrastructure for industrialization such as roads, factories and ports.[114] Expanding this idea to East Asia, he intended to draw on the picture of a self-sufficient East Asian economic sphere. This economic sphere, he believed, would then need to be extended into a *lebensraum* (living space) in East Asia, supported by the historical and cultural affinities among Asian people.[115] Through this thinking process, Moritani's gaze pointed to one specific space as a perfect spot to bring both China and Korea to the construction of an industrialized area that would represent the success of a Japan-led developmentalist approach. It was the *Amrok* river (the Yalu River in China) across the northern border between Chosun Korea and Manchuria.[116]

Moritani was not the only one who considered the Amrok river area a significant site. Immediately after the outbreak of the Sino-Japanese War in 1937, there existed a strong demand to create military supply bases adjacent to Japan's war front in mainland China. As a result, northern Manchuria first received attention from Japanese bureaucrats. This government-led development plan to increase productivity was epitomized by the construction of the Su'pung Dam, a hydro-power plant which is often compared to the Hoover Dam in its size and electricity production capacity.[117] I argue that Japan's wartime development project in the Amrok River appeared to provide a special significance to Moritani. The dam was an ideal example of how the government-led planning economy could bring industrial development and thereby the promotion of living standard to colonial subjects. But more than this, the construction of Su'Pung Dam ironically brought to mind that the hydraulic society of traditional China and Korea, the main cause of the region's underdevelopment and despotic politics, had now become the basis for a world-level industrial plant.

Conclusion

Moritani initially undertook a similar elite path to most Japanese intellectuals until he graduated from Tokyo Imperial University in 1926. At that point he became a product of Taisho liberalism and radicalism, and he stood his Marxist ground until the 1930s. However, Moritani's encounter with colonial Korea caused him to convert from being a theoretical Marxist to an imperial social scientist with a strong Pan-Asian aim. Deeply concerned with the perception of China and Korea as the epitome of "Asiatic" stagnation and underdevelopment, he realized that the construction of an East Asian empire led by Japan would not be feasible without providing alternative narratives to Western universalism and Asian particularity. This explains why he hardly resonated with the other mainstream of Pan-Asianism that emphasized the recovery of traditional Asian values vis-à-vis Westernization. Revisiting Japan's modernization as a successful example of innovative changes within Asia itself, Moritani intended to take colonial Korea as a testing ground to measure whether imperial Japan's ambition to create an East Asian empire would be possible. Therefore, his blueprint for a new Asia and a reconstructed Korea included several highly progressive plans that were aimed to reduce the political and economic distance between Japan and her imperial territories. Unquestionably, Moritani's writing during the wartime period illustrates one version of how Japanese social scientists left the ivory tower and became harbingers of an imperialist "area studies." To borrow from Wallerstein's critique of postwar area studies in the United States, this was to be achieved by producing knowledge and policies that explicitly served Japan's Pan-Asian imperial project.

Moritani's peculiar shift from being an orthodox Marxist to an imperial intellectual through his 19-year stay in colonial Korea is not the only reason this book has paid special attention to his intellectual trajectory. The content of his

Pan-Asian plan was filled with a raft of developmentalist ideas for colonial Korea and China. The illusion that the process of building an empire could be compatible with bringing qualitative and quantitative development to the colony captured the imagination of colonial intellectuals, and Korean social scientists in particular. From this new Korean intellectual commitment to Japan's empire building arises another important question, one of how this imperial social science as presented by Japanese intellectuals was accepted and challenged by colonial intellectuals, who eventually created another set of imperial knowledge, a new form of knowledge that might be best conceptualized as a colonial social science. In its last chapter, this book will trace these intellectual currents in colonial Korea in the late 1920s and 1930s and directly interrogate the content and implications set forth in Korean intellectuals' writing on the idea of Pan-Asian empire, focusing on the renowned converted Marxist, In Jeong Sik.

Notes

1 For an extended study of Kyungsung Imperial University, see Chun-yŏng Chŏng, *Kyungsung jekuk daehak kwa sikminji hegemony*, Ph.D. Dissertation, Seoul National University, 2009. About the establishment of the Imperial University system, see Amano Ikuo, *Teikoku Daigaku: kindai nihon no erito ikusei sochi* [Imperial University: Colonial Control and Producing Elites in Modern Japan] (Tokyo: Iwanami Shoten, 2017). However, Amano's work does not include two imperial universities established in Japan's colony: Kyungsung Imperial University and Taihoku Imperial University in Taipei, Taiwan.

2 To name a few Korean specialists who came to colonial Korea with the opening of Kyungsung Imperial University, Imanishi Ryu (1875~1931) took the Korean History Lecture and Takahashi Toru (1878–1967) taught Korean linguistics and literature. Shigata Hiroshi (1900–1973) took the First Economics Lecture and produced numerous works on the economic history of Korea. See Yun Hae-Dong and Chun-yŏng Chŏng, eds., *Kyŏngsŏng Cheguk Taehak kwa Tongyanghak yŏn'gu* [Kyunsung Imperial University and Oriental Studies] (Seoul: Sŏnin, 2018).

3 Jeong Gun Sik, ed., *Singmin kwŏllyŏk kwa kŭndae chisi: Kyŏngsŏng Cheguk Taehak yŏn'gu* [Colonial Power and Modern Knowledge: A Study of Kyungsung Imperial University] (Seoul: Sŏul Taehakkyo Ch'ulp'an Munhwawŏn, 2011), 8.

4 On July 3rd 1930, the Seodaemun Branch of the Kyungsung Police Bureau sent a document filed under the title of "documents about thought" to the Kyungsung Local Court about Moritani's recent activities. In this document, Moritani's status was designated as a "figure under special monitoring." Documents from the Prosecution Bureau at the Kyungsung Local Court, database available at the National Institute of Korean History. Lee Chung Woo also introduces Moritani as one of a few Marxist professors at Keijo Imperial University. Lee Chung Woo, *Kyungsung jekuk daehak* [Kyungsung Imperial University] (Seoul: Darakwon, 1980).

5 Moritani Katsumi, *Aziateki seisan yoshiki ron* [On the Asiatic Mode of Production] (Tokyo: Rikuseisha, 1937), 64–65.

6 Moritani Katsumi, "Shakai minshushgi no minzoku riron danben [A Thought on the Theory of Nation in Social Democracy]," in *Chōsen keizai kenkyū* (Kyoto: Irie Shoin, 1929), 7–8. Moritani referred to Kautsky's 1887 work on modern nationality in *Die Neue Zeit*.

7 Moritani Katsumi, "Shakai minshushgi no minzoku riron danben," 8–22. For a study of the Kautsky and Bauer debate, see Sakuma Periwal, ed., *Notions of Nationalism* (London: Central European University: Oxford University Press, 1995).

8 Ibid. Bauer's own definition of national character is as follows: "We will call the complex of physical and intellectual characteristics that distinguishes one nation from another its national character. Over and above these differences, all peoples share certain characteristics that identify us as human beings." Otto Bauer, *The Question of Nationalities and Social Democracy*, trans. Joseph O'Donnell (Minneapolis: University of Minnesota Press, 2000), 20.

9 Moritani Katsumi, "Shakai minshushgi no minzoku riron danben," 43.

10 Otto Bauer, *The Question of Nationalities and Social Democracy*, 418.

11 Marx wrote:

> England, it is true, in causing a social revolution in Hindostan, was actuated only by the vilest interests, and was stupid in her manner of enforcing them. But that is not the question. *The question is, can mankind fulfill its destiny without a fundamental revolution in the social state of Asia? If not, whatever may have been the crimes of . England she was the unconscious tool of history in bringing about the revolution.*
> (emphasis added). Karl Marx, "Die britische Herrschaft in Indien,"
> in *Karl Marx on India*, trans. Iqbal Husain (New Delhi:
> Tulika Books, 2006), 16–17.

12 Many previous studies on the Asiatic mode of production debate in Japan and China deserve attention and some of them include Joshua A. Fogel, "The Debates over the Asiatic Mode of Production in Soviet Russia, China, and Japan," *American Historical Review* 93, no. 1 (Feb. 1988), 56–79; Timothy Brook, ed., *The Asiatic Mode of Production in China* (New York: M. E. Sharpe, 1989).

13 See "Forms Which Precede Capitalist Production (Concerning the process which precedes the formation of the capital relation or of original accumulation)," in *Grundrisse: Foundations of the Critiques of Political Economy*, ed. Karl Marx, trans. Martin Nicolaus (London and New York: Penguin Books in association with New Left Review, 1993), 471–479.

14 Karl Marx, *Grundrisse: Foundations of the Critiques of Political Economy*, 475.

15 Ludvig Mad'iar, *Puroretaria kagaku kenkyūkai chūgoku mondai kenkyūkai*, trans. *Chūgoku noson keizai kenkyū* (1) [A Study of Agricultural Economy in China] (Tokyo: Kibokaku, 1931).

16 Ibid., 10.

17 Germaine Hoston, *Marxism and the Crisis of Development in Prewar Japan* (Princeton: Princeton University Press, 1986), 140–145.

18 The term *koza-ha* was widely used by students of Japanese Marxism as Marxist social scientists in this group published a monumental eight-volume work, entitled *Nihon shihonshugi hattatsushi kōza* (*Lectures on the Developmental History of Japanese Capitalism*) between 1933 and 1934.

19 Aikawa Haruki, "Ajiateki kannenkeitai heno keikō – 'ajiateki seisanyoshiki to godesteki kenkai' [The Tendency of 'Asiatic' Perspectives – the Asiatic Mode of Production and M. Godes]," *Shisō* 139 (Dec. 1933): 79.

20 Ibid., 80–81.

21 Aikawa Haruki, "Ajiateki seisanyoshiki no nihon rekishi e no「tekiyō」ron ni kanrenshite [On the Application of the Asiatic Mode of Production to Japanese History]," *Rekishikagaku* 2, no. 3 (May 1933): 48.

22 Hayakawa Jirō, "Iwayuru tōyōshi ni okeru「doreishōyushateki kōsei no ketsujō」wo ikani setumei subekika? [How to Explain the Absence of the Formation of Slavery Owners in East Asian History?]" *Yuibutsuron kenkyū* 30 (Apr. 1935): 114–125.

23 Ibid., 117.

24 Ibid., 115–116.

25 Ibid., 116.

26 Hayakawa Jirō, "Doreishoyūshateki kōsei to tōyōteki keitai no mondai [The Problem of the East Asian Formation of Slave Owners]," *Yuibutsuron kenkyū* 33 (July 1935): 75.

27 Ibid.
28 Moritani Katsumi, *Aziateki seisan yoshiki ron*, 38–42.
29 Ibid., 39. The exact sentences written by Marx are as follows:

> The *stationary nature* of this part of Asia, despite all the aimless activity on the
> political surface, can be completely explained by two mutually supporting circum-
> stances: 1. The public works system of the central government and, 2. Alongside
> this, the entire Empire which, apart from a few large cities, is an agglomeration of
> villages, each with its own distinct organisation and each forming its own small
> world. . . . In some of these communities the lands of the village cultivated in com-
> mon, in most of them each occupant tills his own field. Within the same, slavery
> and the caste system. Waste lands for common pasture. Home-weaving and spin-
> ning by wives and daughters. These idyllic republics, of which only the village
> boundaries are jealously guarded against neighbouring villages, continue to exist in
> well-nigh perfect form in the North Western parts of India only recently occupied
> by the English. No more solid basis for *Asiatic despotism and stagnation* is, I think,
> conceivable.

    Marx-Engels Correspondence 1853, London, 14 June 1853, Karl Marx and Frederick
    Engels, *Collected Works* 39 (New York: International Publishers, 1975–2004), 344.
30 Moritani Katsumi, *Aziateki seisan yoshiki ron*, 70–72.
31 Ibid., 73.
32 Lee Chung Won, "Aziateki seisanyoshikiron to chōsenhōkenshakaishi [The Asiatic
    Mode of Production and the Social History of Feudal Chosun Korea]," *Yuibutsuron
    kenkyū* 13 (Apr. 1935).
33 Ibid., 128.
34 Ibid., 129. These are (1) artificial irrigation, (2) Asiatic or oriental despotism, (3)
    national ownership of land, (4) taxes = land taxes, (5) existence of agricultural com-
    munity, (6) irreversible and repetitive stagnation, and (7) combination of agriculture
    and familial handcraft industry.
35 Ibid., 137.
36 Ibid., 146.
37 Ibid.
38 Ibid.
39 Hirano Yoshitarō, *Nihon shihonshugi shakaino kikō* [The Structure of Capitalist Soci-
    ety in Japan] (Tokyo: Iwanami Shoten, 1934), 293.
40 Nagaoka Shinkichi, "Kōzaha riron no denkai to ajia ninshiki – hirano yoshitarō no baai
    [The Development of Theories in the Lecturer-Faction and Its Asian Perception – the
    Case of Hirano Yoshitarō]," *Keizaigaku kenkyū* 34, no. 4 (Mar. 1985): 460.
41 Hirano Yoshitarō, "Shina kenkyū ni taisuru hutatsu no michi [The Two Ways of Study
    on China]," *Yuibuturon kenkyū* 20 (June 1934): 5–27.
42 Ibid., 5.
43 Ibid.
44 Hirano Yoshitarō, "Kaitai wo maeni seru kyūshina no keizai, shakai – adamu smisu no
    shinaron [The Economy and Society of Old China on the Verge of Transition: Adam
    Smith's Writing on China]," *Chūōkōron* 49, no. 1 (Jan. 1934): 15–36.
45 Hani Goro, *Meiji ishinshi kenkyū* [A Study of the Meiji Restoration] (Tokyo: Iwa-
    nami Shoten, 1978), 77–83. Hani's original texts were published four times in *Shigaku
    zasshi* no. 2, no. 3, no. 6, and no. 8 (all in 1932).
46 Ibid., 106.
47 Ibid., 49.
48 Ibid., 115.
49 Karl Wittfogel, *Oriental Despotism: A Comparative Study of Total Power* (New
    Haven: Yale University Press, 1957). For a detailed study on Karl Wittfogel's

scholarship in the context of the Cold War, see Ishii Tomoaki, *Karl bitfogeru no toyoteki shakairon* [Karl Wittfogel's Theory of Oriental Society] (Tokyo: Shakaihy-oronsha, 2008).

50   Wittfogel's works started to appear in Japanese language in 1929. The publications of his works before 1934 were as follows: Karl Wittfogel, *Son issen to shina kakumei* [Sun Yat Sen and Chinese Revolution], trans. Eiichi Tsutsui (Tokyo: Nagata Shoten, 1929); Karl Wittfogel, "Marukusushigi ni okeru futotekikeikino igi [The Significance of Climate in Marxism]," trans. Sakada Yoshiochō, *Shisō* 103 (Dec. 1930): 110–123; Hermann Duncker, Alfons Goldschmidt and Karl August Wittfogel, eds., *Marukusu shugi rōdōsha kyōtei: Kokusai rōdōsha undōshi* (*Marxistische Arbeiter Schulung. Geschichte der Internationalen Arbeiterbewegung*) [Educating Workers in Marxism: The International History of Workers' Movement], trans. Buhei Kitajima (Tokyo: Chu-gai Shobo, 1931), 2 vols; Karl Wittfogel, *Geopolitik, Geographischer Materialismus und Marxismus, Chirigaku hihan* [Critiques of Geography], trans. Kawanishi Seikan (Kyoto: Yukosha, 1933); Karl Wittfogel, *Jinrui shakai hattatsushi gaiyō* [An Introduc-tion to the History of Progress in Human Society], trans. Mizuno Chikara, Nijima Shigeru and Kume Makoto (*Vom Urkommunismus bis zur proletarischen Revolution*) (Tokyo: Ōhata Shoten, 1934).

51   Karl Wittfogel, *Kaitai katei ni aru shina no keizai to shakai* [Chinese Society and Economy in the Process of Dismantling] (*Wirtschaft und Gesellschaft Chinas; Versuch der wissenschaftlichen Analyse einer grossen asiatischen Agrargesellschaft*, 1931), trans. Hirano Yoshitarō (Tokyo: Chūōkōronsha, 1934), 2 vols.

52   The other two translators were Ota Morimichi who translated the first part of volume one and Yokokawa Jiro who translated the second volume. Hirano Yoshitarō, *Kaitai katei ni aru shina no keizai to shakai*, 2. In 1935, Yokokawa published a book that included his translations of Wittfogel's four articles. Karl Wittfogel, *Shina keizaishi kenkyū* [A Study on the Economic History of China], trans. Yorokawa Jirō (Tokyo: Sōbunkaku, 1935).

53   Karl Wittfogel, Moritani Katsumi and Hirano Yoshitarō, trans., *Tōyōteki shakai no riron* [Theories of Oriental Society] (Tokyo: Nihonhyōronsha, 1939). The English translation appears in several works, including M. Fried, ed., *Readings in Anthro-pology* (New York: Crowell, 1968), 2 vols., 180–198; Anne M. Bailey and Josep R. Llobera, eds., *The Asiatic Mode of Production: Science and Politics* (London: Rout-ledge, 1981), 141–157.

54   Karl Wittfogel, "Marukusushugini okeru futotekikeikino igi (fudoseijigaku, chiriteki-yuibuturonn narabini marukusushugi)," 110–123.

55   Ibid., 118–119.

56   Ibid., 118.

57   Karl Wittfogel, *Chirigaku hihan.*

58   Ibid., 56–57.

59   Karl Wittfogel, *Shina shakai no kagakuteki kenkyū* [A Scientific Study on Chinese Society], trans. Hirano Yoshitarō (Tokyo: Iwanami Shoten, 1939), 57. This book was a compilation of Wittfogel's writings on China in the late 1930s. The first chapter of this book, which contains the core part of Wittfogel's methodology on China stud-ies, was the translation of Wittfogel's 1938 report, "New Light on Chinese Society, an investigation of China's Socio-economic Structure," published by the International Secretarist, Institute of Pacific Relations.

60   Moritani Katsumi, "Chōsen shakai to shizen kankyo [Korean Society and Natural Environment] (1)," *Tōa* 7, no. 12 (1934): 43–45.

61   Karl Wittfogel, *Kaitai katei ni aru shina no keizai to shakai*, trans. Hirano Yoshitarō, 238–471.

62   Ibid.

63   Hirano Yoshitarō, "Shina kenkyū ni taisuru hutatsu no michi," 20–27.

64 Anne M. Bailey and Josep R. Llobera, eds., *The Asiatic Mode of Production: Science and Politics*, 156–157.

65 Fukuritsu Shōji, "Wittofoguru hakase no nihon hōmon [Dr. Wittfogel's Visit to Japan]," *Shinagaku* 8, no. 1 (1935): 133–141.

66 Karl Wittfogel, *Shina shakai no kagakuteki kenkyū*, 189–191.

67 Ibid. Wittfogel's view on the stage of Japanese economic development can be found in other writings. In "The Foundations and Stages of Chinese Economic History," he wrote on Japan as follows:

> Attempted explanations based on metaphysical or racial considerations are evidently incapable of making intelligible why *Japan, at the end of the nineteenth century, could so promptly evolve into industrial capitalism, while China has not even yet been able to do so.* But comparison of the socio-economic systems of the two countries quickly shows that Japan, in contrast to China, was not an "Asiatic" country in our sense. It had indeed an "Asiatic" tinge (irrigational economy on a small scale), but was nevertheless fundamentally more akin to the European nations: her advanced feudal economy in the nineteenth century had already taken the preliminary steps toward the evolution of industrial capitalism.
>
> (emphasis added). Karl Wittfogel, "The Foundations and Stages of Chinese Economic History," in *Zeitschrift für Sozialforschung 4* (Paris: Librairie Félix Alcan, 1935), 57–58.

68 Moritani Katsumi, *Shina shakai keizaishi* (Tokyo: Shōkasha, 1934). For a recent study of Moritani's concept of the Orient, see Koyasu Nobukuni, "Chūgoku ron wo yomu: showa (jihen = senso) ki ni okeru 'Tōyōteki shakai' no koso – moritani katsumi <Tōyōteki shakai no riron> wo yomu" [Reading a Theory of China: A Concept of Asiatic Society in Interwar Japan; Reading <Theories of Asiatic Society> by Moritani Katsumi]," *Gendai shisō* 40, no. 6 (May 2012): 54–62.

69 Moritani Katsumi, "Shikendai to kaitaiki to okeru kyurai no chōsen shakai [The Problem of the Economy of Colonial Korea at the New Stage]," in *Aziateki seisan yoshiki ron*, 265. The original article was contributed to the journal *Toa* (East Asia) with a slightly different title in July 1934.

70 Fukuda Tokuzō, *Keizaigaku zenshu* 4 [Completed Works of Economics] (Tokyo: Kaizōsha, 1925), 1–56, 77–162. I revisit Fukuda's impact on Korean studies in early twentieth- century Japan in Chapter 5.

71 See "Introduction" in Tsuda Sokichi, *Shina shisō to nihon* [Chinese Thought and Japan] (Tokyo: Iwanami Shoten, 1938). In 1940, Minoda Muneki, an ultra-nationalist critic, accused Tsuda of *lese majesty* for the Emperor, problematizing Tsuda's empirical research on the genealogy of the Japanese emperor system. As a result, Tsuda was deprived of his professorship at Waseda University and the publication of his major books was banned. However, it is important to note that a prosecution on Tsuda does not mean that he resisted against Japan's war during the wartime period.

72 Samuel P. Huntington, *The Clash of Civilizations and the Remaking of World Order* (New York: Simon & Schuster, 1996).

73 Moritani Katsumi, *Ajiateki seisan yoshiki ron*, 127–134.

74 Ibid., 132.

75 Ibid., 133–134.

76 Ibid., 134.

77 Moritani Katsumi, "Toyoron [On the Orient]," *Hitostubashi shibun*, May 10, 1939; *Tōyōteki seikatsuken* (Tokyo: Ikuseisha Kōdōgaku, 1942), 9.

78 Moritani Katsumi, *Tōyōteki seikatsuken*, 19.

79 Ibid., 41.

80 Ibid.

81 Moritani Katsumi, "Iwayuru aziateki seisan yoshiki to chosen [The So-called Asiatic Mode of Production and Chosun Korea]," *Keijo gakubo* 17 (June 1938), in *Tōyōteki seikatsuken*, 173–177.

82 Moritani Katusumi, "Tōa nogyo ni okeru chōsen nogyo no ichi [The Position of Agriculture in Colonial Korea in East Asian Agriculture]," *Shokuryoseisaku* 5, no. 1 (Jan. 1939): 13–18; also in *Tōyōteki seikatsuken*, 183–184.

83 Moritani, "Shindankai ni okeru chosenkeizai no mondai [The Problem of the Economy of Colonial Korea at the New Stage]," *Shunjū* (Aug. 1941), in *Tōyōteki seikatsuken*, 242.

84 Moritani Katsumi, "Tōa kyōdōtai no rinen to naisenittai [The East Asian Community and the Theory of Japan and Korea as One Body]," *Ryokki* 4, no. 8 (1939): 18–19.

85 Ibid., 20.

86 Ibid., 21.

87 A roundtable discussion, "Hanto no nōsonmondai wo kataru [Discussing Agricultural Problems in Chosun Korea]," *Ryokki* 6, no. 2 (Feb. 1941): 149.

88 Ibid. See also Iwata Tatsuo, "Chōsen nōgyō saihenseini oite no kakusho [A Statement on the Reconstruction of Agriculture in Chosun Korea]," *Chōsen gyōsei* 21, no. 8 (1941): 6.

89 Hirano Yoshitarō, "Ranryo higashiind no tōchi-gyōsei no kihon seisaku [The Basic Policy of Governmental Administration in Dutch East Indies]," *Hōritujihō* 14, no. 1 (Jan. 1942): 27.

90 Ibid.

91 Hirano Yoshitarō and Kiyono Kenji, *Taiheyō no minzoku = seijigaku* [Nation of the Asia-Pacific Ocean = Political Science] (Tokyo: Nihonhyōronsha, 1942), 234.

92 Hirano Yoshitarō, "Shina ni okeru kyōto no shakaiseikatsu wo kiritsusuru minzoku dōtoku [Ethnic Ethics That Regulates the Life of Social Corporation in Chinese Village Communities]," *Hōritujihō* 15, no. 11 (Nov. 1943): 7–14.

93 Ibid., 10–13.

94 Ibid.

95 See Chapter 2, "Shina shakai no kitetoshite no kotooyobisonojiji," in *Dai ajia shugi no rekishiteki kiso* [The Historical Basis of Greater Asianism], ed. Hirano Yoshitarō (Tokyo: Nihonhyōronsha, 1945), 135–168.

96 Ibid., 140.

97 Moritani Katsumi, *Tōyōteki seikatsuken*, 192.

98 A number of writings on economic control appeared in major journals during the wartime period. See, for example, Hijikata Seibi, *Nihon keizai no michi* [The Way of the Japanese Economy] (Tokyo: Nihonhyōronsha, 1938).

99 Moritani Katsumi, "Kenkyūseikatsu wo kaerimite [A Reflection on My Own Research]," in *Chūkoku shakaikeizaishi: moritani katsumi ikoronbunshu* [The Socio-Economic History of China: A Collection of Essays by Moritani Katsumi], ed. Koyasu Michiko (Kawasaki: Koyasu Michiko, 1965), 150–151.

100 It appeared that Moritani was interested in the notion of social nation (社会国家), that is, the state intervenes in the everyday life of the ordinary people through social, labor and population policies. Takaoka Hiroyuki, *Sōryokusen taisei to fukushi kokka: senjiki nihon no shakai kaikaku kōsō* [From the Total War System to Welfare State: The Notion of Social Reforms in Wartime Japan] (Tokyo: Iwanami Shoten, 2011).

101 Moritani Katsumi, "Shakaiseisaku no rekishito kainen kosei [The History of Social Policy and Its Conceptual Formation]," *Keijōteikoku daigaku hōgakukai ronshū* 15, no. 2 (1944): 125.

102 Moritani Katsumi, "Shakaiseisaku no honjitue no tankyu – josetu [In Search for the Essence of Social Policy: An Introduction]," *Keijōteikoku daigaku hōgakukai ronshū* 13, no. 2 (1942): 226.

103 Mori Kojiro, *Shakai seisaku yoron* [The Essence of Social Policy] (Tokyo: Nihonhyoronsha, 1935).
104 Ōkochi Kazuo, *Senji shakai seisakuron* [On Wartime Social Policy] (Tokyo: Nihonhyoronsha, 1940), 21.
105 Moritani Katsumi, "Shakai seisaku no atarashi hoko to chōsen [A New Direction to Social Policy and Chosun Korea]," *Chōsen shakai jigyo* 18, no. 11 (1940): 14–19.
106 Moritani Katsumi, *Tōyōteki seikatsuken*, 280–298.
107 Ibid., 298–304.
108 Chōsen sotokubu, *The Official Gazette of the Governor General's Office of Chosun Korea*, no. 4177, Dec. 23, 1940.
109 *The Official Gazette of the Governor General's Office of Chosun Korea*, no. 5502, June 5, 1945.
110 Moritani Katsumi, "Toa no kokudo keikaku [National Land Planning in East Asia]," *Seikeiorai* (Feb. 1941), in *Tōyōteki seikatsuken*, 354–356.
111 Ibid., 355.
112 Ibid., 356.
113 The German title of Pollock's work was *Die planwirtschaftlichen Versuche in der Sowjetunion, 1917–1927* and it was published in 1929; Moritani translated it into Japanese, titled *Sovieto renpō keikaku keizai shiron* [The History of Planned Economy in the Soviet Union] (Tokyo: Dōjinsha Shoten, 1932).
114 Moritani Katsumi, "Kōgyo richi gairon [An Introduction to the Theory of Industrial Location]," in *Senji sangyō keieikōwa*, ed. Chōsen shōko kaigisho (Kyungsung: Chōsen Kōrōnsha, 1944), 264–266.
115 Moritani Katsumi, "Tōa kyōei keizairon [A Theory of Economic Co-Prosperity in East Asia]," *Chūōkōron* 56, no. 10 (Oct. 1941): 29.
116 Ibid.
117 For a recent study on the construction of Sup'ung Dam, see Aaron Moore, " 'The Yalu River Era of Developing Asia': Japanese Expertise, Colonial Power, and the Construction of Sup'ung Dam," *Journal of Asian Studies* 72, no. 1 (Feb. 2013): 115–139.

Bibliography

A roundtable discussion. "Hanto no nōsonmondai wo kataru [Discussing Agricultural Problems in Chosun Korea]." *Ryokki* 6, no. 2 (Feb. 1941): 148–158.

Aaron, Moore. " 'The Yalu River Era of Developing Asia': Japanese Expertise, Colonial Power, and the Construction of Sup'ung Dam." *Journal of Asian Studies* 72, no. 1 (Feb. 2013): 115–139.

Aikawa, Haruki. "Ajiateki kannenkeitai heno keikō – 'ajiateki seisanyoshiki to godesteki kenkai' [The Tendency of 'Asiatic' Perspectives – the Asiatic Mode of Production and M. Godes]." *Shisō* 139 (Dec. 1933): 67–87.

———. "Ajiateki seisanyoshiki no nihon rekishi e no tekiyō 」 ron ni kanrenshite [On the Application of the Asiatic Mode of Production to Japanese History]." *Rekishikagaku* 2, no. 3 (May 1933): 41–48.

Amano, Ikuo. *Teikoku Daigaku: kindai nihon no erito ikusei sochi* [Imperial University: Colonial Control and Producing Elites in Modern Japan]. Tokyo: Iwanami Shōten, 2017.

Bailey, Anne M. and Josep R. Llobera, eds. *The Asiatic Mode of Production: Science and Politics*. London: Routledge, 1981.

Bauer, Otto. *The Question of Nationalities and Social Democracy*. Translated by Joseph O'Donnell. Minneapolis: University of Minnesota Press, 2000.

Brook, Timothy, ed. *The Asiatic Mode of Production in China*. New York: M. E. Sharpe, 1989.

Chŏng, Chun-yŏng. *Kyungsung jekuk daehak kwa sikminji hegemony* [Kyungsung Imperial University and Colonial Hegemony]. Ph.D. Dissertation, Seoul National University, 2009.

Chōsen sotokubu. *Chōsen sotokubu kanpo* [The Official Gazette of the Governor General's Office of Chosun Korea], no. 4177, Dec. 23, 1940.

———. *Chōsen sotokubu kanpo* [The Official Gazette of the Governor General's Office of Chosun Korea], no. 5502, June 5, 1945.

Duncker, Hermann, Alfons Goldschmidt and Karl August Wittfogel, eds. *Marxistische Arbeiter Schulung. Geschichte der Internationalen Arbeiterbewegung*. Trans. Kitajima, Buhei. *Marukusu shugi rōdōsha kyōtei: Kokusai rōdōsha undōshi* [Educating Workers in Marxism: The International History of Workers' Movement]. Tokyo: Chugai Shobo, 1931, 2 vols.

Fogel, Joshua A. "The Debates over the Asiatic Mode of Production in Soviet Russia, China, and Japan." *American Historical Review* 93, no. 1 (Feb. 1988): 56–79.

Fukuda, Tokuzō. *Keizaigaku zenshu* 4 [Completed Works of Economics]. Tokyo: Kaizōsha, 1925.

Fukuritsu, Shōji. "Wittofoguru hakase no nihon hōmon [Dr. Wittfogel's Visit to Japan]." *Shinagaku* 8, no. 1 (1935): 133–141.

Hani, Goro. *Meiji ishinshi kenkyū* [A Study of the Meiji Restoration]. Tokyo: Iwanami Shōten, 1978.

Hayakawa, Jirō. "Doreishoyūshateki kōsei to tōyōteki keitai no mondai [The Problem of the East Asian Formation of Slave Owners]." *Yuibutsuron kenkyū* 33 (July 1935): 61–79.

———. "Iwayuru tōyōshi ni okeru ʃdoreishōyushateki kōsei no ketsujoʃ wo ikani setumei subekika? [How to Explain the Absence of the Formation of Slavery Owners in East Asian History?]." *Yuibutsuron kenkyū* 30 (Apr. 1935): 114–125.

Hijikata, Seibi. *Nihon keizai no michi* [The Way of the Japanese Economy]. Tokyo: Nihonhyōronsha, 1938.

Hirano, Yoshitarō and Kiyono Kenji. *Dai ajia shugi no rekishiteki kiso* [The Historical Basis of Greater Asianism]. Tokyo: Nihonhyōronsha, 1945.

———. "Kaitai wo maeni seru kyūshina no keizai, shakai – adamu smisu no shinaron [The Economy and Society of Old China on the Verge of Transition: Adam Smith's Writing on China]." *Chūōkōron* 49, no. 1 (Jan. 1934): 15–36.

———. *Nihon shihonshugi shakaino kikō* [The Structure of Capitalist Society in Japan]. Tokyo: Iwanami Shōten, 1934.

———. "Ranryo higashiind no tōchi-gyōsei no kihon seisaku [The Basic Policy of Governmental Administration in Dutch East Indies]." *Hōritujihō* 14, no. 1 (Jan. 1942): 26–34.

———. "Shina kenkyū ni taisuru hutatsu no michi [The Two Ways of Study on China]." *Yuibuturon kenkyū* 20 (June 1934): 5–27.

———. "Shina ni okeru kyōto no shakaiseikatsu wo kiritsusuru minzoku dōtoku [Ethnic Ethics That Regulates the Life of Social Corporation in Chinese Village Communities]." *Hōritujihō* 15, no. 11 (Nov. 1943): 7–14.

———. *Taiheyō no minzoku = seijigaku* [Nation of the Asia-Pacific Ocean = Political Science]. Tokyo: Nihonhyōronsha, 1942.

Hoston, Germaine. *Marxism and the Crisis of Development in Prewar Japan*. Princeton: Princeton University Press, 1986.

Huntington, Samuel P. *The Clash of Civilizations and the Remaking of World Order*. New York: Simon & Schuster, 1996.

Ishii, Tomoaki. *Karl bitfogeru no toyoteki shakairon* [Karl Wittfogel's Theory of Oriental Society]. Tokyo: Shakaihyoronsha, 2008.

Iwata, Tatsuo. "Chōsen nōgyō saihenseini oite no kakusho [A Statement on the Recon-struction of Agriculture in Chosun Korea]." *Chōsen gyōsei* 21, no. 8 (1941): 1–9.

Jeong, Gun Sik, ed. *Singmin kwŏllyŏk kwa kŭndae chisi: Kyŏngsŏng Cheguk Taehak yŏn'gu* [Colonial Power and Modern Knowledge: A Study of Kyungsung Imperial University]. Seoul: Sŏul Taehakkyo Ch'ulp'an Munhwawŏn, 2011.

Karl, Marx and Frederick Engels. *Collected Works*. New York: International Publishers, 1975–2004, Vol. 39.

Koyasu, Michiko, ed. *Chūkoku shakaikeizaishi: moritani katsumi ikoronbunshu* [The Socio-Economic History of China: A Collection of Essays by Moritani Katsumi]. Kawa-saki: Koyasu Michiko, 1965.

Koyasu, Nobukuni. "Chūgoku ron wo yomu: showa (jihen = senso) ki ni okeru 'Tōyōteki shakai' no koso – moritani katsumi < Tōyōteki shakai no riron> wo yomu [Reading a Theory of China: A Concept of Asiatic Society in Interwar Japan; Reading <Theories of Asiatic Society> by Moritani Katsumi]." *Gendai shisō* 40, no. 6 (May 2012): 54–62.

Lee, Chung Won. "Aziateki seisanyoshikiron to chōsenhōkenshakaishi [The Asiatic Mode of Production and the Social History of Feudal Chosun Korea]." *Yuibutsuron kenkyū* 13 (Apr. 1935): 126–149.

Lee, Chung Woo. *Kyungsung jekuk daehak* [Kyungsung Imperial University]. Seoul: Darakwon, 1980.

Mad'iar, Ludvig. *Puroretaria kagaku kenkyūkai chūgoku mondai kenkyūkai*, trans. *Chūgoku noson keizai kenkyū* (1) [A Study of Agricultural Economy in China]. Tokyo: Kibokaku, 1931.

Marx, Karl. "Die britische Herrschaft in Indien." In *Karl Marx on India*, translated by Iqbal Husain. New Delhi: Tulika Books, 2006.

———. *Grundrisse: Foundations of the Critiques of Political Economy*. Translated by Martin Nicolaus. New York: Penguin Books in association with New Left Review, 1993.

Mori, Kojiro. *Shakai seisaku yoron* [The Essence of Social Policy]. Tokyo: Nihonhyōronsha, 1935.

Moritani, Katsumi. *Aziateki seisan yoshiki ron* [On the Asiatic Mode of Production]. Tokyo: Rikuseisha, 1937.

———. "Chōsen shakai to shizen kankyo (1) [Korean Society and Natural Environment]." *Tōa* 7, no. 12 (1934): 43–51.

———. "Kōgyo richi gairon [An Introduction to the Theory of Industrial Location]." In *Senji sangyō keieikōwa*, edited by Chōsen shōko kaigisho, 249–271. Kyungsung: Chōsen Kōrōnsha, 1944.

———. "Shakai minshushugi no minzoku riron danben [A Thought on the Theory of Nation in Social Democracy]." In *Chōsen keizai kenkyū*, 1–70. Kyoto: Irie Shoin, 1929.

———. "Shakai seisaku no atarashi hoko to chōsen [A New Direction to Social Policy and Chosun Korea]." *Chōsen shakai jigyo* 18, no. 11 (1940): 14–19.

———. "Shakaiseisaku no honjitue no tankyu – josetu [In Search for the Essence of Social Policy: An Introduction]." In *Keijōteikoku daigaku hōgakukai ronshū* 13, no. 2 (1942): 47–61.

———. "Shakaiseisaku no rekishito kainen kosei [The History of Social Policy and Its Conceptual Formation]." In *Keijōteikoku daigaku hōgakukai ronshū* 15, no. 2 (1944): 1–45.

———. *Shina shakai keizaishi* [The Economic History of Chinese Society]. Tokyo: Shōkasha, 1934.

———. "Tōa kyōdōtai no rinen to naisenittai [The East Asian Community and the Theory of Japan and Korea as One Body]." *Ryokki* 4, no. 8 (1939): 18–21.

―――. "Tōa kyōei keizairon [A Theory of Economic Co-Prosperity in East Asia]." *Chūōkōron* 56, no. 10 (Oct. 1941): 20–32.

―――. "Tōa nogyo ni okeru chōsen nogyo no ichi [The Position of Agriculture in Colonial Korea in East Asian Agriculture]." *Shokuryoseisaku* 5, no. 1 (Jan. 1939): 13–18.

―――. *Tōyōteki seikatsuken* [Oriental Living Space]. Tokyo: Ikuseisha Kōdōgaku, 1942.

Moritani, Katsumi and Hirano Yoshitarō, trans. *Tōyōteki shakai no riron* [Theories of Oriental Society]. Tokyo: Nihonhyōronsha, 1939, 2 vols.

Nagaoka, Shinkichi. "Kōzaha riron no denkai to ajia ninshiki – hirano yoshitarō no baai [The Development of Theories in the Lecturer-Faction and Its Asian Perception – the Case of Hirano Yoshitarō]." *Keizaigaku kenkyū* 34, no. 4 (Mar. 1985): 1–11.

Ōkochi, Kazuo. *Senji shakai seisakuron* [On Wartime Social Policy]. Tokyo: Nihonhyoronsha, 1940.

Periwal, Sakuma, ed. *Notions of Nationalism*. London: Central European University; Oxford University Press, 1995.

Pollock, Friedrich. *Die planwirtschaftlichen Versuche in der Sowjetunion, 1917–1927*. Trans. Katsumi, Moritani. *Sovieto renpō keikaku keizai shiron* [The History of Planned Economy in the Soviet Union]. Tokyo: Dōjinsha Shoten, 1932.

Takaoka, Hiroyuki. *Sōryokusen taisei to fukushi kokka: senjiki nihon no shakai kaikaku kōsō* [From the Total War System to Welfare State: The Notion of Social Reforms in Wartime Japan]. Tokyo: Iwanami Shōten, 2011.

Tsuda, Sōkichi. *Shina shisō to nihon* [Chinese Thought and Japan]. Tokyo: Iwanami Shōten, 1938.

Wittfogel, Karl, ed. *Geopolitik, Geographischer Materialismus und Marxismus*. Vienna: Agis Verlag, 1929. Trans. Kawanishi, Seikan. *Chirigaku hihan* [Critiques of Geography]. Kyoto: Yūkōsha, 1933.

―――. "Marukusushigi ni okeru futotekikeikino igi [The Significance of Climate in Marxism]." Translated by Sakada Yoshiochō. *Shisō* 103 (Dec. 1930): 110–123.

―――. *Oriental Despotism: A Comparative Study of Total Power*. New Haven: Yale University Press, 1957.

―――. *Shina keizaishi kenkyū* [A Study on the Economic History of China]. Translated by Yoshitarō Hirano. Tokyo: Sōbunkaku, 1935.

―――. *Shina shakai no kagakuteki kenkyū* [A Scientific Study on Chinese Society]. Translated by Yoshitarō Hirano. Tokyo: Iwanami Shōten, 1939.

―――. *Sun Yat Sen: Aufzeichnungen eines chinesischen Revolutionärs*. Trans. Eiichi, Tsutsui. *Son issen to shina kakumei* [Sun Yat Sen and Chinese Revolution]. Tokyo: Nagata Shoten, 1929.

―――. "The Foundations and Stages of Chinese Economic History." In *Zeitschrift für Sozialforschung 4*, 1–60. Paris: Librairie Félix Alcan, 1935.

―――. *Vom Urkommunismus bis zur proletarischen Revolution*. Berlin: Verl. Junge Garde, 1922. Trans. Mizuno, Chikara, Nijima Shigeru and Kume Makoto. *Jinrui shakai hattatsushi gaiyō* [An Introduction to the History of Progress in Human Society]. Tokyo: Ōhata Shoten, 1934.

―――. *Wirtschaft und Gesellschaft Chinas; Versuch der wissenschaftlichen Analyse einer grossen asiatischen Agrargesellschaft*. Leipzig: Hirschfeld, 1931. Trans. Hirano, Yoshitarō. *Kaitai katei ni aru shina no keizai to shakai* [Chinese Society and Economy in the Process of Dismantling]. Tokyo: Chūōkōronsha, 1934, 2 vols.

Yun, Hae-Dong and Chun-yŏng Chŏng, eds. *Kyŏngsŏng Cheguk Taehak kwa Tongyanghak yŏn'gu* [Kyunsung Imperial University and Oriental Studies]. Seoul: Sŏnin, 2018.

5 In Jeong Sik and the search for a Korean subjectivity

In the pages that follow, the final chapter of this book will deal with the question of how Korean social scientists searched for a Korean subjectivity in the interwar period, 1931–1945. Anti-colonial movements in Korea took on substantial theoretical divisions and differentiations during the 1920s. The failure of the 1919 March 1st Independence Movement compelled Korean intellectuals and activists into new realms of life and thought. The famous writer Yi Kwang Su portrayed his frustrations in the provocative work, *Minjokkaejoron* (On National Reconstruction), published three years after the beginning of the March 1st Movement. Summing up his feelings, Yi wrote: "Anyone who contemplates how to transform a multitudinous populace one individual at a time – to inspire twenty million people into leading civilized, rich, and powerful lives – might in truth be a bit stupefied."[1] The academics and activists who consented to Yi's standpoint in one way or another shaped one prominent intellectual stream of responses to Japanese colonialism. Instead of seeking direct liberation, they favored the idea of "autonomous rule" (*jachiron*) under Japanese control as a means to more usefully strengthen Korean power. As Michael Robinson succinctly notes, this group of intellectuals shared the assumption that "national development had to proceed further before Korea would be ready and able to maintain her political independence as a modern nation-state."[2]

Contrary to this position, some radical intellectuals concretized their own narrative of liberation in the 1920s. Heavily influenced by the spread of international communist movements in the aftermath of the 1917 Bolshevik Revolution, Korean Marxists established a threshold for communist anti-colonial movements in 1925 by constructing the first nation-wide communist organization, the Chosun Communist Party. Most intellectuals and activists involved in this party rejected the collaborative notion of autonomous rule by what they called "bourgeois" nationalists. Instead, they shared the conviction that a direct social revolution would bring to the Korean people both independence from colonialism and a solution to the iniquitous inconsistencies of capitalism.

At the turn of the 1930s, both Marxist and non-Marxist radical intellectuals shared similar concerns regarding the question of how a project of national liberation could be explained in a scientific language. And if a desire for national liberation was an *a priori* fact that could not be abandoned even despite this prolonged period of Japanese colonial rule, how, in more concrete terms, might intellectuals stimulate the general masses and organize liberating forces? From the perspective of Marxism, this question was paraphrased in a more theoretical way, one that questioned if the language of liberation in Marxism was really applicable to the reality of colonial Korea, and if a direct socialist revolution could in theory take place only in countries that are both independent as well as matured in terms of economic capitalist development. Such inquiries prodded Korean Marxists and radical intellectuals to carry out extensive research as to the nature of Korean history and society. As a result, numerous works were produced on the subject of "Chosun Korea" in the early 1930s and the intellectuals behind this new trend of knowledge production defined it as *chosunkak undong* (Korean studies movements).[3] Notwithstanding the academic scientific concerns of the movement's founders, as their very deliberately selected nomenclature might indicate, the optimistic final destination of the Chosun studies movement was to provide the Korean people with a new route toward liberation and the establishment of a modern nation-state.

At stake here is the question of how these radical intellectuals, whose academic inquiries were designed to focus on Korea, were unavoidably forced to also consider the rapidly changing topography of the Japanese empire. As discussed before, the Manchurian Incident marked a turning point, provoking the emergence of various regionally focused discourses from Japanese intellectuals, and Korean intellectuals' search for a Korean subjectivity was equally newly conditioned. And while Japanese Marxists' perspectives were essentially subordinate to ideas of so-called Emperor-way fascism as early as 1934, Korean intellectuals were also placed in a position of having to respond to, and within, Japan's project of Pan-Asian empire building. If radical Korean intellectuals, like their Japanese counterparts, in their sympathies also resonated with the logic of a Pan-Asian empire, how should their writings in this tumultuous period be historicized? In this respect, this chapter will reveal another facet of the primary question posited in this book, that is, the addressing of exactly why and how radical and liberal intellectuals ended up endorsing a Pan-Asian imperial project.

To this end, this book first pays attention to the boom of Chosun studies in the mid-1930s, as it was established as an intellectual campaign to put forth a comprehensive set of knowledge on Korean history and society, by focusing on the works of the Korean social scientists behind this movement. Second, this chapter examines the question of how scientific Korean studies encountered imperial discourses and produced a Koreanized vision of a Pan-Asian empire, and to address this question, this chapter will focus on the writings of In Jeong Sik (1907 – ?), a prominent Marxist agricultural economist who collaborated with the Japanese empire.

Discovering Chosun Korea: *Chosunhak* movements

From the beginning, the *Chosunhak* movements were a highly politically motivated intellectual engagement with colonial reality. Going beyond an attempt to reconfirm some intrinsic nativist sense of Korean identity, these intellectuals strove to find a more sophisticated set of explanations that would promote the status of ethnic affinity among Koreans to the level of an autonomous political awareness. They were convinced that through this, a new route for anti-colonial movements could be created, and at the same time a postcolonial independent nation-state could also be imagined. However, there was little consensus over what should constitute the primary contents of this new Korean subjectivity, and several different groups of intellectuals developed Korean studies in their own way. Despite such theoretical diversity, Korean intellectuals broadly found that history would offer a powerful tool to support their search for a Korean subjectivity. By tracing the trajectory of Korea's various encounters with the world civilization over time, they believed that a source for overcoming the reality of colonialism could be discovered. This observation gave rise to a boom of historiographical studies in the various fields of Korean literature, philosophy and history.

Notions of universality and particularity generated disagreements over the essence of Korean society and history. A group of intellectuals, mostly trained in Marxism and radical political economy, put forward a social scientific methodology and stressed that Korean history must be rewritten in the more general context of universal development as characterized by a globally shared idea of "world history." Accordingly, they made savage critiques of Korean historians whose scholarship had focused on discovering the authentic characteristics of the Korean people. For instance, the creation myth of Dan'gun emerged as a controversial issue among Korean intellectuals. A renowned historian and intellectual Choi Nam Sun began extensively writing on Dan'gun and argued that *Gojoseon*, the first ancient Korean state, was founded by Dan'gun in 2333 BCE. Given that Dan'gun was regarded as a mythical creature in Korean historiography, Choi boldly attempted to bring myth to the realm of official history. Behind this seemingly unscientific approach to the origin of the Korean ethnic community lay an explicit intention to ward off the specter of China in Korean history. As such, this was a challenge to the popular perception that the formation of Korean history and culture was heavily influenced by Chinese civilization.

Choi stressed that the Gojoseon state existed almost 4000 years ago and was independent of ancient Chinese influence. He attributed Gojoseon's success to Dan'gun's founding philosophy *Hongik Ingan* (Live and work for the benefit of all mankind) which, he believed, epitomized the spiritual authenticity of the Korean people.[4] Such a tendency, concerned with rediscovering the spiritual origins of the Korean people, above all signified a facet of Korean nationalism that was intended to separate ancient and contemporary Korean history and culture from the influence of China and Japan. Choi also aimed to refute the idea of *nissendōsoron* (Japan and Korea having the same ancestor) which was presented by Japanese intellectuals in a political attempt to deny the indigenous origins of the Korean people.[5] He believed that an independent Korean subjectivity, in particular designed to function as an anti-colonial force, could only be located by rehabilitating the Korean spirit that originated from the Dan'gun period, and therefore called for Dan'gun to be placed at the center of Chosun studies movements.[6]

Another group of Korean social scientists, however, accused these national-ist historians of "pseudo-scientific" practice, and warned that centering ahis-torical objects such as Dan'gun at the heart of Korean studies would distort the real nature of Korean history. Simply put, the presence of Dan'gun and spiritual nationalism was seen by these social scientists as a failure of scientific thinking in Korea nationalist scholarship. A renowned economic historian Paik Nam Un (1894–1979) articulated that cause-and-effect relationships in human society over time can only be thoroughly explored by a scientific approach whose primary function is, he stressed, to provide a "tool to put human and natural experiences in order and represent them in an organized way."[7] Accordingly, he contended that writing the history of Korea from the origins of Dan'gun is a fallacy, and the idea of Dan'gun represented a mere single element in the development of Korean history.[8] Instead, he offered the historical interpretation that Dan'gun was merely a tribal chief during the primitive community era and thus he should not be con-sidered literally as the founding father of the Korean people.[9] Heavily influenced by Marxist historical materialism, Paik and like-minded social scientists stressed that proper and urgent inquiries into the nature of Korean society must be focused on examining the processes of the historical development of Chosun Korea, and thereby envisioning a revolutionary blueprint for a contemporary liberated Korea. How, then, did Paik propose a new direction for the writing of Korean history within the global context of universal historical development? In his 1933 semi-nal work, *The Social and Economic History of Chosun Korea*, he articulated the direction for his idea of Chosun studies.

> Studies of the history of Chosun must set up as their mission empirically and practically exploring the processes of its historical and social development in the past, and theorizing its movements in practice. This is possible only by analyzing class relations in the life of Korean people and historical changes in social systems, and *universally* abstracting its formality based on historical dialectics, which is the *universal rule of movements in human society*. In so doing, studies of Korean history as part of the whole history of human beings can examine the processes of the influx and development of modern capital-ism on a *world-historical* scale.[10]

(emphasis added)

To be sure, Paik was conscious that the universal rule of economic development in historical materialism had been applied differently to each society. In the case of Korean history, Paik contended that the Silla Kingdom period (676–918) of premodern Korea corresponded to the feudal stage of historical development. Accordingly, Paik centered his concerns on scientifically proving the hypothesis that slavery and private ownership had existed in premodern Korean society. As is well known, Marx emphasized that the advent of slavery and private land owner-ship were preconditions to the rise of a commodity-based commercial economy, the latter of which became a watershed for emergence of the capitalist economy proper. Therefore, Paik was closely attentive to the point that during the Silla

Kingdom period, the state initiated private land ownership and there existed an aristocratic class who also possessed private slaves.[11] To prove his arguments, Paik referred to major primary sources on premodern Korean history in Chinese and Korean languages and through this, his work was widely accepted by both Korean Marxist social scientists and cultural intellectuals as a monumental social scientific study on the history of Korea. Arguably, it was the publication of Paik's work in fall 1933 that initiated the boom of the *Chosunhak* movement from a Marxist perspective.

In spite of his harsh critique of spiritual nationalism, nationalist sentiment remained deeply ingrained in Paik's Korean history writing. His zeal for rewriting the social-economic history of Korea was in large part motivated by his discontent with the existing colonial gaze on Korean history propagated and dominated by Japanese intellectuals. Immediately after Japan's colonization of Korea in 1910, a series of Japanese academic works on Korea was produced and their common primary narrative was designed to prove the stagnant nature of Korean society and thereby justify Japan's annexation of Korea.

Paik comprehended that these Japanese intellectuals served the goals of the Japanese empire by providing a theoretical justification for Japan's colonialism in Asia. The notion of Korea as stagnated was linked to a political judgment that she was doomed to become the object of Western imperialism due to her inability to deal with any external pressures, and thus Japan, as a neighbor of Korea, was entitled to "advance" Korea under imperial dominion, in the name of civilization and enlightenment. Given that Japanese intellectuals such as Fukuzawa Yukichi had previous theorized early Meiji discourses in support of Japan's colonization of Asia, it is not surprising that similar colonial perspectives gained a wide audience among Japanese intellectuals in the early twentieth century. The primary gravity of the stagnation theory in Japanese academia in the 1910s and 1920s, however, lies in the fact that even progressive and liberal social scientists made a significant contribution to the spread of this theory. Interestingly enough, Fukuda Tokuzō, Paik's own teacher at Tokyo University of Commerce (present-day Hitotsubashi University), was one of these Marxist social scientists whose radical thinking was paradoxically utilized to completely denounce Korean society. In 1903–1905, a period during which Japan was finalizing her colonial project in Korea, Fukuda published three provocative articles, titled "Economic Units and Organizations in Korea."[12] They were written after Fukuda's short visit to Korea in 1903. Fukuda's narrative symbolizes how the notion of universality had already penetrated the mindset of Japanese social scientists by the early 1900s. The first 20 pages of his work was dedicated to explicating the processes of universal development in the world economy. According to him, a modern economic system is characterized by transforming individual economic units such as urban economy into a national economy (*kokumin keizai*).[13] He stressed that the rise of a modern national economy, however, did not naturally occur in all economic organizations, and profound deviations exist among each racial community.[14]

Based on these observations, Fukuda first critically reviewed the Euro-centric tendency within the studies of economics. He argued that it had been widely considered that only Western countries had reached the level of a genuine modern national economy.[15] Fukuda, however, was vocal in challenging such a viewpoint and maintained that the developmental degree of the Japanese national economy was commensurate with that of the West. In order to make his argument sound impartial, he exemplified works on economic development in Japan by Western scholars. Among them, Fukuda found that Karl Rathgen's (1856–1921) works would perfectly correspond to his intention. Rathgen, a German economist, was one of the several Western scholars who had a profound knowledge of Japan. Teaching law and public administration at Tokyo Imperial University, Rathgen spent eight years in Japan between 1882 and 1890. Upon his return to Germany, he published a series of books on the development of the Japanese economy and called for Western scholars to pay attention to the Japanese experience in a highly positive tone.[16] To highlight Rathgen's discussion, Fukuda directly brought several German paragraphs from Rathgen's books to his articles and provided Japanese translations.[17] Rathgen's work played a pivotal role in demonstrating Fukuda's thesis that an evolved national economy had emerged outside the West and thus Fukuda, as a Japanese social scientist, believed that he was now entitled to evaluate Korean society from an "objective" universal standpoint. Importantly, Fukuda's writings on Korean economy were contextualized in such a clear-cut epistemology of universality and particularity, and he literally applied this logic to his observations of Korean society in more general terms.[18]

For this reason, the tone of Fukuda's writing on Korea was already determined by this direction and he faithfully concretized his stagnation theory in regard to the Korean economy. He first fired against the nature of the commercial economy in Chosun Korea. The widespread phenomenon of high-rate loan, Fukuda contended, had prevented a monetary commercial economy from emerging. Due to the fact that surplus values were not circulated in the commercial market and rather enriched only a small group of loan-sharking brokers, he analyzed that the economy in Chosun Korea was dominated by what he termed a low-level ambition to fulfill individuals' interest-seeking goals rather than upgrade the whole economy to a national one.[19] He continued to argue that the stagnant economic system was exactly mirrored in the political system in which the monarch could not even usefully execute its power as the highest authority, but in political and functional administrative terms was simply manipulated by a group of aristocrats (*yangban*).[20] All in all, Fukuda boldly concluded that a true sense of feudalism did not even exist in Chosun Korea, not to mention a national economy, and concluded that the status of Korean society during the Chosun period corresponded to that of tenth- and eleventh- century Japan, when the Fujiwara family ruled the Japanese archipelago prior to the rise of the Kamakura Bakuhu.[21]

Therefore, Paik clearly articulated in his *The Social and Economic History of Chousn Korea* that the primary purpose of his rewriting Korean history was to theoretically confute such colonial discourses as propounded by Japanese intellectuals. Paik was not hesitant to problematize Fukuda Tokuzō's scholarship and this illustrates that Paik's Marxist writings were deeply rooted in an anti-colonial interpretation of Korean history. In clearing away the specter of stagnation theory,

Paik chose instead to prove that Korean history had already internally taken universal steps toward economic development. He was convinced that the key to this battle with Japanese colonial theories was contingent on whether he could draw a comprehensive genealogy of socio-economic development in Korea from antiquity to the present. Just as the Silla Kingdom period attests to the fact that a feudalistic economic structure was shaped in seventh-century Korea, he maintained that feudalism had evolved during the Koryo Kingdom period (918–1392) and the rise of commercialization in late Chosun dynasty contained the sprouts of an early capitalist economy. In so doing, Paik endeavored to place Korean history within the universal timeline of modernization from a Marxist perspective.

For this reason, it was natural that Paik and like-minded Korean social scientists problematized the trend of spiritual and mystic nativist approaches to Korean studies led by nationalist intellectuals. They observed that writing Korean history based on the metaphysical and unscientific discovery of purely "Korean" historical elements would result in derailing Korean society from an empowering universal developmental path. In a 1937 article, the Marxist social scientist Lee Chung Won argued against spiritual nationalism and his main target was Jung In Bo's nationalist Chosun studies. According to Lee, Jung and like-minded nationalist intellectuals had problematically mystified Korean history through their unscientific concepts of *ul* (spirit) and created a false lineage of Korean history from Dan'gun to modern Korea.[22] Similar to Choi Nam Sun's Dan'gun studies in the early 1930s, Jung's notion of the "Korean spirit" was characterized by this intellectual zeal for tracing the origins of a homogeneous Korean entity through the creation myth of Dan'gun. Putting aside the question of whether Dan'gun was a historical reality or merely an imagined mythical creature, Lee usefully observed that the notion of the "Korean spirit" intended to emphasize this unscientific but highly heroic myth to exalt the self-esteem of the Korean people who had suffered from psychological defeatism since Japan's colonization of Korea in 1910. However, Lee held that such a mythical spiritism must be an object of scientitic criticism and it would eventually become absorbed by national facism.[23]

Fighting the double-layered domination of colonialism: shadows of an anti-colonial social science

Two conspicuously different interpretations of Korean history and culture – characterized by the spiritualist and social scientific approaches – were Korean intellectual responses to the reality of Japanese colonialism. But, on top of the highly visible practical problem of addressing Japanese colonialism as it functioned in their contemporary world, these intellectuals located a different history of deep-rooted colonial sentiment to be overcome in their Chosun studies. Just as Choi Nam Sun's Dan'gun studies focused on the rise of an ancient Korean state independent of early Chinese empires, Korean Marxist social scientists paid attention to the various legacies of Chinese civilization in Korean history. As Paik pointed out in his *The Social and Economic History of Chousn Korea*, Korean history had been indiscreetly written by simply imitating Chinese historiography. This approach had predominantly narrated the rise and fall of kingdoms and empires, placing an excessive emphasis on the role of the elite and ruling classes, and thereby marginalizing ordinary people who he believed should be valorized as primary historical forces.[24] As I will discuss in detail, Paik's recognition of the sinocentric aspect in Korean history, however, did not come from a perspective of Korean inferiority, that is, the Korean people had simply accepted "advanced" Chinese civilization and voluntarily joined the sinocentric world order. Paik was clearly aware that the narrative of Korea as a Chinese satellite state had been frequently appropriated by both Western and Japanese Marxist social scientists. The chain-reaction of colonial thinking, Paik logically deduced, was that once contemporary China was labelled as an example of a stagnated, undeveloped and thus "Asiatic" society, Korea was automatically categorized as part of this "China group" and as a result deprived of any recourse to independent academic elucidation.[25]

As discussed in Chapter 4, the Asiatic Mode of Production debate is characterized by the perception that a genuine form of feudalism and the commercial economy did not exist in Asia due to its ecological and socio-political limits. At the center of the AMP debate was the thesis that several elements in traditional Chinese society – primarily the lack of private land ownership, state control of the land, political despotism and irrigation-oriented hydraulic production – all pointed to the conclusion that the Chinese case was incommensurate with the universal developmental path. This analysis also provided an evident example of Asia's *general* stagnation vis-à-vis the West, with the potential exception of Japan. Unquestionably, Paik was aware that an emphasis on the similarity between traditional China and Korea would bring his Korean historiography to another stage of confrontation and discrimination, one facing a much more profound Marxist theoretical fundamentalism addressed not just against Korea but against Asia as a whole, holding that except for Japan, Asia was entirely doomed to become a victim of modern imperialism due to its economic stagnation. Marxist writing on Korean studies in the mid-1930s could not unravel this conundrum without directly confronting, and refuting, the logic of the Asiatic Mode of Production.

Paik intended to minimize the possibility that these loaded colonial and imperial perspectives could reasonably intervene to offer a productive description of Korean history. To do so, Paik maintained a consistent comparative perspective through his book, and this was to juxtapose traditional Korea with ancient Greek and Rome. Of course, since Greek and Roman society was reasonably conceived of by Paik as representing the origins of Western universality, accordingly a dominant "Western" epistemology continued to shape the exterior of his Korean history writing. But by demonstrating that traditional Korea had undertaken a historical path of development comparable to the celebrated societies of Greece and Rome, Paik believed that his mission to universalize Korean history and detach contemporary Korean society from the influence of "stagnated" Chinese civilization might be achieved.

However, the direct projection of Korean history into the realm of Western history brought about several questions. First and foremost, missing in Paik's writing of Korean history was an East Asian perspective. Since the primary purpose of his writing was to position Korean society on a universal path to historical develop- ment, he did not find it imperative to investigate Korean history from the perspec- tive of its relations with East Asia. But most problematically, his methodology did not free him from the haunting question of the Asiatic mode of production, a mode that had characterized Korean history. Since the form of land ownership in traditional China was a state monopoly, the private land ownership essential for the necessary economic progression of feudalism was rendered impossible. The thesis of the historical absence of feudal relations in Asia, together with the domi- nant reality of China and Korea as its (pseudo) colonial vassal state, contributed substantially to the acceptance of Asian stagnation theory. How, then, did Paik respond to these challenges? In 1932, a year before the publication of *The Social and Economic History of Chosun Korea*, he touched on the issue of the Asiatic mode of production:

> The Asiatic mode of production means that (1) countries like China, India and Egypt were politically centralized despotic states, (2) land property was public as a whole, (3) irrigation was controlled by the state or local govern- ments, and (4) those who managed the state were the ruling class. . . . In that the state only exploited the economy of the masses but also their personality, there were slaves and serfdom. Although ordinary people did not own land, the state controlled land. (For this reason) it is superficial that this system was not feudalistic simply because of its being centralized. A look at the contents of this system tells us that it was also feudal in nature.[26]

Paik logically contended that the primary elements of feudalism were slavery and serfdom. The essence of feudalism, he wrote, was the fact that "peasants were attached to the land and they paid land taxes instead of rents for land, and part of their labor power was used for landlords and another part for their own sur- vival."[27] Accordingly, he interpreted the Chosun dynasty period as part of a feudal era and confessed that he had to refute even his teacher Dr. Fukuda Tokuzō; "who argued that feudalism did not exist in Chosun Korea."[28]

Nonetheless, he was very attentive to Western and Japanese Marxist social sci- entists who had persistently attempted to theorize the AMP as an example of *par- ticular* social relations, to label China and Korea as underdeveloped societies. As for critiques of the precise particularities in Chosun Korea and its relatively slow transformation into a modern economy, he wrote:

> The only particularity in historical science is the particularity in the stage of the historical development of a society. . . . The whole process of his- torical development in Chosun, given that there are slight differences in geographical conditions, [. . .] is not something to be distinguished from the rule of historical development in other cultural nations, but something that Chosun has experienced in a very similar way to other nations through the one-dimensional rule of world history. The *slow tempo* in Chosun's

developmental process and the light and shade in its culture are by no means essentially *particular*.[29]

(emphasis added)

As he reiterated, "Blacks are blacks, but they become slaves only under certain conditions."[30] For him, particularity at a certain point of historical time was defined as a mere reflection of certain socio-economic conditions, and he was opposed to the idea that the amalgam of particularities represents particularism as a whole.

To further examine the limits of Marxist social scientific scholarship in colonial Korea, it is important to bring the lens of temporality to it. The boom of scientific Chosun studies actually began with the publication of Paik Nam Um's *The Social and Economic History of Chosun Korea* in the fall of 1933. At this time, most Japanese Marxist social scientists were engaged in fierce scholarly debates over the nature and development of Asian society, namely the Asiatic Mode of Production (AMP) debate. The Comintern announced a series of theses that reconfirmed that a two-stage revolution – a democratic bourgeois revolution followed by a socialist revolution – would be vital in East Asia since the capitalist economy had not matured enough to forge a direct socialist revolution.[31] Theoretically speaking, the two-revolution theory was systemized through the notion of the Asiatic mode of production, that is, a peculiar village-community-oriented mode of production and the state's direct control of land ownership, as precluding the emergence of the private ownership and commercial capital essential for the capitalist economy. To prove that Chosun Korea had followed universal developmental stages and to theorize a direct socialist revolution accordingly, Korean Marxist social scientists had to overcome the shadow of the Asiatic mode of production that was cast across Marxist scholarship in East Asia.

Among the few Korean Marxist social scientists who responded to the Asiatic mode of production debate, Roh Tong Kyu's writings deserve attention. In a 1934 article published in the Korean language journal *Shin Dong-A* (New East Asia), Roh touched on this issue for the first time.[32] In the article, Roh conceptualized the Asiatic mode of production as having nine major characteristics.[33] However, these characteristics, as Roh himself pointed out, were too indiscriminate to determine the constitution of a certain society. Therefore, he maintained that the Asiatic mode of production must be discussed from the perspective of two questions. The first being, is the Asiatic mode of production an independent mode of production opposed to or different from slavery, feudalism and capitalism? And the second, can the so-called "Oriental society" that Western capitalism discovered be usefully categorized as either a feudal or Asiatic society?[34]

Roh's questions hinted that the direction of his theorization would be significantly different from that of Japanese Marxist social scientists. To begin with, the temporal scope of the Asiatic mode of production in his discussion was not limited to an ancient period or the slavery system, nor did he avoid discussing it in relation to capitalism in contemporary Asian society. Therefore, to answer his questions, Roh utilized a strategy of "double translation." In the approach, he introduced a series of opinions on Asiatic society promulgated by Western scholars, focusing on Hegel, Marx, Mad'iar and Godes. He then moved on to the Japanese Marxists' interpretation and critique of these Western thinkers. Repeating Godes' definition of the Asiatic mode of production, Roh reconfirmed that feudalism occurs when producers create surplus products. However, the whole process of creating surplus value in Asian society, Roh argued, was controlled by oppressive relationships between landowners and producers. Based on this analysis, he concluded that the Asiatic mode of production was not an independent mode of production. Although surplus value took the form of taxes, not commodities derived from the land, and peasants paid taxes to the government, these relations in themselves could not constitute an ostensibly different mode of production. For this reason, Roh emphasized that the issue of an Asiatic society must now be confined to two remaining characteristics – artificial irrigation and centralized despotism.[35]

Central to Roh's analysis of Asiatic society was his intention to differentiate the mode of production from the political structure, and by emphasizing that surplus value was created in the agricultural sector, he attempted to demonstrate that Asian society had actually experienced economic development. Therefore, the uniqueness of Asiatic society, for him, was not related to the mode of production itself, but understood as the question of why and how the state emerged as a dominant political unit. However, it was the relationship between village community and the state that Western Marxist theoreticians portrayed as Asiatic, since neither private ownership nor autonomous political subjects could be found in this structure. As he himself acknowledged, Roh was actually heavily influenced by the Japanese *koza-ha* Marxist intellectual Hayakawa Jirō, who positioned the Asiatic mode of production between primitive community and slavery.[36] Hayakawa contended that both class struggle and private ownership occurred as primitive communities were dismantled. However, what is important here is the fact that Hayakawa's argument focused on Japan, while it was widely accepted that the structure of Korean agriculture was much closer to that of China.[37] In this regard, Roh's argument was left on somewhat shaky ground, since he had simply repeated the *koza-ha* Marxists' discussion of Asiatic society without explaining why the village community model continued to exist in Korean agriculture.

Roh's thesis indicates that Korean Marxist social scientists in the mid-1930s were at least aware of the ongoing debates over the Asiatic mode of production. However, Marxist social scientist intellectuals in mid-1930s Korea predominantly focused on establishing an independent historiography immune from the sorts of external evaluations that would result in a circulative denigration of Korean society as stagnant. These conditions gave rise to two distinctive tendencies in Korean Marxist scholarship in the mid-1930s. First, some Korean social scientists centered their concerns on refuting any theories that had denounced the presence of slavery and feudal systems in Korea. They believed that the locus of the AMP debate lay in proving feudalism as a historical reality, thereby allowing the nation forward progress to the next chapter of Korean history which would be universal development toward the capitalist economy. Paik Nam Un's work best exemplifies this tendency.

One the other hand, another group of social scientists acknowledged that "Asi-atic" modes of production did actually exist in *ancient* Korea, but they had already disappeared to be replaced by capitalist modes of production. Lee Chung Won's interpretation of the Asiatic mode of production illuminates the separation between the past and the present well. Despite acknowledging that "Asiatic" elements – a despotic political system and the absence of private land ownership – existed in premodern China and Korea, Lee contended that the sprouts of commercializa-tion and capitalism could be found in the late Chosun dynasty without providing a detailed explanation of how they emerged in nineteenth-century Korea.[38] In this respect, both Paik and Lee, in spite of their different approaches to ancient Korean history, shared the epistemology that contemporary Korea was immune from the specter of Asiatic and stagnant elements.

However, the in-depth social scientific analysis they brought to the study of premodern Korean history did not appear in their writings on early twentieth-century Korean society. In 1937, four years after the publication of *The Social and Economic History of Chosun Korea* that covered the Silla Kingdom period, Paik wrote another book *The Feudal Socio-Economic History of Chosun Korea*. Nam-ing this book as the second volume of *The Social and Economic History of Cho-sun Korea*, Paik attempted to present his revised understanding of the major issues in premodern history and also revealed his interpretation of the Korean economy in the early twentieth century. The most provocative counterargument against the universal development of the Korean economy was the existence of the village community as a unit in premodern Korean. Western Marxist social scientists often pointed out that this particular collective form of living, primarily concerned with the self-sufficient modes of life, was the main reason behind the absence of a commercialized economy in Asia. The problematic obstacle of the village com-munity question in Korean historiography lay in the fact that an acknowledgment of village community in Korea would result in the affirmation of the similarity between premodern China and Korea, thus binding the two countries within the representative idea of Asiatic society. Paik's 1933 work revealed the clear inten-tion that Korean historiography must be separated from both the exiting percep-tion of China carried by Western scholars and the Sino-centric perspective. In *The Feudal Socio-Economic History of Chosun Korea*, Paik admitted that the basic unit of agricultural production in the *feudal* system of the Koryo Dynasty (918– 1392) was the village community and it was directly controlled by the state.[39] Ironically, the village community was described by him as a space where peasants cultivated land and distributed products on a *communal* basis, which reminds us of Marx's categorization of Asiatic society. Since these peasants were still power-fully bound to the power of the state which had effectively monopolized all of the arable land, the feudalistic mode of production based on land ownership could not have occured in the village community. Paik strove to answer this seemingly impossible question by conceptualizing the land taxes peasants paid to the state as similar in their role to the taxes that peasants paid to landlords in the typical feudal relations of production.[40] However, this mechanical analogy between the Asian village community and the European model of feudalism could not answer the question of why the village community had continued to exist, if Korean society had undertaken the universal path of economic development Paik contended.

A weakness in a single area of the work does not of course denounce the value of its entirety. However, what was perhaps most problematic in regards to Paik's speculation on the village community was the timing of his engagement. His *The Feudal Socio-Economic History of Chosun Korea* was published in 1937, several months before the outbreak of the Sino-Japanese War, indicating that Japan was rapidly putting its imperialist ambitions into practice. Importantly, Japanese Marxist scholarship had also experienced significant changes over the four-year time period between the rise of scientific *Chosun* studies around 1933 and Paik's 1937 work. Beginning in 1934, a massive conversion took place, first among Marxist activists and eventually influencing the academic sector. While a number of Japanese Marxist social scientists still refused to completely denounce Marxism, they had gradually come to realize that they would not be able to avoid the moment of their ideology being verified by the question of its ability to endorse Japanese imperialism.

Under these rapidly changing circumstances, ones that necessitated an increasing engagement with the ultra-nationalist forces defining imperial Japan, Japanese Marxist social scientists' perceptions of Asia were drastically internally revised even before they surrendered to Japanese imperialism. At the center of this ideological modification was the need to separate Japan's past and present from its geo-cultural Asian context, and thereby particularizing the rest of Asia in an affirmation of Japan's path of manifest destiny to universal modernity. To put it another way, the particularization of Asia that had already taken place in other academic disciplines now arrived as a task for Japanese Marxist social science. First and foremost, scholarly attention was given to identifying elements that clearly constituted the stereotype of either the Asiatic society or Asiatic modes of production, such as irrigation, despotic monarchy and village community.

In Jeong Sik: from an Anti-Japanese marxist to *Tenkō*

If radical social scientists in Japan surrendered to imperialism and accepted a particularistic view on the rest of Asia based on the superiority of Japan, what roads were open to social scientists in colonial Korea? Considering that direct intellectual resistance became almost impossible in the fascistic transformation of the Japanese empire, colonial academics were left at a crossroads. Under these circumstances, many Korean intellectuals chose to endorse Japan's imperial order by the late 1930s. However, the patterns of response to imperial Japan varied. Some leading Korean intellectuals such as Choi Nam Sun strove to prove that the Korean spirit and culture need not be antagonistic to Koreans' embracing the imperial-way interpretation of Asia. Revising his theory of Dan'gun as the founder and spiritual leader of Chosun Korea, Choi now converted himself from a Korean cultural nationalist to an advocate of a Japan-led Asian empire by linking the spiritual aspects of ancient Korea to Japan's Imperial-Way Pan-Asianism.[41]

At stake was not just the question of accepting the superiority of Japan and endorsing the notion of a new Asian order led by Japan. Japan's project of building a new Asia around 1937 was premised on the rhetoric of protecting Asian people from Western imperialism by creating a self-sufficient community. Natural as it may sound, the slogan of building a new Asia was often accompanied by explicit anti-Western discourses, such as a critique of liberalism and individualism on the one hand, and an emphasis on Japan's affinity with the rest of Asia on the other. Putting aside the anti-Western sentiments deeply ingrained within Japan's new Asian order, I argue that the clear-cut binary formation of East versus West had an enormous impact on social scientists, and Marxist intellectuals in particular, whose profession it was to explore the paths of universal development. The intellectual ground for universalism within social science shrank remarkably and these conditions foregrounded the limited destiny of some Korean social scientists. Paik Nam Un, for example, simply put down his pen and hardly produced any work until Korea's liberation in 1945. The intellectual vacuum caused by the inability to intellectually uphold a universal worldview was, however, quickly filled by the ideas of another group of young Korean social scientists who intended to locate for their nation a progressive momentum within Japan's new order.

In Jeong Sik (1907 – ?) was one of this new generation of social scientists in colonial Korea. Trained in Marxist political economy in Japan and deeply involved in anti-colonial movements until the mid-1930s, In emerged as one of the most influential converted Marxists during the wartime period. For a fewer than two-year period between late 1938 and 1940, he produced nearly one hundred articles and journalistic essays, along with two sole-authored books. As the volume of his wartime writing indicates, he was involved in almost every single discursive space in colonial Korea from peasant literature to *naisenittai* (Japan and Korea as One Body), the controversial theory of assimilating Koreans as Japanese imperial subjects. Before the outbreak of the Sino-Japanese War in 1937, In, like other Korean Marxist social scientists, maintained a fairly critical stance against Japanese colonialism. He was also opposed to the theory of Asiatic society and the Asiatic mode of production, both of which, he believed, had simply served to intensify the concept of Asian stagnation and underdevelopment. In this respect, In's investigative trajectories cast meaningful questions toward any understanding of the intellectual legacy of Japanese imperialism during the wartime period.

His serial publication titled "A Study on Agricultural Economy in Chosun Korea (*Chosun nongchon kyungje ui yongu*)" produced for the Korean journal, *Chungang*, between February 1936 and September 1936, epitomizes In's understanding of Marxism and the Korean economy in prewar times. A glimpse at his writings shows us that his basic understanding of Korean history was heavily influenced by Paik Nam Un's historical materialism. However, In was aware that since the publication of Paik's work in 1933, Marxist scholarship in Asia had experienced rapid change as the Asiatic mode of production debate came to occupy the central position. For this reason, the first issue he problematized in his serial publication was how the Asiatic mode of production had influenced the Korean Marxist intellectual circle.[42] In pointed out that Korean Marxists "have never provided sincerely meaningful clues" to solve the question of the Asiatic mode of production in spite of the gravity of this issue in Korean society. However, he also rejected any interpretation that the Asiatic mode of production signified a particularity in Asian society.[43]

In acknowledged that unlike medieval Europe, Chinese and Korean peasants paid land taxes and provided forced labor for the state, not feudal lords. This indicates that In also accepted Paik's analysis that the state had productively seized control of the entire land in traditional Korean society. However, In stressed that advocates of the Asiatic mode of production had exaggerated the state ownership of land as if it essentially differentiated Asian society from the West.[44] He instead stressed that the state ownership of land was also part of feudalism, and his concern was transformed from focusing on the presence or absence of feudalism in traditional Korea to considering the specific limits that had prevented Korean agriculture from entering a capitalist stage. To help scientifically analyze the problems of Korean agriculture, In showed a keen comparative interest in British agriculture. According to him, capitalist industrialization in newly emerged cities such as Manchester and Liverpool also gave rise to capitalization which liberated peasants from serfdom and turned them into self-owned independent peasants.[45] While the British case represented a gradual transformation from feudal land ownership to capitalist land ownership, In presented three more types of agricultural land ownership in the world. He labeled the French case as the "Jacobin type," since he observed that the birth of independent land-owned peasants was here triggered by revolution. In contended that the stage of land ownership in Chosun Korea was similar to the "Junker type," which symbolized the development of German agriculture, where the rise of independent peasants was much slower than that of Britain and France due to external and internal factors.[46] German agriculture, In argued, was preconditioned by the limits of the development of capitalist commercial and manufacturing industries due to foreign interference, mostly from Britain and France. He went on to argue that domestic feudal powers were so tightly unified in Germany that traditionally conceived capitalist modes of production had hardly occurred.[47]

In fact, In's analyses of agricultural land ownership and their application to colonial Korea were theoretically influenced by the Japanese *koza-ha* Marxist Yamada Moritarō and his 1934 book *An Analysis of Japanese Capitalism*, although In never directly referred to Yamada's study in his work. Yamada categorized the transformation of land ownership in emerging capitalist countries through his peculiar concept of "type" and emphasized that advanced countries' imperial interference in late-comer countries such as Russia and Japan had a negative impact on the rise of land-owned independent peasants so essential for supporting the classical capitalist mode of production.[48] Yamada developed his theories of land ownership to juxtapose the Russian case to that of agricultural development in Japan and eventually argued that the backwardness of Japanese agriculture was in large part due to external factors.[49] In borrowed Yamada's discussion and applied it to Chosun Korea to explain the causes behind the major problems Korean agriculture was facing.[50]

In's Marxist social scientific writing in the prewar and wartime period was in many cases contextualized by his encounters with Japanese and Western Marxist intellectuals. Importantly, many Korean Marxist intellectuals including Paik Nam Un and In Jeong Sik received their formal education in Japan under the instruction of Japanese Marxist social scientists, and for this reason it was not surprising that the imprint of Japanese Marxism is so clear within In's writing. Arguably, the productive radical intellectual interchange between Korean and Japanese social scientists lasted until 1937, when most Marxist intellectuals converted or surrendered to Japanese imperialism. For this reason, In's analyses of Korean agriculture, in spite of their ostensible dependence on Yamada's theory, also played a role in intensifying his anti-colonial thinking. He observed that Korean agriculture in the late nineteenth century was still defined by its feudal and semi-feudal features such as the absence of independent peasants, a lack of agricultural technologies and serfdom for landlords. Such an analysis was followed by his harsh critiques of Japan: Japanese colonialism in Korea had simply aggravated these problems, although Japan claimed that she would bring some "modern" land ownership systems to colonial Korea.[51]

In Jeong Sik maintained a steadfast anti-colonial stance that can be found in his other writings, and in 1935 and 1936, he actively engaged with a scholarly debate on the impact of the National Land Survey conducted by the Governor General's Office in the 1910s. The Japanese colonial government claimed that collecting information on land ownership would be a touchstone to destroy the feudal land-peasant relations in which most Korean peasants had been tenant farmers, and to bring into being a modern peasant-land owner agricultural system. In found it problematic that there was a growing tendency displayed by Korean Marxist social scientists to regard the arrival of Japanese colonial power as a forward step toward the modernization of Korean agriculture. In 1933, Park Mun Kyu, a graduate of Kyungsung Imperial University, presented a provocative thesis arguing that in spite of its colonial context, the nation-wide land survey carried out by the colonial government in Korea in the 1910s had paved the way for bringing a modern sense of land ownership to Korean agriculture.[52] To be sure, Park's argument was not designed to endorse the "good will" of imperial power per se. According to Park, the colonial government in Korea came to the realistic conclusion that "without destroying old social systems, the accumulation of capital that is essential for colonial governance would not occur."[53] Therefore, the Governor General's Office in Korea, he stressed, had no choice but to focus on restructuring Korean agriculture, given that it had taken the largest portion in the Korean economy and at the same time epitomized the feudality of Korean society.[54] Park's somewhat perplexing thesis stimulated the intellectual nerve of In, who had also grappled with the question of why modern modes of production and land ownership could not emerge in colonial Korea. However, he dispassionately revisited the history of the Japanese land survey project and concluded that colonial power simply took over the role of feudal landlords and thus intensified the preexisting feudal relationships within Korean agriculture.[55]

The clear anti-imperialist and radical Marxist stance displayed throughout In's prewar scholarship amplifies curiosity about the eventual direction his wartime writings undertook. While he was experiencing an ideological transformation, most *koza-ha* Japanese Marxist intellectuals converted from Marxism to being advocates of Japanese imperialism around 1936. As Fujita Shojō's insightful studies of conversion (*tenkō*) show, discarding Marxist ideology for Japanese intellectuals meant that they instead officially accepted both spiritual and militaristic Japanism. The Imperial Way offered a spiritual dimension to adhere to, and openly supporting Japan's war effort was an integral part of this ideological conversion. The fascistic aspect of the Japanese Emperor system was closely associated with the fantasy of Japan's biological and spiritual superiority and such an epistemology was mirrored in the rhetoric of "Eight Corners of the World Under One Roof (*Hakkō ichiu*)," meaning that a new world was to be created under the leadership of the Japanese emperor. Unquestionably, as Fujita pointed out, it appeared that rational, objective and critical thinking in social science had ended with the prevalence of Japanism.[56] However, the collapse of a universal and radical approach to social science as represented by Marxism gave rise to new discursive spaces during the wartime period. At the center of this new set of inquiries shared by another group of social scientists was the question of Asia. Shinmei Masamichi, Rōyama Masamichi and Kada Tetsuji, all so-called bourgeois or mainstream social scientists who were once interested or trained in Marxism but were never categorized as "Marxist intellectuals," had steadily gained currency in Japanese academic circles. They put forward the theory of the East Asian community in 1937. This theory, first presented by these non-Marxist social scientists, would later attract converted Marxists and it directly addressed the issue of the imbalance and inequality between metropole and colony. This work had a tendency to provide a positivist futuristic vision by actively offering transformative perspectives on contemporary situations in both Japan and the colony. In believed that by engaging with these new imperial discourses, he could rationalize his endorsement of the Japanese empire. In other words, the concept of "pan-Asia" displayed in Japanese intellectuals' imperial discourses was appropriated by In and like-minded Korean intellectuals as a "method." However, making one's collaboration with the oppressive colonial power sound plausible necessitated several political processes. Most imperative for In Jeong Sik's conversion to becoming a supporter of imperial Japan was to find a rationale that joining the construction of Japan's Pan-Asian community would also promote the status of colonial Korea. This explains why In's writings in the late 1930s pointed to one issue: relocating the position of colonial Korea within Japan's new order.

Naisenittai: the politics of subject formation in colonial Korea

Like other Korean Marxist intellectuals, In maintained an obvious anti-colonial standpoint until he committed to imperialist conversion around 1937. However, his social scientific thinking was different from that of previous generations such as Paik Nam Un, whose scholarship was characterized by an emphasis on discovering the political dynamics of Korean society from a historical perspective. However, it appears that In was not interested in the idea that the socio-political forces to liberate Korea from colonial oppression might be obtained by revisiting Korea's past. From the beginning, In was inclined to dig only into more contemporary and practical inquiries. In this endeavor his primary questions included: If capitalist modes of life had not occurred in twentieth-century Korea, what would be the main problems left to be solved? How could the living conditions of peasants be improved under colonial rule? And how might feudal peasant-landlord relations be dismantled, and mechanization introduced into Korean agriculture? In that respect, In's Marxist social science was, as Andrew Barshay has pointed out, reminiscent of the Japanese liberal and Marxist intellectuals who conceived of social science not only as a weapon of "knowing modernity," but also as a means of bringing actual change to society.[57]

What differentiated In from his contemporary Japanese social scientists was the fact that he did not have a visible, functional object through which he could find the solutions for his own problem-settings. Historian Peter Duus had argued that beginning in the Taisho period, liberal intellectuals made a clear distinction between state and society, and they were convinced that the state existed to serve society.[58] While seeking for an idealistic dream of socialist revolution, Japanese radical intellectuals had constantly criticized the predominance of state science (*staatslehre*),[59] and called for the state to provide actual solutions for social problems (*shakai mondai*).

Such tensional relationships between the state and radical intellectuals did not exist in colonial Korea. For Korean Marxist social scientists, the colonial state was not an object they could negotiate with in drawing up practical changes for problems in colonial Korea, but an enemy to be completely overthrown. Before converting to Japanese imperialism, In Jeong Sik also shared the perception that the occupying colonial power was the "ultimate evil." However, In was also aware that his analyses of the major problems in the Korean economy in the 1930s had reached a dead end, inasmuch as he realized they couldn't be solved without fundamentally destroying the superstructure of the state itself. Such observations led him to gradually accept the reality that the colonial state would be the only agency through which he could imagine visible changes.

But a grudging acknowledgment of the status quo on the part of colonial intellectuals was not enough to satisfy the demands of imperial Japan. During the time of total war, a new logic of mobilization had to be deployed in colonial Korea. In a full-fledged war against China, colonial Korea emerged as an important geopolitical space in support of Japan's war efforts. Theoretically supported by hard-line ultra-nationalists in Japan proper and following the transformation of the Japanese empire into a total war structure, the Governor General of Korea, Ugaki Kazushige, promulgated the notion of *naisenittai* (Japan and Korea as one body), a virtually coercive assimilation and mobilization policy towards the incorporation of Koreans into imperial subjects. Arguably, this notion of *naisenittai* preconditioned Korean intellectuals' initial responses to Japan's imperial war, and

In was one of the few Korean intellectuals who fully understood the gravity of this unprecedented policy of subject formation.

Japan's bold manifesto in the immediate aftermath of the outbreak of the Sino-Japanese War to completely transform Koreans into Japanese imperial subjects was immediately followed by heated debates over the exact ramifications of the idea of *naisenittai*. Invariably, the logic of Japan and Korea as one body demanded radical changes in everyday life, primarily abolishing the Korean language and indigenous culture, and accepting the Japanese Emperor as the spiritual leader of the Korean people. Naturally, Korean intellectuals' debate converged on the one focal question of how would this new radical identity politics change the nature of Korean society? Most Korean intellectuals observed that under the ostensible empire-colony power structure, the concept of diminishing differences between Koreans and Japanese would take a one-dimensional route: Koreans must embrace the entirety of so-called "Japaneseness" to be completely reborn as Japanese subjects. At stake, and in opposition, was the idea common to both the public masses and the intellectuals that Korean culture and history represented the profoundness and beauty of the Korean people.

To alleviate the predictable psychological and cultural resistance against the extinction of Korean identity, some Japanese intellectuals revisited the theory of *nissendōsoron* (Japan and Korea as having the same ancestor).[60] They stressed that incorporating Japanese and Koreans into one body would be only to reconfirm cultural and biological affinities that already existed among two ethnic communities. On the side of converted Korean intellectuals, the debate over *naisenittai* took more political and practical forms. The question of to what degree Koreans should accept Japanese identity could not be separated from the realistic expectations of how much Koreans' status would be promoted by becoming Japanese. For this reason, Korean intellectuals were aware that they had to even accept some extremist measures such as abolishing the Korean language and wearing a kimono, as gestures to become closer to "Japaneseness." And such demands were considered acceptable, as long as *naisenittai* would bring substantial improvements to colonial Korea.

Hyun Yong Sop (1906–) was one of these Korean intellectuals who insisted on the complete assimilation of Koreans into Japanese culture (*tettei tōkaron*). The problem that captured his attention was the need to effectively dispose of the Korean language as the epitome of "Koreanness." Hyun astutely argued that as long as Koreans continued to speak the Korean language, it would be considered as an adversity to the accomplishment of *naisenittai*. Such an observation led him toward the bold argument that abolishing the Korean language and learning Japanese must be an integral part of what he termed as "the road Korea must take."[61] To be sure, he anticipated that his notion of complete assimilation would invite harsh criticism. Although many intellectuals had already chosen to collaborate with the Japanese empire, convincing the ordinary Korean people of the necessity of a complete self-negation of Korean identity was conceived of as an entirely different matter. Hyun endeavored to rationalize his idea using the argument that abolishing the Korean language would not necessarily erase one's

Korean identity. A famous writer Yi Kwang Su also shared a similar approach, providing a virtual future of Koreans in his novels in which the lives of Koreans obtained a promoted recognition from the majority of the Japanese by completely becoming Japanese.[62]

On the contrary, In did not confine the dimension of the *naisenittai* debate to the degree of the Koreans' assimilation of Japanese identity. While he fully endorsed the whole logic of incorporating Koreans into Japan as an inevitable step towards the construction of a new order in East Asia, he also intended to place it in the broader context of seeking a new Korean subjectivity within the Japanese empire. For this purpose, In attempted to position the products of *naisenittai* as one important step toward the entire reconstruction of East Asia. He wrote:

> That the Japanese nation takes the initiative does not mean that it outwardly forces on other nations its ethnic authenticity as such. If there is any element to the detriment of the whole unification of Asia, it must be *sublimated* although it is part of the authenticity of Japanese nationalism. (for example, the islander-like character of the Japanese people) For that reason, the problem of *naisenittai* and the discourse on the reconstruction of East Asia based on *naisenittairon* are problems of nationalism not only for Korean people but also for Japanese people.[63] (emphasis added)

In's concept of sublimating intrinsic ethnic characteristics within a new East Asian subjectivity is reminiscent of the group of Japanese social scientists who unfolded a highly philosophical discussion of nation (minzoku). As examined in Chapter 2 of this book, Takata Yasuma, Kada Tetsuji and Shinmei Masamichi presented their own notion of minzoku in which a new collective identity of East Asian minzoku should be created by overcoming one's nationalism. To put it another way, Koreans should become the subjects of a Japan-led Asian community while they might maintain their Koreanness. In's logic of identity politics, however, doesn't seem to be underpinned by his metaphysical reading of these Japanese social scientists' theories. Instead, he was attentive to the realistic impact on colonial Korea that Japan's formation of a new Asian order might have. In that respect, In's elucidation of *naisenittai* revealed his anxiety over colonial Korea's status within the Japanese empire. A similar concern was mirrored in his critiques of the Japan-Manchuria-China economic bloc. As is well known, the economic bloc theory was presented by Japanese bureaucrats and economists in the mid-1930s as part of their long-term plan to construct a self-sufficient economic zone in East Asia. Due to a strategic emphasis on Manchurian-Chinese spaces, the status of Korea, In stressed, degenerated into an invisible region that had already become part of Japan proper.[64] He found it critical that Korea should be clearly etched on the political and cultural map of a Japan-led East Asian community.

In this way, the *naisenittai* debate was a discursive and political channel through which In could address his analyses of Korean society and eventually his broader worldviews. Accordingly, he reiterated his belief that the principle that Koreans should follow was the *new* Japanism, replacing the old spiritual Japanism that simply stressed the homogeneity and superiority of the Japanese. In apparently came to coin this "new Japanism" through his close reading of Miki Kiyoshi's work, "Principles of Thought for a New Japan (*Shin nihon no shisō genri*)." In also repeated similar notions of anti-capitalism and anti-nationalism in his writings on new Japanism, following the fact that anti-capitalism and anti-nationalism were the two major ideologies to be overcome within the new political order of East Asia in Miki's writing.[65] In this piece of work, Miki never mentioned colonial Korea, but In attempted to shed new light on Miki's abstract manifestation of a new Asia by linking it to the real issue of subject formation in colonial Korea. The *naisenittai* campaign, he contended, must be regarded as an aspect of a new ethnic movement and at the same time, it should be considered as the integral part in constructing an East Asian Cooperative Community.[66] Through the use of his own critical language, In's arguments appealed to Japanese imperial intellectuals, and the fact that Koreans were now on the brink of becoming Japanese perhaps provided him with a greater space for political enunciation.

Discursive reversal: Asia in colonial Korea and colonial Korea in Asia

While he was deeply involved in discussions about Korea's future within Japan's new order at the macroscopic level, In also intended to expand on his own interpretation of the East Asia Community that was soon to be realized in colonial Korea. For him, it was clear that contemporary colonial Korean society could not be addressed without discussing the many serious questions that existed in relation to agricultural production. From everyday life issues such as peasants' illiteracy, to the politico-economic question of how to deal with the remnants of a semi-feudal system of organization, In believed that many of the most harmful inconsistencies and frustrations in contemporary Korean society were due to the ingrained structural status-quo that characterized the nation's system of agricultural production. Precisely for this reason, he reversed his initial observation and outlined a strong case that the socio-political dynamics for rationalizing the existence of a new Korea within the Japanese empire could be found in the agricultural sectors. Here, it is important to note that his approach to these problems drastically differed from that of previous Korean social scientists whose area of expertise was also agricultural and economic. Paik Nam Un and Lee Hun Goo, for instance, strove to investigate the origins of Korean agriculture by studying the economic history of Korea in the mid-1930s, and as I have discussed, Paik was vocal in his insistence on locating Korean agriculture in the universal stages of *historical* development. On the contrary, In focused on the contemporaneity of failing Korean agriculture and he did not resort to any historical prescription for recovering Korea's immanent powers by looking back into the national past. This focus on contemporaneity explains the absence of reference to historical Korean kingdoms, such as Silla, Koryo and Chosun, in his wartime writing.

This denouncement of historical materialism was followed by an endorsement of the colonial government as the agency best suited to solving the problems of the nation's agrarian production from a social scientific perspective. In a 1938 article titled "The Incompatibility of Marxism in Asia," he stressed that the theory of historical materialism is in itself a euro-centric model, and thus is not useful for analyzing any Asian society that contains "particular" elements.[67] In argued that as long as Marxism's historical materialism was correct and the accumulation of capital had occurred in Korean agriculture, it should have brought a rapid class differentiation to Chosun Korea.[68] However, as he acknowledged, capitalist modes of production never arrived in Korean agriculture, and therefore In concluded that such a linear explanation of historical development itself would not be suitable for Asian society.

In that respect, In's observation of Marxism's theoretical incompatibility with Asian society must be understood as part of a "thought war (*shisōsen*)," the concept that intellectuals must partake in overcoming the ideological remnants of Western structural and theoretical edifices such as capitalism and individualism.[69] Miki's "blueprint" for a new Japan best illustrates the ideological direction of the thought war, and it would be reasonable to assert that In's basic understanding of the geopolitical setting of the world stemmed from the writing of Miki and other Japanese social scientists.

Although In's conversion in support of the empire was theoretically indebted to Japanese Marxist post-conversion writing, as best illuminated in Miki Kiyoshi's manifestation of anti-Marxism and a new Pan-Asian order, he was never satisfied with simply echoing the ideas of these Japanese imperial intellectuals. He was clearly aware that the most appealing way to rationalize his endorsement of the Japanese empire was to expound its utility for providing practical solutions to the impending politico-economic issues that colonial Korean society was facing. Just as In intended to get beyond the *naisenittai* debate by addressing the idea to the broader context of creating a new form of East Asian identity, he strove to shed new light on other unanswered questions regarding the nature of Asian society. Most crucial among them was how to reinterpret the Asiatic mode of production that had haunted Asian Marxist social scientists and theoretically inscribed stagnation and underdevelopment on the map of Asia, with the arguable exception of Japan.

Once again, In utilized the tactic of reversing the perceived images of the discursive subject. First, he was opposed to reiterating the shared perception by Western and Japanese Marxist social scientists that the Asiatic mode of production mainly pertained to a comparative degree of development and underdevelopment within a binary schema of the West and Japan-excluding Asia. Instead, In replaced the issue of the Asiatic mode of production with the universal question of the maldistribution and imbalance between production and producers in the feudal economy. According to him, the fact that peasants, as the majority productive force, did not receive appropriate economic and political compensation for their contribution in a feudal economic structure should be universally and critically applied to the West and Asia.[70] Although he did not omit the particular characteristics of Asian feudal society, such as the nationalized possession of all arable land,[71] the problematic fact of the universal and increasing normalization of peasants' living conditions throughout the global capitalist structure held the central position in his critical reinterpretation of the Asiatic mode of production.

The displacement of the Asiatic mode of production enabled In to provincialize the issue of underdevelopment and economic unevenness *within* the East Asian community. If Japan is the only exception in the doomed-to-stagnation context of Asia, and accomplished an outstanding level of economic development, then the issue of reducing the gap between Japan and the rest of Japan's projected territory within its incipient Asian empire deserves more serious attention in wartime Asian discourses of economic and social development. In order to transform the reality of the stricken Korean economy as it existed within the Japanese empire, Korean intellectuals, In observed, should not hesitate to disclose their scientific assessments that colonial Korea belongs to a group of underdeveloped countries. Rather, In believed that only an acute analysis of the stagnating nature of Korean society would be an effective weapon in provoking the Japanese imperial government to address the urgent need to economically develop colonial Korea. By taking this path of engagement with his colonial masters, In doubtless considered he might be more likely to emerge as an influential social scientist within the discursive space of colonial Korea. Perhaps In even hoped to bring about a theoretical metamorphosis of the notion of the East Asian Community, taking it beyond its origins as a metaphysical and propagandized euphemism for the Japanese Pan-Asian empire, and rejuvenating the idea so that it might inspire positive benefits and reforms relevant to the everyday life of colonial subjects. And at the center of In's "Koreanized" vision of the East Asian Community was the issue of agriculture in colonial Korea.

Diagnosing Korean agriculture

In's argument regarding the Asiatic mode of production in Korean agriculture was intentionally made to address another political goal. He contended that incredibly high land taxes and suppressive peasant-landlord relations had exacerbated the poor living standards of most Korean peasants. In addition to these political inconsistencies, In argued that irrigation-oriented environmental conditions, a constant shortage of precipitation and unexpected floods and draughts – virtually the three major characteristics of the Asiatic mode of production provided by Karl Wittfogel as examined in Chapter 4 – were primary disadvantages that had kept Korean agriculture in stagnation. In also acknowledged that Korean agriculture had not even reached the nominal degree of technological development. Fertilizers were rarely used and the substantial portion of agricultural work depended on manual labor. He stressed that in spite of the lack of mechanization, Korean agriculture had also suffered from serious overpopulation and the average cultivation area per Korean peasant was excessively small. In was singularly obsessed with the necessity of articulating the manifold problems in Korean agriculture. He had no hesitation in accepting the analysis that Asian society, including China and Korea, overtly displayed the symptoms of stagnation and underdevelopment, as extensively addressed by Karl Wittfogel.[72] In was convinced that a meticulous scientific analysis of Korean society would be a powerful tool to highlight Korea's status within the Japanese empire in terms of problems and remedies.

Importantly, he had already described the major issues in Korean agriculture in a similar way before his acquiescence to Japanese imperialism. This indicates that his political conversion, ironically, did not force him to modify his basic understanding of Korean agriculture. What had changed was the abandonment of any radical solution; that is, he no longer believed that a Marxist revolution could realistically offer a panacea for struggling Korean agriculture. Therefore, he had no choice but to leave his utopian ideals and look for solutions in reality, and this awareness of his contemporaneous circumstance can be found in his changed views on Japanese colonialism. For instance, he drastically revised his evaluation of the National Land Survey by the Governor's Office. In 1935 and 1936, he railed against his fellow Marxist social scientists who observed that the land survey paved the way for modern land ownership since such surveys could be followed by the redistribution of agrarian property, which might eventually dismantle the feudal land-peasant relations.[73] He simply rejected such a view, charging it as a dangerous revisionism to so naïvely endorse the colonial power's positive role in Chosun Korea.[74] In 1939, two years after the outbreak of the Sino-Japanese War, he now pointed out that through the land and real estate surveys carried out in Korea by Japan, a modern private ownership had been established in Chosun Korea.[75] As I will discuss in detail, such revised opinions on colonial governance played a pivotal role in his mapping out the future of Korean agriculture.

In incessantly highlighted the agriculture problem as the most pressing issue for colonial Korea in numerous examples of his other writing, to the degree that the repetition of his highly similar arguments in different works took on a monolithic quality. In considering his writings between 1939 and 1940, it might be argued that he deployed a very distinctive but highly deliberate writing style that associated every single social issue with the problem of Korean agriculture. To be sure, he had his own rationale as he produced nearly 100 journal articles and essays that all addressed the one all-absorbing issue of the "Korea problem." Essentially, since In believed that since nearly 80 percent of the Korean population were peasants, it was proper for him to envision the whole of Korean society through the lens of agriculture. Interestingly, much of his writing is read as if he considered Japanese intellectuals and bureaucrats as his potential audience, as well as the potential agents who might put his planned change into practice. For this reason, he had no hesitation in revealing for them the darkest parts of his own nation in a hyperbolic and emotional way. Discontent with the existing literature on Korean agriculture, In vociferously conveyed his diagnosis as to the failure of representation in all previous academic analyses of Korean agrarian production. In doing so, he aimed to exonerate himself from any condemning Korean gazes he might face for his collaboration, and confirm the ontological justification as to why it should be an intellectual like him who must deliver the tragic story of the Korean peasantry.

It was at this point that In showed keen interest in the power of literature. As a matter of fact, Korean Marxist scholarship on national agriculture, before its conversion to the Japanese Imperial perspective, had faithfully followed the logic of social scientific writing at the time. In other words, the object of study must be scientifically analyzed and thus there should not be any room for individual mistakes and subjective stories. This seemingly elaborate and theoretical social scientific writing, In observed, ironically did not address the reality of how the Korean peasantry had lived, and was living. In contrast to this dry scientific gaze, In was amazed by the power of narrative inherent in what he called "peasant literature." He was particularly motivated by American female writer and Nobel Literature Prize laureate Pearl Buck's (1892–1973) masterful writing on Chinese peasants. Just as Thomas More (1478–1535) had an enormous impact on European society with his magnum opus *Utopia*, In praised Buck's *The Good Earth* (1935) as providing "an apex in Asian peasant literature."[76] He evaluated that *The Good Earth* vividly depicted the reality of Chinese peasants who were constrained to abnormally high land taxes and almost slave-like relations of production. In attributed Buck's accomplishments to her acute understanding of the Asiatic characteristics in Chinese agriculture.[77] Following this revelatory encounter with literature, for In the Asiatic mode of production was no longer a doomed theory that pushed Asian society toward the world of inferiority, but one that might offer an effective tool to illuminate the pathetic reality of Asian agriculture, and he intended to mirror the similar circumstances of the Korea peasantry and agrarian production through Buck's vivid narration of Chinese agriculture.

Naturally, In turned to Korean literature, to survey the field. First, he adamantly argued that so-called Korean writers in the field of peasant literature, including famous writers such as Yi Kwang Su and Kim Dong Li, had produced lackluster works that failed to capture the authentic characteristics of Korean peasants. According to him, the Korean peasants that appeared in these writers' works were "neither Korean peasants nor European peasants," and described simply as "people whose work is merely to plow and weed a field and eventually harvest crops." These works, In stressed, should have instead contained the authentic, nativist stories of Korean peasants who had undergone numerous ordeals caused by Asiatic agricultural conditions.[78] In's critiques, however, were not simply linked to his aspiration to have such a writer as Pearl Buck operating in the realm of Korean peasant literature. Instead, he attempted to associate the absence of representation within Korean literature with his critiques of Japan's colonial policies in Korea. The so-called cultural politics imperial Japan brought to colonial Korea in the aftermath of the March 1st Independence Movement in 1919, In observed, had rather widened the gap between the urban and rural populations, marginalizing the majority of the rural peasant masses. The following remark reveals his critical evaluation of the shadow of urbanization very well:

> Culture always requires *universality*. In today's situation culture is focused only in the cities, the impure air in the cities pollutes culture and obstructs its sound development. . . . Only when technologies are modernized and the mode of production is transformed, and peasants will request modern science

and knowledge in their direct production process, then rural areas can be a vast cultural society.[79]

(emphasis added)

As the above statement shows, In believed that culture was a mirror of contemporary society, which is strikingly different from the perception of culture by the group of Korean intellectuals who placed national culture in the realm of a historical, intrinsic and homogeneous unit that represented the idea of national community. Rather, In's concept offered an idea of culture as a testing paper that measured the degree to which modern development had penetrated the everyday life of ordinary people. The proliferation of modern modes of life was certainly recognized by In as an example of modern transformation in colonial Korea, but he was even more attentive to the unevenness between rural and urban areas.

In Jeong Sik observed that bringing modern technological development to Korean agriculture was one of the primary tasks that needed to be completed. In, however, pointed out that a mere mechanization in agriculture would not transform the Korean peasantry into modern individuals, let alone "responsible" subjects of imperial Japan. The literacy degree of Korean peasants, he stressed, was appalling, and for this reason it was inappropriate to discuss "culture" in Korean agriculture.[80] It is at this point that In's speculation on theory and praxis in Korean agriculture through a literary analysis targeted the Japanese audience and highlighted the necessity of establishing mandatory education in Korea. To appeal to the Japanese audience, a political analogy came into play through In's argument. For him, a mandatory education system in colonial Korea was regarded as one of the most pressing and immediate of contemporary social problems. Therefore, he criticized the initial plan of the Governor General's office to bring mandatory elementary education to colonial Korea only by 1950, not the present.[81] The year 1950 was regarded by In as an example of how naively the colonial government perceived the issue, given that elementary mandatory education was introduced as early as the 1870s in Japan proper. By highlighting the gap between metropole and colony in this way, In strove to demonstrate why building a new Asia and promoting the living conditions of Korean peasants were not two different things.

As such, In's writings before the expansion of Japan's war to the Pacific Ocean were characterized by his "Koreanizing" the vision of an East Asian new order. Needless to say, In found that advocates of the East Asian Community (*tōa kyōdōtai*) had a deeper understanding of why constructing a *kyōdōtai* should be so closely related to rehabilitating the colonial economy, and agriculture in particular. However, he was convinced that simply reiterating the normative chant of a Pan-Asian community would not appeal to most colonial subjects whose economic survival lay at the crossroads. Therefore, a corollary of In's politicization of the East Asian Community was to create a new political logic for turning poverty-stricken colonial peasants into modern individuals who would spontaneously collaborate with the Japanese empire. This new project of creating a new type of human being must be accompanied by a series of institutional changes, and In stressed that they should be immediately implemented within Korean agriculture.

For instance, the incredibly high land taxes for tenant farmers in colonial Korea was indicated by him as the main obstacle to Koran peasants' basic access to culture. In argued that in comparison to England and France where peasants pay about 20 percent of their total income for land taxes, nearly half of Korean peasants' income was deducted for land taxes, a rate even higher than that of southeast Asian countries under European colonial rule.[82] Under these conditions, In thought that it would be nonsense to imagine that the Korean peasantry would understand the grand will of building a new Asian order under the leadership of imperial Japan. In sum, In centered his energy post-conversion on persuading Japanese intellectuals and bureaucrats to understand why the "Korea problem" should take the central position in their constructing of a Pan-Asian empire.

Ambiguous identities: "Colonial Korea matters"

As discussed above, In Jeong Sik superficially maintained his critical and radical standpoint after conversion, in that he adamantly called for Korean society to be fundamentally restructured. However, he no longer considered the grassroots energy of the masses to be sufficient to forge social change. A derailment from Marxist revolutionary imagination was substituted by In's endorsement of a top-down power dynamic, that is, the Japanese colonial power would take the "Korea problem" seriously as part of its new empire-building project. Rapid industrialization and advanced techniques in Japan proper, the preponderance of the Japanese forces in Northern China and the plan of transforming Korea into a military base implemented by the Government-General in Korea, all these circumstances served as infallible evidence toward his conviction that Japan could modernize Korea. Stressing that whether or not the long-term project of reconstructing East Asia could be realized was entirely dependent on the leadership of millions of the Japanese people (*naichijin*) who were in the colonies, he did not hide his expectation that Japan would "peacefully" restructure Korean industry.[83] This perspective greatly colored the tone of In's social scientific thinking. The discursive hierarchy between the addresser and the addressed clearly exists in most of his writings. Ironically, this setting reconfirmed his conviction that only a rational and scientific analysis of Korean society could drag out forward-looking responses from Japanese intellectuals and bureaucrats. Nonetheless, In knew that he had to incessantly draw attention to the question of how to locate colonial Korea within the new Pan-Asian empire, since he believed that colonial Korea's position has been ambiguously perceived both strategically and epistemologically by imperial Japan.

In fact, there was a general consensus among Japanese bureaucrats and high-ranking military officials that colonial Korea should play a certain role in operating the Japan-Manchuria-China bloc system, a regional economic unit proposed right after the 1931 Manchurian Incident. However, running two different colonies – Manchukuo and Korea – for the sake of an expanded Japanese empire generated political tensions among the agents of empire. Louise Young persuasively argues that private capital invested in Manchukuo held different priorities from those of the Japanese government and this often resulted in internal conflicts over how to design the basic structure of the Manchukuo economy.[84] Similar tensions, though not exactly analogous with Manchukuo, existed between bureaucrats in colonial Korea and policymakers in Japan proper. Ugaki Kazushige, the 7th Governor-General of Colonial Korea, intended to encourage both industrial and agricultural development by inducing direct investment from private capital in Japan proper in the mid-1930s. This plan was seen by hard-liner ultranationalists in Japan as contradictory to the basic principle of the Japan-Manchukuo-China economic bloc in which each economic unit such as Korea and Taiwan should be under direct control of the Japanese imperial government. Historian Pang Kie Jung has insisted that such internal tensions stemmed from a lack of general understanding regarding Korea's position within the Japanese empire. Colonial Korea was in theory part of Japan proper and ought to follow the economic structure and policy-making processes set by the Japanese government. Pang pointed out that this concept of colonial Korea as part of Japan proper, in relation to its reality as *gaichi*, functioned as an obstacle to consolidating the two economic systems.[85]

Minami Jirō, who had just retired from his position as Commander-in-Chief for the Japanese Kwangtung Army, was appointed as the 8th Governor General of Colonial Korea in 1936. He intended to inherit Ugaki's policy by continuing to promote direct investment from Japan. However, his "developmental" notion was strongly rebutted by military officials and conservative politicians in Japan proper. They already had a clear ideological direction of where colonial Korea should be headed at the time of total war. Their concept of total war was characterized by the observation that the borders between private and public sectors, and between war front and home front, had disappeared in modern warfare. This new approach was reflected in Japan's war against China as she passed the total mobilization law in 1938 which stipulated that all available resources in both Japan proper and the colony must be utilized for Japan's war efforts.

Such a top-down and one-dimensional drive to expand the Japanese empire initiated by hardliner officials and bureaucrats did not receive full support from Japanese intellectuals, not to mention critical colonial intellectuals. Rōyama Masamichi cast a skeptical eye on the project of the Japan-Manchuria-China economic bloc in the mid-1930s. The naïve Japan-centered approach to China and Manchuria, driven by the greedy goal of exploiting their labor and resources in the name of economic unity, he stressed, could not be realized without taking seriously the question of changing the internal power structure between Japan and the rest of Asia. Nowhere was Rōyama's observation of the lack of the recognition of colonial problems more perfectly applicable than colonial Korea, and total mobilization and *naisenittai* were the two official and institutional responses imperial Japan brought to colonial Korea in the late 1930s.

In's discontent with the lack of appreciation for Korea's importance was mirrored in many of his writings during the first years of the Sino-Japanese War. While reconfirming the validity of the *tōa kyōdōtai* notion as the only plausible approach to the colony, he devoted his intellectual energies to highlighting colonial Korea's role in the empire-building project. Unquestionably, he intended to bring actual social, economic and political changes into practice, agricultural reform and development in particular, in return for Koreans' commitment to war and empire building. His 1940 book *The Agricultural Land of Chosun Korea* is a work that reveals his standpoint very well. In this book, he put forward two immediate tasks to be accomplished in Chosun Korea. First, the mechanization of Korean agriculture must be introduced immediately. Since one of the main goals in Japan's reconstructing Korea was to increase agricultural production power, In observed, this would not be conceivable without fundamentally changing the structure of a Korean agriculture that was still dominantly manual-labor oriented.[86] But he did not simply repeat a manifesto. By carrying out extensive fieldwork research on contemporary Korean agriculture, he collected a vast amount of data and evidence to prove his thesis that agriculture itself was on the verge of collapse and this would be eventually detrimental to Japan's war efforts in mainland China. He lamented that rice farming in colonial Korea was so manual-labor oriented that even livestock labor was not frequently used by peasants, while the agricultural machinery such as tractors and combine harvesters that were widely used in Western agriculture were entirely absent.[87] In addition, he pointed out that land-owning farmers barely existed in most areas and that the average tenant taxes were nearly 60 percent of peasants' total income. Under these circumstances, In claimed, peasants were simply incapable of even purchasing the fertilizers essential for improving productivity.[88]

Such observations by In led him to insist that superficial mechanization for the purpose of mobilization and exploitation, however, would not bring imperial Japan what it was looking for in colonial Korea. He was clearly aware that the foremost goal in reconstructing Korean agriculture was to increase productivity for Japan's war efforts in Manchuria and mainland China. In this way, In aimed to draw attention to the "Korea problem" by logically linking it to the entire future of the Japanese empire. He reconfirmed that a substantial increase in agricultural productivity would not take place unless peasant-landlord relations were transformed into a modern system of exchange. He observed that bringing improvement to agriculture pertained in part to a highly psychological process, that is, a strong positive link between the peasant and their land must be established. To do this, he emphasized that peasant land ownership should be encouraged immediately and the adoption of mechanized farming should also be led by these same independent peasant groups. However, In criticized that mechanization was taking place in a very limited context and more importantly, it was predominantly occurring to the benefit of only the landed class.[89]

In this way, In's response to colonial Korea's role for Japan's war efforts took the form of resending his critical insights to his potential Japanese audience. For this reason, nonfictional accounts of the miserable living conditions of Korean peasants were included in *The Agricultural Land of Chosun Korea*. As these peasants' hardships and ordeals were the most effective sources that would enable him to highlight the seriousness of the "Korea problem" in conjunction with Japan's Pan-Asian project.

Colonial Korea as a prizm of Japan's new Asia

Beginning with his analysis of the agricultural problem, In's pro-imperial social science agenda gradually expanded its concern to cover the entire economic structure of colonial Korea. Once again, the epistemology of a colonial intellectual is infused in his writing. By showing that colonial Korea's social issues were closely entangled with domestic and intra-regional problems within the Japanese empire, In attempted to turn colonial Korea into a key strategic domain through which the success and failure of Japan's empire-building project would be forecast. For instance, he pointed out that lack of mechanization would first exacerbate the issue of overpopulation in agriculture. Rural overpopulation, in combination with poorly trained, manual labor was a large burden for the state not just in colonial Korea but in Japan proper. However, In also argued that unplanned mechanization would create another problem in colonial Korea since such mechanization would eventually push the excess rural labor to urban areas and aggravate the issue of unemployment in the city areas.

It is at this juncture that In attempted to make the point that the Korea problem represented a focal point for constructing the imperial Pan-Asian community. The sustainability of an East Asian empire was contingent on its self-sufficiency. Objecting to the superficial notion of the Japan-Manchuria-China economic bloc as a regional unit of self-sufficient economy, Japanese imperial social scientists such as Rōyama Masamichi, Ezawa Jōji and Moritani Katsumi called for the fundamental restructuring of the Japanese and colonial economies. They observed that a key to economic sustainability is to enhance productivity in both agricultural and industrial sectors. For this purpose, the disposition and distribution of available resources should not be controlled by individuals and thus, it was widely accepted that state power must be the highest authority that could provide a maximum level of efficiency through a planned economy.

In observed that the establishment of the Committee for National Land Planning in both Japan proper and colonial Korea was an inevitable consequence of how the rationalist and developmentalist notion had gained currency among various rival imperial discourses. Joining the Committee for National Land Planning in colonial Korea in 1940, In produced numerous articles on restructuring national land and thereby reconstructing the Korean economy. The political distance between In's perception of a Pan-Asian community and that of the Japanese government was shortened most during this brief time period between 1940 and early 1942, shortly after the Pearl Harbor attack. At this point, In might have believed that his constant insistence on rehabilitating agriculture was finally being acknowledged by Japanese bureaucrats and intellectuals, since one of the main goals of national land planning was to reconstruct the struggling agricultural sector.

The institutionalization of the notion of restructuring provided the political ground for In's emphasis on Korea's importance in the general reconstruction plan mapped out by imperial Japan. In aptly associated Korean agriculture with the productivity issue in the East Asian Community as a whole. Now, as a member of the Committee for National Land Problems in colonial Korea, In's first criticism was that Korea was seriously underestimated in spite of its size. For instance, in comparison to the similarly sized *Honshu* Island in Japan, where five independent rural land plans had been drafted, colonial Korea, he stressed, was categorized as a mere sub-area together with the Southern Seas, while national land planning in Manchuria and China was linked to that of Japan proper at the same level.[90] Of course, In was aware that a simple repetition of Korea's position in Japan's empire-building projects would not convince his potential audience. Instead, In intended to present scientific and rational evidence for Korea's strategic importance within the boom of restructuring at the turn of the 1940s. In Jeong Sik (here writing under the Japanese name Kazuo Kiryu), believed that rice produced in Korea could help solve the problem of growing demand for rice in northern China where the flood of immigrants had simply overwhelmed local agricultural production.[91]

The stream of logical thinking apparent within In's writing targeted the conclusive point as to why agricultural and industrial development in colonial Korea should receive firm imperial attention. Here, In put forward his prescription for this intertwined social-scientific issue that, he believed, might be applied to agricultural problems in Japan proper as well. His analysis focused on the uniqueness of population configuration in East Asia. The supply of cheap and affordable labor was made possible by the traditional expanded family structure. However, extra labor flocking to urban areas, In observed, had aggravated unemployment in the cities. Therefore, In insisted that mechanization in agriculture and modern industrialization in urban areas were needed together to form a dualistic approach to solving the overpopulated dysfunctional economic structure of East Asia.[92] In believed that mechanization in agriculture would increase productivity per household, thereby increasing disposable income which could help mitigate the economic hardship suffered by overpopulated peasant families.

"Greater East Asia" and the fate of colonial social science

In this way, numerous "Koreanized" visions of a Pan-Asian community were produced through In Jeong Sik's pro-imperial social scientific perspective between 1938 and late 1941. Apparently, In did not go as far as the outright denunciation of modernization, despite the fact that many Japanese philosophers, and the Kyoto School in particular, had articulated their slogan as one of "overcoming modernity." For In, modernization was no longer a lexicon that represented the maximization of individuals' indefinite pursuit of profit, nor was it regarded as a Western ideology incompatible with the East. As discussed in Chapter 3, Ezawa Jōji attempted to shed new light on this forward-looking perspective by redefining the notion of development. Imagining a shared but positively developed future, Ezawa thought, subjects in Asia might come to share in the "community of destiny." To this end, the logic of promoting everyone's living standard within the colony should occupy a central position in imperial Japan's new economic plans, and In tenaciously immersed himself in these ideological tensions over how best to build an Asian community, believing that the *kyōdōtai* notion would be most suitable to function transformatively within the colonial reality.

In's expectation to promote the status of Korea through Japan-led social and political reforms, however, gradually came to an impasse as the Sino-Japanese War was expanded into a larger total war against the United States. Imperial Japan changed its imperial rhetoric from a Asian new order to a Greater East Asia Co-Prosperity Sphere, which included Southeast Asia and the Southern Seas. No doubt, the maximization of exploiting and mobilizing human and material resources was prioritized as part of this new Asian prospect. This indicated that domestic and practical socio-political reforms would be marginalized. Moreover, Japanese intellectuals' and bureaucrats' concern with China increasingly grew as the Sino-Japanese War became prolonged through the intensification and organization of anti-Japanese sentiment under Mao Zedong's leadership. Under these circumstances, Korean intellectuals' hope to bring colonial Korea to the center of a new empire-building project was fading away.

In early 1942, shortly after the Pearl Harbor attack, a group of Japanese and Korean intellectuals and bureaucrats published collective essays of the status and role of colonial Korea in Japan's expanded Greater East Asian war. The Japanese participants in this book, titled *The Greater East Asian War and Colonial Korea*, represented different views on colonial Korea from Japan proper.[93] Both Japanese and Korean writers, including In Jeong Sik, were fully aware that the primary goal of the Greater East Asia Co-Prosperity Sphere was to construct a self-defensive and self-sufficient regional unit that embraced Southeast Asia. Behind the jubilation over the series of victories by the Japanese Army and Navy in the Pacific and Southeast Asian theaters in early 1942 lay serious expectations of, and anxieties over, the changed status of colonial Korea. Importantly, missing in their discussion was the presence of China in the Asia-Pacific War. Emphasizing the binary warfront of Japan versus the United States, they did not hide their expectation that colonial Korea, which had been part of Japan for more than three decades, would play a central role in supporting imperial Japan's "holy war."

In's writing reveals the mentality of this war-oriented perception of colonial Korea. After a meticulous survey of each region's capacity to export rice, he came to the proud conclusion that only Chosun Korea had surpassed a level of self-sufficiency and therefore could export rice to Japan and the rest of Asia.[94] He asserted that Manchukuo and China did not have any extra capacity beyond a degree of self-sufficiency, and Southeast Asian agriculture had not even reached the stage where discussing a rapid increase in rice production was possible due to the lack of technology and environmental conditions.[95] In's optimistic analysis of Korea's importance within Japan's Pan-Asian empire, however, paradoxically disclosed that his reform-oriented vision of a new Asia was reaching a dead end. Instead of stressing the urgency of structural reforms in agriculture as an integral part of the constructing of the new East Asian Community, In now inverted his argument. That is, Korea's *given* physical capacity of producing extra rice would greatly contribute to Japan's war efforts and thus several reforms such as mechanization and "proper" land taxes were duly expected. In's pro-imperialist social science had begun finally to provide scientific knowledge for the purpose of maximized exploitation and mobilization at the time of the Greater East Asian War. In this process, calls for structural and fundamental social changes were marginalized or considered auxiliary in the context of conducting a total war. Most importantly, In substantially deviated from his early speculations as to the suitability of making Korean peasants full-fledged subjects of Japan's empire. The presence of subservient peasants was now crucially important since they were the main source for fulfilling imperial Japan's demand for rice production.

The downturn of In's colonial social science, and his revised vision of Korea as a faithful space for wartime exploitation is best illuminated in his constant use of the term "proper." In his 1943 book *A Study of the Reconstruction of Korean Agriculture*, published two years after Japan's war fronts had been expanded to the United States of America and Southeast Asia,[96] he expounded on the basic direction for the reconstruction of agriculture in Korea.

> First, the general goal of reconstruction must be set up in an attempt to normalize agricultural living conditions and permanently improve agricultural productivity by reorganizing Korean agriculture. However, such reconstruction would eventually result in two major courses – determining the *proper* size of agricultural management and making landlord-peasant relations *proper*. Other issues include, for example, a *proper* distribution of the peasant population. . . . Surely, the precondition for setting the *proper* size of (agricultural) management is to relocate labor powers within rural areas or send them outside farmland.[97]

(emphasis added)

The above paragraph contains major agricultural issues In himself had raised between 1938 and 1941. The excessive small-sized and rented farmland for Korean peasants, incredibly high rent taxes and the maldistribution of agricultural labor power remained the major issues in early 1940s Chosun Korea. However, he became aware that dealing with these problems was predominantly contingent on Japan's total mobilization projects in its expanded warfronts. For this reason, In attempted to rationalize his call for constructing Korean agriculture by bringing up an abstract concept of "making everything proper." He insisted that lowering tenant land taxes would greatly serve for increasing rice production, since Korean peasants had not been able to accumulate surplus capital necessary for promoting productive powers under high land taxes.[98] Such a standpoint in 1942 and 1943 reveals that In's initial justification of his collaboration with the Japanese empire, that is, promoting the living condition of Korean peasants and promoting the status of colonial Korea within the Japanese empire, was now broken in pieces.

More importantly, the primacy of spiritualism over tangible reality that dominated the notion of the Greater East Asia Co-Prosperity Sphere changed the whole topography of wartime Asian discourses. In contrast to the East Asian Community, which emphasized putting actual policies into practice to narrow the gap between metropole and colony, the official slogan of the Greater East Asia Co-Prosperity

Sphere itself was premised on the spiritual bondage between Japan and the rest of Asia under the auspices of the Emperor. Here, I do not intend to make the preposterous point that the *kyōdōtai* group of social scientists had progressive visions of a new Asia and thus can be called "reformists." Rather, that they were aware that "rational" and developmentalist Pan-Asian discourses would more effectively serve to turn colonial and Chinese subjects into spontaneous forces constructing a Japan-led empire. The official adoption of the Greater East Asia Co-Prosperity Sphere around 1942, therefore indicates that there was little room for colonial intellectuals' addressing their various visions of empire and this was no exception for In Jeong Sik.

The rise of spiritual and cultural Pan-Asianism paved the way for the reevaluating of traditional Chinese values and a modification to the existing master narrative of Chinese society as stagnant and thus incompatible with modern development. In Jeong Sik was attentive to such a tendency since it would have an impact on the status of colonial Korea within the Japanese empire. However, the emphasis on traditional Chinese values in building a Pan-Asian empire would form a distinctively contradictory route to In's developmentalist and reconstruction-oriented future of East Asia. Since the slogan, the Greater East Asia Co-Prosperity Sphere, was officially promulgated by imperial Japan around 1942, several China specialists, many of whom had converted from Marxism to spiritual Pan-Asianism, attempted to reevaluate the significance of the modes of life in traditional China. The renowned economic historian of China, Tachibana Shiraki, was one of these intellectuals. Tachibana found Western perceptions of Asia, and the concept of the Asiatic society by Karl Wittfogel in particular, incompatible with Asia, denigrating it as another addition to the Western misunderstanding of China.[99] In fact, Tachibana had taken a skeptical perspective about Wittfogel when he was first introduced to Japan in the early 1930s. He observed that the autonomous and self-sufficient aspects of a Pan-Asian community could be epitomized by reinterpreting the Chinese village system. Such a perspective constituted his clear-cut perception that world civilization is divided into two main spheres: the East and the West. This explains why Tachibana was deeply involved in the Kingly Way group in Manchuria in the mid-1930s, while Wittfogel's theory of Asiatic society rapidly gained currency in Japan proper. The Kingly Way was conceptualized by Ishihara Kanji, a leading architect of Manchukuo in the early 1930s, and in spite of a complex mixture of different ideological aspects, the Kingly Way put an emphasis on the spiritual harmony of Asian people independent of the West. Tachibana was particularly interested in the Confucian background of the Kingly Way and this informed his vision of agricultural autonomy and harmony.[100] He claimed that Western civilization represented industrialization-driven and profit-oriented society, but also stressed that the core dynamics of China and Asia lie in their agriculture-centered communality and self-sufficiency.

Some converted Marxist social scientists also kept pace with the rise of spiritual values in Pan-Asian discourses. Hirano Yoshitarō, for example, began extensively writing on his reevaluation of the Chinese village community which he himself had problematized in the mid-1930s as the main reason for Chinese underdevelopment. Ancient Chinese moral codes and ethics-oriented collective norms, he stressed, played a pivotal role in maintaining the stability of Chinese village communities with minimal class conflicts. He theorized it as "national morality (*minzoku dotoku*)" and centered his academic concerns on how these traditional Chinese value systems might plausibly decorate the spiritual exterior of the Greater East Asia Co-Prosperity Sphere. Notwithstanding, such academic moves reflected Japan's urgency to convince the Chinese people of Japan's role as a savior from Western imperialism in order to mobilize Chinese subjects for its war efforts.

In's encounter with Tachibana in March 1942 vividly shows the tension he felt as the center of a Pan-Asian empire-building project was shifting from the notion of realistic developmentalism to dogmatic spiritual and ethical values. Tachibana stayed in colonial Korea about a month to carry out field surveys on rural areas and join several meetings, which included a roundtable discussion of Korean agriculture for the journal, *Manchu Review*. In this roundtable discussion, Tachibana maintained his perspective on the historical and structural difference between Chinese agriculture and Western agriculture and made some points about Korean society in this regard. He was particularly interested in the *gye* system, an autonomous village association that shared labor power and resources mostly for agricultural production. Tachibana found it very similar to the Chinese traditional village system and for him, this type of communal labor was an integral part of maintaining self-sufficiency since it was premised on the sense of sharing the destiny of community and thus being collectively responsible for rice production. Theoretically, the notion of communal labor had several aspects that might fit into the slogans of the "community of destiny" and a self-sufficient state for national defense, two core concepts of the Greater East Asia Co-Prosperity Sphere.

While showing his utmost respect to one of the most renowned scholars of Chinese agriculture alive, In, however, did not hide his discontent with Tachibana's understanding of the nature of Korean agriculture. At the center of his rebuttal of the rediscovery and "overestimation" of the traditional village system was a structural analysis of why Korean agriculture must be modernized along with industrialization in urban areas. Unquestionably, In's critical response to Tachibana reveals the discomfort of a colonial intellectual who was concerned that the rise of Chinese traditional values at the center of an ideological Pan-Asianism would marginalize colonial Korea as an auxiliary state. More importantly, an excessive valorization of ethnical and spiritual bondage, such as communal labor, as the driving force for a new Asian unity would greatly dilute realistic demands for mechanization and modernization in agriculture.

In did not reject the necessity of communal labor as such but basically observed that the idea of communal labor only gained currency due to the shortage of labor power in rural areas. The prolonged total war, he stressed, had demanded the mobilizing of all available resources on both the war and home fronts. Wartime mobilization necessarily focused on technology-oriented industrial and military sectors and it absorbed a massive volume of labor power from rural areas which resulted in a serious labor shortage in agriculture. For this reason, he contended that the concept of communal or collective labor had emerged in order to make sure that not a single labor power should be left unused and previously set goals could be accomplished more quickly by converging labor powers to one point.[101] These analyses indicate that he basically referred to the rise of communal labor within wartime agricultural discourses as a socio-economic issue or an issue of management, rather than considering the Asian tradition of communal labor as an ideological key to overcoming capitalistic Western agricultural systems.

As Tachibana and Hirano had already argued, In was also aware that the concept of communal labor was not something new in colonial Korea either. Pointing out that several forms of communal labor did exist in traditional Korea, In, however, attempted to make a few interesting points to scientifically examine the differences regarding communal labor in traditional times and in the period of total war. He maintained that communal labor in traditional Korea had little to do with a labor shortage. Since no sense of private land ownership existed in premodern Korea, communal labor, according to him, came from a charity-based noncapitalist mentality shared by peasants.[102] In went on to argue that the same type of noncapitalist communal labor could not be voluntarily undertaken by present-day peasants, since a great deal of labor power in agriculture already consisted of wage-based work, and therefore workers were subject to profit-oriented modes of life.[103] In sum, bringing up "Asian" modes of life and coloring with them the "anti-modern" and "anti-capitalist" aspect of Japan's Pan-Asian empire building, meant a regression from the state-oriented modernist and developmentalist direction through which colonial Korean social scientists like In had aimed to promote the status of Korea, thereby justifying their conversion.

Summary

In Jeong Sik's encounter with the notion of the East Asia Cooperative Community (*kyōdōtai*) enabled him to articulate colonial problems in the context of social reforms, although imperial Japan always took the political initiative in actually changing Korean society. The intellectual cohabitation between the imperial power and this social scientist converted to the imperial cause did not last long. However, when he could, In Jeong Sik incessantly projected his personal conviction that colonial Korea could obtain substantial packages for development, utilizing the circumstances of total war. Oscillating between "stagnated" China and "advanced" Japan, In attempted to restructure colonial Korea under the umbrella of a Pan-Asian empire. For this purpose, In immersed himself in the pursuit and practice of social scientific knowledge on Korean society. In this process, he neglected the everyday violence and exploitation committed by the occupying imperial power against its colonial subjects, since he had already projected his optimistic picture of a developed Korea onto the fate of a Japan-led Pan-Asia. However, this kind of rationalization could never accomplish fulfillment since In's narrative for the improved future of Korea depended entirely on external imperial power.

Since 1942, In's project of reconstructing Korea faced challenges from the rise of spiritual Pan-Asianism mingled with various Chinese and Japanese traditional thinking systems and value codes such as the Chinese village community, the samurai spirit and the Imperial Way. In addition, aggravated situations on Japan's war fronts resulted in an increasingly explicit and violent demand for human and material resources from the colony. Any imagined "grand" transformation, such as the destruction of peasant-landlord hierarchies, industrial mechanization and the expansion of educational opportunities in Korean agriculture all became impossible. Nevertheless, In continued to rationalize his collaboration with the Japanese empire, now providing practical suggestions for maximizing wartime exploitation in the name of improving labor conditions and management in agriculture. At this point, it suffices to say that In Jeong Sik's writings simply represented the voice of the empire, contradictory to his perception that he was still on the side of Korean peasants. Perhaps predictably, In's pro-imperial social science could not overcome the specter of colonialism and served to rationalize the Japanese empire in the shadow of Pan-Asianism.

Notes

1 Yi Kwang Su, Ellie Choi, trans., "On National Reconstruction," in *Imperatives of Culture: Selected Essays on Korean History, Literature and Society from the Japanese Colonial Era*, eds. Christopher P. Hanscom, Walter K. Lew and Youngju Ryu (Honolulu: University of Hawaii Press, 2013), 14–15. Yi's original writing appeared in *Kaebyok* in May 1922 under the title of *Minjok kaejoron*.
2 Michael Robinson, *Cultural Nationalism in Colonial Korea, 1920–1925* (Seattle and London: University of Washington Press, 1988), 6.
3 For a genealogy of *Chosunhak* movements, See Paek Seung Cheol, "1930 nendai chosunhak undong ui jungae wa minzok insik-kundaekwan [The Development of Korean Studies Movements in the 1930s and Its Concepts of Nation and Modernity]," *Yoksa wa silhak* 36 (2008): 113–148.
4 Choi Nam Sun, "Dangunron [On Dan'gun]," *Dong-A Ilbo* (Mar. 3 – July 25, 1926); "Chosun yoksa gangwha [Lectures on the History of Chosun Korea]," *Dong-A Ilbo* (Jan. 12 – Mar. 15, 1930).
5 For Choi Nam Sun's critiques of *nissendōsoron*, refer to Chapter 2 in Ryu Sihyun, *Choi nam sun yongu* [A Study of Choi Nam Sun] (Seoul: Yoksapipyungsa, 2011).
6 Ibid., 194.
7 Paik Num Un, "Kwahak baljon ui yoksajeok philyonsung [The Historical Inevitability of the Development of Science]," *Tongbang pyongron* (May 1932), in *Hwip'yŏn: Paik Nam Un Chonjip* 4 [The Completed Works of Paik Num Un], ed. Ha Ilsik (Seoul: Iron kwa Silch'ŏn, 1991), 74.
8 Pail Nam Un, "Chosun kyungjesa ui pangbyopron [The Methodology of the Korean Economy]," *Sindong-A* 3, no. 2 (Dec. 1933), in Ha Ilsik, *Hwip'yŏn*, 92.
9 Ibid.
10 Paik Nam Un, *Chōsen shakai keizaishi* [The Social and Economic History of Chosun Korea] (Tokyo: Kaizosha, 1933), 5. For a detailed study of Paik's scholarship, Pang Kie Jung, *Han'guk kŭnhyŏndae sasangsa yŏn'gu: 1930, 40-yŏndae Paek Nam-un ŭi hangmun kwa chŏngch'i kyŏngje sasang* [A Study of the Intellectual History of Modern Korea: The Scholarship and Politico-Economic Thoughts of Paik Nam Un in the 1930s and 1940s] (Seoul: Yŏksa Pip'yŏngsa, 1992). Henry Em has recently published a work that includes a study of Paik Nam Un's studies of Korean history. See Chapter 3

in Henry H. Em, *The Great Enterprise: Sovereignty and Historiography in Modern Korea* (Durham: Duke University Press, 2013), 114–137.

11 See Chapter 17 "Shilla," in *Chōsen shakai keizaishi*. However, Historian Pang Ki Jung points out that Paik's notion of the rise of private land ownership during the Shila period shows logical inconsistencies since Paik failed to explain why slavery and private land ownership coexisted with massive state land ownership. Pang Kie Jung, *Han'guk kŭnhyŏndae sasangsa yŏn'gu*, 156–160.

12 The three articles were published under the same title. Fukuda Tokuzō, "Kankoku no keizai soshiki to keizai tanyi1 [The Economic Structure and Unit of Korea]," *Naigaironso* 2, no. 5 (1903): 71–92; *Naigaironso* 3, no. 6 (1904): 27–49; *Naigaironso* 4, no. 1 (1905): 1–38. These articles were later included in the 4th volume of *The Completed Works of Economics*. Fukuda Tokuzō, *Keizaigaku zenshu* 4 [Completed Works of Economics] (Tokyo: Kaizosha, 1925), 1–56, 77–162.

13 Fukuda Tokuzō, *Keizaigaku zenshu* 4, 77–100.

14 Ibid., 92–93.

15 Ibid., 92–94.

16 Rathgen's works on Japan were mostly published between 1890 and 1911. Karl Rathgen, *Japans Volkswirtschaft und Staatshaushalt* [Japan's Economy and State Budget] (Leipzig: Duncker & Humblot, 1891); *Die Japaner und ihre wirtschaftliche Entwicklung* [The Japanese and Japan's Economic Development] (Leipzig: Teubner, 1905); *Staat und Kultur der Japaner* [State and Culture of the Japanese] (Bielefeld and Leipzig: Velhagen & Klasing, 1907); *Die Japaner in der Weltwirtschaft* [The Japanese in the World Economy] (Leipzig: Teubner, 1911).

17 Fukuda Tokuzō, *Keizaigaku zenshu* 4, 95–99.

18 Eric Grimmer-Solem pointedly argues how German social scientists provided a theoretical basis for what he terms "Japanese exceptionalism." He made the point that the perception of Japan as unique and peculiar among the Orient was linked to the observation that its social and economic constitution should be considered as similar to that of the West. Eric Grimmer-Solem, "German Social Science, Meiji Conservatism, and the Peculiarities of Japanese History," *Journal of World History* 16, no. 2 (June 2005): 187–222.

19 Fukuda Tokuzō, *Keizaigaku zenshu* 4, 113–114.

20 Ibid., 115.

21 Ibid., 119.

22 Lee Chung Won, "Chosun ui ul ui sidaejok gochal [A Historical Analysis of the Korean Spirit]," *Pipan* 5, no. 3 (Mar. 1937): 79. On January 1, 1935, Jung began contributing articles on his theory of "ul (spirit)" under the title of "Ochunneyon gan ui joseon ui ul [The 5000 Years of the Korean Spirit]" for *Tong-A Newspaper* but his contribution ended in 1936 as Japan ordered a discontinuation of *Tong-A Newspaper*.

23 Lee Chung Won, "Chosun ui ul ui sidaejok gochal," 78.

24 Paik Nam Un, *Chōsen shakai keizaishi*, 5–6.

25 In *Chōsen shakai keizaishi*, Paik included the Asiatic mode of production as one of the four major modes of production.

26 Paik Nam Un, "Chosun sakwan surip ui jechang," *Kyongje yongu* 4 (1933), in Ha Ilsik, *Hwip'yŏn*, 83.

27 Ibid., 84.

28 Ibid.

29 Paik Nam Un, *Chōsen shakai keizaishi*, 8–9.

30 Ibid.

31 For a study on Comintern theses on Japan, see Chapter 3 in Germaine Hoston, *Marxism and the Crisis of Development in Prewar Japan* (Princeton: Princeton University Press, 1986), 55–75.

32 Roh Tong Kyu, "Aseajok sangsanyangsik ui daehaya [On the Asiatic Mode of Production]," *Shin Dong-A* 4, no. 7 (July 1934): 100–107.

33 The nine categories Roh indicated are as follows: (1) importance of artificial irrigation; (2) Asiatic despotism; (3) absence of private land ownership; (4) taxes commensurate with the rent from land; (5) development of agricultural community; (6) inseparable association of agriculture and handicraft industry; (7) underdevelopment in urban areas; (8) fixation of the class system such as Caste in India and (9) irreversible repetition of stagnation. Roh Tong Kyu, "Aseajok sangsanyangsik ui daehaya," 102–103.
34 Ibid., 103.
35 Ibid., 107.
36 Ibid.
37 For example, Moritani Katsumi published several articles in 1933 and 1934 and argued that certain characteristics such as irrigation and state land ownership were also found in Korean agriculture. Moritani Katsumi, "Chōsen shakai to shizen kankyō (1)," *Tōa* 7, no. 12 (Dec. 1934); Moritani Katsumi, "Kyūrai no chōsen nogyoshakai ni tssuite no kenkyū no tameni [For the Study of Old Agricultural Society in Chosun Korea]," in *Chōsen shakai keizai shi kenkyū*, ed. Keijōteikokudaigaku hōbungakkai (Tokyo: Tōkō Shoin, 1933), 397–482.
38 Lee Chung Won, "Aziateki seisanyoshikiron to chosenhokenshakaishi [The Asiatic Mode of Production and the Feudal Social History of Chosun Korea]," *Yuibutsuron kenkyū* 13 (Apr. 1935): 126–149.
39 Paik Nam₁ Un, *Chōsenhōken shakai keizaishi* (1) [The Feudal Economic History of Chosun Korea] (Tokyo: Kaizōsha, 1937), 139–142.
40 Ibid.
41 Ryu Sihyun, *Choi nam sun yongu*, 266–272.
42 In Jeong Sik, "Chosun nongchon kyungje ui yongu [A Study of the Agricultural Economy of Chosun Korea]," *Chungang* 28–35 (8 issues) (Feb.–Sep. 1936), in *Singminji sidae sahoe sŏngkyŏk kwa nongŏp munje* [The Social Nature of Colonial Korea and the Problem of Agriculture], ed. Oh Mi Il (Seoul: P'ulpit, 1991), 214.
43 Oh Mi Il, *Singminji sidae sahoe sŏngkyŏk kwa nongŏp munje*, 215.
44 Ibid., 231.
45 Ibid., 242.
46 In Jeong Sik, "Nongop jabonjewha ui jehyung kwa chosun tojijosasaup ui uii [Types of Agricultural Capitalist Systems and the Significance of Land Survey in Chosun Korea]," (4 articles) *Pipan* 4 & 5 (Sep. 1936 – Mar. 1937), in *In Jeong Sik Jeonjip* 1 [Completed Works of In Jeong Sik, hereafter *CWI*], ed. In Jeong Sik Jeonjip Kanhaeng Wiwŏnhoe (Seoul: Hanul Academy, 1992), 193–202.
47 In Jeong Sik, *CWI* 1, 195.
48 Yamada Moritaro, *Nihon shinonshugi bunseki* [An Analysis of Japanese Capitalism] (Tokyo: Iwanami Shoten, 1934). For a study of Yamada's concept of land ownership, see Sawada Koji, "Dochi shoyu = nogyo no genjo bunseki – yamada moritanō si no senzen to sengo no bunseki ni tsuite 2 [Land Ownership: Analyzing the Reality of Agriculture – About Yamada Moritarō's Analyses in Wartime and Postwar Periods]," *Keizai ronso* 25, no. 2 (1989): 33–57.
49 Terade Michio, *Yamada Moritaro: Marukusu shugisha no shirarezaru sekai* [Yamada Moritaro: The Unknown World of a Marxist Intellectual] (Tokyo: Nihonkeizaihyoronsha, 2008), 78.
50 Kim In Soo, "Iron yonswe to junhwang – In Jeong sik ui kyungjeron ul chungsim uiro [A Chain of Theories and Conversion: A Focus on In Jeong Sik's Economic Theories]," *Sahoe wa yoksa* 96 (2012): 78–81.
51 In Jeong Sik, "Toji jeomyu ui kundaesung kwa bongkonsung [The Modernity and Feudality of Landownership]," *Chungang* 31 (May 1936), in In Jeong Sik Jeonjip Kanhaeng Wiwŏnhoe, *CWI* 1, 111–113.
52 Park Mun Kyu, "Noson shakai no bunka no kiten toshite dochichosajigyo ni tuite [The Significance of Land Survey as a Starting Point of Culture in Agricultural Society]," in

Chōsen shakai keizai shi kenkyū 5, ed. Keijoteikokudaigaku hobungakkai (Tokyo: Irie Shoin, 1933).

53 Ibid., 21–22.

54 Ibid.

55 In Jeong Sik, "Toji jeomyu ui kundaesung kwa bongkonsung," *CWI* 1, 113.

56 Fujita Shōzō, *Tenkō no shisōshiteki kenkyū: sono ichimen* [A Study of Conversion from the Perspective of Intellectual History] (Tokyo: Iwanami, 1975).

57 Andrew Barshay, *The Social Sciences in Modern Japan* (Berkeley: University of California Press, 2004), 36–71.

58 Peter Duus, "Liberal Intellectuals and Social Conflicts in Taisho Japan," in *Conflict in Modern Japanese History: The Neglected Tradition*, eds. Testuo Najita and J. Victor Koschmann (Princeton: Princeton University Press, 1982), 419.

59 Andrew Barshay, *The Social Sciences in Modern Japan*, 40.

60 It was in the 1910s and early 1920s that Japanese anthropologists and historians began putting forward the theory of *nissendōsoron*. Torri Ryūzō (1870–1953) was a representative Japanese intellectual who believed that the theory of Japanese and Koreans as having the same ancestor could be scientifically proved. For a study of *nissendōsoron*, see Mitsui Takashi, "Kindai academizu shigaku no nakani *nissendōsoron* – kankoku heigo zengo wo chushinni [The Theory of Japan and Korea as Having the Same Ancestor in the Context of Modern Academism – A Focus on the Period of Japan's Annexation of Korea]," *Chōsenshikenkyuronbunshu* 42 (2004): 42–76.

61 Hyun Yong Sop, *Chōsenjin no susumubeki do* [The Way of Survival for Koreans] (Kyungsung: Ryokkirenmei, 1938).

62 Lee Kyong Hun, *Yi Kwang-su ŭi ch'inil munhak yŏn'gu* [A Study of Lee Kwang Su's Pro-Japanese Literature] (Seoul: T'aehaksa, 1998).

63 In Jeong Sik, "Minjok munjeui bangbeopron [A Methodology for the Problem of Nation]," *Samcholl'i*, 131 (1939), in In Jeong Sik jeonjip Kanhaeng Wiwŏnhoe, *CWI* 2, 49.

64 Ibid.

65 Miki Kiyoshi, "Shin nihon no shisō genri [Principles of a New Japan]," in *Miki Kiyoshi zenshū* 17 (Tokyo: Iwanami, 1968). For an unpublished English translation, see Lewis Harrington, trans., *Principles of Thought for a New Japan*.

66 In Jeong Sik, "Chosun sahoe wa sinilbonjuui – yoksa ui saeronun wondongryok [New Japanism in Korean Society: A New Historical Dynamic]," *Chungsakji* 5 (May 1939), in In Jeong Sik jeonjip Kanhaeng Wiwŏnhoe, *CWI* 2, 56.

67 In Jeong Sik, "Marukusushugi no aseani okeru hutekiousei [The Incompatibility of Marxism in Asia]," *Chikei* 16, no. 12 (1938): 27–30.

68 Ibid., 28.

69 The term "thought war" first emerged after the outbreak of the Sino-Japanese War in 1937 and was widely used by Japanese intellectuals to justify Japan's imperialist war.

70 In Jeong Sik, "Asea ui bonggun sahoe [Feudal Society in Asia]," *Nongup chosun* 3, no. 7 (July 1940), in In Jeong Sik Jeonjip Kanhaeng Wiwŏnhoe, *CWI* 2, 255.

71 *CWI* 2, 258–262.

72 In Jeong Sik, "Mul iyagi [A Story of Water]," *Taeyang* 1, no. 2 (Feb. 1940), in In Jeong Sik Jeonjip Kanhaeng Wiwŏnhoe, *CWI* 2, 160–165.

73 Park Moon Byung, "Nong'op chosun ui gumto [An Analysis of Agriculture in Chosun Korea]," *Chosun Joong Ang Ilbo* (June 1936 – Aug. 1936); for an analysis of Park Moon Byung's writings, see Oh Mi-Il, "1930 nyondae sahoejuiujadului sahoesung-kyoknonjaeng [A Debate over the Nature of Society in Socialist Movements in 1930s Chosun Korea]," *Yŏksapipyong* 10 (1990): 218–251.

74 In Jeong Sik, " 'Nong'op chosun ui gumto' ui gumto [A Reading of "An Analysis of Agricultural Chosun Korea"]," *Pipan* 5, no. 9 (Sep. 1937), in In Jeong Sik Jeonjip Kanhaeng Wiwŏnhoe, *CWI* 1, 222–226.

75 In Jeong Sik, "Shinkisanmaijosankeikaku to sono tenbo [A New Plan to Increase Rice Production and Its Prediction]," *Chōsensotokubu chosagetsuho* 10, no. 9 (Oct. 1939) in In Jeong Sik Jeonjip Kanhaeng Wiwŏnhoe, *CWI* 2, 91.

76 In Jeong Sik, "Chosun nongmin munhak ui kunponjeok kwaje [A Fundamental Mission of Agricultural Literature in Chosun Korea]," *Inmunpyungron* 1, no. 3 (Dec. 1939), in In Jeong Sik Jeonjip Kanhaeng Wiwŏnhoe, *CWI* 2, 131–133.

77 Ibid., 134.

78 Ibid.

79 In Jeong Sik, "Munwhawa sojakryo [Culture and Farm Rent]," *Inmunpyongron* 2, no. 10 (1940), in In Jeong Sik Jeonjip Kanhaeng Wiwŏnhoe, *CWI* 2, 293–297.

80 In Jeong Sik, "Chosun nongmin munhak ui kunponjeok kwaje," *CWI* 2, 137–138.

81 Ibid., 137.

82 Kazuo Kiryu (In Jeong Sik), "Chōsen ni okeru tekisei kosakuriryo no mondai [The Problem of Proper Farm Rent in Chosun Korea] (1)," *Chōsensotokubu shosagetsubo* 12, no. 8 (Aug. 1941), in In Jeong Sik Jeonjip Kanhaeng Wiwŏnhoe, *CWI* 2, 390–393.

83 In Jeong Sik, *Chōsen no nogyochitai* [The Agricultural-Industrial Zone of Chosun Korea] (Tokyo: Seikatsusha, 1940), in In Jeong Sik Jeonjip Kanhaeng Wiwŏnhoe, *CWI* 3, 28.

84 Louise Young, *Japan's Total Empire*: *Manchuria and the Culture of Wartime Imperialism* (Berkeley: University of California Press, 1998), 183–240.

85 Pang Kie Jung, "1930 nendai chosun nonggong pyungjin jungchack kwa kyeongje tongje [The Policy for the Uniform Advancement of Agriculture and Industry and Economic Control in 1930s Chosun Korea]," *Tongbang hakji* 120 (June 2003): 75–120.

86 In Jeong Sik, *Chōsen no nogyochitai, CWI* 3, 3–4.

87 In Jeong Sik, "Dongakwon ui kyeongjejok sungguck kwa chosun ui wichi [The Characteristics of the Economy in East Asian Region and the Status of Chosun Korea]," *Sam'cholli* 140 (Jan. 1940), in In Jeong Sik Jeonjip Kanhaeng Wiwŏnhoe, *CWI* 2, 300.

88 In Jeong Sik, *Chōsen no nogyochitai, CWI* 3, 74–94.

89 Ibid., 5.

90 In Jeong Sik, "Chosun nongup gwa sikryang gwa kuktogyehoek [Agriculture, Food and National Land Planning in Chosun Korea]," *Sam Cholli* (June 1941), in In Jeong Sik Jeonjip Kanhaeng Wiwŏnhoe, *CWI* 2, 349.

91 Kazuo Kiryu (In Jeong Sik), "Chōsen ni okeru kokudo keikaku to nogyokeikaku [National Land and Agricultural Planning in Chosun Korea]," *Chōsensotokubu chosagetsuho* 12, no. 2 (Feb. 1942), in In Jeong Sik Jeonjip Kanhaeng Wiwŏnhoe, *CWI* 2, 308–312.

92 Kazuo Kiryu, "Chōsen ni okeru kokudo keikaku to nogyokeikaku," *CWI* 2, 312–318.

93 Okubo Koichi, et al., eds., *Daitōasenso to hanto* [The Greater Asian War and Chosun Korea] (Kyungsung: Jinbunsha, 1942).

94 In Jeong Sik, "Tōa kyōeiken no shokuryomondai to hanto no nogyo [The Food Problem in the East Asia Co-Prosperity Sphere and Agriculture in Chosun Korea]," *Kokumin bungaku* 2, no. 5 (May 1942), in In Jeong Sik Jeonjip Kanhaeng Wiwŏnhoe, *CWI* 2, 526.

95 Ibid., 522–527.

96 In Jeong Sik, *Chōsen noson saihensei no kenkyū* [A Study on the Reconstruction of Agriculture in Chosun Korea] (Kyungsung: Jinbunsha, 1943), also available in *CWI* 3.

97 Ibid., 370.

98 Ibid., 378–380.

99 Tachibana Shiraki, "Tōyo shakai no kōzo [The Formation of Oriental Society]," *Tairiku* (Mar. 1942), also in *Tachibana Shiraki chosakushū* 3 (Tokyo: Keisō Shobō, 1966), 10–15.

100 For a study of the Kingly Way, see Chapter 4, "'The Long-Term Policy of National Management Will Always Be in Unison with the Japanese Empire': The Paradise of the Kingly Way Stumbles and the Path Toward the Merging of Japan and Manzhouguo," in *Manchuria Under Japanese Dominion*, ed. Yamamuro Shinichi, trans. Joshua Fogel (Philadelphia: University of Pennsylvania Press, 2006), 127–197. About Tachibana's encounter with Ishihara Kanji, see Hamaguchi Yuko, "Tachibana Shiraki to Ishihara Kanji – manshujihen sengo wo chushinni [Tachibana Shiraki and Ishihara Kanji – With a Focus on the Manchurian Incident Periods]," *Kunjishigaku* 24, no. 2 (Sep. 1988): 19–33.
101 Kazuo Kiryu (In Jeong Sik), "Chōsen ni okeru nogyorodo ni saihenseikate [The Process of Restructuring Agriculture Labor in Chosun Korea] (1)," *Manshuhyōron* 23, no. 15 (1942), in In Jeong Sik Jeonjip Kanhaeng Wiwŏnhoe, *CWI* 2, 594.
102 Kazuo Kiryu (In Jeong Sik), "Chōsen ni okeru nogyorodo ni saihenseikate [The Process of Restructuring Agriculture Labor in Chosun Korea] (2)," *Manshuhyōron* 23, no. 16 (1942), in In Jeong Sik Jeonjip Kanhaeng Wiwŏnhoe, *CWI* 2, 603–604.
103 Ibid., 604.

Bibliography

Barshay, Andrew. *The Social Sciences in Modern Japan*, 127–197. Berkeley: University of California Press, 2004.
Choi, Nam Sun. "Chosun yoksa gangwha [Lectures on the History of Chosun Korea]." *Dong-A Ilbo*, Jan. 12 – Mar. 15, 1930.
———. "Dangunron [On Dan'gun]." *Dong-A Ilbo*, Mar. 3 – July 25, 1926.
Duus, Peter. "Liberal Intellectuals and Social Conflicts in Taisho Japan." In *Conflict in Modern Japanese History: The Neglected Tradition*, edited by Testuo Najita and J. Victor Koschmann, 412–440. Princeton: Princeton University Press, 1982.
Eric, Grimmer-Solem. "German Social Science, Meiji Conservatism, and the Peculiarities of Japanese History." *Journal of World History* 1 & 6, no. 2 (June 2005): 187–222.
Fujita, Shōzō. *Tenkō no shisōshiteki kenkyū: sono ichimen* [A Study of Conversion from the Perspective of Intellectual History]. Tokyo: Iwanami, 1975.
Fukuda, Tokuzō. "Kankoku no keizai soshiki to keizai tanyi 1 [The Economic Structure and Unit of Korea]." *Naigaironso* 2, no. 5 (1903): 71–92.
———. "Kankoku no keizai soshiki to keizai tanyi 2 [The Economic Structure and Unit of Korea]." *Naigaironso* 3, no. 6 (1904): 27–49.
———. "Kankoku no keizai soshiki to keizai tanyi 3 [The Economic Structure and Unit of Korea]." *Naigaironso* 4, no. 1 (1905): 1–38.
———. *Keizaigaku zenshu* 4 [Completed Works of Economics]. Tokyo: Kaizosha, 1925.
Germaine, Hoston. *Marxism and the Crisis of Development in Prewar Japan*. Princeton: Princeton University Press, 1986.
Ha, Ilsik, ed. *Hwip'yŏn: Paik Nam Un Chonjip* 4 [The Completed Works of Paik Num Un]. Seoul: Iron kwa Silch'ŏn, 1991.
Hamaguchi, Yuko. "Tachibana Shiraki to Ishihara Kanji – manshujihen sengo wo chushinni [Tachibana Shiraki and Ishihara Kanji – With a Focus on the Manchurian Incident Periods]." *Kunjishigaku* 24, no. 2 (Sep. 1988): 19–33.
Henry, Em. *The Great Enterprise: Sovereignty and Historiography in Modern Korea*. Durham: Duke University Press, 2013.
Hyun, Yong Sop. *Chōsenjin no susumubeki do* [The Way of Survival for Koreans]. Kyungsung: Ryokkirenmei, 1938.

In, Jeong Sik (In Jeong Sik Jeonjip Kanhaeng Wiwŏnhoe). *In Jeong sik jeonjip* [Completed Works of In Jeong Sik]. Seoul: Hanul, 1992, 5 vols.

——— (Kazuo Kiryu). "Asea ui bonggun sahoe [Feudal Society in Asia]." *Nongup chosun* 3, no. 7 (July 1940) in In, Jeong Sik. *In Jeong Sik Jeonjip* 2. 255–262.

———. "Chōsen ni okeru nogyorodo ni saihenseikate [The Process of Restructuring Agriculture Labor in Chosun Korea]." *Manshuhyōron* 23, no. 15 (1942), in In, Jeong Sik. *In Jeong SikJjeonjip* 2. 594–601.

———. "Chōsen ni okeru nogyorodo ni saihenseikate [The Process of Restructuring Agriculture Labor in Chosun Korea] (2)." *Manshuhyōron* 23, no. 16 (1942), in In, Jeong Sik. *In Jeong Sik Jeonjip* 2. 602–621.

———. "Chōsen ni okeru tekisei kosakuriryo no mondai [The Problem of Proper Farm Rent in Chosun Korea] (1)." *Chōsensotokubu shosagetsubo* 12, no. 8 (Aug. 1941), in In, Jeong Sik. *In Jeong Sik Jeonjip* 2. 378–405.

———. *Chōsen no nogyochitai* [The Agricultural-Industrial Zone of Chosun Korea]. Tokyo: Seikatsusha, 1940, in In, Jeong Sik. *In Jeong Sik Jeonjip* 3.

———. *Chōsen noson saihensei no kenkyū* [A Study on the Reconstruction of Agriculture in Chosun Korea]. Kyungsung: Jinbunsha, 1943. Also available in In, Jeong Sik. *In Jeong Sik Jeonjip* 3.

———. "Chōsen ni okeru kokudo keikaku to nogyokeikaku [National Land and Agricultural Planning in Chosun Korea]." *Chosensotokubu chosagetsuho* 12, no. 2 (Feb. 1942), in In, Jeong Sik. *In Jeong Sik Jeonjip* 2. 308–312.

———. "Chosun nongchon kyungje ui yongu [A Study of the Agricultural Economy of Chosun Korea]." *Chungang* 28–35 (8 issues) (Feb.–Sep. 1936). In *Singminji sidae sahoe sŏngkyŏk kwa nongŏp munje* [The Social Nature of Colonial Korea and the Problem of Agriculture], edited by Oh Mi Il, 214–281. Seoul: P'ulpit, 1991.

———. "Chosun nongmin munhak ui kunponjeok kwaje [A Fundamental Mission of Agricultural Literature in Chosun Korea]." *Inmunpyungron* 1, no. 3 (Dec. 1939), in In, Jeong Sik. *In Jeong Sik Jeonjip* 2. 131–133.

———. "Chosun nongup gwa sikryang gwa kuktogyehoek [Agriculture, Food and National Land Planning in Chosun Korea]." *Sam Cholli* (June 1941), in In, Jeong Sik. *In Jeong Sik Jeonjip* 2. 347–352.

———. "Chosun sahoe wa sinilbonjuui – yoksa ui saeronun wondongryok [New Japanism in Korean Society: A New Historical Dynamic]." *Chungsakji* 5 (May 1939): 19–23, in In, Jeong Sik. *In Jeong Sik Jeonjip* 2. 52–56.

———. "Dongakwon ui kyeongjejok sungguck kwa chosun ui wichi [The Characteristics of the Economy in East Asian Region and the Status of Chosun Korea]." *Sam'cholli* 140 (Jan. 1940): 66–72, in In, Jeong Sik. *In Jeong Sik Jeonjip* 2. 298–304.

———. "Marukusushugi no aseani okeru hutekiousei [The Incompatibility of Marxism in Asia]." *Chikei* 16, no. 12 (1938): 27–30.

———. "Minjok munjeui bangbeopron [A Methodology for the Problem of Nation]." *Samcholl'i,* 131 (1939): 62–65, in In, Jeong Sik. *In Jeong Sik Jeonjip* 2. 48–51.

———. "Mul iyagi [A Story of Water]." *Taeyang* 1, no. 2 (Feb. 1940): 59–64, in In, Jeong Sik. *In Jeong Sik Jeonjip* 2. 160–165.

———. "Munwhawa sojakryo [Culture and Farm Rent]." *Inmunpyongron* 2, no. 10 (1940), in In, Jeong Sik. *In Jeong Sik Jeonjip* 2. 293–297.

———. " 'Nong'op chosun ui gumto' ui gumto [A Reading of 'An Analysis of Agricultural Chosun Korea']." *Pipan* 5, no. 9 (Sep. 1937), in In, Jeong Sik. *In Jeong Sik Jeonjip* 1. 222–226.

————. "Nongop jabonjewha ui jehyung kwa chosun tojijosasaup ui uii [Types of Agricultural Capitalist Systems and the Significance of Land Survey in Chosun Korea]." (4 articles) *Pipan* 4 & 5 (Sep. 1936 – Mar. 1937), in *In Jeong Sik Jeonjip* 1. 193–202.

————. "Shinkisanmaijosankeikaku to sono tenbo [A New Plan to Increase Rice Production and Its Prediction]." *Chōsensotokubu chosagetsuho* 10, no. 9 (Oct. 1939): 11–19, in In, Jeong Sik. *In Jeong Sik Jeonjip* 2. 85–104.

————. "Tōa kyōeiken no shokuryomondai to hanto no nogyo [The Food Problem in the East Asia Co-Prosperity Sphere and Agriculture in Chosun Korea]." *Kokumin bungaku* 2, no. 5 (May 1942), in In, Jeong Sik. *In Jeong Sik Jeonjip* 2. 516–529.

————. "Toji jeomyu ui kundaesung kwa bongkonsung [The Modernity and Feudality of Land Ownership]." *Chungang* 31 (May 1936): 46–54, in In, Jeong Sik. *In Jeong Sik Jeonjip* 1. 111–119.

Kim, In Soo. "Iron yonswe to junhwang – in Jeong sik ui kyungjeron ul chungsim uiro [A Chain of Theories and Conversion: A Focus on In Jeong Sik's Economic Theories]." *Sahoe wa yoksa* 96 (2012): 71–112.

Lee, Chung Won. "Aziateki seisanyoshikiron to chosenhokenshakaishi [The Asiatic Mode of Production and the Feudal Social History of Chosun Korea]." *Yuibutsuron kenkyū* 13 (Apr. 1935): 126–149.

————. "Chosun ui ul ui sidaejok gochal [A Historical Analysis of the Korean Spirit]." *Pipan* 5, no. 3 (Mar. 1937): 78–83.

Lee, Kyong Hun. *Yi Kwang-su ǔi ch'inil munhak yŏn'gu* [A Study of Lee Kwang Su's Pro-Japanese Literature]. Seoul: T'aehaksa, 1998.

Michael, Robinson. *Cultural Nationalism in Colonial Korea, 1920–1925*. Seattle and London: University of Washington Press, 1988.

Miki, Kiyoshi. "Shin nihon no shisō genri [Principles of a New Japan]." In *Miki Kiyoshi zenshū* 17, edited by Hyōe Ōuchi, 507–533. Tokyo: Iwanami, 1968.

Mitsui, Takashi. "Kindai academizu shigaku no nakani *nissendōsoron* – kankoku heigo zengo wo chushinni [The Theory of Japan and Korea as Having the Same Ancestor in the Context of Modern Academism – A Focus on the Period of Japan's Annexation of Korea]." *Chosenshikenkyuronbunshu* 42 (2004): 42–76.

Moritani, Katsumi. "Chōsen shakai to shizen kankyō (1) [Natural Environment in Korean Society]." *Tōa* 7, no. 12 (Dec. 1934): 43–51.

————. "Kyūrai no chōsen nogyoshakai ni tssuite no kenkyū no tameni [For the Study of Old Agricultural Society in Chosun Korea]." In Keijōteikokudaigaku hōbungakkai ed., *Chōsen shakai keizai shi kenkyū* [A Study of the Social Economic History of Chosun Korea], 397–482. Tokyo: Tōkō Shoin, 1933.

Oh, Mi-Il. "1930 nyondae sahoejuiujadului sahoesungkyoknonjaeng [A Debate over the Nature of Society in Socialist Movements in 1930s Chosun Korea]." *Yŏksapipyong* 10 (1990): 218–251.

Okubo, Koichi et al., eds. *Daitōasenso to hanto* [The Greater East Asian War and Chosun Korea]. Kyungsung: Jinbunsha, 1942.

Paek, Seung Cheol. "1930 nendai chosunhak undong ui jungae wa minzok insikkundaekwan. [The Development of Korean Studies Movements in the 1930s and Its Concepts of Nation and Modernity]." *Yoksa wa silhak* 36 (2008): 113–148.

Paik, Nam Un. *Chōsen shakai keizaishi* [The Socio-Economic History of Chosun Korea]. Tokyo: Kaizosha, 1933.

————. *Chōsenhōken shakai keizaishi* (1) [The Feudal Economic History of Chosun Korea]. Tokyo: Kaizōsha, 1937.

Pang, Kie Jung. "1930 nendai chosun nonggong pyungjin jungchack kwa kyeongje tongje [The Policy for the Uniform Advancement of Agriculture and Industry and Economic Control in 1930s Chosun Korea]." *Tongbang hakji* 120 (June 2003): 75–120.

———. *Han'guk kŭnhyŏndae sasangsa yŏn'gu: 1930, 40-yŏndae Paek Nam-un ŭi hangmun kwa chŏngch'i kyŏngje sasang* [A Study of the Intellectual History of Modern Korea: The Scholarship and Politico-Economic Thoughts of Paik Nam Un in the 1930s and 1940s]. Seoul: Yŏksa Pip'yŏngsa, 1992.

Park, Moon Byung. "Nong'op chosun ui gumto [An Analysis of Agriculture in Chosun Korea]." *Chosun Joong Ang Ilbo*, June–Aug. 1936.

Park, Mun Kyu. "Noson shakai no bunka no kiten toshite dochichosajigyo ni tuite [The Significance of Land Survey as a Starting Point of Culture in Agricultural Society]." In *Chōsen shakai keizai shi kenkyū* 6, edited by Keijoteikokudaigaku hobungakkai. Tokyo: Irie Shoin, 1933.

Rathgen, Karl. *Die Japaner in der Weltwirtschaft*. Leipzig: Teubner, 1911.

———. *Die Japaner und ihre wirtschaftliche Entwicklung*. Leipzig: Teubner, 1905.

———. *Japans Volkswirtschaft und Staatshaushalt*. Leipzig: Duncker & Humbolt, 1891.

———. *Staat und Kultur der Japaner*. Bielefeld and Leipzig: Velhagen & Klasing, 1907.

Roh, Tong Kyu. "Aseajok sangsanyangsik ui daehaya [On the Asiatic Mode of Production]." *Shin Dong-A* 4, no. 7 (July 1934): 100–107.

Ryu, Sihyun. *Choi namsun yongu* [A Study of Choi Nam Sun]. Seoul: Yoksapipyungsa, 2011.

Sawada, Koji. "Dochi shoyu = nogyo no genjo bunseki – yamada moritanō si no senzen to sengo no bunseki ni tsuite 2 [Land Ownership: Analyzing the Reality of Agriculture – About Yamada Moritarō's Analyses in Wartime and Postwar Periods]." *Keizai ronso* 25, no. 2 (1989): 33–57.

Tachibana, Shiraki. "Tōyo shakai no kōzo [The Formation of Oriental Society]." *Tairiku* (Mar. 1942). In *Tachibana Shiraki chosakushū* 3 [Completed Works of Tachibana Shiraki], 10–15. Tokyo: Keisō Shobō, 1966.

Terade, Michio. *Yamada Moritaro: Marukusu shugisha no shirarezaru sekai* [Yamada Moritaro: The Unknown World of a Marxist Intellectual]. Tokyo: Nihonkeizaihyoronsha, 2008.

Yamada, Moritaro. *Nihon shinonshugi bunseki* [An Analysis of Japanese Capitalism]. Tokyo: Iwanami Shōten, 1934.

Yamamuro, Shinichi. "'The Long-Term Policy of National Management Will Always Be in Unison with the Japanese Empire': The Paradise of the Kingly Way Stumbles and the Path Toward the Merging of Japan and Manzhouguo." In *Manchuria Under Japanese Dominion*, translated by Joshua Fogel, 127–197. Philadelphia: University of Pennsylvania Press, 2006.

Yi, Kwang Su and Ellie Choi, trans. "On National Reconstruction." In *Imperatives of Culture: Selected Essays on Korean History, Literature and Society from the Japanese Colonial Era*, edited by Christopher P. Hanscom, Walter K. Lew and Youngju Ryu, 1–28. Honolulu: University of Hawaii Press, 2013.

Young, Louise. *Japan's Total Empire: Manchuria and the Culture of Wartime Imperialism*. Berkeley: University of California Press, 1998.

Epilogue

From the moment Japan invaded Manchuria and China in 1931, the Japanese government was forced to respond to Chinese anti-imperialist nationalism and confront the Western powers that were hostile to its imperial ambition. These conditions radically altered the intellectual terrain of Japanese academia and compelled Japanese scholarly attempts to rationally justify the situation as the birth of a new form of pan-Asian empire.

Whereas liberal thinkers up until the late 1920s had steadfastly focused on only domestic issues, a group of social scientists after 1931 were now preoccupied with attempting to locate the conceptual basis of a regional order, one through which the conventional empire-colony power structure might be transcended. Most right-wing intellectuals in Japan focused on refiguring the concept of the Imperial Way into a wider, regionally apposite theory, through the binary logic of an anti-Western imperialism and simplistic pan-Asianism, a notion through which Imperial Japan was defined as an agency that would protect all Asian people from Western oppression. In contrast, the social scientists this book has investigated were acutely aware that repeating this one-dimensional perception of the West and the East would not convince the Chinese and colonial subjects to support the construction of an East Asian imperial bloc under Japanese leadership. Nor did they think that reproducing the rhetoric of a colonial civilizing mission would help to rationalize any intellectual commitment to empire. As they faced the challenge to overcome the limits inherent in the liberal social scientific tradition of the Taisho period, and address the emergence of a pro-imperial reactionary political discourse, these social scientists were compelled to contrive a new logical basis for their academic practice of social science. This book has conceptualized this quest as an attempt to create an East Asian empire.

In order to locate Asia as a social scientific object to be conceptually possessed and refigured, they first had to challenge an array of irrational and nonobjective concepts such as blood, religion, customs and community, which had previously fallen outside the remit of any social scientific study. Additionally, their project toward the creation of an imperial social science also had to confront the binary formation of the West as universal and the East as particular. As this book has shown in several chapters, these imperial social scientists did not intend to posit the counter claim for a superior *universal* East Asian empire. Rather than appropriate and reproduce the schematic configuration of East and West, they strove to logically support an idea of a universal community through the investigation of the unscientific elements of human society. In this way, individual subjective and ubiquitous modes of life became part of their social scientific study. These imperial social scientists believed that they could create a theory which posited that the amalgam of individuals' subjective and at times unpredictable behavior could become the basis for an abstract subject formation that would conceptually facilitate the possibility of a singular East Asian nation or *minzoku*. They believed that this theory would explain how all Asian subjects in this new East Asian (Imperial) Community might productively share in the sense of a single *community of destiny*.

Rōyama Masamichi, Kada Tetsuji, Shinmei Masamichi and Takata Yasuma were the new generation of social scientists whose primary intellectual inquiry was to logically contrive how this new community of destiny would replace the old imperial structure. They aimed to rationalize their involvement in the production of this pro-imperial knowledge by positioning their intellectual endeavor in the broader context of offering a challenge to the Euro-centric bourgeois social scientific academic tradition, and they were firmly opposed to the Marxist concept of world history as class struggle. In producing a new set of imperial knowledge, they faced two major challenges. The first was to conceptually and practically dismantle the empire-colony power structure. Second, and more importantly, was the need to locate a logical understanding of subject formation beyond the conceptual limits of capitalism. They were convinced that the issue of ethnic and racial hierarchy as constructed between the positions of metropole and colony could not be addressed by adopting simple political measures such as conceding to the colonized an independent national identity. The deconstruction of colonial inequality, and the inspiration of a colonized individual's desire to become a member of the planned East Asian regional community entailed profound discussions of subject formation that extended far beyond the binary configuration of empire and colony. Both Shinmei and Takata produced extensive amounts of writing on how to theorize the formation of the East Asian *minzoku*, and they contended that the creation of a pan-regional form of identity would productively deconstruct the schematic racial hierarchy between metropole and colony. It might have seemed that what was presented was a plan in support of global racial liberation, and this was certainly a dimension which attracted radical intellectuals from around the world such as W.E.B. Du Bois.[i] But this idea was primarily formed to convince all Asian subjects to voluntarily mobilize themselves in support of the construction of the new Japanese empire. The rationalized plan for a multi-ethnic and regional empire that was presented arguably provided a crucial platform for Japan's wartime mobilization effort. A number of youths in colonial Korea and Taiwan volunteered to join the Imperial Army, seduced by the logic of this plan, and the propounding of the virtues of imperial citizenship. As such, this new notion of a multi-ethnic empire was not confined to the realm of abstract theory, but penetrated the mindset of colonial subjects in reality.

Nonetheless, rationalizing colonial subjects' commitment to the Japanese empire called for the imperial government to implement new policies to realistically convince people of the veracity of Japan's rhetoric, as it proclaimed the new Japanese empire as a "Greater Asia." Without this, the whole question of fighting for the empire would be reduced to the schematic binary of the East against the West, and to the abstract duty of all Asians to stand united against Western imperialism. But as was discussed above, this rationale was also frequently appropriated and reproduced by Japanese intellectuals and politicians throughout the early twentieth century, and arguably it never bore tangible fruit in convincing the rest of Asia to acquiesce under Japan's leadership. Despite this fact, too many discourses in support of the pan-Asian empire during the interwar period never attempted to surpass this level of argument. Since the concept of the East Asian Community was dominant, and indistinguishably appropriated by both right-wing and left-wing pro-colonial intellectuals, students of Japanese imperialism and twentieth-century East Asian history might simplistically consider the episteme of this period as characterized by the Asian intellectual denunciation of any form of Western modernity.

While one group of social scientists concentrated their academic inquiry toward the contriving of a logical and theoretical rationale for the new multi-ethnic Japanese empire, another group who shared a similar pro-imperial perspective considered the issues that would reshape the reality of social, political and economic structures within Japanese Imperial East Asia. Again, the seemingly progressive blueprints for a new empire, produced by both groups, were aimed to maximize voluntary mobilization and optimize the economic and social exploitation of the colony. In compelling fashion, these social scientists denounced profit-oriented individual activity as a result of Western inspired values that needed to be overcome. Instead, they shared the perspective that in order to sustain the empire, or the symbolic Pan-Asian community of destiny, an individual had to embody a productivist ethos. This was despite the fact that the logic of productivism was inseparable from the principle of the capitalist developmentalist economy, something that they also adhered to. However, the theoretical and practical turn to colonial development also generated tensional spaces between the various intellectual advocates of the East Asian Community. For example, Hirano Yoshitarō, a converted *koza-ha* Marxist, could not abandon his theoretical adherence to the value of the so-called Asian village community, so clearly labeled as the historical locus of stagnation and underdevelopment in Asia by Marxist theory. He tried to break through this conundrum by providing an alternative historical analysis. By constantly reproducing images of harmony and social equilibrium from pre-modern Asian communities, Hirano linked this idealistic historical vision to an idealized version of the contemporary Japanese empire in which the harmonious family unit is expanded up through society to the level of the Emperor. Despite such efforts, the developmentalist perspective never faded and maintained a primary theoretical position for most Japanese and colonial social scientists. Ezawa Jōji believed that the existing economic gap between metropole and colony could be reduced straightforwardly through increased industrialization, construction and national land planning. It was at this point that he encountered geopolitics as a new platform from which to productively refigure a new idea of East Asian geography and economics.

The notion of developmentalism and the productivist ethos are perhaps most vividly illuminated in the writings and political behavior of Moritani Katsumi and In Jeong Sik. They grappled with the similar question of how to develop the colonial economy so that colonial subjects might be led to successfully realize their subjective potential as imperial citizens devoted to the Japanese empire. They were also deeply involved in intellectual and political endeavors to position colonial Korea productively within the newly envisioned East Asian empire. In this regard, Moritani represented a pro-Japanese standpoint compared to that of In Jeong Sik, who was primarily focused on promoting the status of colonial Korea. But both men were convinced that colonial Korea might function as a litmus paper through which the grand task of building a new empire would be tested. Both called for imperial Japan to allow more social and economic opportunity for colonial Koreans, from agricultural mechanization to mandatory education. Toward this, a state-led developmentalist perspective was centrally important within their discourses on East Asia. Unsurprisingly, this pro-developmentalist dimension within most conceptions of the East Asian Community found its historical rationale in Japan's "successful" top-down modernization from the Meiji period onward. Moritani contended that Japan's transformation into a modern society showed how institutional and bureaucratic renovation could overcome the perceived image of stagnation attached to traditional Asian society. Both Moritani and In Jeong Sik aimed to clear away any skepticism cast on the idea of Asia's immanent development. Precisely for this reason, colonial Korea emerged as a crucial space where the project of building an East Asian Community could become a realizable dream. The illusion presented by these imperial social scientists, that the colony could also attain the status of the metropole, was, however, nothing but a vivid example of how the social sciences were deployed in the service of colonial subjugation and imperial war. In Jeong Sik's writings indicate the problematic nature of any cooperative pro-colonial social science, as he faithfully represented Imperial Japan's interests to maximize the mobilization and exploitation of Korean subjects.

Hegemonic Asia again: East Asian regionalism under US hegemony

The project of building a Pan-Asian empire in East Asia came to an end with Japan's unconditional surrender in 1945, and the clear-cut binary of victor and loser defined the way in which the Asia-Pacific War would be historicized. The American occupation of Japan was justified by the official US definition of the war as a clash between democracy and barbarity. According to this logic, a new Japan needed to be imagined, from the blank starting point of it lacking even the roots of democracy. One may speculate as to the role of the General Headquarters (GHQ) in the first years of the US occupation, as the highest authorities in Japan put into practice several forward-looking changes to engender an authentic sense of democracy. These included the release of intellectuals and activists imprisoned for their political ideas and the theoretical problematizing of the seldom-challenged emperor system in public discourse. On the other hand, dozens of high-ranking bureaucrats and politicians were put on trial. These officials were sentenced based on their degree of involvement in and personal responsibility for any crimes against humanity committed by Japan over the course of the Asia-Pacific War. In addition, an act of "purging from public service" was issued and those who were involved in imperial wartime institutions such as think-tanks were deprived of their positions in government and academia. Not one of the social scientists explored above could avoid this fate, and their postwar academic career restarted only in 1952 with the lifting of the act of purging from public service.

Notably, the initial project to implant an American version of democracy into Japan was drastically modified as the East Asian region became the central theater of the Cold War. Socialist political figures were highly successful in the 1947 general election and this left-wing boom in postwar Japanese politics gave the United States a significant warning signal. The arrival of communist China in 1949, and its unexpected ability to thwart the allied forces led by the United States during the Korean War, had a profound impact on the foreign policy of the United States in the mid-1950s. In these sharpening ideological conditions of the Cold War, the productive role of an economically prosperous Japan as a platform from which to realize US interest in East Asia became crystal clear. Notably, newly decolonized areas, and Southeast Asia in particular, emerged as the central geopolitical area where ideological conflicts between the United States, the Soviet Union and China collided. Now it was social scientists in the United States who came to the fore as the producers of the rational knowledge that could be utilized to guide America's early Cold War strategies in East and Southeast Asia. As is well known, anxieties over the spread of communism associated with strong anti-Western nationalism propelled American social scientists to provide an urgent prescription for Asian instability. Their solution was to induce rapid, state-driven economic development through US direct and indirect investment. As Michael Latham's recent study demonstrates well, the concept of modernization was theorized as an ideology to integrate people in the third world – Asia, Africa and Latin America – into a group of favorable partners who would recognize the possibility of a US-led new world of affluence and prosperity.[2] To this end, it was extremely important for American intellectuals and policymakers to make sure that their strategy of modernization was not contradictory to nationalist ideology and indigenous agency in the third world, given that ethnic nationalism tended to view foreign intervention as imperialistic. Leading American Cold War foreign policymakers believed that a certain degree of controlled economic development in the third world could be achieved by investing American foreign capital and establishing functioning political organizations that were pro-American.

John Dower's study explains that the presence of the United States and its decisive influence in postwar Japan gave rise to several streams of thought among intellectuals, politicians and the masses regarding how to locate Japan's position in Asia.[3] Among them, the so-called civil society school led by liberal and progres-sive intellectuals such as Maruyama Masao deserves attention. Rejecting the idea of rearmament and upholding the spirit of the postwar Peace Constitution, the lat-ter of which became the central object of growing conservatism in contemporary Japan, the civil society group basically took a critical stance regarding the legacy of Japan's war. At the center of this approach was Maruyama's interpretation of Japanese imperialism as illustrated in his writings of the late 1940s and early 1950s. His thesis can be characterized by his negative critique of wartime ultra-nationalism and the Emperor system. Both of these, he believed, reinforced each other and played a major role in the formation of wartime totalitarianism. Impor-tantly, Maruyama never explicitly endorsed the American version of democracy as an ideal alternative, although his postwar writing was preoccupied with the question of how an authentic modernity could come to Japanese society. In this way, his critique of the Emperor-system and ultranationalism became a pivotal moment preceding his advocacy of democracy and civil society in the 1950s and 1960s. To this end, Maruyama had to also intellectually displace wartime social scientific scholarship which, he believed, had provided the theoretical rationale for wartime fascism.

In his 1947 writing for *Sekai*, one of the most influential liberal journals in postwar Japan, Maruyama argued pointedly that prewar Japanese political science "had no tradition worth reviving."[4] Maruyama, an intellectual icon of postwar Japanese democracy and the "civil society" school, sought a new path in liberal social science, building on his critical assessment of wartime Japanese social sci-ences. In this respect, Maruyama expanded his critique to include the general academic field of Japanese wartime social science.[5] However, one may wonder why Maruyama particularly problematized only the field of wartime Japanese social sciences, given that the issues of colonialism and imperialism had existed throughout modern intellectual history, ever since Japan began to colonize its neighbors in the 1870s. For this reason, one could conclude that Maruyama's denouncement of prewar Japanese science was not premised on his recognition of modern Japanese history on the whole as one of colonialism. Instead it was informed by his intention to rehabilitate what he believed to be the objective and rational traditions of Japanese social science, and thereby establish the historical intellectual ground for a new beginning of democratic Japan.

At stake was the fundamental limit of Maruyama's postwar social scientific thinking to delineate the continuity of colonialism and imperialism within Cold War East Asia. Since the standpoint of Maruyama and like-minded liberal intel-lectuals was pegged to a desire to bring democratization only to *Japan proper*, they paid little attention to the question of how Japan was expected to sustain America's regional hegemony. While the civil society group showed a funda-mental lack of any regional awareness, another group of more regionally ori-ented social scientists, many of whom were deeply involved in wartime imperial discourses, were gradually strengthening their academic and political clout. In 1954, Rōyama Masamichi returned to academia, appointed as the dean at Ochano-mizu University, a prestigious women's university. Through the 1950s, Rōyama produced many volumes of writing on the changing topography of the East Asian international order. He was no longer in a position to address his wartime ideas of Pan-Asian regionalism in the context of postwar East Asia under American hegemony. But as Sakai Tetsuya succinctly pointed out, Rōyama remained convinced that the significance of a pan-Asian regional awareness had never faded away.[6]

Rōyama showed a keen interest in the growing nationalist sentiments present within other Asian countries, as they progressed through various stages of post-colonial political awareness. He was acutely aware that Mao Zedong's communist New Democracy movement was strongly associated with Chinese ethnic nationalism, and of the various anti-colonial movements against European colonial power in Southeast Asia. He considered that both cases exemplified the fact that nationalism had become the central agency behind the geopolitical changes shaping post-war Asia. However, he did not endorse the radical dimension of Asian nationalism at face value. Rōyama observed that the bondage between foreign power and the indigenous bourgeois class had shaped the basic politico-economic structure in Asia during the colonial period, and that nationalism gained momentum as this bondage collapsed.[7] He considered that the prevalent and seemingly strongly rooted Asian nationalist sentiment was actually a form of self-recognition that during the colonial period, technological development and the accumulation of capital had never occurred. Therefore, most Asian countries had fallen into poverty.[8] Based on these observations, he concluded that the success of nationalist movements in Asia was contingent on whether they could be harmoniously and productively associated with democracy and industrialization. He warned that nationalism was subject to transition into simple chauvinistic racism if it only fulfilled the monopolization of power by a certain group. For Rōyama, Mao's communist China was an example of how such nationalism could serve politically flagrant ends.[9] Therefore, Rōyama was insistent that a functional regional order needed to be urgently established to monitor and mediate the unstable imbalances inside single Asian nation-states.

It is important to note that Rōyama highlighted democracy and industrialization as two key features that would engender success for Asia's nationalist political movements. On the surface, he seemed to echo Maruayma's notion of democracy, in that he agreed that democracy must take root for the successful production of a modern nation-state. However, it appeared that his ideas on democracy were related to dominant patterns of pro-US Cold War ideology. In other words, Rōyama believed that Asian nations under American leadership must take on "democracy" as a *fait accompli* to become part of the developed "free" world. Acknowledging the newness of the India-centered "third-way" of conceiving Asia as a neutral zone in the midst of polarized Cold War international politics, Rōyama argued that Japan and Asia must instead join the collective security system led by the United States.[10] As such, he was overtly critical of the limits of the Bandung group as an alternative regional power.

Returning to Rōyama's notion of industrialization and regional development as a prerequisite to the functioning of a modern nation-state, I argue that it valuably illuminates the mentality of postwar Japanese social scientists. First, Rōyama demonstrated cohesive continuity in his internationalist thinking from the prewar to the postwar periods. As discussed in Chapters 1 and 3 of this book, Rōyama, together with Ezawa Jōji and other like-minded social scientists, attempted to rationalize the efficacy of a developmentalist approach to the incorporation of China and the other Japanese colonies into a Pan-Asian empire during the war-time period. In this notion it was of course Japan's advanced economic power that would enable the rest of Asia to become industrialized in the late 1930s and early 1940s. While Japan's regional hegemony disappeared, Rōyama still believed that his developmentalist perspective could effectively serve to remap the postwar Asian regional order.

Let us not forget that the affinity Rōyama, and other like-minded Japanese intel-lectuals, had for a developmentalist perspective never went as far as to consider the utilization of American economic power to help reconstruct the damaged Jap-anese economy. Instead, their developmentalist gaze was directed to other Asian countries outside of Japan. Interestingly, this epistemological conception was entirely different from that of the American social scientists who were involved in drafting US foreign policy in the 1950s and 1960s. Rōyama's developmental-ist approach to postwar Asia was a Japanized comprehension of how American policy in Asia should function. In fact, he did not think that an advanced country's economic intervention in less developed countries would be necessarily an impe-rialistic action. For this reason, he could withhold a value judgment on whether US intervention in Asia would be another example of imperialism, just as he failed to acknowledge that his notion of the East Asian Cooperative Community during the wartime period was an evolved version of colonial violence. Driving Rōyama's conception of the postwar international order was his awareness of the growing cleavage between theory and practice. Although the United Nations was established as an authoritative international organization after the Second World War and accordingly, the nominal principle of equal sovereignty was ensured, Rōyama was skeptical of the efficiency of the United Nations as a mediator of world peace. While the hierarchy and division between advanced powers and weak states, and the ideological rivalry between communist and liberal capitalism clearly existed in real politics, he anticipated that a functioning Cold War period international order would be greatly influenced by successful economic develop-ment in the Third World.[11]

Interestingly, the Korean War reinforced Rōyama's pragmatic conception of the postwar international order. For him, the outbreak and ending of the Korean War was a vivid example of how Cold War international politics in the 1950s would be shaped. He defined the Korean War as the first "war of attrition," that is, neither American nor communist alliances accomplished their intended goal in spite of their endless supply of resources. Accordingly, he analyzed that this type of "hot" war would provide a similar lesson to the two superpowers, this being that both the United States and the Soviet Union must concentrate on developing the econo-mies of their international partners to ensure their ideological superiority. This observation was naturally linked to the strategic importance of the Asian region. As in Asia, emergent nationalist forces frequently deployed the rhetoric of anti-colonial liberation and planned economic development, following the example of both Soviet and Chinese communism.

In this way, Rōyama's diagnosis of the postwar order in Asia contained several compelling points that American intellectuals and policymakers might favorably refer to. As Latham notes, the ideology of modernization was for the United States a "means for the continued assertion of the privileges and rights of a dominant power during an era in which the nations of Africa, Asia, Latin America and the Middle East increasingly demanded independence."[12] As early as the late 1950s, Rōyama presented his interpretation of a new East Asian order. This promised that as long as the American project of economic modernization in the Third World could provide some degree of economic development, US influence in Asia would not necessarily be considered as imperialist in design.

However, Rōyama never volunteered to simply spread the message of American idealism in Asia. Instead, he intended to reposition Japan in the new international order, an order in which he still believed, a developmental perspective was significant. For him, the frustrated project of the East Asian Community during the wartime period bore a striking resemblance to the postwar developmentalist approach to Asia undertaken by the United States, in that both put a great emphasis on nominally boosting the economy of "underdeveloped regions," in order to pursue regional alliances. For this reason, he made it clear that his critical interpretation of wartime Japanese social science was fundamentally different from the postwar liberal evaluation, offered by figures such as Maruyama. This liberal and progressive social scientific analysis problematized the absolute conception of state power that was in full bloom during the Taisho period, something that Rōyama considered was further concretized in the notion of the East Asian Cooperative Community. If the "*kyōdōtai*" group of social scientists epitomized the progress of Japanese social science in the early twentieth century, in their imagining of a utopian vision of a new Asia, Rōyama reasoned that the successful modernization of the Japanese state from Meiji Japan onwards also gave rise to internationalist and "forward-looking" regionalism in the social sciences during the Taisho and wartime periods. The liberal and internationalist tendency within Japanese social science, he asserted, was frustrated by retroactive and ultranationalist forces during the wartime period. In this respect, Rōyama was not hesitant to endorse imperial Japan's solitary accomplishment within Asia of both an institutional democracy and a substantial level of industrialization. Returning to his emphasis on democracy and industrialization as two major keys to establishing a functioning nation-state in Asia, I argue that Rōyama was confident that Japan had already demonstrated a successful combination of nationalism concurrent with democracy and industrialization. Japan was therefore well positioned to offer an exemplary answer to the puzzle of how to productively address anti-colonial nationalism and underdevelopment in America's plan for a new Asian order.

While Rōyama presented a theoretical roadmap for the location of Japan's position in the postwar regional order in Asia, other social scientists who belonged to the "*kyōdōtai*" group more pragmatically understood the benefits of the developmentalist perspective. In 1951, Kada Tetsuji, a representative wartime social scientist who advocated for the East Asian Community, was appointed as the founding director of the Institute of Asian Affairs (*Ajia mondai chōsakai*) at Keio University. In fact, the foundational base of the Institute of Asian Affairs was the Imperial Asian Research Institute which Kada directed during the wartime period but was dismantled in 1945. The establishment of the Institute of Asian Affairs therefore symbolized the triumphant return of a prominent social scientist ousted for his wartime writing, and more importantly signaled Japanese social scientists' interest to continue to intervene in the broad scheme of Asian affairs. In 1953, Kishi Nobusuke, one of the primary architects of Manchukuo during the wartime period and accused as a class A war criminal, was appointed as the chairman of the board for this organization.[13]

Kada, Kishi and other like-mined former *kyōdōtai* bureaucrats and social scientists were well aware that their wartime developmental perspective could not be reapplied to Asian countries within the changed Cold War setting. In particular, South Korea was conceived of as an area of extreme exception due to its strong anti-Japanese sentiment. But although the 1950s South Korean government in public vehemently opposed any notion of a postwar Asian order in which Japan would take a leading role, behind closed doors they faithfully followed the general direction of American's foreign policy in Asia. Recognizing anti-Japanese sentiment in all its former colonies, the United States developed a particular strategic plan toward Southeast Asia. The official US governmental report drafted by William Rostow, the champion of the American developmentalist modernization project, drew attention to underdeveloped countries in the Third World. Similarly, Kada and like-minded Japanese social scientists shared in the perception that Southeast Asia would emerge as a key area to both US foreign policy and Japan's role in postwar Asia. Its official journal, *Ajia mondai*, served as an academic platform to provide knowledge about South and Southeast Asia for policy development. The English title of this journal – *Journal of Asia Kyōkai: The Society for Economic Cooperation in Asia* – indicated that this academic organization was armed with a clear intention to strategically tie noncommunist areas in Asia to American regional hegemony through economic aid. Social scientists affiliated with this organization were acutely aware that their role was to ascertain how Japan might remain as a regional leading power within a new Asian order led by the United States.

Pan-Asianism has had a significant impact on the formation of modern Asian society and its challenge to Western hegemony throughout the twentieth century. However, it never contained a monolithic notion of an Asian unity against the West. Intellectuals and politicians have redefined its implications based on their understanding of the existing order. These strategists were constantly aware that the rhetoric of a unified Asia would be utilized as a panacea to justify their political position, even as far as to support colonialism and imperialism. Japanese intellectuals' use and abuse of Pan-Asian regionalism during the wartime period illustrates how the seemingly enchanting notion of Asian liberation and self-sufficiency helped to create a collective regional unconsciousness, a fact which in turn led to the sacrifice of countless numbers of Asian subjects in the violence of an imperial war. With the onset of the Cold War period, the specter of colonial development never faded from the memory of postwar, post-Imperial Japanese intellectual thought. As such, the legacy of Japanese imperial social science continued to linger through the inception of an oppressive hegemonic Asian regionalism into the 1950s and 1960s.

Notes

1 As for Du Bois's writings on China and Japan during the wartime period, see Bill V. Mullen and Cathryn Watson, eds., *W.E.B. Du Bois on Asia: Crossing the World Color Line* (Oxford: University of Mississippi Press, 2005).

2 Michael Latham, *Modernization as Ideology* (Durham: University of North Carolina Press, 2000).

3 John Dower, "Peace and Democracy in Two Systems: External Policy and Internal Conflict," in *Postwar Japan as History*, ed. Andrew Gordon (Berkeley: University of California Press, 1993), 3–33.

4 Maruyama states,

> [T]here has undoubtedly been a brilliant revival in other social sciences, but political science in this country, to put it bluntly, really has no tradition worth reviving. *For Japanese political science everything depends on what happens in the future.*
> (emphasis added) Maruyama Masao, trans., Arthur Tiedemann, "Politics as a Science in Japan: Retrospect and Prospects," in *Thought and Behaviour in Modern Japanese Politics*, ed. Maruyama Masao, trans. Ivan Morris (Oxford: Oxford University Press, 1969), 226.

5 Extensive self-examination does seem to have taken place in other branches of social sciences too, once the hollow sounding tunes heard briefly in the intermediate post-war period subsided. A year and a half after the war ended social scientists were asking themselves whether their sciences could really serve as guiding influences in contemporary reality. . . . They realized that the problem was not to be solved by merely returning to "the good old days" and treating the decade of reaction as a historical vacuum, Maruyama wrote (Ibid., 226–227).

6 Sakai Tetsuya, *Kindai nihon no kokusai jitsujoron* [Theories of International Order in Modern Japan] (Tokyo: Iwanami Shoten, 2007).

7 Rōyama Masamichi, *Kokusai seiji to nihon gaiko* [International Politics and Japanese Diplomacy] (Tokyo: Chūokōronsha, 1959), 164–165.

8 Ibid.

9 Ibid., 153.

10 Ibid., 170–171.

11 Ibid., 83.

12 Michael Latham, *Modernization as Ideology*, 16.

13 For a detailed survey of *Ajia Mondai Chōsakai*, see Suehiro Akira, "Sengo nihon no ajia kenkyū [Research on Asia in Postwar Japan]," *Shakai kagaku kenkyū* 48, no. 4 (1997): 42–50.

Bibliography

Dower, John. "Peace and Democracy in Two Systems: External Policy and Internal Conflict." In *Postwar Japan as History,* edited by Andrew Gordon, 3–33. Berkeley: University of California Press, 1993.

Latham, Michael. *Modernization as Ideology.* Durham: University of North Carolina Press, 2000.

Masao, Maruyama. *Thought and Behaviour in Modern Japanese Politics.* Translated by Ivan Morris. Oxford: Oxford University Press, 1969.

Mullen, Bill V. and Cathryn Watson, eds. *W.E.B. Du Bois on Asia: Crossing the World Color Line.* Oxford: University of Mississippi Press, 2005.

Rōyama, Masamichi. *Kokusai seiji to nihon gaiko* [International Politics and Japanese Diplomacy]. Tokyo: Chūokōronsha, 1959.

Sakai, Tetsuya. *Kindai nihon no kokusai jitsujoron* [Theories of International Order in Modern Japan]. Tokyo: Iwanami Shōten, 2007.

Suehiro, Akira. "Sengo nihon no ajia kenkyū [Research on Asia in Postwar Japan]." *Shakai kagaku kenkyū* 48, no. 4 (1997): 42–50.

Index